Bilingual Course of Exercise and Sport Physiology

运动生理学双语教程

汪军　主编

北京体育大学出版社

策划编辑：佟　晖
责任编辑：佟　晖
责任校对：潘海英
版式设计：李　鹤

图书在版编目（CIP）数据

运动生理学双语教程 = Bilingual Course of Exercise and Sport Physiology : 英汉对照 / 汪军主编. -- 北京 : 北京体育大学出版社, 2023.10
ISBN 978-7-5644-3900-2

Ⅰ. ①运… Ⅱ. ①汪… Ⅲ. ①运动生理学 - 高等学校 - 教材 - 英、汉 Ⅳ. ①G804.2

中国国家版本馆CIP数据核字(2023)第185701号

运动生理学双语教程
YUNDONG SHENGLIXUE SHUANGYU JIAOCHENG　　**汪军　主编**

出版发行：北京体育大学出版社
地　　址：北京市海淀区农大南路1号院2号楼2层办公B-212
邮　　编：100084
网　　址：http：//cbs.bsu.edu.cn
发 行 部：010-62989320
邮 购 部：北京体育大学出版社读者服务部 010-62989432
印　　刷：北京建宏印刷有限公司
开　　本：787mm × 1092mm　1/16
成品尺寸：185mm × 260mm
印　　张：24
字　　数：676千字
版　　次：2023年10月第1版
印　　次：2023年10月第1次印刷
定　　价：120.00元

本书编写组

主　编：汪　军

编　委：（以姓氏笔画为序）

于　亮　石丽君　刘晨喆　许寿生

李　丽　李　岩　吴　迎　周　越

赵　丽　赵　磊

CONTENTS 目录

1 / An Introduction to Exercise and Sport Physiology
15 / 运动生理学导论

19 / Chapter 1　Structure and Function of Exercising Muscle
43 / 第一章　肌肉的结构和功能

50 / Chapter 2　Fuel for Exercise: Bioenergetics
60 / 第二章　人体运动的能源：生物能量学

65 / Chapter 3　Neural Control of Exercising Muscle
73 / 第三章　运动中肌肉的神经调控

77 / Chapter 4　Hormonal Control During Exercise
98 / 第四章　运动中的激素调控

105 / Chapter 5　Exercise and Oxygen Transport
124 / 第五章　运动与氧气运输

128 / Chapter 6　Exercise and Respiratory System
145 / 第六章　运动与呼吸系统

149 / Chapter 7　Cardiorespiratory Responses to Acute Exercise
175 / 第七章　一次性运动的心肺功能反应

181 / Chapter 8　Principles of Exercise Training
198 / 第八章　运动训练原则

203 / Chapter 9　Adaptations to Resistance Training
222 / 第九章　机体对抗阻训练的适应

228 / Chapter 10　Adaptations to Aerobic and Anaerobic Training
258 / 第十章　机体对有氧训练和无氧训练的适应

266 / Chapter 11　Exercise at Altitude
287 / 第十一章　高原环境与运动训练

294 / Chapter 12　Exercise in Hot and Cold Environments
319 / 第十二章　冷热环境与运动训练

329 / Chapter 13　Prescription of Exercise for Health and Fitness
342 / 第十三章　健身运动处方

346 / Chapter 14　Cardiovascular Disease and Physical Activity
357 / 第十四章　心血管疾病与体力活动

361 / Chapter 15　Obesity, Diabetes, and Physical Activity
374 / 第十五章　肥胖、糖尿病与体力活动

An Introduction to Exercise and Sport Physiology

The human body is an amazing machine. As you sit reading this introduction, countless perfectly coordinated and integrated events are occurring simultaneously in your body. These events allow complex functions, such as hearing, seeing, breathing, and information processing, to continue without any conscious effort. If you stand up, walk out the door, and jog around the block, almost all your body's systems will be activated, enabling you to successfully shift from rest to exercise. If you continue this routine regularly for weeks or months and gradually increase the duration and intensity of your jogging, your body will adapt so that you can perform better. Therein lie the two basic components of the study of exercise physiology: the acute responses of the body to exercise in all its forms and the adaptation of the body's systems to repeated or chronic exercise, often called exercise training.

For example, as a point guard directs her team down the basketball court on a fast break, her body makes many adjustments that require a series of complex interactions involving many body systems. Adjustments occur even at the cellular and molecular levels. To enable the coordinated leg muscle actions as she moves rapidly down court, nerve cells from the brain, referred to as motor neurons, conduct electrical impulses down the spinal cord to the legs. On reaching the muscles, these neurons release chemical messengers that cross the gap between the nerve and muscle, each neuron exciting several individual muscle cells or fibers. Once the nerve impulses cross this gap, they spread along the length of each muscle fiber and attach to specialized receptors. Binding of the messenger to its receptor sets into motion a series of steps that activate the muscle fiber's contraction processes, which involve specific protein molecules—actin and myosin—and an elaborate energy system to provide the fuel necessary to sustain a single contraction and subsequent contractions. It is at this level that other molecules, such as adenosine triphosphate (ATP) and phosphocreatine (PCr), become critical for providing the energy necessary to fuel contraction.

1 Focus of Exercise and Sport Physiology

Exercise and sport physiology have evolved from the fundamental disciplines of anatomy and physiology. Anatomy is the study of an organism's structure, or morphology. While anatomy focuses on the basic structure of various body parts and their interrelationships, physiology is the study of body function. Physiologists study how the body's organ systems, tissues, cells, and the molecules within cells work and how their functions are integrated to regulate the body's internal environment, a process called homeostasis. Because physiology focuses on the functions of body structures, understanding anatomy is essential to learning physiology. Furthermore, both anatomy and physiology rely on a working knowledge of biology, chemistry, physics, and other basic sciences.

Exercise physiology is the study of how the body's functions are altered when we are physically active, since exercise presents a challenge to homeostasis. Because the environment in which one performs exercise has a large impact, environmental physiology has emerged as a subdiscipline of exercise physiology. Sport physiology further applies the concepts of exercise physiology to enhancing sport performance and optimally training athletes. Thus, sport physiology derives its principles from exercise physiology. Because exercise physiology and sport physiology are so closely related and integrated, it is often hard to clearly distinguish between them. Because the same underlying scientific principles apply, exercise and sport physiology are often considered together.

2 Acute and Chronic Responses to Exercise

The study of exercise and sport physiology involves learning the concepts associated with two distinct exercise patterns. First, exercise physiologists are concerned with how the body responds to an individual bout of exercise, such as running on a treadmill for an hour or lifting weights. An individual bout of exercise is called acute exercise, and the responses to that exercise bout are referred to as acute responses. When examining the acute response to exercise, we are concerned with the body's immediate response to, and sometimes its recovery from, a single exercise bout.

The other major area of interest in exercise and sport physiology is how the body responds over time to the stress of repeated bouts of exercise, sometimes referred to as chronic adaptation or training effects. When one performs regular exercise over a period of days and weeks, the body adapts. The physiological adaptations that occur with chronic exposure to exercise or training improve both exercise capacity and efficiency. With resistance training, the muscles become stronger. With aerobic training, the heart and lungs become more efficient and endurance capacity of the muscles increases. These adaptations are highly specific to the type of training the person does.

3 The Evolution of Exercise Physiology

3.1 Early History of Exercise Physiology

Although exercise physiology is a relative newcomer to the world of science, one of its first publications appeared in 1793, when a paper by Seguin and Lavoisier described the oxygen consumption of a young man measured both in the resting state and while he repeatedly lifted a 7.3 kg weight for 15 min. At rest the man used 24 L of oxygen per hour (L/h) , which increased to 63 L/h during exercise. Lavoisier believed that the site of oxygen utilization and carbon dioxide production was in the lungs. Even though this concept was doubted by other physiologists of the time, it remained accepted doctrine until the middle of the 1800s, when several German physiologists demonstrated that combustion of oxygen occurred in cells throughout the entire body.

Arguably the first published textbook on exercise physiology, *Physiology of Bodily Exercise*, was written in French by Fernand LaGrange in 1889. Considering the small amount of research on exercise that had been conducted up to that time, it is intriguing to read the author's accounts of such topics as "Muscular Work", "Fatigue", "Habituation to Work", and "The Office of the Brain in Exercise." This early attempt to explain the response to exercise was, in many ways, limited to speculation and theory. Although some basic concepts of exercise biochemistry were emerging at that time, LaGrange was quick to admit that many details were still in the formative stages.

Because the early text by LaGrange offered only limited physiological insights regarding bodily functions during physical activity, some argue that the third edition of a text by F.A. Bainbridge titled *The Physiology of Muscular Exercise*, published in 1931, should be considered the earliest scientific text on this subject. Interestingly, that third edition was written by A.V. Bock and D.B. Dill, at the request of A.V. Hill, three key pioneers of exercise physiology discussed in this introductory chapter.

During the late 1800s, many theories were proposed to explain the source of energy for muscle contraction. Muscles were known to generate much heat during exercise, so some theories suggested that this heat was used directly or indirectly to cause muscle fibers to shorten. After the turn of the century, Walter Fletcher and Sir Frederick Gowland Hopkins observed a close relation between muscle action and lactate formation. This observation led to the realization that energy for muscle action is derived from the breakdown of muscle glycogen to lactic acid, although the details of this reaction remained obscure. Because of the high energy demands of exercising muscle, this tissue served as an ideal model to help unravel the mysteries of cellular metabolism. In 1921, A.V. Hill was awarded the Nobel Prize for his findings on energy metabolism. At that time, biochemistry was in its infancy, although it was rapidly gaining recognition through the research efforts of such other Nobel laureates as Albert Szent-Gyorgyi, Otto Meyerhof, August Krogh, and Hans Krebs, all of whom were actively studying how living cells generate and use energy.

3.2 Era of Scientific Exchange and Interaction

From the early 1900s through the 1930s, the medical and scientific environment in the United States was changing. This was an era of revolution in the education of medical students, led by changes at Johns Hopkins. More medical and graduate programs based their educational endeavors on the European model of experimentation and development of scientific insights. There were important advances in physiology in areas such as bioenergetics, gas exchange, and blood chemistry that served as the basis for advances in the physiology of exercise. Building on collaborations forged in the late 1800s, interactions of laboratories and scientists were promoted, and international meetings of organizations such as the International Union of Physiological Sciences created an atmosphere for free scientific exchange, discussion, and debate. Research laboratories and collaborations created during this period would go on to do some of the most important exercise physiology research of the 20th century. For example, the research on athletes, the Harvard Fatigue Laboratory (HFL) and the Scandinavian influence, etc.

3.3 Development of Contemporary Approaches

Much advancement in exercise physiology must be credited to improvements in technology. In the late 1950s, Henry L. Taylor and Elsworth R. Buskirk published two seminal papers describing the criteria for measuring maximal oxygen uptake and establishing that measure as the gold standard for cardiorespiratory fitness. In the 1960s, development of electronic analyzers to measure respiratory gases made studying energy metabolism much easier and more productive than before.

This technology and radio telemetry (which uses radio-transmitted signals) , used to monitor heart rate and body temperature during exercise, were developed as a result of the U.S. space program. Although such instruments took much of the labor out of research, they did not alter the direction of scientific inquiry. Until the late 1960s, most exercise physiology studies focused on the whole body's response to exercise. Most investigations involved measurements of such variables as oxygen uptake, heart rate, body temperature, and sweat rate. Cellular responses to exercise received little attention.

3.3.1 Biochemical Approaches

In the mid-1960s, three biochemists emerged who were to have a major impact on the field of exercise physiology. John Holloszy at Washington University in St. Louis, Missouri, America, Charles "Tip" Tipton at the University of Iowa, and Phil Gollnick at Washington State University first used rats and mice to study muscle metabolism and examine factors related to fatigue. Their publications and their training of graduate and postdoctoral students resulted in a more biochemical approach to exercise physiology research. Holloszy was ultimately awarded the 2000 Olympic Prize for his contributions to exercise physiology and health.

Before the 1960s, there were few biochemical studies on the adaptations of muscle to training. Although the field of biochemistry can be traced to the early part of the 20th century, this special area of chemistry was not applied to human muscle until Bergstrom and Hultman reintroduced and popularized the needle biopsy procedure in 1966. Initially, this procedure was used to examine glycogen depletion during exhaustive exercise and its resynthesis during recovery. In the early 1970s, as noted earlier, several exercise physiologists used the muscle biopsy method, histological staining, and the light microscope to determine human muscle fiber types.

Around the time Bergstrom reintroduced the needle biopsy procedure, exercise physiologists who were well trained as biochemists emerged. In Stockholm, Bengt Saltin realized the value of this procedure for studying human muscle structure and biochemistry. He first collaborated with Bergstrom in the late 1960s to study the effects of diet on muscle endurance and muscle nutrition. About the same time, Reggie Edgerton (University of California at Los Angeles, America) and Phil Gollnick were using rats to study the characteristics of individual muscle fibers and their responses to training. Saltin subsequently combined his knowledge of the biopsy procedure with Gollnick's biochemical talents. These researchers were responsible for many early studies on human muscle fiber's characteristics and use during exercise. Although many biochemists have used exercise to study metabolism, few have had more impact on the current direction of human exercise physiology than Bergstrom, Saltin, Tipton, Holloszy, and Gollnick.

3.3.2 Other Tools and Techniques

The history of exercise physiology has, in some ways, been driven by advancements in technologies adapted from basic sciences. The early studies of energy metabolism during exercise were made possible by the invention of gas-collecting equipment and chemical analysis of oxygen and carbon dioxide. Chemical determination of blood lactic acid seemed to provide some insights regarding the aerobic and anaerobic aspects of muscular activity, but these data told us little regarding the production and removal of this by-product of exercise. Likewise, blood glucose measurements taken before, during, and after exhaustive exercise proved to be interesting data but were of limited value for understanding the energy exchange at the cellular level.

Over the last 30 years, muscle physiologists have used various chemical procedures to understand how muscles generate energy and adapt to training. Test tube experiments (in vitro) with muscle biopsy samples have been used to measure muscle proteins (enzymes) and determine the muscle fiber's capacity to use oxygen. Although these studies provided a snapshot of the fiber's potential to generate energy, they often left more questions than answers. It was natural, therefore, for the sciences of cell biology to move to an even deeper level. It was apparent that the answers to those questions must lie within the fiber's molecular makeup.

Although not a new science, molecular biology has become a useful tool for exercise physiologists who wish to delve more deeply into the cellular regulation of metabolism and adaptations to the stress of exercise. Physiologists like Frank Booth and Ken Baldwin have dedicated their careers to understanding the molecular regulation of muscle fiber characteristics and function and have laid the groundwork for our current understanding of the genetic controls of muscle growth and atrophy.

Well before James Watson and Francis Crick unraveled the structure of deoxyribonucleic acid (DNA) in 1953, scientists appreciated the importance of genetics in predetermining the structure and function of all living organisms. The newest frontier in exercise physiology combines the study of molecular biology and genetics. Since the early 1990s, scientists have attempted to explain how exercise causes signals that affect the expression of genes within skeletal muscle.

In retrospect, it is apparent that since the beginning of the 20th century, the field of exercise physiology has evolved from measuring whole-body function (i.e., oxygen consumption, respiration, and heart rate) to molecular studies of muscle fiber genetic expression. There is little doubt that exercise physiologists of the future will need to be well-grounded in biochemistry, molecular biology, and genetics.

3.4 Integrative Physiology

With the announcement of the sequencing of the human genome in 2001, it was hoped that one day, scientists could simply analyze cheek cells from a mouth swab and, by looking at your gene sequence, predict whether you were at risk for developing diabetes or cardiovascular disease. More promising was the idea that detection of these predictive genetic variations could aid in developing more effective treatments for these debilitating diseases.

In the era of mega-genomic data, where does the study of physiology fit in? And is it still relevant to human health and disease? One outspoken advocate or the field of integrative physiology is Dr. Michael J. Joyner. Dr. Joyner is an award-winning, distinguished investigator at the Mayo Clinic who has critically questioned the functional value of so-called reductionist thinking in molecular biology. In contrast to examining biological processes at the lowest common level (e. g., how genes code for proteins in cells) , integrative physiology examines how whole organisms' function and adapt to internal and external stresses (including exercise). This approach is informed by the concepts of homeostasis, regulated organ systems, and redundancy in physiological systems. Moreover, integrative physiologists strive to ask hypothesis-driven research questions and design defensible experiments to test those hypotheses.

The importance of seeking to study biological questions from an integrative, regulated approach is highlighted by the influences of culture and behavior on disease pathology. The challenge for integrative physiologists is to incorporate key findings from genetics and molecular biology and to examine how behavioral patterns, including physical activity, diet, and stress, interplay with this genetic variation to affect health and disease.

3.5 Translational Physiology

Exercise physiologists, by the nature of the topics we study and the variety of approaches we use in those studies, make valuable contributions to what has become known as translational physiology. Translational physiology is a term that was originally used in the early 1990s to refer to the research process needed to link cancer risk with its predisposing genetic factors. The field of translational physiology has broadened substantially from that time to include the processes by which basic research findings are extended to the clinical research setting, then to the realm of clinical practice, and finally to health policy. This translational research continuum, however, works best in a bidirectional manner, such that population-based problems, like obesity, also drive the basic research questions that exercise physiologists ask. In turn, these basic research findings eventually drive changes in clinical practice and overall community health.

A good example of opportunities in translational physiology is in the field of aging. Advancing age by itself is a risk factor for many chronic diseases and presents a significant challenge to our health care system and to society in general. In order to fully understand the underlying physiology of aging and be able to engage in appropriate interventions to keep the aging population healthy, we must understand the aging process from the molecular level all the way to the community and population levels. Being able to successfully contribute to the translational physiology process requires a broad skill set to critically examine data and approach scientific problems with new goals in mind, from bench to bedside and from bedside to community.

4 Exercise Physiology in the 21st Century

The field of exercise physiology is rapidly evolving. Ever-expanding technological developments and new approaches to science have substantial implications for health, medicine, and biomedical research. Exercise physiology and our understanding of the physiological processes that underpin physical activity are often at the forefront of this new age of science.

4.1 Exercise in Personalized Medicine

In 2007, the United States Congress passed the Genomics and Personalized Medicine Act. The intent of this legislation was to implement and support research related to formulating a personalized prescription to fit each patient's unique genetic and environmental characteristics in order to optimize health care strategies. This personalized medicine concept first emerged in the field known as pharmacogenomics, which provided scientific insights into why some individuals respond favorably to certain drugs while others do not respond (or may even respond adversely). It could be possible for a physician to prescribe an appropriate dosage to optimize the drug's therapeutic effectiveness for each individual patient.

Similarly, there has been a recent push to personalize each individual's exercise prescription. Exercise is a powerful intervention for the treatment of many different medical conditions—cardiovascular disease, diabetes mellitus, osteoporosis, metabolic diseases, and many more. However, there is significant heterogeneity or variability in people's abilities to perform exercise and adapt to the effects of exercise training, especially in individuals with different clinical disease manifestations. Moreover, researchers are just beginning to understand and formulate optimal training programs or personalized dosages of exercise to produce beneficial responses in these patients.

4.2 The "-Omics" Revolution

As a part of the Human Genome Project, scientists sequenced all 3.2 billion nucleotides that compose the human genome. This was mostly completed in 2003 (the last chromosome was sequenced in 2006) at an estimated cost of $2.7 billion. Today, the entire human genome can be sequenced for less than $1,000. This has opened up new fields of science, often called -omics. This new research area in turn has fostered the development of new technologies aimed at the universal detection of gene sequences and variants (genomics) , the expression of genes at the messenger RNA (mRNA) level (transcriptomics) , the proteins that are produced (proteomics) , and other products of metabolic reactions (i.e., metabolites, studied in metabolomics) involved in all aspects of physiological function (Figure 0.1). One purported appeal of -omics research is that a highly complex system (e.g., the exercising human) can be more fully understood if it is examined at each of the most basic levels of inquiry. As it is applied to exercise physiology, the primary goal of -omics research is to illuminate exercise physiology and behavior in order to better understand the preventive and therapeutic values of exercise.

Epigenetics and Bioinformatics are all very important in exercise physiology.

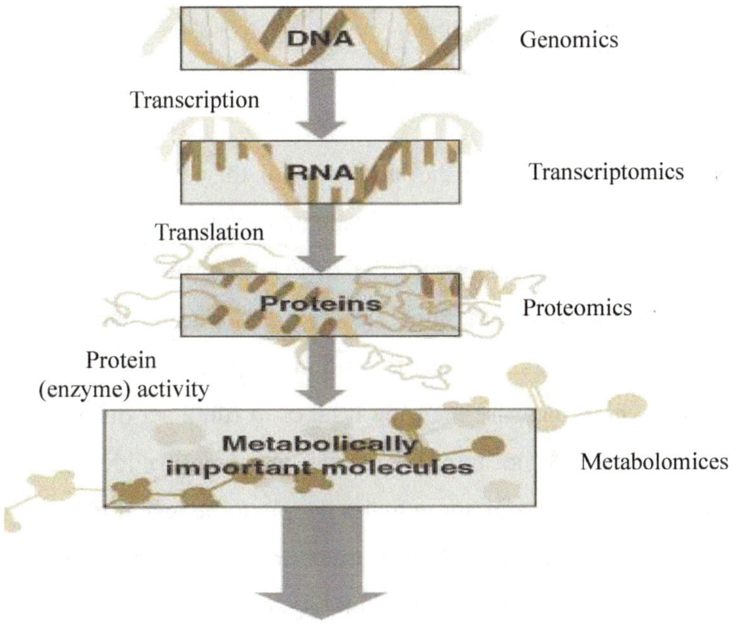

Figure 0.1 The link between genomics, transcriptomics, proteomics, and metabolomics in the context of exercise physiology.

5 Research: The Foundation for Understanding

Exercise and sport scientists actively engage in research to better understand the mechanisms that regulate the body's physiological responses to acute bouts of exercise, as well as its adaptations to training and detraining. Most of this research is conducted at major research universities, medical centers, and specialized institutes using standardized research approaches and select tools of exercise physiologists.

5.1 The Research Process

Science and research (the process by which science is developed) involve a process designed to pose and answer appropriate questions, develop testable hypotheses, test those hypotheses appropriately, generate usable data, interpret those data, and either accept or refute the original hypotheses. Scientists are constantly challenged to make careful observations either from nature or the scientific literature, then ask focused questions that can be examined using a well-designed and well-controlled experimental process. The usual result of this overall process is submitting a research manuscript to an appropriate scientific journal, where it is peer reviewed, revised, and (hopefully) published. As other scientists read the research paper, they may in turn craft their own follow-up questions, and the process continues.

5.2 Research Settings

Research can be conducted either in the laboratory or the field. Laboratory tests are usually more accurate because more specialized and sophisticated equipment can be used and conditions can be carefully controlled. As an example, the direct laboratory measurement of maximal oxygen uptake ($\dot{V}O_{2\,max}$) is considered the most accurate estimate of cardiorespiratory endurance capacity. However, some field tests, such as the 1.5 mi (2.4 km) run, are also used to estimate $\dot{V}O_{2\,max}$. These field tests, which measure the time it takes to run a set distance or the distance that can be covered in a fixed time, are not totally accurate, but they provide a reasonable estimate of $\dot{V}O_{2\,max}$, are inexpensive to conduct, and allow many people to be tested in a short time. Field tests can be conducted in the workplace, on a running track or in a swimming pool, or during athletic competitions. To measure $\dot{V}O_{2\,max}$ directly and accurately, one would need to go to a university or clinical laboratory.

5.3 Research Tools: Ergometers

When physiological responses to exercise are assessed in a laboratory setting, the participant's physical effort must be controlled to provide a measurable exercise intensity. This is generally accomplished through use of ergometers. An ergometer (ergo = work; meter = measure) is an exercise device that allows the intensity of exercise to be controlled (standardized) and measured.

5.3.1 Treadmills

Treadmills are the ergometers of choice for most researchers and clinicians. With these devices, a motor drives a large belt on which a subject can either walk or run; thus, these ergometers are often called motor-driven treadmills. Belt length and width must accommodate the individual's body size and stride length.

Treadmills offer a number of advantages. Walking is a natural activity for almost everyone, so individuals normally adjust to the skill required for walking on a treadmill within a few minutes. Also, most people can achieve their peak values for most physiological variables (heart rate, ventilation, oxygen uptake) on the treadmill, although some athletes (e.g., competitive cyclists) achieve higher values on ergometers that more closely match their mode of training or competition.

5.3.2 Cycle Ergometers

For many years, the cycle ergometer was the primary testing device in use, and it is still used extensively in both research and clinical settings. Cycle ergometers can be designed to allow subjects to pedal either in the normal upright position or in reclining or semi-reclining positions.

Cycle ergometers in a research setting generally use either mechanical friction or electrical resistance. With mechanical friction devices, a belt encompassing a flywheel is tightened or loosened to adjust the resistance against which the cyclist pedals. The power output depends on the combination of the resistance and the pedaling rate—the faster one pedals, the greater the power output. To maintain the same power output throughout the test, one must maintain the same pedaling rate, so pedaling rate must be constantly monitored.

With electrically braked cycle ergometers, the resistance to pedaling is provided by an electrical conductor that moves through a magnetic or electromagnetic field. The strength of the magnetic field determines the resistance to pedaling. These ergometers can be controlled so that the resistance increases automatically as pedal rate decreases, and decreases as pedal rate increases, to provide a constant power output.

Similar to treadmills, cycle ergometers offer some advantages and disadvantages compared to other ergometers. Exercise intensity on a cycle ergometer does not depend on the subject's body weight. This is important when one is investigating physiological responses to a standard rate of work (power output). As an example, if someone lost 5 kg, data derived from treadmill testing could not be compared with data obtained before the weight loss because physiological responses to a set speed and grade on the treadmill vary with body weight. After the weight loss, the rate of work at the same speed and grade would be less than before. With the cycle ergometer, weight loss does not have as great an effect on physiological response to a standardized power output. Thus, walking or running is often referred to as weight-dependent exercise, while cycling is weight independent.

Cycle ergometers also have disadvantages. If the subject does not regularly engage in that form of exercise, the leg muscles will likely fatigue early in the exercise bout. This may prevent a subject from attaining a true maximal intensity. When exercise is limited in this way, responses are often referred to as peak exercise intensity rather than maximal exercise intensity. This limitation may be attributable to local leg fatigue, blood pooling in the legs (less blood returns to the heart) , or the use of a smaller muscle mass during cycling than during treadmill exercise. Trained cyclists, however, tend to achieve their highest peak values on the cycle ergometer.

5.3.3 Other Ergometers

Other ergometers allow athletes who compete in specific sports or events to be tested in a manner that more closely approximates their training and competition. For example, an arm ergometer may be used to test athletes or nonathletes who use primarily their arms and shoulders in physical activity. Arm ergometry has also been used extensively to test and train athletes paralyzed below arm level. The rowing ergometer was devised to test competitive rowers.

When one is choosing an ergometer, the concept of specificity is particularly important with highly trained athletes. The more specific the ergometer is to the actual pattern of movement used by the athlete in his or her sport, the more meaningful the test results will be.

5.4 Research Designs

In exercise physiology research, there are two basic types of research design: cross-sectional and longitudinal. With a cross-sectional research design, a cross section of the population of interest (that is, a representative sample) is tested at one specific time, and the differences between subgroups from that sample are compared. With a longitudinal research design, the same research subjects are retested periodically after initial testing to measure changes over time in variables of interest.

5.5 Research Controls

When we conduct research, it is important to be as careful as possible in designing the study and collecting the data. Changes in a variable over time resulting from an intervention such as exercise can be very small. Yet, even small changes in a variable such as HDL-C can mean a substantial reduction in risk for heart disease. Recognizing this, scientists design studies aimed at providing results that are both accurate and reproducible. This requires that studies be carefully controlled.

Research controls are applied at various levels. Starting with the design of the research project, the scientist must determine how to control for variation in the subjects used in the study. The scientist must determine if it is important to control for the subjects' sex, age, or body size. To use age as an example, for certain variables, the response to an exercise training program might be different for a child or an aged person compared with a young or middle-aged adult. Is it important to control for the subject's smoking or dietary status? Considerable thought and discussion are needed to make sure that the subjects used in a study are appropriate for the specific research questions being asked.

For almost all studies, it is critical to have a control group. Experimental designs often employ a placebo group. Thus, in a study in which a subject might expect to have a benefit from the proposed intervention, such as the use of a specific food or drug, a scientist might decide to use three groups of subjects: an intervention group that receives the actual food or drug, a placebo group that receives an inert substance that looks exactly like the actual food or drug, and a control group that receives nothing. The last group often serves as a time control, accounting for nonexperimentally induced changes that may occur over the course of the study period. If the intervention and placebo groups improve their performance to the same level and the control group does not improve performance, then the improvement is likely the result of the placebo effect, or the expectation that the substance will improve performance. If the intervention group improves performance, and the placebo and control groups do not, then we can conclude that the intervention does improve performance.

One other way of controlling for the placebo effect is to conduct a study that uses a crossover design. In this case, each group undergoes both treatment and control trials at different times. For example, one group is administered the intervention for the first half of the study (e.g., 6 months of a 12-month study) and serves as a control during the last half of the study. The second group serves as a control during the first half of the study and receives the intervention during the second half. In some cases, a placebo can be used in the control phase of the study.

It is equally important to control data collection. The equipment must be calibrated so the researcher knows that the values generated by a given piece of equipment are accurate, and the procedures used in collecting data must be standardized.

Finally, it is important to know that all test results are reproducible.

5.6 Confounding Factors in Exercise Research

Many factors can alter the body's acute response to a bout of exercise. For example, environmental conditions such as the temperature and humidity of the laboratory and the amount of light and noise in the test area can markedly affect physiological responses, both at rest and during exercise. Even the timing, volume, and content of the last meal and the quantity and quality of sleep the night before must be carefully controlled in research studies.

IN CLOSING

In this introduction, we highlighted the historical roots and scientific underpinnings of exercise and sport physiology. We learned that the current state of knowledge in these fields builds on the past and is a bridge to the future—many questions remain unanswered. New and exciting approaches and techniques are being developed continually. While reductionist (e.g., genomics) approaches are growing in popularity, being able to integrate those findings into a systems and whole-body perspective will never go out of style. Exercise and sport physiology is an important part of integrative and translational physiology. We briefly defined the acute responses to exercise bouts and chronic adaptations to long-term training.

KEY TERMS

acute exercise; bioinformatics; chronic adaptation; control group; crossover design; cross-sectional research design; cycle ergometer; environmental physiology; epigenetics; ergometer; exercise physiology; homeostasis; integrative physiology; longitudinal research design; sport physiology; training effect; translational physiology; treadmill

STUDY QUESTIONS

(1) What is exercise physiology? How does sport physiology differ?

(2) Provide an example of "studying acute responses to a single bout of exercise."

(3) Describe what is meant by "studying chronic adaptations to exercise training."

(4) What is an ergometer? Name the two most commonly used ergometers and explain their advantages and disadvantages.

(5) What factors must researchers consider when designing a research study to ensure that they get accurate and reproducible results?

(6) List several environmental conditions that could affect one's response to an acute bout of exercise.

(7) What are the advantages and disadvantages of a cross-sectional versus a longitudinal study design?

运动生理学导论

一、运动生理学的研究对象和任务

运动生理学是从解剖学和生理学两门基础学科演变而来的。解剖学研究的是有机体的结构或者形态，该学科关注人体各部分的基本结构和不同结构之间的相互关系；生理学研究的则是人体的功能。生理学家研究人体的器官系统、组织、细胞以及细胞内分子如何工作，如何整合其功能来调节人体内环境。由于运动会给内稳态带来挑战，运动生理学（exercise physiology）所研究的就是人体在运动时身体功能会如何变化。竞技运动生理学（sport physiology）进一步强调应用，目的是增强运动表现、优化运动训练，其起源于运动生理学，两者紧密联系，很难区分。

二、人体对运动的急性反应和慢性适应

研究运动生理学，主要关注两个概念：人体对一次性运动所做出的急性反应和长时间运动训练时各器官系统的适应。对于急性反应，重点关注人体在一次性运动时做出的即刻反应，有时则会关注一次性运动后的恢复情况，即慢性适应。长期的运动训练使机体产生生理上的适应，从而提高运动表现和训练效果，不同的训练类型会产生高度特异性的适应。

三、运动生理学的发展历史

1.运动生理学的早期历史

关于运动生理学最早的出版物是由塞金和拉瓦锡在1793年发表的论文，他们认为人体氧

气的利用和二氧化碳的产生都发生在肺部。而在19世纪中期，几名德国的生理学家证明有氧氧化发生在人体全身各处的细胞中。第一本有关运动生理学的教科书《身体运动的生理学》由费尔南德·拉格朗日于1889年编写。也有人认为，贝恩布里奇在1931年出版的《肌肉活动的生理学》（第三版）应被认为是该领域最早的学术著作。19世纪末期，运动生理学研究者提出了许多解释肌肉收缩能量来源的理论。但进入20世纪，有研究者发现肌肉活动和乳酸形成之间存在的紧密联系。1922年，希尔因其在能量代谢方面的发现被授予诺贝尔奖。

2.学科交叉以及相互促进的时代

从20世纪初到20世纪30年代，生理学取得了重要的进步，这些进步是运动生理学发展的基础。国际生理科学联合会等机构举办的国际会议为学术交流和讨论创造了条件。其间建立起来的实验室和合作机构，为20世纪一些最重要的运动生理学研究做出了贡献。这一时期出现了大量的研究成果和研究机构，譬如对运动员耐力和力量的研究、哈佛大学疲劳实验室和斯堪的纳维亚对运动生理学的影响，等等。

3.当代研究方法的进展

运动生理学的许多进步必须要归功于技术的进步。20世纪60年代，用于测量呼吸气体的电子气体分析仪的发展，使得能量代谢的研究比以往更为简便和高效；无线电遥测技术用于监测运动过程中的心率和体温等。其他如生物化学技术的使用、肌肉活检技术、遗传学的发展等都为运动生理学的进步提供了条件。20世纪60年代末期，大多数运动生理学研究都集中在全身对运动的反应上，并且大多数研究都涉及对摄氧量、心率、体温、出汗率等这类变量的测量。

4.整合生理学

在如今的“组学”时代，生理学究竟适用在何处？生理学还与人体的健康和疾病相关吗？整合生理学研究的是整个机体如何运转并适应内部和外界的压力。这种方法的基本原理基于内稳态、受调节的器官系统、存在冗余的生理系统等。此外，整合生理学家致力于提出假设驱动的研究问题，并设计可靠的实验来验证这些假设。整合生理学家所面临的问题是统合遗传学和分子生物学的主要发现，以及研究行为模式（包括体力活动、饮食、压力）如何与基因变异相互作用，从而影响人体的健康和疾病。

5.转化生理学

转化生理学的领域包括，首先将基础研究成果扩展到临床研究环境，其次继续扩展到临床实践领域，最后扩展到健康政策的过程。转化研究的流程最适用于双向作用。比如，肥胖这种基于人群的疾病，推动了运动生理学家们提出的基本研究问题；反过来，基础研究的结果最终也会推动临床实践，以及整体社区健康状况的变化。

四、21世纪的运动生理学

运动生理学领域正在迅速发展。不断发展的技术和新的研究方法对健康、医学、生物医学研究具有重大的影响。

1.运动与个性化医疗

个性化医疗的概念最早出现在药物基因组学，它为一部分人为什么对某些药物产生积极反应，而另一部分人没有反应（甚至可能产生不良反应）提供了科学见解。医生可以根据每名患者的不同情况，开出不同剂量的药物，优化治疗效果。同样，近年来运动生理学研究者也在推动个性化运动处方的制定。

2. “组学”变革

随着人类基因组测序成本的降低，“组学”研究在运动生理学领域也有了较大发展。反过来，这个新的研究领域又促进了新的科学技术的发展，包括基因组学、转录组学、蛋白质组学和代谢组学。当“组学”研究用于运动生理学时，其主要目标就是阐明运动生理学和运动行为，以便更好地了解运动在疾病预防和治疗方面的价值。另外，表观遗传学、生物信息学等相关理论在运动生理学领域也有较大的应用。

五、研究：为认识打下基础

运动科学家们需要积极参与研究，以便更好地认识人体对一次性运动的调控机制和长期运动的生理学适应。

1.研究过程

科学的研究过程包括提出和回答问题、做出可检验的假设、正确地对假设进行检验、生成可用数据、解释这些数据，以及接受或驳回原始假设等。

2.研究场景

研究可以在实验室或者场地条件下进行。实验室研究通常更加精确，因为实验设备更专业、精密，实验环境也能得到更好的控制。场地测试可以在工作地点进行，也可以在跑道或游泳池内进行，还可以在比赛中进行。

3.研究工具：测功仪

在实验室环境下评估人体对运动的生理反应时，必须对受试者的功率输出进行控制，以提供可测量的运动强度，通常借助测功仪来完成。测功仪包括跑台、功率自行车等。

4.研究设计

在运动生理学研究中，研究设计有两种基本类型：横向研究和纵向研究。使用横向研究设计，可以在一个特定时间测试目标总体（代表性样本）的横向水平，然后比较该样本的组间差异。通过纵向研究设计，可以在初次测试后定期对相同的研究对象进行重新测试，以观察相关变量随着时间的变化。

5.研究控制

在进行研究时，实验设计和收集数据务必谨慎。研究控制需用在不同层次，如在制订研究计划时，科学家必须要确定如何控制研究受试者的变化，包括性别、年龄、体型等。研究中需要进行大量的思考和讨论，以确保研究的受试者适合所提出的特定研究问题。对几乎所有研究来说，设计对照组是至关重要的。数据的收集过程同样重要，如实验设备必须要校准、收集数据的过程要做到标准化等。最后，所有测试结果都应该是可重复的。

6.运动研究中的干扰因素

许多因素都会改变身体对运动的急性反应。如实验室温度、湿度，以及测试地区的光照、噪声之类的环境因素等，都能影响安静和运动时的生理反应。甚至运动前最后一餐的时间、量、种类，以及前一夜的睡眠时长和质量，在研究中都必须谨慎控制。

Chapter 1
Structure and Function of Exercising Muscle

When the heart beats, when partially digested food moves through the intestines, and when the body moves in any way, muscle is involved. These many and varied functions of the muscular system are performed by three distinct types of muscle (Figure 1.1): smooth muscle, cardiac muscle, and skeletal muscle.

Smooth muscle is sometimes called involuntary muscle because it is not under direct conscious control. It is found in the walls of most blood vessels, where its contraction or relaxation leads to vessel constriction or dilation, respectively, to regulate blood flow. It is also found in the walls of most internal organs, allowing them to contract and relax, for example, to move food through the digestive tract, to expel urine, or to give birth.

Cardiac muscle is found only in the heart, composing the vast majority of the heart's structure. It shares some characteristics with skeletal muscle, but like smooth muscle, it is not under conscious control. Cardiac muscle in essence controls itself, with some fine-tuning by the nervous and endocrine systems.

Skeletal muscles are under conscious control and are so named because most attach to and move the skeleton. Together with the bones of the skeleton, they make up the musculoskeletal system. The human body contains more than 600 skeletal muscles, such as deltoids, pectorals (or "pecs") , and biceps. The thumb alone is controlled by nine separate muscles.

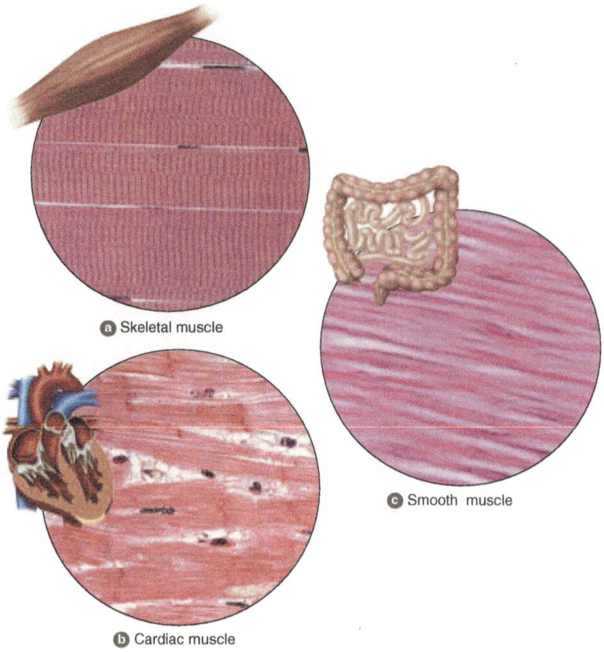

Figure 1.1 Microscopic photographs of the three types of muscle.

Exercise requires movement of the body, which is accomplished through the action of skeletal muscles. Because exercise and sport physiology depend on human movement, the primary focus of this chapter is on the structure and function of skeletal muscle. Although the anatomical structures and control of smooth, cardiac, and skeletal muscle differ in many respects, their principles of action—for example, creating tension, shortening, and lengthening—are similar.

1 Anatomical Structure of Skeletal Muscle

When we think of muscles, we visualize each muscle as a single unit. This is natural because a skeletal muscle most often acts as a single entity. But skeletal muscles are far more complex than that.

If a person were to dissect a muscle, he or she would first find out an outer connective tissue covering known as the epimysium (Figure 1.2). It surrounds the entire muscle and functions to hold it together and give it shape. Once through the epimysium, one would see small bundles of fibers wrapped in a connective tissue sheath. These bundles are called fascicles (or fasciculi) , and the connective tissue sheath surrounding each fascicle is the perimysium.

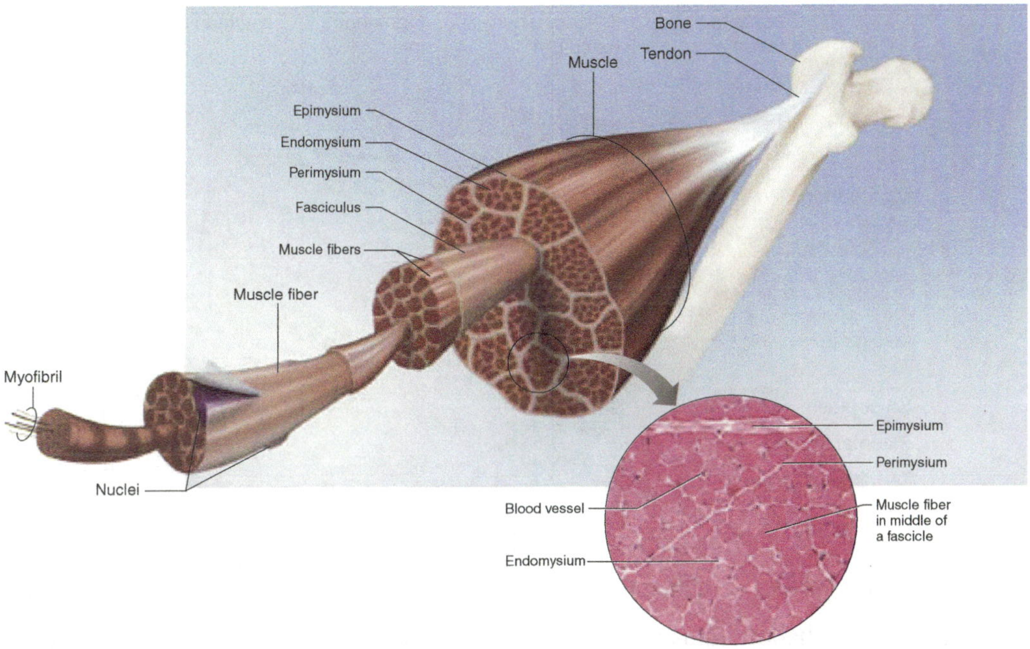

Figure 1.2 The basic structure of muscle.

Finally, by cutting through the perimysium and using a microscope, one would see the individual muscle fibers, each of which is a muscle cell. A sheath of connective tissue, called the endomysium, also covers each muscle fiber. The longest human muscle fibers are about 12 cm (4.7 in.) , which corresponds to about 500,000 sarcomeres, the basic functional unit of the myofibril. The number of fibers in different muscles ranges from several hundred (e.g., in the tensor tympani, attached to the eardrum) to more than a million (e.g., in the medial gastrocnemius muscle).

Muscle fibers range in diameter from 10–120μm, so they are nearly invisible to the naked eye. The following sections describe the structure of the individual muscle fiber.

Each individual muscle fiber is surrounded by a plasma membrane, called the plasmalemma (Figure 1.3). The plasmalemma is part of a larger unit referred to as the sarcolemma. The sarcolemma is composed of the plasmalemma and the basement membrane (some textbooks use the term sarcolemma to refer to just the plasmalemma). At the end of each muscle fiber, its plasmalemma fuses with the tendon, which inserts into the bone. Tendons are made of fibrous cords of connective tissue that transmit the force generated by muscle fibers to the bones, thereby creating motion. So typically, individual muscle fibers are ultimately attached to bone via the tendon.

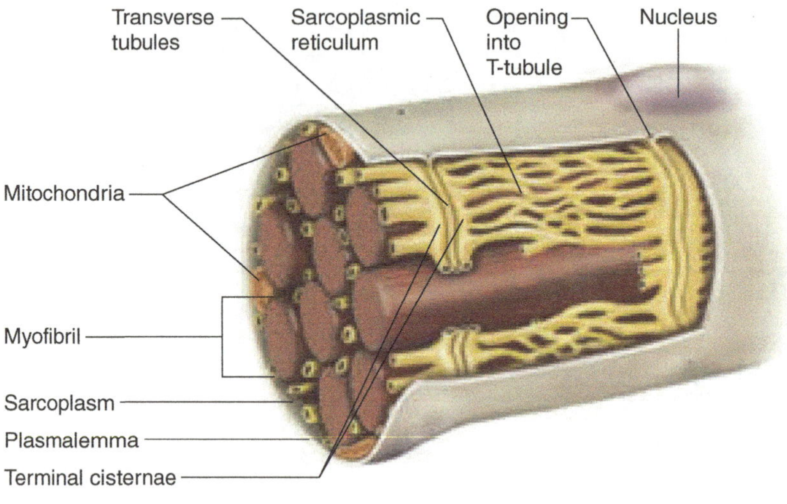

Figure 1.3 The structure of a single muscle fiber.

The plasmalemma has several unique features that are critical to muscle fiber function. It appears as a series of shallow folds along the surface of the fiber when the fiber is contracted or in a resting state, but these folds disappear when the fiber is stretched. This folding allows stretching of the muscle fiber without disrupting the plasmalemma. The plasmalemma also has junctional folds in the innervation zone at the motor end plate, which assists in the transmission of the action potential from the motor neuron to the muscle fiber, as discussed later in this chapter. Finally, the plasmalemma helps to maintain acid-base balance and transport of metabolites from the capillary blood into the muscle fiber.

Satellite cells are located between the plasmalemma and the basement membrane. These cells are involved in the growth and development of skeletal muscle and in muscle's adaptation to injury, immobilization, and training. This is discussed in greater detail in subsequent chapters.

Inside the plasmalemma, a muscle fiber contains successively smaller subunits, as shown in Figure 1.3. The largest of these are myofibrils, the contractile element of the muscle, which are described later. At present, myofibrils are considered to be rod-shaped structures paralleled to the long axis of myofibrils. A gelatin-like substance fills the spaces within and between the myofibrils. This is the sarcoplasm. It is the fluid part of the muscle fiber—its cytoplasm. The sarcoplasm contains mainly dissolved proteins, minerals, glycogen, fats, and necessary organelles. It differs from the cytoplasm of most cells because it contains a large quantity of stored glycogen as well as the oxygen-binding compound myoglobin, which is similar in structure and function to the hemoglobin found in red blood cells.

(1) Transverse Tubules

The sarcoplasm also houses an extensive network of transverse tubules (T-tubules) , which are extensions of the plasmalemma that pass laterally through the muscle fiber. These tubules are interconnected as they pass among the myofibrils, allowing nerve impulses received by the plasmalemma to be transmitted rapidly to individual myofibrils. The tubules also provide pathways from outside the fiber to its interior, enabling substances to enter the cell and waste products to leave the fibers.

(2) Sarcoplasmic Reticulum

A longitudinal network of tubules, known as the sarcoplasmic reticulum (SR) , is also found within the muscle fiber. These membranous channels parallel the myofibrils and loop around them. The SR serves as a storage site for calcium, which is essential for muscle contraction. Figure 1.3 depicts the T-tubules and the SR. Their functions are discussed in more detail later in this chapter when we consider the process of muscle contraction.

2 Myofibrils

Each muscle fiber contains several hundred to several thousand myofibrils. These small fibers are made up of the basic contractile elements of skeletal muscle—the sarcomeres. Under the electron microscope, myofibrils appear as long strands of sarcomeres.

2.1 Sarcomeres

Under a light microscope, skeletal muscle fibers have a distinctive striped appearance. Because of these markings, or striations, skeletal muscle is also called striated muscle. This striation pattern is also seen in cardiac muscle, so it too can be considered striated muscle.

Refer to Figure 1.4, showing myofibrils within a single muscle fiber, and note the striations. Note that dark regions, known as A-bands, alternate with light regions, known as I-bands. Each dark A-band has a lighter region in its center, the H-zone, which is visible only when the myofibril is relaxed. There is a dark line in the middle of the H-zone called the M-line. The light I-bands are interrupted by a dark stripe referred to as the Z-disk, also known as the Z-line.

A sarcomere is the basic functional unit of a myofibril and the basic contractile unit of muscle. Each myofibril is composed of numerous sarcomeres joined end to end at the Z-disks. Each sarcomere includes several elements found between each pair of Z-disks, in this sequence:

- An I-band (light zone)
- An A-band (dark zone)
- An H-zone (in the middle of the A-band)
- An M-line in the middle of the H-zone

Looking at individual myofibrils through an electron microscope, one can differentiate two types of small protein filaments that are responsible for muscle contraction. The thinner filaments are composed primarily of actin, and the thicker filaments are primarily myosin. The striations seen in muscle fibers result from the alignment of these filaments, as illustrated in Figure 1.4. The light I-band indicates the region of the sarcomere where there are only thin filaments. The dark A-band represents the regions that contain both thick and thin filaments. The H-zone is the central portion of the A-band and contains only thick filaments. The absence of thin filaments causes the H-zone to appear lighter than the adjacent A-band. In the center of the H-zone is the M-line, which is composed of proteins that serve as the attachment site for the thick filaments and assist in stabilizing the structure of the sarcomere. Z-disks, composed of proteins, appear at each end of the sarcomere. Along with two additional proteins, titin and nebulin, they provide points of attachment and stability for the thin filaments.

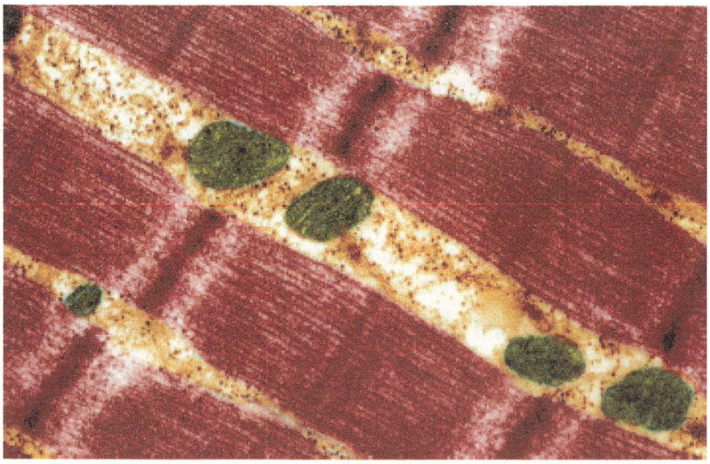

Figure 1.4 An electron micrograph of myofibrils.

Note the striping or striations. The blue regions are the A-bands, and the pink regions are the I-bands.

2.2 Thick Filaments

About two-thirds of all skeletal muscle protein is myosin, the principal protein of the thick filament. Each myosin filament typically contains about 200 myosin molecules.

Each myosin molecule is composed of two protein strands twisted together (Figure 1.5). One end of each strand is folded into a globular head, called the myosin head. Each thick filament contains many such heads, which protrude from the thick filament to form cross bridges that interact during muscle contraction with specialized active sites on the thin filaments. There is an array of fine filaments, composed of titin, that stabilize the myosin filaments along their longitudinal axis (Figure 1.5). Titin filaments extend from the Z-disk to the M-line.

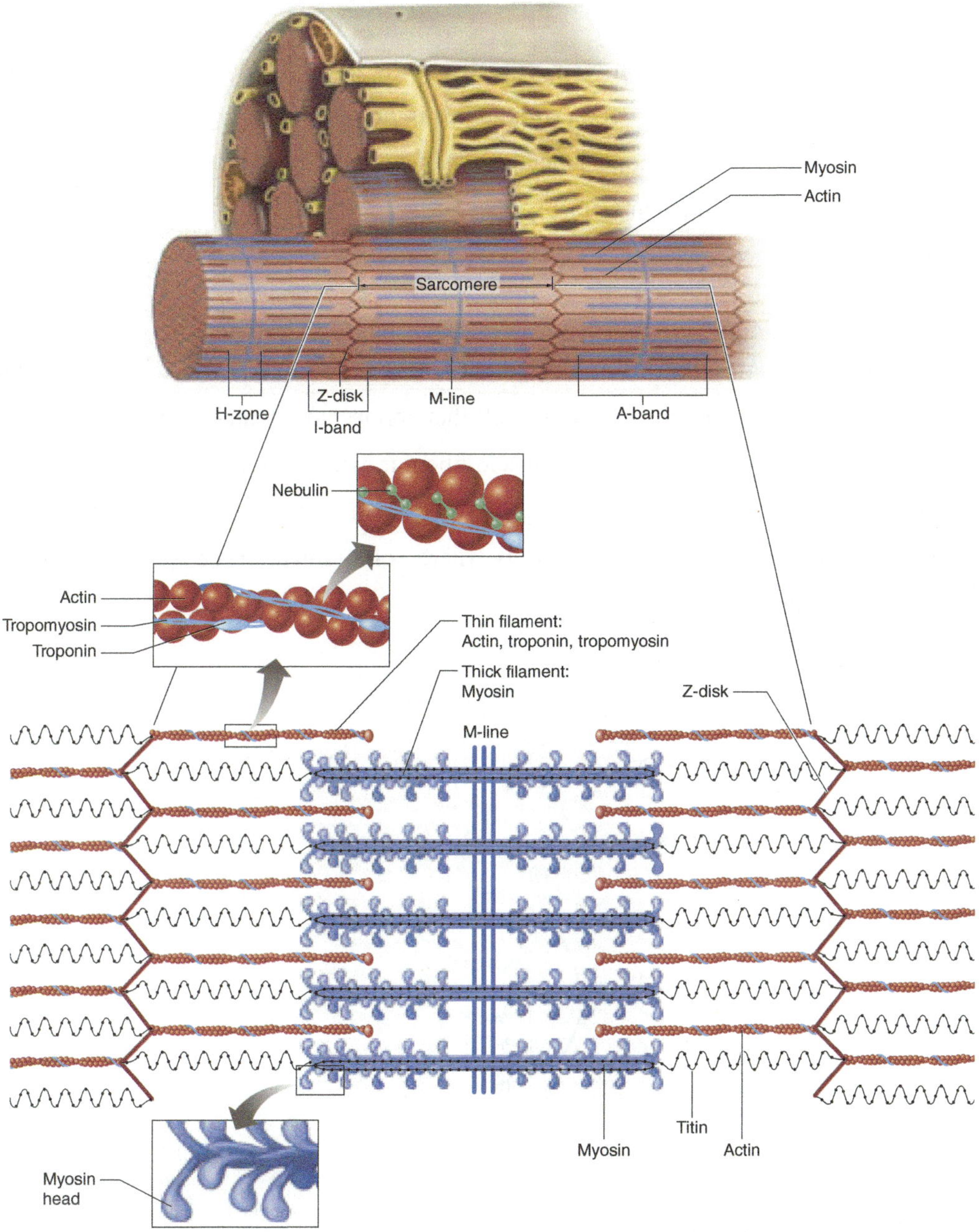

Figure 1.5 The sarcomere contains a specialized arrangement of actin (thin) and myosin (thick) filaments. The role of titin is to position the myosin filament to maintain equal spacing between the actin filaments. Nebulin is often referred to as an "anchoring protein" because it provides a framework that helps stabilize the position of actin.

2.3 Thin Filaments

Each thin filament, although often referred to simply as an actin filament, is actually composed of three different protein molecules—actin, tropomyosin, and troponin. Each thin filament has one end inserted into a Z-disk, with the opposite end extending toward the center of the sarcomere, lying in the space between the thick filaments.

3 Muscle Fiber Contraction

The initiation of contraction of a skeletal muscle occurs in response to a signal from the nervous system. An α-motor neuron is a nerve cell that connects with and innervates many muscle fibers. A single α-motor neuron and all the muscle fibers it directly signals are collectively termed a motor unit (Figure 1.6). The synapse or gap between the α-motor neuron and a muscle fiber is referred to as a neuromuscular junction. This is where communication between the nervous and muscular systems occurs.

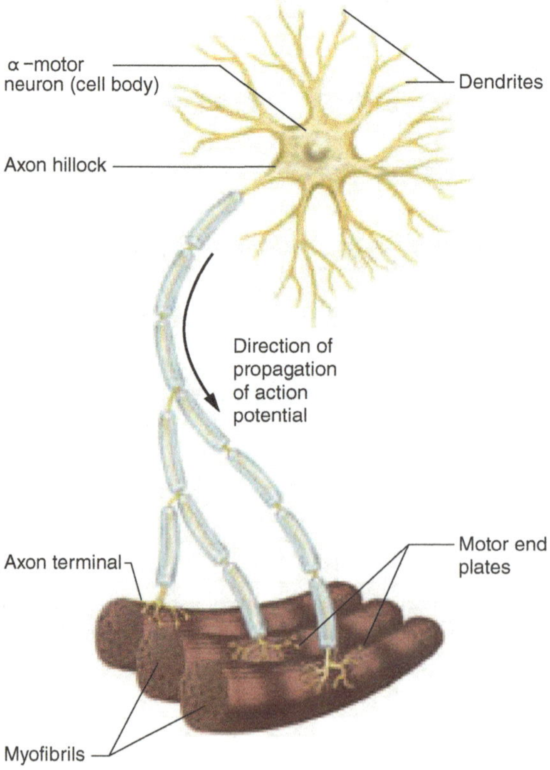

Figure 1.6 A motor unit includes one α -motor neuron and all of the muscle fibers it innervates.

3.1 Excitation-Contraction Coupling

The complex sequence of events that triggers a muscle fiber to contract is termed excitation–contraction coupling because it begins with the excitation of a motor nerve and results in contraction of the muscle fibers. The process, depicted in Figure 1.7, is initiated by a nerve impulse, or action potential, from the brain or spinal cord to an α-motor neuron. The action potential arrives at the α-motor neuron's dendrites, specialized receptors on the neuron's cell body. From here, the action potential travels down the axon to the axon terminals, which are located very close to the plasmalemma.

When the action potential arrives at the axon terminals, these nerve endings release a signaling molecule or neurotransmitter called acetylcholine (ACh) , which crosses the synaptic cleft and binds to receptors on the plasmalemma (Figure 1.7a). If enough ACh binds to the receptors, the action potential will be transmitted the full length of the muscle fiber as ion gates open in the muscle cell membrane and allow sodium to enter. This process is referred to as depolarization. An action potential must be generated in the muscle cell before the muscle cell can act.

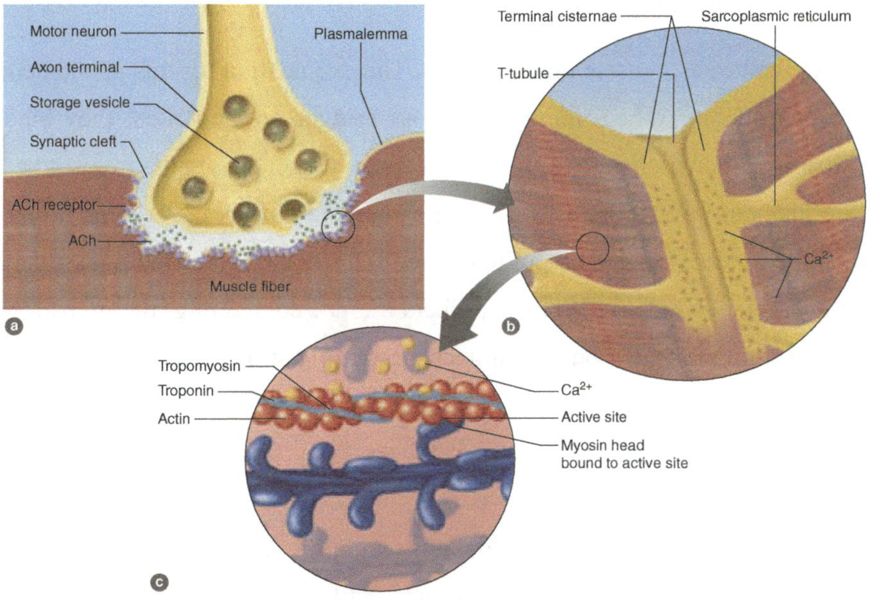

Figure 1.7 The sequence of events leading to muscle action, known as excitation contraction coupling. (a) In response to an action potential, a motor neuron releases acetylcholine (ACh) , which crosses the synaptic cleft and binds to receptors on the plasmalemma. If enough ACh binds, an action potential is generated in the muscle fiber. (b) The action potential triggers the release of calcium ions (Ca^{2+}) from the terminal cisternae of the sarcoplasmic reticulum into the sarcoplasm. (c) The Ca^{2+} binds to troponin on the actin filament, and the troponin pulls tropomyosin off the active sites, allowing myosin heads to attach to the actin filament.

3.2 Role of Calcium in the Muscle Fiber

In addition to depolarizing the fiber membrane, the action potential travels over the fiber's network of tubules (T-tubules) to the interior of the cell. The arrival of an electrical charge causes the adjacent SR to release large quantities of stored calcium ions (Ca^{2+}) into the sarcoplasm (Figure 1.7b).

In the resting state, tropomyosin molecules cover the myosin-binding sites on the actin molecules, preventing the binding of the myosin heads. Once calcium ions are released from the SR, they bind to the troponin on the actin molecules. Troponin, with its strong affinity for calcium ions, is believed to then initiate the contraction process by moving the tropomyosin molecules off the myosin-binding sites on the actin molecules. This is shown in Figure 1.7c. Because tropomyosin normally covers the myosin-binding sites, it blocks the attraction between the myosin cross-bridges and actin molecules. However, once the tropomyosin has been lifted off the binding sites by troponin and calcium, the myosin heads can attach to the binding sites on the actin molecules.

3.3 The Sliding Filament Theory: How Muscles Creating Movement

When muscle contracts, muscle fibers shorten. The explanation for this phenomenon is termed the sliding filament theory. When the myosin cross-bridges are activated, they bind with actin, resulting in a conformational change in the cross-bridge, which causes the myosin head to tilt and to drag the thin filament toward the center of the sarcomere (Figures 1.8). This tilting of the head is referred to as the power stroke. The pulling of the thin filament past the thick filament shortens the sarcomere and generates force. When the fibers are not contracting, the myosin head remains in contact with the actin molecule, but the molecular bonding at the site is weakened or blocked by tropomyosin.

Immediately after the myosin head tilts, it breaks away from the active site, rotates back to its original position, and attaches to a new active site farther along the actin filament. Repeated attachments and power strokes cause the filaments to slide past one another, giving rise to the term sliding filament theory. This process continues until the ends of the myosin filaments reach the Z-disks, or until the Ca^{2+} is pumped back into the SR. During this sliding (contraction) , the thin filaments move toward the center of the sarcomere and protrude into the H-zone, ultimately overlapping. When this occurs, the H-zone is no longer visible.

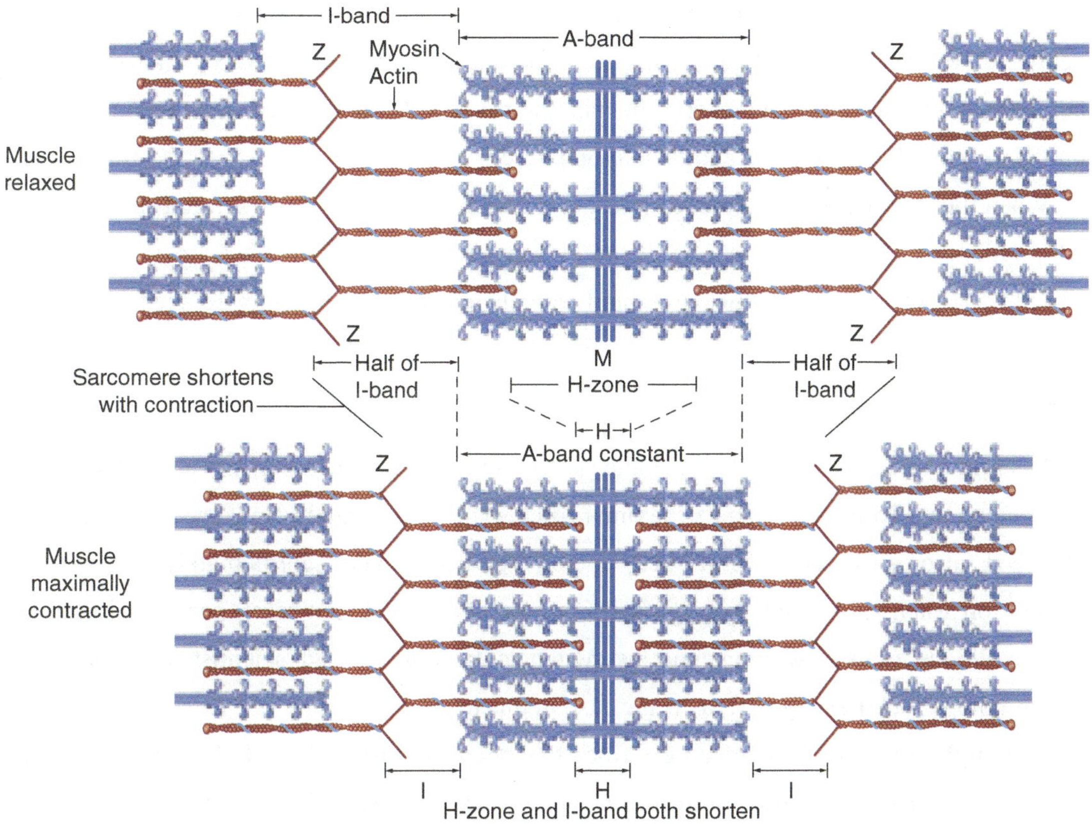

Figure 1.8 A sarcomere in its relaxed (top) and contracted (bottom) state, illustrating the sliding of the actin and myosin filaments with contraction.

Recall that the sarcomeres are joined end to end within a myofibril. Because of this anatomical arrangement, as sarcomeres shorten, the myofibril shortens, causing muscle fibers within a fascicle to shorten. The result of many such fibers shortening is an organized muscle contraction.

3.4 Energy for Muscle Contraction

Muscle contraction is an active process, meaning that it requires energy. In addition to the binding site for actin, a myosin head contains a binding site for the molecule adenosine triphosphate (ATP). The enzyme adenosine triphosphatase (ATPase) , which is located on the myosin head, splits the ATP to yield adenosine diphosphate (ADP) , inorganic phosphate (Pi) , and energy. The energy released from this breakdown of ATP is used to power the tilting of the myosin head. Thus, ATP is the chemical source of energy for muscle contraction.

3.5 Energy for Muscle Relaxation

Muscle contraction continues as long as calcium is available in the sarcoplasm. At the end of a muscle contraction, calcium is pumped back into the SR, where it is stored until a new action potential arrives at the muscle fiber membrane. Calcium is returned to the SR by an active calcium-pumping system. This is another energy-demanding process that also relies on ATP. Thus, energy is required for both the contraction and relaxation phases.

When the calcium is pumped back into the SR, troponin and tropomyosin return to the resting conformation. This blocks the linking of the myosin cross-bridges and actin molecules and stops the use of ATP. As a result, the thick and thin filaments return to their original relaxed state.

4 Muscle Fiber Types

Not all muscle fibers are alike. A single skeletal muscle contains fibers having different speeds of shortening and ability to generate maximal force: type I (also called slow or slow-twitch) fibers and type II (also called fast or fast-twitch) fibers. Type I fibers take approximately 110 ms to reach peak tension when stimulated. Type II fibers, on the other hand, can reach peak tension in about 50 ms. While the terms slow twitch and fast twitch continue to be used, scientists now prefer to use the terminology type I and type II, as is the case in this textbook.

Although only one form of type I fiber has been identified, type II fibers can be further classified. In humans, the two major forms of type II fibers are fast-twitch type a (type Ⅱa) and fast-twitch type x (type Ⅱx). Figure 1.9 is a micrograph of human muscle in which thinly sliced (10 μm) cross sections of a muscle sample have been chemically stained to differentiate the fiber types. The type I fibers are stained black; type Ⅱa fibers are unstained and appear white; and type Ⅱx fibers appear gray. Although not apparent in this Figure, a third subtype of fast-twitch fibers has also been identified: type Ⅱc.

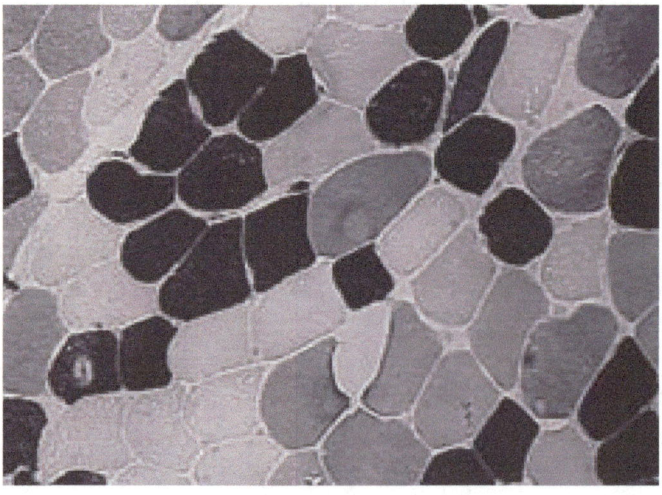

Figure 1.9 A photomicrograph showing type I (black), type Ⅱa (white), and type Ⅱx (gray) muscle fibers.

The differences in the type Ⅱa, type Ⅱx, and type Ⅱc fibers are not fully understood, but type Ⅱa fibers are believed to be the most frequently recruited. Only type I fibers are recruited more frequently than type Ⅱa fibers. Type Ⅱc fibers are the least often used. On average, most muscles are composed of roughly 50% type I fibers and 25% type Ⅱa fibers. The remaining 25% are mostly type Ⅱx, with type Ⅱc fibers making up only 1%–3% of the muscle. Because knowledge about type Ⅱc fibers is limited, we will not discuss them further. The exact percentage of each of these fiber types varies greatly in various muscles and among individuals, so the numbers listed here are only averages. This extreme variation is most evident in athletes, as we will see later in this chapter when we compare fiber types in athletes across sports and events within sports.

In the early 1900s, a needle biopsy procedure was developed to study muscular dystrophy. In the 1960s, this technique was adapted to sample muscle for studies in exercise physiology, specifically to help determine muscle fiber types.

A muscle biopsy (Figure 1.10) involves removing a very small piece of muscle tissue from the muscle belly for analysis. The area from which the sample is taken is first numbed with a local anesthetic, and then a small incision (approximately 1 cm, or 0.4 in.) is made with a scalpel through the skin, subcutaneous tissue, and connective tissue. A hollow needle is then inserted to the appropriate depth into the belly of the muscle. A small plunger is pushed through the center of the needle to snip off a very small sample of muscle. The biopsy needle is withdrawn, and the sample, weighing 10–100 mg, is removed, cleaned of blood, mounted, and quickly frozen. It is then thinly sliced, stained, and examined under a microscope.

This method allows us to study muscle fibers and gauge the effects of acute exercise and chronic training on fiber composition. Microscopic and biochemical analyses of the samples aid our understanding of the muscles' ability to produce energy for contraction.

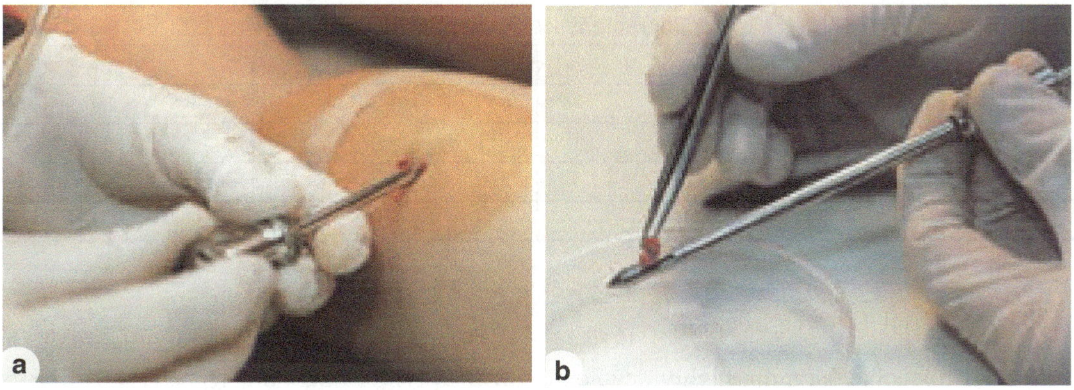

Figure 1.10 (a) The use of a biopsy needle to obtain a sample from the leg muscle of an elite female runner. (b) A close-up view of a muscle biopsy needle and a small piece of muscle tissue.

4.1 Characteristics of Type I and Type II Fibers

Different muscle fiber types play different roles in exercise and sport. This is largely due to differences in their inherent characteristics.

4.1.1 ATPase

Type I and type II fibers differ in their speed of contraction. This difference results primarily from different forms of myosin ATPase. Recall that myosin ATPase is the enzyme that splits ATP to release energy to drive contraction. Type I fibers have a slow form of myosin ATPase, whereas type II fibers have a fast form. In response to neural stimulation, ATP is split more rapidly in type II fibers than in type I fibers. As a result, cross-bridges cycle more rapidly in type II fibers.

One of the methods used to classify muscle fibers is a chemical staining procedure applied to a thin slice of tissue. This staining technique measures the ATPase activity in the fibers. Thus, the type I, type Ⅱa, and type Ⅱx fibers stain differently, as depicted in Figure 1.9. This technique makes it appear that each muscle fiber has only one type of ATPase, but fibers can have a mixture of ATPase types.

Table 1.1 summarizes the characteristics of the different muscle fiber types. The table also includes alternative names that are used in other classification systems to refer to the various muscle fiber types.

Table 1.1 Classification of Muscle Fiber Types

Fiber classification			
System 1 (preferred)	Type I	Type Ⅱa	Type Ⅱx
System 2	Slow-twitch (ST)	Fast-twitch a (FTa)	Fast-twitch x (FTx)
System 2	Slow oxidative (SO)	Fast oxidative/glycolytic (FOG)	Fast glycolytic (FG)
Characteristics of fiber types			
Oxidative capacity	High	Moderately high	Low
Glycolytic capacity	Low	High	Highest
Contractile speed	Slow	Fast	Fast
Fatigue resistance	High	Moderate	Low
Motor unit strength	Low	High	High

4.1.2 Sarcoplasmic Reticulum

Type II fibers have a more highly developed SR than type I fibers do. Thus, type II fibers are more adept at delivering calcium into the muscle cell when stimulated. This ability is thought to contribute to the faster speed of contraction (V_O) of type II fibers. On average, human type II fibers have a V_O that is five to six times faster than that of type I fibers. Although the amount of force (P_O) generated by type IIand type I fibers with the same diameter is about the same, the calculated power ($\mu N \cdot$ fiber length$^{-1} \cdot s^{-1}$) of a type II fiber is three to five times greater than that of a type I fiber because of a faster shortening velocity. This may explain in part why individuals who have a predominance of type II fibers in their leg muscles tend to be better sprinters than individuals who have a high percentage of type I fibers, all other things being equal.

4.1.3 Motor Units

Recall that a motor unit is composed of a single α-motor neuron and the muscle fibers it innervates. The α-motor neuron appears to determine whether the fibers are type I or type II. The α-motor neuron in a type I motor unit has a smaller cell body and typically innervates a cluster of ≤300 muscle fibers. In contrast, the α-motor neuron in a type II motor unit has a larger cell body and innervates ≥300 muscle fibers. This difference in the size of motor units means that when a single type I α-motor neuron stimulates its fibers, far fewer muscle fibers contract than when a single type II α-motor neuron stimulates its fibers. Consequently, type II muscle fibers reach peak tension faster and collectively generate more force than type I fibers. The difference in maximal isometric force development between type IIand type I motor units is attributable to two characteristics: the number of muscle fibers per individual motor unit and the difference in the size of type IIand type I fibers. Type I and type II fibers of the same diameter generate about the same force. On average, however, type II fibers tend to be larger than type I fibers, and type II motor units tend to have more muscle fibers than the type I motor units do.

4.2 Distribution of Fiber Types

As mentioned earlier, the percentages of type I and type II fibers are not the same in all the muscles of the body. Generally, arm and leg muscles have similar fiber compositions within an individual. An endurance athlete with a predominance of type I fibers in his or her leg muscles will likely have a high percentage of type I fibers in the arm muscles as well. A similar relationship exists for type II fibers. There are some exceptions, however. The soleus muscle (beneath the gastrocnemius in the calf) , for example, is composed of a very high percentage of type I fibers in everyone.

4.3 Fiber Type and Exercise

Because of these differences in type I and type II fibers, one might expect that these fiber types would also have different functions when people are physically active. Indeed, this is the case.

4.3.1 Type I Fibers

In general, type I muscle fibers have a high level of aerobic endurance. Type I fibers are very efficient at producing ATP from the oxidation of carbohydrate and fat, which is discussed in Chapter 2.

Recall that ATP is required to provide the energy needed for muscle fiber contraction and relaxation. As long as oxidation occurs, type I fibers continue producing ATP, allowing the fibers to remain active. The ability to maintain muscular activity for a prolonged period is known as muscular endurance, so type I fibers have high aerobic endurance. Because of this, they are recruited most often during low-intensity endurance events (e.g., marathon running) and during most daily activities for which the muscle force requirements are low (e.g., walking).

4.3.2 Type II Fibers

Type II muscle fibers, on the other hand, have relatively poor aerobic endurance when compared to type I fibers. They are better suited to perform anaerobically (without oxygen). This means that in the absence of adequate oxygen, ATP is formed through anaerobic pathways, not oxidative pathways.

Type Ⅱa motor units generate considerably more force than type I motor units do, but type Ⅱa motor units also fatigue more easily because of their limited endurance. Thus, type Ⅱa fibers appear to be the primary fiber type used during shorter, higher-intensity endurance events, such as the mile run or the 400 m swim.

Although the significance of type Ⅱx fibers is not fully understood, they apparently are not easily activated by the nervous system. Thus, they are used rather infrequently in normal, low-intensity activity but are pre-dominantly used in highly explosive events such as the 100 m dash and the 50 m sprint swim. Characteristics of the various fiber types are summarized in Table 1.2.

Tabe 1.2 Structural and Functional Characteristics of Muscle Fiber Types

Characteristic	Fiber type		
	Type I	Type IIa	Type IIx
Fibers per motor neuron	≤300	≥300	≤300
Motor neuron size	Smaller	Larger	Larger
Motor neuron conduction velocity	Slower	Faster	Faster
Contraction speed /ms	110	50	50
Type of myosin ATPase	Slow	Fast	Fast
Sarcoplasmic reticulum development	Low	High	High

4.4 Determination of Fiber Types

The characteristics of muscle fibers appear to be determined early in life, perhaps within the first few years. Studies with identical twins have shown that muscle fiber type, for the most part, is genetically determined, changing little from childhood to middle age. These studies reveal that identical twins have nearly identical proportions of fiber types, whereas fraternal twins differ in their fiber type profiles.

The genes we inherit from our parents likely determine which α-motor neurons innervate our individual muscle fibers. After innervation is established, muscle fibers differentiate (become specialized) according to the type of α-motor neuron that stimulates them. Some recent evidence, however, suggests that endurance training, strength training, and muscular inactivity may cause a shift in the myosin isoforms. Consequently, training may induce a small change, perhaps less than 10%, in the percentage of type I and type II fibers. Further, both endurance and resistance training have been shown to reduce the percentage of type Ⅱx fibers while increasing the fraction of type Ⅱa fibers.

Studies of older men and women have shown that aging may alter the distribution of type I and type II fibers. As we grow older, muscles tend to lose type II motor units, which increases the percentage of type I fibers.

5 Skeletal Muscle and Exercise

Having reviewed the overall structure of muscle, and the process by which it develops force, we now look more specifically at the types of muscle fibers, and how muscle functions during exercise. Strength, endurance, and speed depend largely on the muscle's ability to produce energy and force. This section examines how muscle accomplishes this task.

5.1 Muscle Fiber Recruitment

When an α-motor neuron carries an action potential to the muscle fibers in the motor unit, all fibers in the unit develop force. Activating more motor units is the way muscles produce more force. When little force is needed, only a few motor units are recruited. Recall from our earlier discussion that type Ⅱa and type Ⅱx motor units contain more muscle fibers than type I motor units do. Skeletal muscle contraction involves a progressive recruitment of type I, followed by type II motor units, depending on the requirements of the activity being performed. As the intensity of the activity increases, the number of fibers recruited increases in the following order, in an additive manner: type I → type Ⅱa → type Ⅱx.

Motor units are generally activated on the basis of a fixed order of fiber recruitment. This is known as the principle of orderly recruitment, in which the motor units within a given muscle appear to be ranked. Let's use the biceps brachIIas an example: Assume a total of 200 motor units, which are ranked on a scale from 1–200. For an extremely fine muscle contraction requiring very little force production, the motor unit ranked number 1 would be recruited. As the requirements for force production increase, numbers 2, 3, 4, and so on would be recruited, up to a maximal muscle contraction that would activate most, if not all, of the motor units. To produce a given force, the same motor units are usually recruited each time and in the same order.

A mechanism that may partially explain the principle of orderly recruitment is the size principle, which states that the order of recruitment of motor units is directly related to the size of their motor neuron. Motor units with smaller motor neurons will be recruited first. Because the type I motor units have smaller motor neurons, they are the first units recruited in graded movement (going from very low to very high rates of force production). The type II motor units then are recruited as the force needed to perform the movement increases. It is unclear at this time how the size principle relates to complex athletic movements.

During events that last several hours, exercise is performed at a submaximal pace, and the tension in the muscles is relatively low. As a result, the nervous system tends to recruit those muscle fibers best adapted to endurance activity: the type I and some type Ⅱa fibers. As the exercise continues, these fibers become depleted of their primary fuel supply (glycogen) , and the nervous system must recruit more type Ⅱa fibers to maintain muscle tension. Finally, when the type I and type Ⅱa fibers become exhausted, the type Ⅱx fibers may be recruited to continue exercising.

This may explain why fatigue seems to come in stages during events such as the marathon. It also may explain why it takes great conscious effort to maintain a given pace near the finish of the event. This conscious effort results in the activation of muscle fibers that are not easily recruited. Such information is of practical importance to our understanding of the specific requirements of training and performance.

5.2 Fiber Type and Athletic Success

From what we have just discussed, it appears that athletes who have a high percentage of type I fibers might have an advantage in prolonged endurance events, whereas those with a predominance of type II fibers could be better suited for high-intensity, short-term, and explosive activities. But does the relative proportion of an athlete's muscle fiber types determine athletic success?

The muscle fiber makeup of successful athletes from a variety of athletic events and of non-athletes is shown in Table 1.3. As anticipated, the leg muscles of distance runners, who rely on endurance, have a predominance of type I fibers. Studies of elite male and female distance runners revealed that many of these athletes' gastrocnemius (calf) muscles may contain more than 90% type I fibers. World champions in the marathon are reported to possess 93%–99% type I fibers in their gastrocnemius muscles. In contrast, the gastrocnemius muscles are composed principally of type II fibers in sprint runners, who rely on speed and strength. World-class sprinters have only about 25% type I fibers in this muscle. Also, although muscle fiber cross-sectional area varies markedly among elite distance runners, type I fibers in their leg muscles average about 22% more cross-sectional area than type II fibers.

Tabe 1.3 Percentages and Cross-Sectional Areas of Type I and Type II Fibers in Selected Muscles of Male and Female Athletes

Athlete	Sex	Muscle	% type I	% type II	Cross-sectional area /μm^2	
					Type I	Type II
Sprint runners	M	Gastrocnemius	24	76	5,878	6,034
	F	Gastrocnemius	27	73	3,752	3,930
Distance runners	M	Gastrocnemius	79	21	8,342	6,485
	F	Gastrocnemius	69	31	4,441	4,128
Cyclists	M	Vastus lateralis	57	43	6,333	6,116
	F	Vastus lateralis	51	49	5,487	5,216
Swimmers	M	Posterior deltoid	67	33	—	—
Weightlifters	M	Gastrocnemius	44	56	5,060	8,910
	M	Deltoid	53	47	5,010	8,450
Triathletes	M	Posterior deltoid	60	40	—	—
	M	Vastus lateralis	63	37	—	—
	M	Gastrocnemius	59	41	—	—
Canoeists	M	Posterior deltoid	71	29	4,920	7,040
Shot-putters	M	Gastrocnemius	38	62	6,367	6,441
Nonathletes	M	Vastus lateralis	47	53	4,722	4,709
	F	Gastrocnemius	52	48	3,501	3,141

Swimmers tend to have higher percentages of type I fibers (60%–65%) in their arm muscles than untrained subjects (45%–55%).

The fiber composition of muscles in distance runners and sprinters is markedly different. However, it may be a bit risky to think we can select champion distance runners and sprinters solely on the basis of predominant muscle fiber type. Other factors, such as cardiovascular function, motivation, training, and muscle size, also contribute to success in such events of endurance, speed, and strength. Thus, fiber composition alone is not a reliable predictor of athletic success.

5.3 Muscle Contraction

We have examined the different muscle fiber types. We understand that all fibers in a motor unit, when stimulated, act at the same time and that different fiber types are recruited in stages, depending on the force required to perform an activity. Now we can turn our attention to how whole muscles work to produce movement.

5.3.1 Types of Muscle Contraction

Muscle movement generally can be categorized into three types of contractions—concentric, static, and eccentric. In many activities, such as running and jumping, all three types of contraction may occur in the execution of a smooth, coordinated movement. For the sake of clarity, though, we will examine each type separately.

A muscle's principal action, shortening, is referred to as a concentric contraction, the most familiar type of contraction. To understand muscle shortening, recall our earlier discussion of how the thin and thick filaments slide across each other. In a concentric contraction, the thin filaments are pulled toward the center of the sarcomere. Because joint movement is produced, concentric contractions are considered dynamic contractions.

Muscles can also act without moving. When this happens, the muscle generates force, but its length remains static (unchanged). This is called a static (isometric) muscle contraction because the joint angle does not change. A static contraction occurs, for example, when one tries to lift an object that is heavier than the force generated by the muscle, or when one supports the weight of an object by holding it steady with the elbow flexed. In both cases, the person feels the muscles tense, but there is no joint movement. In a static contraction, the myosin cross-bridges form and are recycled, producing force, but the external force is too great for the thin filaments to be moved. They remain in their normal position, so shortening can't occur. If enough motor units can be recruited to produce sufficient force to overcome the resistance, a static contraction can become a dynamic one.

Muscles can exert force even while lengthening. This movement is an eccentric contraction. Because joint movement occurs, this is also a dynamic contraction. An example of an eccentric contraction is the action of the biceps brachii when one extends the elbow slowly to lower a heavy weight. In this case, the thin filaments are pulled farther away from the center of the sarcomere, essentially stretching it.

5.3.2 Generation of Force

Whenever muscles contract, whether the contraction is concentric, static, or eccentric, the force developed must be graded to meet the needs of the task or activity. The amount of muscle force developed is dependent on the number and type of motor units activated, the frequency of stimulation of each motor unit, the size of the muscle, the muscle fiber and sarcomere length, and the muscle's speed of contraction.

5.3.3 Motor Units and Muscle Sizes

More force can be generated when more motor units are activated. Type II motor units generate more force than type I motor units because a type II motor unit contains more muscle fibers than a type I motor unit. In a similar manner, larger muscles, having more muscle fibers, can produce more force than smaller muscles.

5.3.4 Frequency of Stimulation of Motor Units: Rate Coding

A single motor unit can exert varying levels of force dependent on the frequency at which it is stimulated. This is illustrated in Figure 1.11. The smallest contractile response of a muscle fiber or a motor unit to a single electrical stimulus is termed a twitch. A series of three stimuli in rapid sequence, before complete relaxation from the first stimulus, can elicit an even greater increase in force or tension. This is termed summation. Continued stimulation at higher frequencies can lead to the state of tetanus, resulting in the peak force or tension of the muscle fiber or motor unit. Rate coding is the term used to refer to the process by which the tension of a given motor unit can vary from that of a twitch to that of tetanus by increasing the frequency of stimulation of that motor unit.

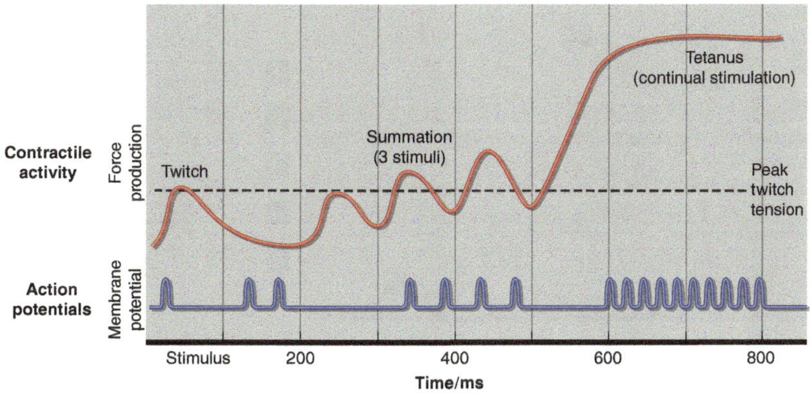

Figure 1.11 Variation in force of tension produced based on electrical stimulation frequency, illustrating the concepts of a twitch, summation, and tetanus.

5.3.5 Length-Tension Relation

Each muscle fiber has an optimal length for generating force. Recall that each muscle fiber is composed of sarcomeres connected end to end and that these sarcomeres are made up of both thick and thin filaments. The optimal sarcomere length is defined as that length where there is optimal overlap between the thick and thin filaments. This maximizes the potential for cross-bridge interaction, as illustrated in Figure 1.12. When a sarcomere is overly stretched (1) or shortened (5) , little or no force can be developed since there is little cross-bridge interaction. The muscle's resting length is determined by the tendons that attach muscles to the bones on either end. As it turns out, this natural resting length maximizes the muscle's ability to generate force, referred to as the length-tension relation.

The implication of this relation is that muscle length, and therefore joint angle, will provide a mechanical advantage for force generation of a particular muscle or muscle group. The length-tension curve shown in Figure 1.12 illustrates this phenomenon. Maximal tension can be achieved at sarcomere lengths between 2.0 and 2.25μm, where the overlap between myosin and actin is optimal (i.e., the highest number of cross-bridges can be formed). As the sarcomere becomes elongated (> 2.25μm) , the number of possible cross-bridges decreases, and therefore tension development (the descending limb of the curve) decreases accordingly. When sarcomeres are shortened to lengths < 2.0μm, the ability of myosin to interact with actin decreases because there are fewer myosin heads available to interact with actin (actin moves close to the M-line where there are few myosin heads; Figure 1.12). Another possible explanation for the reduced ability to produce force at lengths < 2.0μm is the physical constraint imposed by myosin reaching the Z-line of the sarcomere.

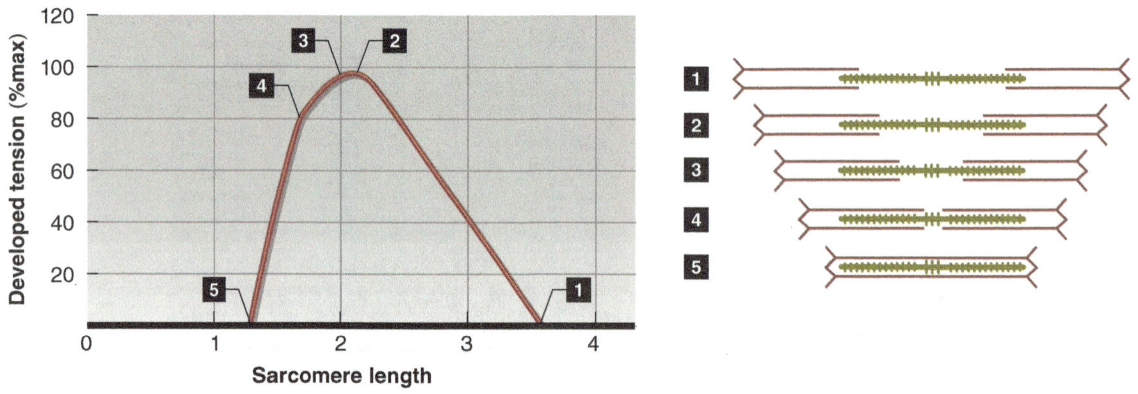

Figure 1.12 Variation in force of tension produced (% of maximum) with changes in sarcomere length, illustrating the concepts of optimal length for force production.

5.3.6 Force-Velocity Relation

The ability of the muscle to develop force also depends on the speed of contraction. When people try to lift a very heavy object, they tend to do it slowly, maximizing the force they can apply to it. If they grab it and quickly try to lift it, they will likely fail, if not injure themselves. The force–velocity relation of a muscle illustrates muscle force as a function of the speed of contraction. During concentric (muscle-shortening) contractions, maximal force development decreases progressively as the speed of contraction increases. However, with eccentric (muscle-lengthening) contractions, the opposite is true.

This relation between force development and speed of contraction can be explained by the number of total cross-bridges attached at various speeds of contraction. When a muscle is contracting slowly, there is more time for cross-bridge formation than when contractions occur at higher speeds. In other words, when cross-bridges are formed at higher velocities, the ability of the muscle to produce force is reduced.

The force-velocity relation applies to both shortening and lengthening contractions. As depicted in Figure 1.13, increasing the velocity of contraction while shortening (moving rightward along the *x*-axis) reduces force. Another way to think of the force-velocity relation is in terms of applying an external force to the muscle, such as performing a biceps curl. As the load gets heavier, the speed of contraction gets slower. When the load applied equals the maximal isometric force of the muscle, contraction velocity equals zero (by definition, an isometric contraction involves no movement). Now, let's explore what will happen when the load applied to the muscle is higher than the maximal isometric force and the muscle lengthens. In this case, the ability of the muscle to produce force will increase as a function of speed (moving leftward along the x-axis in Figure 1.13) because as the load increases beyond maximal isometric, the speed of contraction will also increase.

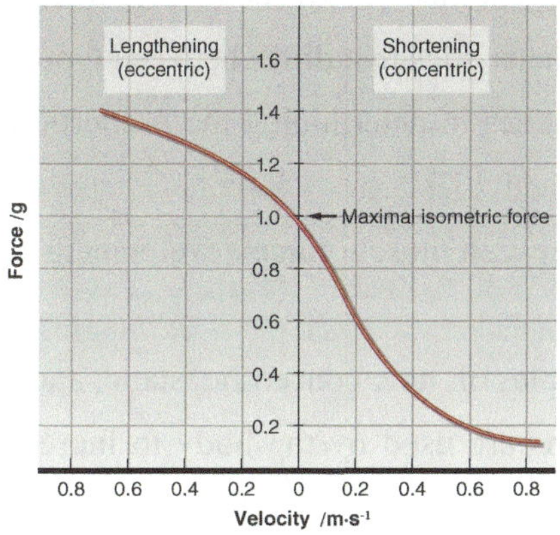

Figure 1.13 The relation between muscle lengthening and shortening velocity and force production. Note that the capacity for the muscle to generate force is greater during eccentric (muscle-lengthening) actions than during concentric (muscle-shortening) actions.

IN CLOSING

In this chapter, we reviewed the components of skeletal muscle. We considered the differences in fiber types and their impact on physical performance. We learned how muscles generate force and produce movement. Now that we understand how movement is produced, we turn our attention to how movement is fueled. In the next chapter, we focus on metabolism and energy production.

KEY TERMS

actin; action potential; adenosine triphosphatase; adenosine triphosphate; α-motor neuron; concentric contraction; dynamic contraction; eccentric contraction; endomysium; epimysium; fasciculus; fast-twitch (type II) fiber; motor unit; muscle fiber; myofibril; myosin; cross-bridge; nebulin; perimysium; plasmalemma; principle of orderly recruitment; rate coding; sarcolemma; sarcomere; sarcoplasm; sarcoplasmic reticulum (SR) ; satellite cells; contractile; velocity; size principle; sliding filament theory; slow-twitch (type I) fiber; static (isometric) contraction; summation; tetanus; transverse tubules (T-tubules)

STUDY QUESTIONS

(1) List and describe the anatomical components that make up a muscle fiber.

(2) List the components of a motor unit.

(3) What are the steps in excitation-contraction coupling?

(4) What is the role of calcium in muscle contraction?

(5) Describe the sliding filament theory. How do muscle fibers shorten?

(6) What are the basic characteristics that differ between type I and type II muscle fibers?

(7) What is the role of genetics in determining the proportions of muscle fiber types and the potential for success in selected activities?

(8) Describe the relation between muscle force development and the recruitment of type I and type II motor units.

(9) Explain, and give examples of, how concentric, static, and eccentric contractions differ.

(10) What two mechanisms are used by the body to increase force production in a single muscle?

(11) What is the optimal length of a muscle for maximal force development?

(12) What is the relation between maximal force development and the speed of shortening (concentric) and lengthening (eccentric) contractions?

第一章
肌肉的结构和功能

平滑肌不受意识的支配，为非随意肌。大多数血管壁上有平滑肌，它们的收缩和舒张可调节血管内的血流量。多数内脏器官管壁也有平滑肌，通过它们的收缩和舒张，可完成食物在消化道的运动、尿液的排出和胎儿的分娩等。

心肌仅在心脏可见，是构成心脏壁的主要成分。心肌的某些特性与骨骼肌类似，但与平滑肌一样，也属于非随意肌。心肌的运动是在神经系统和内分泌系统的微细调节下进行自我调控的。

骨骼肌受意识的支配，为随意肌。由于其附着在骨骼上，并可引起骨骼的运动，故此得名。人体全身共有600多块骨骼肌，如三角肌、胸大肌、肱二头肌等。其中控制拇指运动的肌肉就有9块之多。

一、骨骼肌的解剖学结构

在解剖一块肌肉时首先会发现，每块肌肉的外面覆有结缔组织，称为肌外膜。肌外膜包绕整块肌肉。切开肌外膜，可见许多由结缔组织包绕的肌纤维束，称为肌束。包绕在肌束外面的结缔组织，称为肌束膜。

切开肌束膜，显微镜下才可以看到单个的肌细胞（亦称肌纤维）。每条肌纤维外面也覆有结缔组织，称为肌内膜。肌纤维的直径为10～120微米，用肉眼几乎无法看到。显微镜下，肌纤维可见许多明暗相间的横纹。肌节是肌纤维的结构和功能单位。

每条独立的肌纤维被质膜所包裹。质膜是肌膜的一部分，肌膜由质膜和基底膜组成（有些教科书使用“肌膜”一词来指代“质膜”）。

在质膜内部，每条肌纤维还包含有许多小的亚单位。其中最大的为肌原纤维，是肌肉的收缩成分。肌原纤维内及肌原纤维之间都有凝胶样物质，这种物质称为肌浆。它是肌纤维胞质内的液态部分，主要包含可溶性蛋白质、无机物、糖原、脂肪及细胞器。肌浆包括横小管、肌浆网等结构。

二、肌原纤维

肌原纤维是由骨骼肌的基本收缩成分——大量肌节连接而成的。

（一）肌节

一条肌纤维内有许多肌原纤维，并可见横纹，即明暗带相间出现。暗带也叫A带，明带也叫I带。暗带中央还有一个色浅区域，称为H带，H带仅在肌原纤维舒张时可见。H带的中央有一条色深的线，叫M线。明带的中央有一条色深的区域，叫Z盘或Z线。肌节为肌原纤维的基本功能单位，也是肌肉的基本收缩单位。每条肌原纤维由大量的肌节组成，肌节与肌节借Z线连接。肌节指的是相邻两条Z线之间的部分。

（二）粗肌丝

粗肌丝的主要蛋白为肌球蛋白，约占骨骼肌总蛋白的2/3。每个肌球蛋白大约由200个肌球蛋白分子组成。肌球蛋白分子由两条蛋白链互相缠绕而成。蛋白链的一端折叠形成球形，为肌球蛋白头。粗肌丝有许多突出于表面的肌球蛋白头，其形成横桥，在骨骼肌收缩时，横桥与细肌丝的特定激活位点结合。肌联蛋白与肌球蛋白并行，具有稳定肌球蛋白分子的作用。肌联蛋白从Z线延续到M线。

（三）细肌丝

细肌丝主要是由肌动蛋白组成，也有原肌球蛋白和肌钙蛋白。每一个细肌丝一端插入Z盘，另一端延伸至肌节的中心，与粗肌丝镶嵌。

三、肌纤维的收缩

骨骼肌收缩是对神经系统发来的信号做出反应。α运动神经元与肌纤维相连接，并支配肌纤维的活动。一个α运动神经元及其所支配的所有肌纤维合称一个运动单位。α运动神经元与肌纤维之间的间隙（突触）称为神经肌肉接头，是神经和肌肉进行信息交流的部位。

（一）兴奋–收缩耦联

触发肌纤维收缩的复杂过程被称为兴奋–收缩耦联，是由神经冲动或动作电位引发的，从大脑或脊髓到α运动神经元。动作电位到达α运动神经元的树突，激活神经元细胞体上的受体，从这开始，动作电位沿着轴突到轴突末梢。轴突末梢位于非常接近质膜的地方。

动作电位到达轴突终末时，神经末梢会分泌神经递质——乙酰胆碱，乙酰胆碱将与肌膜上的受体结合。乙酰胆碱和肌膜上的受体大量结合后，动作电位将传遍整条肌纤维，肌膜上的离子通道开放，钠离子进入，此过程称为去极化。在肌纤维收缩之前必定有动作电位产生。

（二）钙在肌纤维中扮演的角色

动作电位除引起肌细胞膜去极化，还沿着T小管形成的网络传遍肌纤维内部。产生的电流可以使其相邻的肌浆网释放大量的钙离子进入到肌浆。

在静息状态下，原肌球蛋白覆盖肌动蛋白的肌球蛋白结合位点，阻止肌球蛋白头与此位点结合。当钙离子从肌浆网释放出来后，与附着在肌动蛋白的肌钙蛋白结合，可使原肌球蛋白从肌动蛋白的肌球蛋白结合位点移开，肌球蛋白头就会与肌动蛋白的结合位点结合，从而触发肌肉的收缩过程。

（三）肌丝滑行理论：肌肉如何产生运动

肌球蛋白与肌动蛋白结合，导致肌球蛋白横桥的构象发生变化，横桥被激活，引起肌球蛋白头发生屈动，拉动细肌丝移向肌节中央。这个头部倾斜的过程称为做功冲程。细肌丝滑向粗肌丝，肌节缩短并产生力量。肌纤维放松时，肌球蛋白头仍可能与肌动蛋白分子接触，但其结合位点会被原肌球蛋白覆盖。

肌球蛋白头屈动后，即与结合位点分离，回到原来的位置，再与另一个肌动蛋白结合位点结合。如此反复，肌丝之间产生滑动，就构成了肌丝滑动的原理。这种收缩过程会一直持续，直到肌球蛋白分子的一端到达Z线或者钙离子被泵回到肌浆网。在肌丝滑动（肌肉收缩）过程中，细肌丝滑向肌节中央，伸入到H带，与H带重叠，此时，H带便消失。

（四）肌肉收缩的供能

肌肉收缩是一个主动过程，需要消耗能量。肌球蛋白头除与肌动蛋白结合，还必须结合三磷酸腺苷（ATP），为肌肉的收缩提供能量。位于肌球蛋白头部的ATP酶，可以分解ATP以产生二磷酸腺苷（ADP）和无机磷，并释放能量。ATP分解释放的能量可以引起肌球蛋白头的屈动。ATP是肌肉收缩的化学性能量来源。

（五）肌肉舒张的供能

只要肌浆中钙离子一直存在，肌肉收缩就会一直持续。当钙离子泵回到肌浆网储存起来，肌肉收缩即结束，直到新的动作电位再次传到肌细胞膜。钙离子泵回肌浆网，是钙泵的主动运输过程，需要ATP供能才可以完成。因此，肌肉的收缩和舒张都需要消耗能量。

当钙离子泵回到肌浆网，原肌球蛋白和肌钙蛋白恢复到安静状态的构象。此时，肌球蛋白横桥与肌动蛋白分子的结合会受阻，ATP供能也停止，细肌丝和粗肌丝也恢复到最初的静息状态。

四、肌纤维的类型

Ⅰ型肌纤维为慢缩型，Ⅱ型肌纤维为快缩型。慢缩型肌纤维在受到刺激时约需110毫秒达到最大收缩状态，而快缩型肌纤维仅需50毫秒。

Ⅰ型肌纤维只有一种，Ⅱ型肌纤维还可以分出许多亚型，主要有Ⅱa型和Ⅱx型两种。人类Ⅱx型肌纤维的数量与动物Ⅱb型肌纤维大致相等。一般认为Ⅱa型肌纤维是最常被募集的，但Ⅰ型肌纤维的募集多于Ⅱa型肌纤维，Ⅱc型肌纤维是最少被募集的。通常，大多数肌纤维含有50%的Ⅰ型肌纤维和25%的Ⅱa 型肌纤维；余下的25%大部分都是Ⅱx型肌纤维；Ⅱc型肌纤维仅占 1%～3%。不同个体、不同部位的肌肉，各型肌纤维所占的比例不完全一样，因此上述的比例只是平均值。运动员的肌纤维类型差异最大。

（一）Ⅰ型和Ⅱ型肌纤维的特征

1. ATP酶

Ⅰ型肌纤维和Ⅱ型肌纤维的收缩速度不同，主要是因为肌球蛋白ATP酶不同。肌球蛋白ATP酶分解ATP释放能量，引起骨骼肌收缩。Ⅱ型肌纤维分解ATP的速度较Ⅰ型肌纤维分解ATP的速度快，因此，Ⅱ型肌纤维横桥的循环使用更快。

2. 肌浆网

Ⅱ型肌纤维较Ⅰ型肌纤维的肌浆网发达。因此，Ⅱ型肌纤维在受到刺激时，钙离子更容易进入肌细胞，这也是Ⅱ型肌纤维在收缩时具有较快收缩速度的原因。人类Ⅱ型肌纤维收缩速度为Ⅰ型肌纤维的5～6倍。Ⅱ型肌纤维和Ⅰ型肌纤维产生的收缩力基本相同，但因为Ⅱ型肌纤维有较快的收缩速度，所以其产生的功率为Ⅰ型肌纤维的3～5倍。

3. 运动单位

运动单位是指一个α运动神经元及其所支配的所有肌纤维。α运动神经元决定着所支配的肌纤维是Ⅰ型还是Ⅱ型。Ⅰ型肌纤维内的运动单位，其α运动神经元胞体较小，支配的肌纤维数不多于300条；而Ⅱ型肌纤维内的运动单位，其α运动神经元胞体较大，支配的肌纤维数不少于300条。运动单位的大小不同，意味着Ⅰ型α运动神经元刺激肌纤维时，只能引起较少肌纤维收缩，而Ⅱ型α运动神经元刺激肌纤维时，能引起较多肌纤维收缩。Ⅱ型肌纤维达到最大收缩力的速度快于Ⅰ型肌纤维，且产生的力量也较大。Ⅱ型肌纤维和Ⅰ型肌纤维运动单位之间最大等长力量发展的差异可归因于两点：每个运动单位的肌纤维数量，以及Ⅱ型肌纤维和Ⅰ型肌纤维的大小。相同直径的Ⅰ型肌纤维和Ⅱ型肌纤维产生大约相同的力。平均来讲，Ⅱ型肌纤维体积往往大于Ⅰ型肌纤维，而且Ⅱ型肌纤维运动单位往往比Ⅰ型肌纤维运动单位具有更多的肌纤维。

（二）肌纤维类型的分布

如前所述，身体的所有肌肉都含有不同比例的Ⅰ型肌纤维和Ⅱ型肌纤维。一般来说，人体上肢和下肢的肌肉具有相似的肌纤维组成，研究表明均是Ⅰ型肌纤维较多，Ⅱ型肌纤维较少。但也有一些例外，如比目鱼肌，Ⅰ型肌纤维占有非常高的比例。

（三）肌纤维类型与运动

1. Ⅰ型肌纤维

通常，Ⅰ型肌纤维具有很高的有氧耐力，Ⅰ型肌纤维中糖和脂肪氧化产生ATP的速度非常快。

如前所述，肌肉在收缩和舒张过程中都需要ATP提供能量。只要有氧化存在，Ⅰ型肌纤维就可以持续产生ATP，维持肌肉运动。维持肌肉进行长时间运动的能力，称为肌肉的耐力，所以Ⅰ型肌纤维具有较高的有氧耐力。

2. Ⅱ型肌纤维

Ⅱ型肌纤维与Ⅰ型肌纤维相比，有氧耐力相对较弱，更加适合于在无氧状态下工作。

Ⅱa型肌纤维运动单位较Ⅰ型肌纤维运动单位产生更大的力量，但因为其耐力较弱，所以更容易疲劳。因此，Ⅱa型肌纤维适合于短距离、高强度的运动，如1英里（约1609米）跑或400米游泳。

Ⅱx型肌纤维不易被神经系统激活。Ⅱx型肌纤维很少参与日常的低强度活动，但在100米跑和50米游泳等高强度运动中发挥重要作用。

（四）肌纤维类型的鉴定

对同卵双胞胎的研究发现，肌纤维类型主要是由基因决定的。父母遗传的基因决定着α运动神经元支配的肌纤维类型。一旦神经支配建立，肌纤维就会分化为α运动神经元支配的类型。最新研究显示，耐力训练、力量训练和肌肉制动均会引起肌纤维类型的转变。

对老年人的研究表明，年龄的增长可引起肌纤维类型发生转变。随着年龄的增长，Ⅱ型肌纤维比例将会减少，Ⅰ型肌纤维比例将会增加。

五、骨骼肌与运动

（一）肌纤维的募集

当α运动神经元向运动单位中的肌纤维传递动作电位时，运动单位中的所有纤维都会产生力。激活更多的运动单位可以使肌肉产生更多力量。当产生较小的力量时，只有一小部分的运动单位被募集。随着运动强度的增加，募集的肌纤维数量按以下顺序，以递增的方式增加：Ⅰ型→Ⅱa型→Ⅱx型。

特定肌肉内的运动单位是按照一定方式募集的。以肱二头肌为例，假设共有200个运动单位，从1～200排列，如果需要一个非常精确的肌肉收缩产生极其小的力量，仅需要运动单位1被募集；当需要的力量增加时，运动单位2、3、4等逐渐被募集；达到最大收缩时，几乎所有的运动单位都会被募集。如果产生一个特定的力，每次都会动员同样的运动单位，并且是按照同样顺序动员的。

大小原则能够部分解释运动单位有序募集的机制，即运动单位的有序募集与运动神经元的大小直接相关。小的运动神经元首先被动员。

（二）肌纤维类型与竞技场上的成功

需要很强耐力的长跑运动员，其腿部肌肉中Ⅰ型肌纤维占优势。研究表明，优秀的男女长跑运动员的腓肠肌均含有超过90%的Ⅰ型肌纤维。据报道，马拉松世界冠军的腓肠肌中含有93%～99%的Ⅰ型肌纤维。相比之下，短跑运动员的腓肠肌主要由Ⅱ型肌纤维组成，短跑更依赖于速度和力量。世界一流的短跑运动员的腓肠肌中只有大约25%的Ⅰ型肌纤维。游泳运动员上肢含有较多的Ⅰ型肌纤维（60%～65%），而未经训练的人仅含有45%～55%的Ⅰ型肌纤维。

长跑运动员和短跑运动员的肌纤维组成明显不同，但是仅靠优势肌纤维类型来选材有很大风险，因为肌肉的耐力、速度和力量也受心血管功能、动机、训练水平和肌肉体积等影响。所以，把肌纤维类型的组成作为运动员选材的唯一条件是不可靠的。

（三）肌肉收缩

一个运动单位支配的所有肌纤维，在受到刺激时，根据运动过程中所需的力量不同，在不同阶段募集的肌纤维类型不同。现在来介绍肌肉作为整体是如何产生运动的。

1.肌肉收缩的分类

肌肉收缩时长度缩短称为向心收缩。肌肉作向心收缩时，细肌丝滑向肌节中央。由于向心收缩可引起关节的运动，所以也称为动力性收缩。

肌肉在收缩时，也可不引起运动，此时肌肉收缩产生力，但其长度不变，称为静力收缩或等长收缩。静力收缩时，肌球蛋白横桥循环利用产生力量，但由于外力太大以至于细肌丝不能被移动，粗、细肌丝还保持其正常结构，肌肉不能缩短。

肌肉在被拉长的过程中产生力量，这种方式称为离心收缩。此时可引起关节运动，因此也属于动力收缩。肌肉作离心收缩时，细肌丝从肌节中央滑出，肌纤维被拉长。

2.力的产生

肌力的大小，取决于激活的运动单位类型和数量、每个运动单位的刺激频率、肌肉体积的大小、肌纤维和肌节的长度和肌纤维收缩的速度。

3. 运动单位与肌肉体积

激活的运动单位越多，产生的力越大。Ⅱ型肌纤维运动单位产生的力大于Ⅰ型肌纤维运动单位产生的力，因为Ⅱ型肌纤维运动单位比Ⅰ型肌纤维运动单位含有更多的肌纤维。同样运动模式下，体积大的肌肉含有的肌纤维多，产生的力就大于体积小的肌肉。

4. 运动单位的刺激频率：速率编码

单一运动单位产生肌力的大小取决于其受刺激的频率。一条肌纤维或一个运动单位受到单个电刺激引起的最小收缩反应称为单收缩。快速、连续的三个刺激（后一刺激落在前一刺激的舒张期），后一次就会产生比前一次更大的肌张力，称为收缩的总和。高频率的持续收缩可以引起强直收缩，导致肌纤维或运动单位产生最大收缩力。速率编码是指通过增加刺激频率，使一个运动单位从单收缩到强直收缩的过程。

5. 长度–张力关系

每个肌纤维都有产生力量的最佳长度。最佳肌节长度定义为粗肌丝和细肌丝之间最佳重叠的长度。当肌节过度伸展或缩短时，因为没有横桥之间的相互作用，所以几乎没有力产生。这种初始的静息长度最大限度地提高了肌肉产生力的能力，称为长度–张力关系。

这种关系的含义是，肌肉长度和关节角度将为肌群中特定肌肉的力量产生提供优势。最大张力产生在2.0 ~ 2.25 微米的肌节长度之间，其中肌球蛋白和肌动蛋白之间的重叠是最优的（可以形成最高数量的横桥）。

6. 力–速度关系

肌力的产生还与肌肉的收缩速度有关。向心收缩时，收缩速度越快，产生的最大肌力越小；进行离心收缩时正好相反。

力量发展与收缩速度之间的关系可以用在不同收缩速度下的总的横桥数目来解释。当肌肉缓慢收缩时，横桥形成的时间比快速收缩时更长。换句话说，当以较高的速度摆动横桥时，肌肉产生的力就会减小。

Chapter 2
Fuel for Exercise: Bioenergetics

Nutrients from ingested foods are provided in the form of carbohydrates, fats, and proteins. These three basic fuels, or energy substrates, can ultimately be broken down to release the stored energy. Each cell contains chemical pathways that convert these substrates to energy that can then be used by that cell and other cells of the body, a process called bioenergetics. All of the chemical reactions in the body are collectively called metabolism.

Because all energy eventually degrades to heat, the amount of energy released in a biological reaction can be measured from the amount of heat produced. Energy in biological systems is measured in calories. By definition, 1 calorie (cal) equals the amount of heat energy needed to raise 1 g of water 1 ℃, from 14.5 ℃ to 15.5 ℃. In humans, energy is expressed in kilocalories (kcal) , where 1 kcal is the equivalent of 1,000 cal.

Some free energy in the cells is used for growth and repair throughout the body. Such processes build muscle mass during training and repair muscle damage after exercise or injury. Energy also is needed for active transport of many substances, such as sodium, potassium, and calcium ions, across cell membranes to maintain homeostasis. Myofibrils use energy to cause sliding of the actin and myosin filaments, resulting in muscle action and force generation, as described in Chapter 1.

1 Energy Substrates

The energy in food's molecular bonds is chemically released within our cells and then stored in the form of the high-energy compound introduced in Chapter 1, adenosine triphosphate (ATP) , which is discussed in detail later in this chapter.

At rest, the energy that the body needs is derived almost equally from the breakdown of carbohydrates and fats. Proteins serve important functions as enzymes that aid chemical reactions and as structural building blocks but usually provide little energy for metabolism. During intense, short-duration muscular effort, more carbohydrate is used, with less reliance on fat to generate ATP. Longer, less intense exercise uses both carbohydrate and fat for sustained energy production.

1.1 Carbohydrate

The amount of carbohydrate used during exercise is related to both the carbohydrate availability and the muscles' well-developed system for carbohydrate metabolism. All carbohydrates are ultimately converted to the simple six-carbon sugar, glucose, a monosaccharide (one-unit sugar) that is transported through the blood to all body tissues. Under resting conditions, ingested carbohydrate is stored in muscles and liver in the form of a more complex polysaccharide (multiple linked sugar molecules) , glycogen. Glycogen is stored in the cytoplasm of muscle cells until those cells use it to form ATP. Additional glycogen stored in the liver is converted back to glucose as needed and then transported by the blood to active tissues, where it is metabolized.

Muscle and liver glycogen stores are limited, especially if the diet contains an insufficient amount of carbohydrate, and can be depleted during prolonged, intense exercise. Thus, we rely heavily on dietary sources of starches and sugars to continually replenish our carbohydrate reserves. Without adequate carbohydrate intake, muscles can be deprived of their primary energy source. Furthermore, carbohydrates are the only energy source used by brain tissue; therefore, severe carbohydrate depletion results in negative cognitive effects.

1.2 Fat

Fats provide a large portion of the energy used during prolonged, less intense exercise. Body stores of potential energy in the form of fat are substantially larger than the reserves of carbohydrate, in terms of both weight and energy availability. Table 2.1 provides an indication of the total body stores of these two energy sources in a lean person (12% body fat). For the average middle-aged adult with more body fat (adipose tissue) , the fat stores would be approximately twice as large, whereas the carbohydrate stores would be about the same. But fat is less readily available for cellular metabolism because it must first be reduced from its complex form, triglyceride, to its basic components, glycerol and free fatty acids (FFAs). Only FFAs are used to form ATP (Figure 2.1).

Table 2.1 Body Stores of Fuels and Associated Energy Availability

Carbohydrates		
Liver glycogen	110 g	451 kcal
Muscle glycogen	500 g	2,050 kcal
Glucose in body fluids	15 g	62 kcal
Fat		
Subcutaneous and visceral	7,800 g	73,320 kcal
Intramuscular	161 g	1,513 kcal
Total	8,586 g	77,396 kcal

Note: These estimates are based on a body weight of 65 kg (143 lb) with 12% body fat.

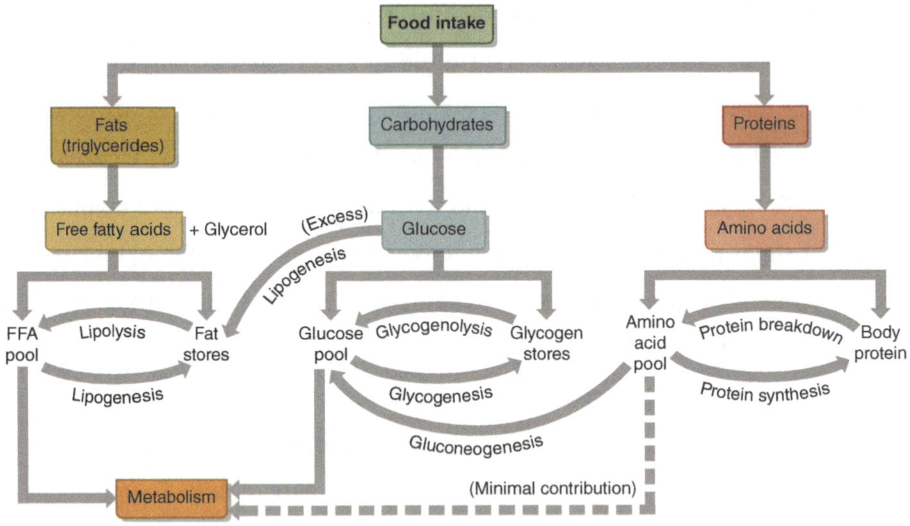

Figure 2.1 Cellular metabolism results from the breakdown of three fuel substrates provided by the diet. Once each is converted to its usable form, it either circulates in the blood as an available "pool" to be used for metabolism or is stored in the body.

Substantially more energy is derived from breaking down a gram of fat (9.4 kcal/g) than from the same amount of carbohydrate (4.1 kcal/g). Nonetheless, the rate of energy release from fat is too slow to meet all of the energy demands of intense muscular activity.

Other types of fats found in the body serve non-energy-producing functions. Phospholipids are a key structural component of all cell membranes and form protective sheaths around some large nerves. Steroids are found in cell membranes and also function as hormones or as building blocks of hormones, such as estrogen and testosterone.

1.3 Protein

Protein can be used as a minor energy source under some circumstances, but it must first be converted into glucose (Figure 2.1). In the case of severe energy depletion or starvation, protein may even be used to generate FFAs for energy. The process by which protein or fat is converted into glucose is called gluconeogenesis. The process of converting protein into fatty acids is termed lipogenesis. Protein can supply up to 10% of the energy needed to sustain prolonged exercise. Only the most basic units of protein—the amino acids—can be used for energy. A gram of protein yields about 4.1 kcal.

2 Controlling the Rate of Energy Production

To be useful, free energy must be released from chemical compounds at a controlled rate. This rate is determined primarily by two things, the availability of the primary substrate and enzyme activity. The availability of large amounts of a substrate increases the activity of that particular pathway. An abundance of one particular fuel (e.g., carbohydrate) can cause cells to rely more on that source than on alternatives. This influence of substrate availability on the rate of metabolism is termed the mass action effect.

Specific protein molecules called enzymes also control the rate of free-energy release. Many of these enzymes speed up the breakdown (catabolism) of chemical compounds. Chemical reactions occur only when the reacting molecules have sufficient initial energy to start the reaction or chain of reactions. Enzymes do not cause a chemical reaction to occur and do not determine the amount of usable energy that is produced by these reactions. Rather, they speed up reactions by lowering the activation energy that is required to begin the reaction (Figure 2.2).

Biochemical pathways that result in the production of a product from a substrate almost always involve multiple steps. Each individual step is typically catalyzed by a specific enzyme. Therefore, increasing the amount of enzyme present or the activity of that enzyme (for example, by changing the temperature or pH) results in an increased rate of product formation through that metabolic pathway. Additionally, many enzymes require other molecules called cofactors to function, so cofactor availability may also affect enzyme function and therefore the rate of metabolic reactions.

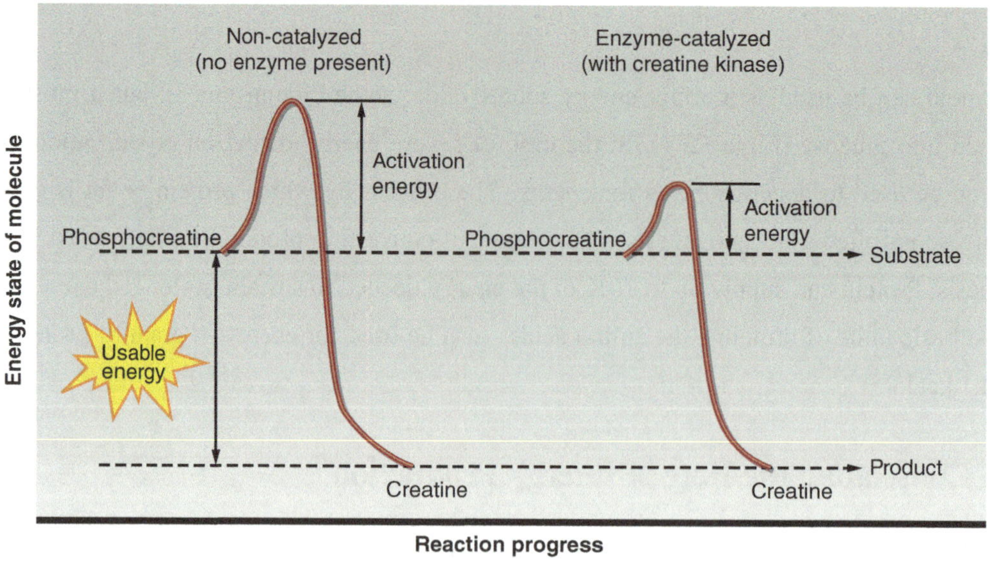

Figure 2.2 Enzymes control the rate of chemical reactions by lowering the activation energy required to initiate the reaction. In this example, the enzyme creatine kinase binds to its substrate phosphocreatine to increase the rate of production of creatine.

3 Storing Energy: High-energy Phosphates

The immediately available source of energy for almost all bodily functions, including muscle contraction, is ATP. To generate ATP, a phosphate group is added to the relatively low-energy compound, ADP, in a process called phosphorylation. This process requires a considerable amount of energy. Some ATP is generated independent of oxygen availability, and such metabolism is called substrate-level phosphorylation. Other ATP-producing reactions (discussed later in the chapter) occur without oxygen, while still others occur with the aid of oxygen, a process called oxidative phosphorylation.

4 The Basic Energy Systems

Cells can store only very limited amounts of ATP and must constantly generate new ATP to provide needed energy for all cellular metabolism, including muscle contraction. Cells generate ATP through any one of (or a combination of) three metabolic pathways:

- The ATP-PCr system
- The glycolytic system (glycolysis)
- The oxidative system (oxidative phosphorylation)

The first two systems can act in the absence of oxygen and are jointly termed anaerobic metabolism. The third system requires oxygen and therefore comprises aerobic metabolism.

4.1 ATP-PCr System

The simplest of the energy systems is the ATP-PCr system, shown in Figure 2.3. In addition to storing a very small amount of adenosine triphosphate (ATP) directly, cells contain another high-energy phosphate molecule that stores energy called phosphocreatine (PCr; sometimes called creatine phosphate). This simple pathway involves donation of a Pi from PCr to ADP to form ATP. Unlike what occurs with the limited freely available ATP in the cell, energy released by the breakdown of PCr is not directly used for cellular work. Instead, it regenerates ATP to maintain a relatively constant supply under resting conditions.

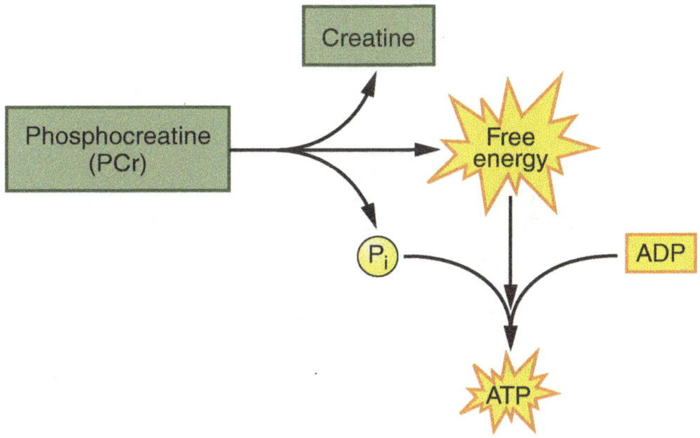

Figure 2.3 In the ATP-PCr system,adenosine triphosphate (ATP) can be recreated via the binding of an inorganic phosphate (Pi) to adenosine diphosphate (ADP) with energy derived from the breakdown of phosphocreatine (PCr).

The release of energy from PCr is catalyzed by the enzyme creatine kinase, which acts on PCr to separate Pi from creatine. The energy released can then be used to add a Pi molecule to an ADP molecule, forming ATP. As energy is released from ATP by the splitting of a phosphate group, cells can prevent ATP depletion by breaking down PCr, providing energy and Pi to reform ATP from ADP.

Creatine kinase activity is enhanced when concentrations of ADP or Pi increase, and is inhibited when ATP concentrations increase. When intense exercise is initiated, the small amount of available ATP in muscle cells is broken down for immediate energy, yielding ADP and Pi. The increased ADP concentration enhances creatine kinase activity, and PCr is catabolized to form additional ATP. As exercise progresses and additional ATP is generated by the other two energy systems—the glycolytic and oxidative systems—creatine kinase activity is inhibited. This process of breaking down PCr to allow formation of ATP is rapid and can be accomplished without any special structures within the cell. The ATP-PCr system is classified as substrate-level metabolism.

Although it can act in the presence of oxygen, the process does not require oxygen.

During the first few seconds of intense muscular activity, such as sprinting, ATP is maintained at a relatively constant level, but PCr declines steadily as it is used to replenish the depleted ATP (Figure 2.4). At exhaustion, however, both ATP and PCr levels are low and are unable to provide energy for further muscle contraction and relaxation. Thus, the capacity to maintain ATP levels with the energy from PCr is limited. The combination of ATP and PCr stores can sustain the muscles' energy needs for only 3–15 s during an all-out sprint. Beyond that time, muscles must rely on other processes for ATP formation: glycolytic and oxidative pathways.

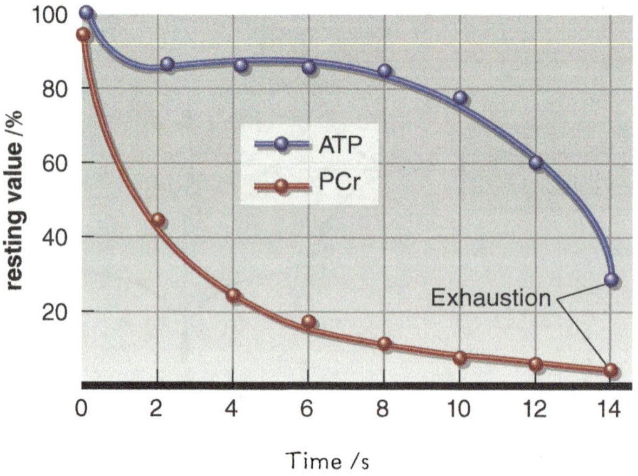

Figure 2.4 Changes in type Ⅱ (fast-twitch) skeletal muscle adenosine triphosphate (ATP) and phosphocreatine (PCR) during 14 s of maximal muscular effort (sprinting). Although ATP is being used at a very high rate, the energy from PCr is used to synthesize ATP, initially preventing the ATP level from decreasing. However, at exhaustion, both ATP and PCr levels are low.

4.2 Glycolytic System

The ATP-PCr system has a limited capacity to generate ATP for energy, lasting only a few seconds. The second method of ATP production involves the liberation of energy through the breakdown ("lysis") of glucose. This system is called the glycolytic system because it entails glycolysis, the breakdown of glucose through a more complex pathway than the ATP-PCr system that involves a sequence of glycolytic enzymes.

Glucose accounts for about 99% of all sugars circulating in the blood. Blood glucose comes from the digestion of carbohydrate and the breakdown of liver molecule to two three-carbon molecules of pyruvic acid. The process can begin with either glucose circulating in the blood or glycogen (a chain of glucose molecules, the storage form of glucose in muscle and liver).

Glycogen is synthesized from glucose by a process called glycogenesis and is stored in the liver or in muscle until needed. At that time, the glycogen is broken down to glucose-1-phosphate, which enters the glycolysis pathway, a process termed glycogenolysis. Before either glucose or glycogen can be used to generate energy, it must be converted to a compound called glucose-6-phosphate. Even though the goal of glycolysis is to release ATP, the conversion of a molecule of glucose to glucose-6-phosphate requires the expenditure or input of one ATP molecule. In the conversion of glycogen, glucose-6-phosphate is formed from glucose-1-phosphate without this energy expenditure. Glycolysis technically begins once the glucose-6-phosphate is formed.

Glycolysis requires 10–12 enzymatic reactions for the breakdown of glycogen to pyruvic acid, which is then converted to lactic acid. All steps in the pathway and all of the enzymes involved operate within the cell cytoplasm. The net gain from this process is 3 moles (mol) of ATP formed for each mole of glycogen broken down. If glucose is used instead of glycogen, the gain is only 2 mol of ATP because 1 mol was used for the conversion of glucose to glucose-6-phosphate.

This energy system obviously does not produce large amounts of ATP. Despite this limitation, the combined actions of the ATP-PCr and glycolytic systems allow the muscles to generate force even when the oxygen supply is limited. These two systems predominate during the early minutes of high-intensity exercise.

Another major limitation of anaerobic glycolysis is that it causes an accumulation of lactic acid in the muscles and body fluids. Glycolysis produces pyruvic acid. This process does not require oxygen, but the presence of oxygen determines the fate of the pyruvic acid. Without oxygen present, the pyruvic acid is converted directly to lactic acid, an acid with the chemical formula $C_3H_6O_3$ that quickly dissociates, forming lactate. In all-out sprint events lasting 1 or 2 min, the demands on the glycolytic system are high, and muscle lactic acid concentrations can increase from a resting value of about 1 mmol/kg of muscle to more than 25 mmol/kg. This acidification of muscle fibers inhibits further glycogen breakdown because it impairs glycolytic enzyme function. In addition, the acid decreases the fibers' calcium-binding capacity and thus may impede muscle contraction.

A muscle fiber's rate of energy use during exercise can be 200 times greater than at rest. The ATP-PCr and glycolytic systems alone cannot supply all the needed energy. Furthermore, these two systems are not capable of supplying all of the energy needs for all-out activity lasting more than 2 min or so. Prolonged exercise relies on the third energy system, the oxidative system.

4.3 Oxidative System

The final system of cellular energy production is the oxidative system. This is the most complex of the three energy systems, and only a brief overview is provided here. The process by which the body breaks down substrates with the aid of oxygen to generate energy is called cellular respiration. Because oxygen is required, this is an aerobic process. Unlike the anaerobic production of ATP that occurs in the cytoplasm of the cell, the oxidative production of ATP occurs within special cell organelles called mitochondria. In muscles, these are adjacent to the myofibrils and are also scattered throughout the sarcoplasm (Figure 1.3).

5 Interaction of the Energy Systems

The three energy systems do not work independently of one another, and no activity is 100% supported by any single energy system. When a person exercises at the highest intensity possible, from the shortest sprints (less than 10 s) to endurance events (greater than 30 min) , each of the energy systems is contributing to the total energy needs of the body. Generally, one energy system dominates energy production, except when there is a transition from the predominance of one energy system to another. As an example, in a 10 s, 100 m sprint, the ATP-PCr system is the predominant energy system, but both the anaerobic glycolytic and the oxidative systems provide a small portion of the energy needed. At the other extreme, in a 30 min, 10,000 m (about 10,936 yd) run, the oxidative system is predominant, but both the ATP-PCr and anaerobic glycolytic systems contribute some energy as well.

The ATP-PCr energy system can provide energy at a fast rate but has a very low capacity for energy production. Thus it supports exercise that is intense but of very short duration. By contrast, fat oxidation takes longer to gear up and produces energy at a slower rate; however, the amount of energy it can produce is unlimited. The characteristics of the muscle fiber's energy systems are listed in Table 2.2.

Table 2.2 Characteristics of the Various Energy Supply Systems

Energy system	Oxygen necessary	Overall chemical reaction	Relative rate of ATP formed per second	ATP formed per molecule of substrate	Available capacity
ATP-PCr	No	PCr to Cr	10	1	<15 s
Glycolysis	No	Glucose or glycogen to lactate	5	2–3	~ 1 min
Oxidative (from carbohydrate)	Yes	Glucose or glycogen to CO_2 and H_2O	2.5	36–39*	~ 90 min
Oxidative (from fat)	Yes	FFA or triglycerides to CO_2 and H_2O	1.5	>100	Days

* Production of 36–39 ATP per molecule of carbohydrate excludes energy cost of transport through membranes. The net production is slightly lower (see text).

IN CLOSING

In this chapter, we focused on energy metabolism and the synthesis of the storage form of energy in the body, ATP. We described in some detail the three basic energy systems used to generate ATP and their regulation and interaction. Finally, we highlighted the important role that oxygen plays in the sustained generation of ATP for continued muscle contraction and the three fiber types found in human skeletal muscle. We next look at the neural control of exercising muscle.

KEY TERMS

activation energy adenosine diphosphate (ADP) ; aerobic metabolism; anaerobic metabolism; ATP-PCr system; bioenergetics; carbohydrate catabolism; creatine kinase; cytochrome; enzyme free fatty acids (FFAs) ; gluconeogenesis; glucose glycogen; glycogenolysis; glycolysis; kilocalories (kcal); lipogenesis; lipolysis; metabolism; mitochondria; oxidative phosphorylation; oxidative system; phosphocreatine (PCr) ; phosphorylation; rate-limiting enzyme; substrate; triglycerides

STUDY QUESTIONS

(1) What is ATP, how is it formed, and how does it provide energy during metabolism?

(2) What is the primary substrate used to provide energy at rest? During high-intensity exercise?

(3) What is the role of PCr in energy production, and what are its limitations? Describe the relationship between muscle ATP and PCr during sprint exercise.

(4) Describe the essential characteristics of the three energy systems.

(5) Why are the ATP-PCr and glycolytic energy systems considered anaerobic?

(6) What role does oxygen play in the process of aerobic metabolism?

(7) Describe the by-products of energy production from ATP-PCr, glycolysis, and oxidation.

(8) What is lactic acid, and why is it important?

(9) Discuss the interaction among the three energy systems with respect to the rate at which energy can be produced and the sustained capacity to produce that energy.

(10) How do type I muscle fibers differ from type II fibers in their respective oxidative capacities? What accounts for those differences?

第二章
人体运动的能源：生物能量学

消化的食物营养分为糖、脂肪、蛋白质等形式。这三种基本的燃料，或者称为能源物质，最终都能分解、释放出其储存的能量。每个细胞都有化学通路可以将这些底物转变成能量，以供这个细胞和机体别的细胞利用，这就是生物能量学。体内所有的这些化学反应总的来讲就是新陈代谢。

由于所有能量最终都产生热，生物反应释放能量的多少可以用产生的热量来计算。能量的单位为卡（cal），1卡的定义是使1克水升高1 ℃（从14.5 ℃升高到15.5 ℃）所耗用的能量。人类表示能量时常用千卡（kcal），即1千卡等价于1000卡。

细胞内的一些自由能可用于机体的生长和各处的修复。这些过程可增加训练后的肌肉质量和修复运动或受伤导致的骨骼肌损伤。能量还可用来参与许多物质的跨膜主动转运，如钠离子、钾离子和钙离子，主动转运对于细胞存活和稳态保持是至关重要的。肌原纤维利用能量产生肌动蛋白和肌球蛋白的肌丝滑行，其结果即生成肌肉动作和力量。

一、能源物质

食物分子键的能量在细胞内通过化学过程释放出来，以高能化合物的形式储存。三磷酸腺苷（ATP）将在本章详述。

人在安静休息时，身体需要的能量几乎均由糖和脂肪分解而来。蛋白质主要是作为机体重要的酶助力生化反应，也是身体结构的组成部分，但是在新陈代谢中通常很少提供能量。进行高强度、短时程的运动时，主要依靠更多的糖来生成ATP供能，较少依靠脂肪；进行持续时间长一些、强度低一些的运动时，糖、脂肪都作为主要供能物质提供持久的能量。

1.糖

运动中糖的利用量不仅与糖的供给量有关，而且与肌肉高度发达的糖代谢系统有关。

所有的糖类最终转变成简单的六碳糖（葡萄糖）——一种通过血液运送到全身组织的单糖。在休息状态下，摄入的糖在肌肉和肝脏中以结构更加复杂的糖原形式储存起来。糖原储存于肌细胞胞浆中，直至被细胞用来生成ATP。其他储存在肝脏的糖原在机体需要时被转化为葡萄糖，然后通过血液到达活动的组织参与代谢。

肌糖原和肝糖原的储量有限，在长时间、高强度运动中易被耗竭，尤其是在饮食含糖不足时更是如此。所以，机体非常依赖淀粉或者蔗糖来持续地补充糖的储量。如果没有充足的糖摄入，肌肉就失去了其最重要的能源。此外，糖是脑组织可用的唯一能源，所以，严重的糖耗竭会损害脑的认知功能。

2.脂肪

在长时间、强度较小的运动中，脂肪供能占有相当大的比例。就存储量和潜在能量而言，机体以脂肪形式储存的能量远远大于糖的储能。对于一个含有较多体脂的中年人，脂肪的储量将会增加一倍，而糖的储量基本不变。但脂肪不能被细胞便捷利用，因为其必须从复杂的甘油三酯分解成甘油和游离脂肪酸（FFAs）这两个基本构件，只有游离脂肪酸可被用来生成ATP参与供能。

总的来说，分解1克脂肪（9.4 千卡/克）可以比1克糖（4.1 千卡/克）获得更多能量。但是，脂肪释放能量的速度太慢，不能满足高强度运动时肌肉的能量需要。

体内有些形式的脂肪不能提供能量。磷脂是所有细胞膜的主要结构成分，也构成某些大神经元的保护性髓鞘。类固醇也存在于细胞膜内，具有激素的功能，同时还是雌激素和雄激素的原料。

3.蛋白质

在一些特殊情况下，蛋白质能够作为能源物质少量供能，但其必须先转化为葡萄糖才可供能。在能量耗竭或非常饥饿时，蛋白质还可以转化为游离脂肪酸供给细胞代谢所需的能量。蛋白质或脂肪转化成葡萄糖的过程，称为糖异生。蛋白质转化为脂肪酸的过程，称为脂肪形成。长时间运动中，蛋白质可提供最多10%的能量，只有组成蛋白质的最基本单位——氨基酸才可以供能。1克蛋白质可产生大约4.1千卡能量。

二、能量生成率的控制

为了方便能量利用，自由能必须以可控速率从化合物释放出来供能，此速率一定程度上取决于两个方面：主要能源物质的供应情况和酶的活性。大量能源物质可供利用，能提高代谢通路的活性。一种能源底物（例如，糖）的丰足供应可以使细胞更多地依赖于它，胜过其他的替代物。能源底物供应量影响代谢速率的现象称为质量作用效应。

酶是一种特殊蛋白质分子，也可控制自由能释放的速率。很多酶可以加快化合物的分解代谢，只有当参与反应的分子有足够的启动能量时，化学反应或反应链才开始。酶不能启动化学反应，也不能决定这些反应所产生能量的可利用量。但是，酶可以通过降低启动反应所必需的活化能而加快反应。

从底物开始到产物生成的生物化学反应路径涉及多个步骤，每个步骤都有特定酶起催化作用，因此，提高酶的数量或者该酶的活性（例如，改变反应温度或pH值）可以增加该代谢途径的产物生成率。此外，很多酶需要其他辅助因子共同作用，辅助因子的量也会影响酶的功能，继而影响代谢反应的效率。

三、能量储存：高能磷酸盐

包括肌肉收缩在内的大多数代谢都需要ATP作为即时的能量来源。磷酸基团结合能量相对较低的化合物ADP形成ATP的过程，称为磷酸化。这个过程需要一定量的能量。一些ATP的形成过程与氧供无关，这样的代谢过程称为底物水平磷酸化。其他生成ATP的反应需要氧气才能进行，需氧才能进行的过程称为氧化磷酸化。

四、基本供能系统

细胞只能储存非常有限量的ATP，必须持续地生成新的ATP为细胞代谢提供所需的能量，包括肌肉收缩。细胞可以通过以下三种代谢途径的任意一种（或联合几种）生成ATP：ATP-PCr系统；糖酵解系统；有氧代谢系统。

前两个系统可以在缺氧状况下进行，被称为无氧代谢。第三个系统需要氧气供应，因此称为氧化代谢。

1.ATP-PCr系统

最简单的供能系统是ATP-PCr系统。细胞内除储存少量ATP，还有另一种高能磷酸分子——磷酸肌酸（PCr）。与ATP可自由供能不同，PCr分解释放的能量不能直接用于细胞的工作，而是用来重新合成ATP，以维持机体休息状态下相对持久的能量供应。

肌酸激酶可促进磷酸肌酸分解成肌酸和无机磷酸，并释放能量。释放出来的能量可使无机磷酸结合到ADP分子上形成ATP。ATP被利用时，脱掉一个无机磷酸，释放能量。细胞可通过分解磷酸肌酸提供能量和无机磷酸，使ADP重新合成ATP，从而维持ATP水平的稳定。

肌酸激酶在ADP或磷酸（Pi）增多时活性增强，而ATP浓度升高时活性降低。在高强度运动开始时，肌细胞中可以供能的少量ATP分解成直接的能量，生成ADP和Pi，ADP浓度的升高使肌酸激酶活性增强，催化PCr去生成更多的ATP。当运动持续进行，ATP的补给通过糖酵解和氧化系统而实现时，肌酸激酶的活性受到抑制。

PCr分解以生成ATP的过程非常迅速，而且不需要细胞内的特定结构即可完成。ATP-PCr

系统归属于底物水平磷酸化。此过程不需要氧即可进行，但也可在有氧条件下进行。

像短跑这样的高强度运动，在其最初的几秒内，ATP含量维持在一个相对恒定的水平，但PCr含量却不断下降，因为其要补充消耗的ATP。力竭时，ATP和PCr含量均显著降低，以至于不能继续提供能量来维持肌肉的收缩和舒张。因此，分解磷PCr来维持ATP含量的作用是有限的。体内的ATP和PCr总的储存量，仅能提供全速奔跑3～15秒的能量供应。超出这个时间，肌肉将通过糖酵解和有氧氧化产生ATP参与供能。

2.糖酵解系统

ATP-PCr系统生成ATP的能力有限，仅能持续几秒钟。生成ATP的第二个途径涉及到葡萄糖的分解释出能量，这个系统称为糖酵解系统。因为这个系统中葡萄糖通过一系列糖酵解酶催化而分解产能，是比ATP-PCr系统更复杂的通路。

血液中循环的糖，99%是葡萄糖，血液中的葡萄糖来源于食物中糖的消化和肝糖原的分解。葡萄糖合成糖原的过程称为糖原合成作用。糖原储存在肝脏和肌肉内，在机体需要时，糖原分解形成葡萄糖-1-磷酸，随后进入到糖酵解通路，此过程称为糖原分解作用。

糖酵解将糖原变为丙酮酸需要10～12个酶动力学的反应，丙酮酸之后变成乳酸。反应的所有步骤和有关的所有酶都在胞浆中进行。每摩尔的糖原分解过程可以净得到3摩尔的ATP。如果是葡萄糖而不是糖原，净得的ATP量只有2摩尔，因为在葡萄糖转变成葡萄糖-6-磷酸的过程中要消耗1摩尔的ATP。

很明显，糖酵解系统不能大量产生ATP。虽然有这种局限性，但ATP-PCr系统和糖酵解系统仍可在氧不足的情况下提供能量，使肌肉产生力量，高强度运动的前几分钟主要由这两个系统供能。

无氧糖酵解的另一个主要局限性是可以导致肌肉和体液内的乳酸蓄积。糖酵解途径可产生丙酮酸，此过程不需要氧，但氧是否存在决定着丙酮酸的去向。在无氧条件下，丙酮酸直接转变成了乳酸（分子式是$C_3H_6O_3$）。无氧糖酵解产生乳酸，但它很快解离，生成乳酸盐。

持续1～2分钟的全速奔跑项目对糖酵解系统需求很高，肌乳酸浓度可从休息时约1 毫摩尔/千克升高到25 毫摩尔/千克之多。肌纤维的内环境酸化可抑制糖酵解酶的活性，从而限制更多的糖原分解。此外，乳酸也会降低肌纤维的钙离子结合能力，阻碍肌肉收缩。

运动时肌纤维的能耗可达安静时的200倍，单靠ATP-PCr系统和糖酵解系统不能提供运动所需的全部能量。在持续2分钟左右的全速运动中，这两个系统不能够供应所需的全部能量。长时间的运动要靠第三个供能系统——有氧代谢系统。

3.有氧代谢系统

细胞内产生能量的最后一个系统就是有氧代谢系统。这个系统是三大供能系统中最复杂的一个。机体在有氧条件下分解底物产生能量的过程，称为细胞呼吸，此过程需要氧的参与，因此称为有氧过程。与在胞浆中无氧代谢产生ATP不同，氧化生成ATP是在一种被叫作线粒体的细胞器中进行的。肌肉内线粒体与肌原纤维毗邻，散布在肌浆中。

五、供能系统的交互作用

三大供能系统并非相互独立起作用的，也没有哪些运动是百分之百通过某个单一系统供能的。当一个人进行高强度的运动时，从短距离的冲刺（少于10秒）到耐力运动（大于30分钟），三个供能系统会共同参与机体的能量供应。通常以一个供能系统供能为主，除非出现主要供能系统向另一个系统的转变。例如，10秒内即可完成的百米跑，ATP-PCr系统为主要供能系统，但糖酵解系统和有氧代谢系统也同时供应少部分的能量；又如，30分钟内可完成的10 000米跑，以有氧代谢系统供能为主，但ATP-PCr系统和糖酵解系统也参与能量供应。

ATP-PCr系统能在最短时间内供能，但总产能非常低，因此该系统主要适合高强度短时间的运动供能。相反，脂肪氧化供能系统的产能速率较慢，但产能的总额是无上限的。

Chapter 3
Neural Control of Exercising Muscle

1 Spinal Control of Posture and Locomotion

In this section we discuss mechanoreceptors that provide sensory information to the spinal cord about the physiologic and mechanical environment associated with the control of movement.

All modes of sensory information in some way can feed into the motor system and thus can initiate, modulate, and control to varying degrees the execution of a motor task.

The following section addresses the sensory information associated with the mechanical (mechanoreceptors) and chemical (chemoreceptors) events associated with muscular activity. The different types of receptors probably provide ensembles or patterns of activity from specific receptors at specific locations and within a specific temporal characterization that have "meaning" to the spinal cord and the brain. With respect to proprioception, the mechanoreceptors, spindles, and Golgi tendon organs (GTOs) provide an abundance of sensory input for the spinal cord to integrate and interpret. An important component of the neural control of movement lies within the skeletal muscles, tendons, and joints where a wide range of mechanoreceptors provide the CNS(central nervous system) with the kinematics and kinetic states of the movement.

Not only are the brain and spinal cord receiving and integrating information continuously, they are receiving very complex patterns from sensory receptors (e.g., vision, audition, smell, taste, touch, and proprioception). Based on the number of sensory axons in peripheral nerves to all of the skeletal muscles and joints, more than one-half of the axons in the muscle nerves are sensory and most of the body mass is comprised of muscle. Thus, if one considers only the muscle nerves, one must expect that exercise and motor training can play a significant role in shaping how the CNS functions. Among these sensory axons are a number of types of mechanoreceptors that are capable of detecting changes in muscle length, force, and pressure. In addition, some nerve branches are essentially all or predominantly sensory and they project to tendons, joints, and skin. One of the most studied mechanoreceptors is the skeletal muscle spindle that provides proprioceptive information to the CNS. During exercise, the brain also receives input from axons that convey touch, sound, vision, smell, and taste and these sources of information influence the physiology of the CNS. There are many examples of ways these sensory systems affect our motor performance, reflecting the fact that each of these sensory modes has input to the motor system. A loud sound can increase voluntary strength. Cutaneous cues shape our reactions in maintaining posture and in the kinematics of locomotion. Vision is a major source of input for guiding virtually all movements. Sound can direct our posture and head position. Even olfactory input can initiate locomotor movements.

1.1 Muscle Spindles

A muscle spindle consists of about four to six small muscle fibers surrounded by a collagenous sheath. The maximum diameter of the collagenous sheath usually approximates the size of the extrafusal muscle fibers. The muscle fibers within the capsule are striated, similar to the extrafusal muscle fibers—these are intrafusal muscle fibers. The ends of these intrafusal fibers commonly project beyond the clearly defined spindle capsule. The intrafusal fibers are innervated by μ-motoneurons and each intrafusal muscle fiber is surrounded by several sensory axons called primary and secondary spindle afferents. These sensory axons generate action potentials when the length of the intrafusal fiber changes. Stretch of the intrafusal fibers can be caused by two events: (a) activation of the μ-motoneurons, which will cause shortening of the distal ends of the intrafusal fibers and, therefore, stretch the center where the annulospiral sensory nerve endings are; and (b) passively lengthening or shortening the intrafusal fibers because they lie parallel and are physically attached indirectly to the extrafusal muscle fibers. Very small changes in length can stimulate the primary (also referred to as Ia afferents) and secondary sensory fibers from the spindle. In general, the primary afferents from the muscles spindles demonstrate a more dynamic response, whereas the secondary fibers have a more static response to changes in length. The primary Ia fibers are the main afferents responding to a tendon tap and vibration.

1.2 Afferents During Locomotion

This emphasizes the variation in details of the activation patterns of γ-and α-motoneurons, not only among different afferent fibers but even from step to step for the same afferent. This step-to-step variability is a steadfast feature of locomotor networks even under the most controlled conditions possible. The likelihood that the μ-motoneurons innervating the intrafusal muscle fibers were sufficiently active during all phases of the step cycle to sustain some sensitivity of the spindle to the intramuscular mechanical events.

One of the most common ways to demonstrate the responsiveness of muscle spindles to stretch is to tap the tendon to trigger a muscle contraction. Tapping the tendon induces a monosynaptic reflex by activating the spindle afferents that project to the dendrites of the motoneurons associated with the same muscle containing the spindle. Each spindle afferent sends axonal branches to nearly every motoneuron within that motor pool and to a significant proportion of the motoneurons that innervate synergistic muscles. In addition, the same Ia afferent from the spindle projects to interneurons that inhibit the motoneurons innervating antagonistic muscles.

The density of muscle spindles varies widely among muscles. Muscles or muscle regions having a high percentage of slow fibers usually have a relatively high incidence of spindles and thus are highly sensitive to length changes. The intrinsic muscles of the hip, for example, have a high spindle density, are extremely sensitive to length changes and provide very important information for modulating the motor output during routine motor tasks such as stepping. These length sensors provide important cues as to when the stance and swing phases of a step should begin and terminate and when the body weight is being shifted from one leg to the other while standing.

1.3 Other Mechanoreceptors

Another mechanoreceptor within the muscle tendon unit is the GTO. In spite of the name, most GTOs are within the muscle. They are able to detect small changes in force generated within the muscle. The high level of sensitivity to force of the GTOs contrasts with the traditional concept that they are activated only by high forces and that their function is to prevent tendon injury by inhibiting the muscle from generating excessive forces. The sensory information generated by GTOs will excite some muscles and inhibit others, with these effects being highly state-dependent. For example, the specific neurons that are excited or inhibited can change with the phase of a step cycle and probably other physiologic conditions. A third type of muscle mechanoreceptor is referred to as free nerve endings because there is no remarkable specialization at the ends of these axons. These free endings generate action potentials when excited by mechanical as well as biochemical or metabolic stimuli (metaboreceptors). Free nerve endings actually constitute most of the sensory endings from muscle. Their function is not well understood, although they are thought to be actively involved in muscle spasticity in individuals with a spinal cord injury.

From the perspective of the systems level, all of the muscle spindle afferents, GTOs, and free nerve endings serve as mechanoreceptors that provide important information associated with proprioception.

Proprioception is a broad term often used to convey the idea that there are sensory receptors that provide precise information to the spinal cord and brain regarding the exact biomechanical state of the musculoskeletal system at any given time.

2 Supraspinal Control of Posture and Locomotion

In general, the functional organization of the neural control of locomotion in humans and quadrupeds is similar. Although the spinal cord has neuronal systems that alternate the activation patterns of the musculature to produce stance and swing phases during locomotion, the brain also has neuronal systems that can accomplish these tasks. These supraspinal neuronal networks are highly responsive to sensory information from the periphery.

2.1 Descending Pathways For Controlling Locomotion

The primary anatomical descending pathways for initiating locomotion are the corticospinal, reticulospinal, vestibulospinal, and rubrospinal tracts. The motor cortex gives rise to the corticospinal tract that decussates and influences the spinal circuitry associated primarily with the contralateral limbs. Some of these neurons have rhythmic firing patterns during locomotion. This rhythm seems to be generated by the spinal circuitry driven by CPG (central pottern generator) as well as by sensory feedback.

In quadrupeds, the motor cortex has a minimal role in generating the basic locomotor pattern, but it appears to be involved in corrective actions and in making adjustments to weight-bearing levels.

The motor cortex, however, does play an important role in executing more skilled movements that are less repetitive and in adjusting the basic activation patterns during locomotion in a more variable environment. Although corticospinal neurons may provide instruction for refining or modifying locomotor movements, it is clear that the basic locomotor patterns can be relatively normal without corticospinal input. In primates, including humans, lesions of the motor cortex or spinal cord may produce a greater disruption of the basic locomotor patterns than in lower mammalian species. Most of the dysfunction occurs in the distal musculature that controls the wrist, ankle, and digits.

The medial reticular formation of the pons and medulla gives rise to neurons that form the reticulospinal tract. These axons descend within the ventrolateral funiculi of the spinal cord and a single neuron can project to multiple levels of the spinal cord. The neurons that form the reticulospinal tract receive input from the brainstem including the MLR (mesencephalic locomotor region, a 1-mm long strip of cells in the nucleus cuneiformis) and from the cerebellum. The MLR, just rostral to the medial reticular formation, provides input to the neurons that form the reticulospinal tract. Stimulation of the MLR can elicit locomotion. Stimulation of the MLR region activates reticulospinal neurons that, in turn, can stimulate the spinal centers producing locomotion.

The vestibulospinal tract seems to facilitate extensor motoneurons, whereas the reticulospinal tract mainly facilitates flexor and inhibits extensor motoneurons. The rubrospinal and corticospinal tracts mainly facilitate flexor motoneurons.

Thus, these descending tracts seem to have a modulatory effect on the motoneurons during specific phases of the step cycle. It should be noted that the rhythm and firing of these descending tracts are due, in large part, to the influences from ascending input derived from the spinal cord circuitry. This phasic input (cyclic input associated with stepping) can occur independently of the afferent input from the periphery. For example, in paralyzed and decerebrated cats in which phasic afferent inflow from the periphery is precluded, phasic descending and ascending activity between the spinal cord and supraspinal centers is still present during spontaneous motor activity.

2.2 Role of Cerebellum In Locomotion

The cerebellum also plays an important role in motor control. A major function of the cerebellum is to assist in the control of limb movements by modulating supraspinal motor centers. It mediates sensory feedback from the spinal cord and modifies the motor output accordingly. The cerebellum also receives information from CPGs of the limbs to modulate the motor output. In addition, the cerebellum compares different inputs and, based on these comparisons, provides a means of correcting intended movements.

3 Automaticity in Posture and Locomotion

This section addresses the relative importance of different supraspinal nuclei in initiating and controlling locomotion. It is apparent that these centers can control different muscle groups (e.g., extensors vs. flexors). Each of these control centers has a strong gating function whereby its input is timed closely with the phase of the step cycle. Clearly, specific regions within the brainstem can initiate and control very complex motor behaviors, apparently with little or no necessity for “conscious” control, resulting in the generation of largely automatic responses.

Actually, there seems to be a continuum of consciousness ranging from a totally simple reflex without any conscious awareness or capability of control to modulation of a task in which one is fully and continuously aware of every aspect of the movement. What is the level of consciousness when one begins to step compared to the level of automaticity during a simple monosynaptic reflex? Even the efficacy of a monosynaptic response can be modulated by conscious control by a rat, monkey, or human. A human with a low thoracic spinal cord injury and with no supraspinal control below the lesion can learn to stand and initiate steps using sensory information associated with unilaterally bearing weight and manipulating the hip position. This spinal stepping can be initiated consciously and voluntarily, although the subject initiates the process “reflexively”. Thus, the subject manipulates the afferent inflow by controlling critical biomechanical as well as neurophysiologic signals by manipulating other parts of the body.

A variety of approaches have been used to identify how one initiates a movement. Functional MRI (fMRI) is being used to examine where within the CNS the decision is made to initiate a movement. A number of studies suggest that the “urge” to move precedes the actual initiation of movement by about 200 ms. Thus, there seems to be a readiness potential that precedes the subjective decisions. fMRI shows elevated blood flow in the dorsal prefrontal cortex, intraparietal sulcus, and supplementary motor area in preparation for a movement.

3.1 Automaticity Derived from the Brainstem to Control Locomotion

For example, once the decision to walk across a room is made, very little conscious effort is required to perform the details of that task. It seems that the CNS is designed so that much of the intricate decision making associated with posture and locomotion occurs automatically. Both supraspinal and spinal sources contribute to the pathways responsible for this automaticity. For example, a subthalamic cat, decerebrated just rostrally to the mammillary bodies, can walk in response to exteroceptive stimulation and can sometimes walk spontaneously. A cat decerebrated at the caudal border of the mammillary bodies cannot walk with or without exteroceptive stimulation. Therefore, the subthalamic locomotor region lies between these two transection levels. When the subthalamic locomotor region remains intact, the animal can walk by itself, go to a plate of food, and even kill and eat a mouse. Such a cat, however, cannot perform locomotion voluntarily.

There is a strong element of automaticity in the neural control of most movements, both from the brain and spinal cord.

3.2 Automaticity and Autonomic Function During Locomotion

Automaticity is also evident in the coordination of the neural control of locomotion with that of respiration and cardiovascular function. For example, not only does the stimulation of the MLR generate remarkably normal locomotion, it also leads to a modulation of cardiovascular and respiratory function that is appropriate for locomotion. When the MLR of a mesencephalic cat is stimulated and the limbs are stepping on a treadmill, a 20%–35% higher arterial blood pressure, a 70%–90% greater cardiac output, and an increase of 15%–20% in heart rate relative to the resting conditions have been observed. In addition, pulmonary ventilation can increase threefold as a result of increased tidal volume and frequency of breathing. These observations demonstrate the highly integrated and automated nature of the neural system to control locomotion with some assurance that the cardiovascular and respiratory systems will be modulated accordingly.

3.3 Levels of Automaticity

Clearly, there are a number of levels of automaticity (absence of conscious detailed control) of the neural control of posture and stepping. For example, decerebrated cats can run without hitting obstacles and jump over obstacles. When the MLR is stimulated, the decerebrated cat can generate locomotion and demonstrate awareness of spatial orientation. In animals that have a chronic lesion (several weeks) in the subthalamic locomotor region, locomotor behavior is nearly normal.

Spinal automaticity remains in the absence of supraspinal input, as occurs after a complete transection of the spinal cord. A large body of data demonstrates that the spinal cord is much more than a static conduit for communication between the brain and muscles. It was shown in the mid-1970s that kittens whose spinal cords were transected at a neonatal age can be trained to take steps on all four limbs. A significant level of automaticity was also evident when it was learned that stimulating the dorsum of the lumbosacral spinal cord in a tonic pattern generates stepping motions in paraplegic mammals including humans. Also, rhythmic locomotor patterns can be induced by the spinal cord when selected regions of the brainstem are stimulated tonically even in the absence of sensory feedback from the spinal cord. The spinal cord can also generate patterns resembling locomotion in the absence of sensory feedback when the spinal cord is stimulated pharmacologically (e.g., as with L-Dopa).

From a teleologic perspective, one can question the concept of automaticity with respect to how useful these autonomic responses are. All sensory and motor systems, however, have evolved so that they can function within their known environments. Similar sensory and motor components among a wide range of animals with vastly different musculoskeletal structures have evolved in a manner that enables many postural and locomotor tasks to occur quite automatically within Earth's gravitational fields. The automaticity aspect of these functions reflect the successful evolution that enables postural and locomotor responses to occur without relying on more complicated, and probably more unpredictable, delayed decision making by higher neural centers. A greater reliance on the brain would require additional time and would impose disadvantages in the execution of a variety of postural and locomotor tasks, particularly when the response time is critical for survival. In this sense, "evolutionary learning" has played a key role in the automaticity of neural control during the execution of motor tasks. This plasticity includes the ability to learn and forget motor tasks that are practiced.

Thus, the nervous system, even without conscious control, not only demonstrates a sophisticated level of automaticity, but it is also smart and highly adaptable or plastic.

IN CLOSING

In this chapter, we examined how the nervous system is organized and how that organization functions to control movement. We covered the central nervous system as it relates to movement and the sensory and effector arms of the peripheral nervous system. We have seen how muscles respond to neural stimulation, whether through reflexes or under complex control of the higher brain centers, and the role of individual motor units in determining this response. Thus, we have learned how the body functions to allow people to move. In the next chapter, we examine the role of hormones in the body's response to exercise. Furthermore, the details of these responses to specific combinations of sensory input are routinely modified based on our experiences.

KEY TERMS

motor reflex; muscle spindle; Golgi tendon organs; spinal cord; motor cortex; brainstem; cerebellum; corticospinal; reticulospinal; vestibulospinal; rubrospinal tracts

STUDY QUESTIONS

(1) What brain centers have major roles in controlling movement, and what are these roles?

(2) How do the sympathetic and parasympathetic systems differ? What is their significance in performing physical activity?

(3) Explain how reflex movement occurs in response to touching a hot object.

(4) Describe the role of the muscle spindle in controlling muscle contraction.

(5) Describe the role of the Golgi tendon organ in controlling muscle contraction.

(6) How similar are the mechanisms of spinal learning to those in the hippocampus?

第三章 运动中肌肉的神经调控

一、脊髓对运动和姿势的调控

本章介绍了骨骼肌运动过程中机械感受器和化学感受器的作用。不同类型的感受器将不同位置和不同时间序列的信息传入脑和脊髓，这些信息（如视觉、听觉、嗅觉、味觉、触觉和本体感觉）对大脑和脊髓调控骨骼肌的运动具有重要意义。其中，肌梭和腱梭（高尔基腱器官）等本体感受器为脊髓整合和处理相关信息提供了丰富的感觉输入。

1.肌梭

位于肌梭的囊内的肌纤维被称为梭内肌。梭内肌受到脊髓γ运动神经元的支配。γ运动神经元的激活可以引起梭内肌收缩，从而拉伸位于梭内肌纤维中间的感觉神经末梢。因为梭内肌与梭外肌平行，两者呈并联关系，所以当梭外肌长度变化时，梭内肌会被动地被拉长或缩短。

2.运动期间感觉输入的特征

运动过程中脊髓灰质前角中α运动神经元和γ运动神经元激活模式的变化，不仅依赖于不同传入神经传入的神经冲动，也依赖于同一个传入神经在节律性运动中的动态变化。在类似于走路这种节律性运动中，即使在严格的调控下，每一步之间也会发生变化，这是运动控制系统的特征。支配梭内肌的γ运动神经元在行走周期的所有阶段都会激活以维持肌梭对机械刺激的敏感性。证明肌梭对肌肉牵伸反应最好的例子之一就是牵拉肌腱触发肌肉收缩。敲击肌腱时激活肌梭，肌梭与支配同一块肌肉梭外肌的α运动神经元形成单突触联系。肌梭的传入神经纤维会发出轴突分支，这些分支一方面与运动池内支配受牵拉肌肉的α运动神经元形成突触联系，另一方面也与支配协同肌的α运动神经元形成突触联系。此外，肌梭Ia类神经纤维投射至抑制性中间神经元，该抑制性中间神经元与支配拮抗肌的α运动神经元形成突触联系，进而抑制拮抗肌的活动。

不同骨骼肌含有的肌梭的数量有很大差异。通常慢肌含有更多的肌梭，因此慢肌对肌纤维的长度变化敏感度更高。

3.其他机械感受器

除肌梭，肌肉内还存在另一种机械感受器——腱梭（GTO），又称高尔基腱器官。GTO对肌张力高度敏感，但传统理论认为只有较大的肌张力才能将GTO激活，抑制肌肉过度收缩从而避免肌腱出现损伤。

肌肉内第三种类型的机械感受器是游离的神经末梢，它们的轴突末梢没有形成特化的装置。这些游离的神经末梢可以被肌肉内的机械刺激、生化反应和代谢（化学感受器）所激活。

综上所述，肌梭、腱梭（高尔基腱器官）和游离的神经末梢都是肌肉内的机械感受器，它们向中枢传递与本体感觉有关的信息。本体感觉是指本体感受器向脊髓和大脑传入的运动系统实时的生物力学状态。

二、脑对姿势和躯体运动的调控

人类和四足动物的神经系统对运动的控制是类似的。虽然行走的站立和摆动时相是脊髓作为中枢控制完成的，但是脑作为高级中枢也可以完成这些活动。脑对外周的感觉信息输入高度敏感。

1.运动控制的下行通路

运动控制的下行通路包括皮质脊髓束、网状脊髓束、前庭脊髓束和红核脊髓束等。皮质脊髓束起自运动皮质，下行过程中大部分纤维交叉至对侧，终于相应节段的脊髓灰质前角，控制对侧肢体的随意运动。其中，部分神经元在运动过程中具有节律性的发动模式，这种节律模式产生于脊髓中枢模式发生器，而脊髓中枢模式发生器的活动依赖于外周的感觉信息的反馈。

虽然，运动皮层在调控技巧性运动和在复杂多变的环境中调控基础运动的过程中起重要作用，但基础运动的正常控制不依赖于皮质脊髓束。

网状脊髓束起自脑桥和延髓网状结构的内侧核群，行于脊髓白质的前索和外侧索，一个神经元可以与多个节段的脊髓形成突触联系。

前庭脊髓束的功能是易化伸肌运动神经元。网状脊髓束的功能是易化屈肌运动神经元并抑制伸肌运动神经元。红核脊髓束和皮质脊髓束的功能是易化屈肌运动神经元。

2.小脑在运动中的作用

小脑在运动控制中也起重要作用。小脑的主要功能是协助脑完成对肢体运动的调控。它接受感觉反馈信息的传入，将不同的感觉信息进行比较，进而按照预期的动作编排对动作进行校正。

三、姿势和运动的自动化

本节将讨论不同脑区在运动发起和运动控制中的作用。脑中与运动控制相关的中枢可以对不同的肌群进行调控（如屈肌群和伸肌群）。这些与运动控制相关的中枢在行走动作的各个时相发挥重要作用。脑干的某些区域在不需要意识的参与下就能发起并控制十分复杂的运动，这在动作自动化过程中发挥重要作用。

即使是行走这样的自动化动作也需要运动皮层在意识的参与下发起。意识是一个宽泛的概念，涉及从没有意识控制的最简单的运动反射到完成一种精细的运动调控（意识到运动的各个方面）。与单突触反射的自动化相比，一个人开始行走时需要多大程度的意识的参与？对于老鼠、猴子或人类来说，单突触反射也可以受到意识的控制。一项针对下段胸髓损伤（损伤节段以下失去脑的控制）受试者的研究发现，他们可以利用单侧承重或调整髋关节位置的感觉信息传入，学会站立并发起行走动作。虽然受试者“条件反射式”地发起行走动作，但是该过程是有意识的且自愿开始的。因此，受试者可以通过对身体其他部分重要的生物力学信号和神经生理信号的控制来操纵感觉信息的传入。

功能磁共振成像（fMRI）被用于研究中枢神经系统内哪个区域决定发起运动。许多研究表明，发起运动的“愿望”在运动起始前200毫秒出现。fMRI结果显示，在准备发起运动时，背侧前额叶皮层、顶内沟和补充运动区的血流量增加。因此，似乎在做出主观决定之前就有一种准备就绪的可能性。

1.来自脑干的自动化控制运动

中枢神经系统的设计使得与姿势和运动相关的许多错综复杂的决策自动发生。脑和脊髓都在这种自动化的进程中发挥重要作用。例如，一只猫在乳头体吻侧水平进行去大脑手术后，只保留丘脑下位中枢的支配，这只猫不仅可以对外周刺激发生反应而发起行走动作，也可以自发地发起行走动作；而在乳头体的尾部边缘处去大脑的猫不能在外周刺激的情况下发起行走动作，也不能自发地发起行走动作。因此，底丘脑运动区位于这两个横断面之间。当底丘脑运动区保持完整时，猫可以独立行走，可以去找一盘食物，甚至可以杀死并吃掉一只老鼠。

2.自主神经在运动过程中的作用

在运动过程中，自主神经也被激活，从而协调呼吸系统和心血管系统配合运动的完成。例如，刺激中脑运动区（MLR）不仅可以产生正常的运动，还可以调节呼吸和心血管系统的活动以适应运动。这些研究结果表明神经系统具有高度整合和自动化的能力，在控制运动的同时，应整合心血管系统和呼吸系统的功能活动以满足运动所需。

3.自动化水平

对于姿势和行走的神经控制在很大程度上是自动化的（非意识参与下的精细调控）。例如，去大脑的猫可以在不碰到障碍物的情况下跑步并跳过障碍物。当MLR受到刺激时，去大脑的猫可以产生运动并表现出空间定向的意识。在底丘脑运动区中具有慢性病变（数周）的动物中，运动行为几乎正常。

在完全横断脊髓后，失去来自于脑的信息输入时，脊髓的自动化仍存在。研究表明，脊髓不仅仅是在脑和肌肉之间进行信息传输的静态装置。即使在没有来自脊髓的感觉反馈输入的情况下，对脑干的特定区域进行紧张性刺激，也可以诱导脊髓产生节律性运动模式。当脊髓受到药物刺激时（如左旋多巴），脊髓也可以在没有感觉反馈输入的情况下产生类似的运动模式。即使没有来自大脑的输入，脊髓也能够整合和响应来自外围的感觉信息。

在具有截然不同的肌肉骨骼结构的动物中，感觉和运动成分经过进化使许多姿势和运动任务能够在地球的引力场内自动发生，而不依赖于由更高的神经中枢产生的更复杂、可能更难以预测的延迟的决策。对大脑的更多依赖需要额外的时间，并且在执行各种姿势和运动任务时会带来不利因素，特别是当响应时间对于生存至关重要时。从这个意义上说，“进化学习”在运动任务执行过程中神经控制的自动化方面发挥了关键作用。

因此，即使没有意识的控制，神经系统也能表现出复杂的自动化水平，而且具有智能、高度适应性和可塑性。

Chapter 4 Hormonal Control During Exercise

During exercise and exposure to extreme environments, the body is required a multitude of physiological adjustments. Energy production must increase and metabolic by-products must be cleared. Cardiovascular and respiratory function must be constantly adjusted to match the demands placed upon these and other body systems, such as those regulating temperature. While the body's internal environment is in a constant state of flux even at rest, during exercise these well-orchestrated changes must occur rapidly and frequently.

Much of the regulation required during exercise is accomplished by the nervous system. But another physiological system—the endocrine system—affects virtually every cell, tissue, and organ in the body. It constantly monitors the body's internal environment, noting all changes that occur and rapidly releasing hormones to ensure that homeostasis is not dramatically disrupted. In this chapter, we focus on hormonal control of metabolism and body fluids. Additional hormones, including those that regulate growth and development, muscle mass, and reproductive function, are covered in other chapters of this book.

1 The Endocrine System

As the body transitions from a resting to an active state, the rate of metabolism must increase to provide the necessary energy. This requires the coordinated integration of many physiological and biochemical systems. Although the nervous system is responsible for much of this communication, fine-tuning the physiological responses to any disturbance in homeostasis is primarily the responsibility of the endocrine system. The endocrine and nervous systems, often collectively called the neuroendocrine system, work in concert to initiate and control movement and all of the physiological processes that support exercise. The nervous system functions quickly, having short-lived, localized effects, whereas the endocrine system responds more slowly but has longer-lasting effects.

The endocrine system is defined as all tissues or glands that secrete hormones. The major endocrine glands are illustrated in Figure 4.1. Endocrine glands typically secrete their hormones directly into the blood where they act as chemical signals throughout the body. When secreted by the specialized endocrine cells, hormones are transported via the blood to specific target cells—cells that possess specific hormone receptors. On reaching their destinations, hormones can control the activity of the target tissue. Historically a hormone denoted a chemical made by a gland that traveled to a remote tissue in the body to exert its action. Now hormones are more broadly defined as any chemical that controls and regulates the activity of certain cells or organs. Some hormones affect many body tissues, whereas others target very specific cells of the body.

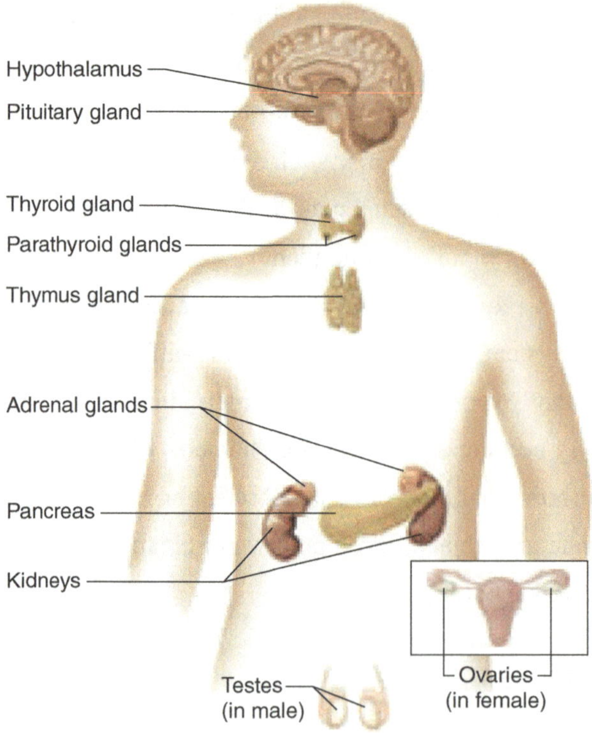

Figure 4.1 Location of the major endocrine organs of the body.

1.1 Hormones

Hormones are involved in most physiological processes, so their actions are relevant to many aspects of exercise and sport. In the following sections, the chemical nature of hormones and the general mechanisms through which they act are discussed. An overview of the major endocrine glands and their hormones is presented for completeness. With respect to exercise, the focus is on two major aspects of hormonal control, the control of exercise metabolism and the regulation of body fluids and electrolytes during exercise.

1.2 Chemical Classification of Hormones

Hormones can be categorized as two basic types: steroid hormones and nonsteroid hormones. Steroid hormones have a chemical structure similar to cholesterol, since most are derived from cholesterol. For this reason, they are soluble in lipids so they diffuse rather easily through cell membranes. This group includes the hormones secreted by

- the adrenal cortex (such as cortisol and aldosterone)
- the ovaries (estrogen and progesterone)
- the testes (testosterone)
- the placenta (estrogen and progesterone)

Nonsteroid hormones are not lipid soluble, so they cannot easily cross cell membranes. The nonsteroid hormone group can be subdivided into two groups: protein or peptide hormones and amino acid-derived hormones. The two hormones produced by the thyroid gland (thyroxine and triiodothyronine) and the two from the adrenal medulla (epinephrine and norepinephrine) are amino acid hormones. All other non-steroid hormones are protein or peptide hormones. The chemical structure of a hormone determines its mechanism of action on target cells and tissues.

1.3 Hormone Secretion and Plasma Concentration

Control of hormone secretion must be rapid in order to meet the demands of changing bodily functions. Hormones are not secreted constantly or uniformly, but often in a pulsatile manner, that is, in relatively brief bursts. Therefore, plasma concentrations of specific hormones fluctuate over short periods of an hour or less. But these concentrations also fluctuate over longer periods of time, showing daily or even monthly cycles (such as monthly menstrual cycles). How do endocrine glands know when to release their hormones and how much to release?

Most hormone secretion is regulated by a negative feedback system. Secretion of a hormone causes some change in the body, and this change in turn inhibits further hormone secretion. In the body, secretion of a specific hormone is similarly turned on or off (or up or down) by specific physiological changes.

Negative feedback is the primary mechanism through which the endocrine system maintains homeostasis. Using the example of plasma glucose concentrations and the hormone insulin, when the plasma glucose concentration is high, the pancreas releases insulin. Insulin increases cellular uptake of glucose, lowering plasma concentration of glucose. When plasma glucose concentration returns to normal, insulin release is inhibited until the plasma glucose level increases again.

The plasma concentration of a specific hormone is not always the best indicator of that hormone's activity because the number of receptors on target cells can be altered to increase or decrease that cell's sensitivity to the hormone. With fewer receptors, fewer hormone molecules can bind. This is referred to as downregulation, or desensitization. In people with insulin resistance, for example, the number of insulin receptors on their cells appears to be reduced. Their bodies respond by increasing insulin secretion from the pancreas, so their plasma insulin concentrations increase. To obtain the same degree of plasma glucose control as normal, healthy people, these individuals must release much more insulin.

In a few instances, a cell may respond to the pro-longed presence of large amounts of a hormone by increasing its number of available receptors. When this happens, the cell becomes more sensitive to that hormone because more can be bound at one time. This is referred to as upregulation. In addition, one hormone occasionally can regulate the receptors for another hormone.

1.4 Hormone Actions

Because hormones travel in the blood, they contact virtually all body tissues. How, then, do they limit their effects to specific targets? This ability is attributable to the specific hormone receptors possessed by the target tissues. Each cell typically has from 2,000–10,000 receptors. The combination of a hormone bound to its receptor is referred to as a hormone-receptor complex.

Recall that steroid hormones are lipid soluble and can therefore pass through cell membranes whereas nonsteroid hormones cannot. Receptors for nonsteroid hormones are located on the cell membrane, while those for steroid hormones are found either in the cytoplasm or in the nucleus of the cell. Each hormone is usually highly specific for a single type of receptor and binds only with its specific receptors, thus affecting only tissues that contain those specific receptors. Once hormones are bound to a receptor, numerous mechanisms allow them to control the actions of cells.

1.4.1 Steroid Hormones

The general mechanism of action of steroid hormones is illustrated in Figure 4.2. Once inside the cell, a steroid hormone binds to its specific receptors. The hormone-receptor complex then enters the nucleus, binds to part of the cell's DNA, and activates certain genes. This process is referred to as direct gene activation. In response to this activation, mRNA is synthesized within the nucleus. The mRNA then enters the cytoplasm and promotes protein synthesis. These proteins may be

- enzymes that can have numerous effects on cellular processes
- structural proteins for tissue growth and repair, or
- regulatory proteins that can alter enzyme function

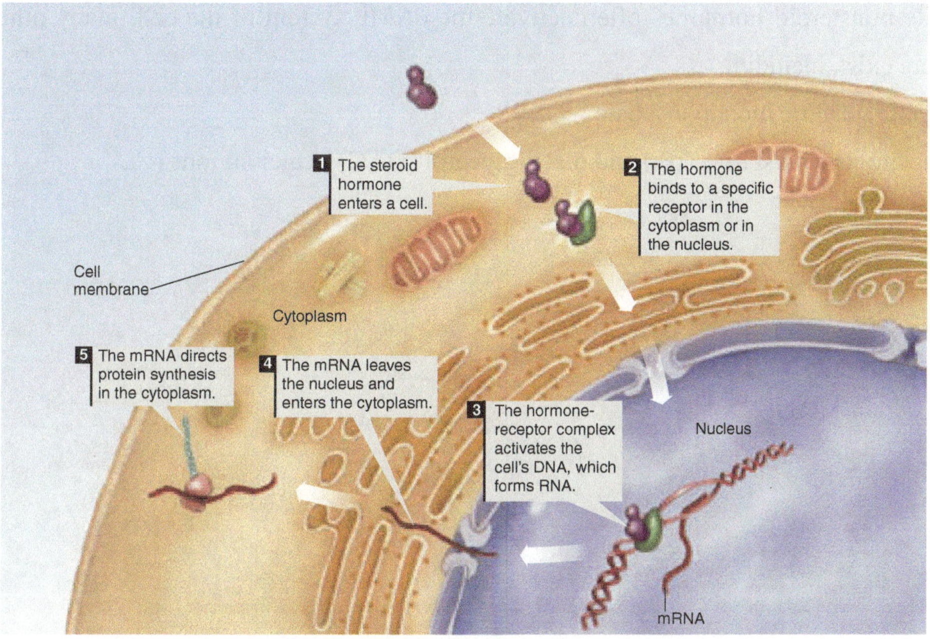

Figure 4.2 The general mechanism of action of a typical steroid hormone, leading to direct gene activation and protein synthesis.

1.4.2 Nonsteroid Hormones

Because nonsteroid hormones cannot cross the cell membrane, they bind with specific receptors on the cell membrane. A nonsteroid hormone molecule binds to its receptor and triggers a series of reactions that lead to the formation of an intracellular second messenger. In addition to their job as a signal-relaying molecule, second messengers also help intensify the strength of the signal. One important second messenger in many cells is cyclic adenosine monophosphate (cyclic AMP, or cAMP) , and its mechanism of action is depicted in Figure 4.3. In this case, attachment of the hormone to the appropriate membrane receptor activates an enzyme, adenylate cyclase, situated within the cell membrane. This enzyme catalyzes the formation of cAMP from cellular adenosine triphosphate (ATP). Cyclic AMP then can produce specific physiological responses that can include

- activation of cellular enzymes
- change in membrane permeability
- promotion of protein synthesis
- change in cellular metabolism, or
- stimulation of cellular secretions

Some of the hormones that achieve their effects through cAMP as a second messenger are epinephrine, glucagon, and luteinizing hormone.

While nonsteroid hormones often activate the cAMP system of the cell, many other second messengers exist, including

- cyclic guanine monophosphate (cGMP)
- inositol trisphosphate (IP_3) and diacylglycerol (DAG) , calcium ions (Ca^{2+})

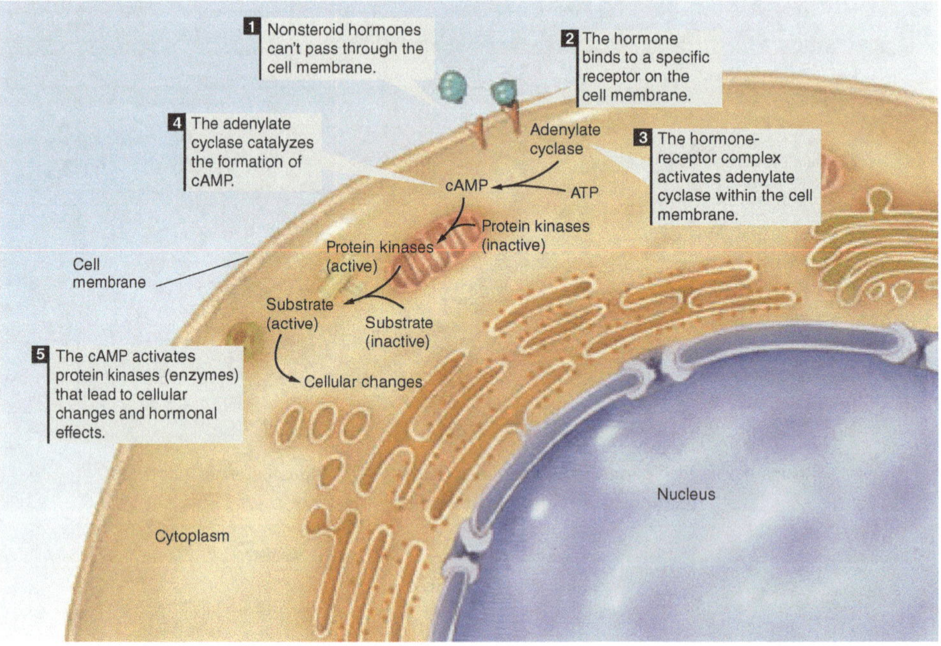

Figure 4.3 The mechanism of action of a nonsteroid hormone, in this case activating a second messenger (cyclic adenosine monophosphate, or cAMP) within the cell to activate cellular functions.

2 Endocrine Glands and Their Hormones: An Overview

The endocrine glands and their respective hormones are listed in Table 4.1. This table is focus on those endocrine glands and hormones of greatest importance to sport and physical activity. Because hormones play such an important role in regulation of many physiological variables during exercise, it is not surprising that hormone release changes during acute bouts of activity. The hormonal responses to an acute bout of exercise and to exercise training are summarized in Table 4.2.

This table is limited to those hormones that play major roles in sport and physical activity. Further details of these exercise-induced hormonal responses are provided in the following discussion of specific endocrine glands and their hormones.

Table 4.1 The Endocrine Glands and Their Hormones, Target Organs, Controlling Factors, and Functions

Endocrine gland	Hormone	Target organ	Controlling factor	Major functions
Anterior pituitary	Growth hormone (GH)	All cells in the body	Hypothalamic GH–releasing hormone; GH–inhibiting hormone (somatostatin)	Promotes development and enlargement of all body tissues until maturation; increases rate of protein synthesis; increases mobilization of fats and use of fat as an energy source; decreases rate of carbohydrate use
	Thyrotropin (TSH)	Thyroid gland	Hypothalamic TSH–releasing hormone	Controls the amount of thyroxin and triiodothyronine produced and released by the thyroid gland
	Adrenocorticotropin (ACTH)	Adrenal cortex	Hypothalamic ACTH–releasing hormone	Controls the secretion of hormones from the adrenal cortex
	Prolactin	Breasts	Prolactin–releasing and inhibiting hormones	Stimulates milk production by the breasts
	Follicle-stimulating hormone (FSH)	Ovaries, testes	Hypothalamic FSH–releasing hormone	Initiates growth of follicles in the ovaries and promotes secretion of estrogen from the ovaries; promotes development of the sperm in the testes
	Luteinizing hormone (LH)	Ovaries, testes	Hypothalamic FSH–releasing hormone	Promotes secretion of estrogen and progesterone and causes the follicle to rupture, releasing the ovum; causes testes to secrete testosterone
Posterior pituitary	Antidiuretic hormone (ADH or vasopressin)	Kidneys	Hypothalamic secretory neurons	Assists in controlling water excretion by the kidneys; elevates blood pressure by constricting blood vessels
	Oxytocin	Uterus, breasts	Hypothalamic secretory neurons	Controls contraction of uterus; milk secretion
Thyroid	Thyroxine (T_4) and triiodothyronine (T_3)	All cells in the body	TSH, T_3, and T_4 concentrations	Increase the rate of cellular metabolism; increase rate and contractility of the heart
	Calcitonin	Bones	Plasma calcium concentrations	Controls calcium ion concentration in the blood
Parathyroid	Parathyroid hormone (PTH or parathormone)	Bones, intestines, and kidneys	Plasma calcium concentrations	Controls calcium ion concentration in the extracellular fluid through its influence on bones, intestines, and kidneys

continued

Endocrine gland	Hormone	Target organ	Controlling factor	Major functions
Adrenal medulla	Epinephrine	Most cells in the body	Baroreceptors, glucose receptors, brain and spinal centers	Stimulates breakdown of glycogen in liver and muscle and lipolysis in adipose tissue and muscle; increases skeletal muscle blood flow; increases heart rate and contractility; increases oxygen consumption
	Norepinephrine	Most cells in the body	Baroreceptors, glucose receptors, brain and spinal centers	Stimulates lipolysis in adipose tissue and in muscle to a lesser extent; constricts arterioles and venules, thereby elevating blood pressure
Adrenal cortex	Mineralocorticoids (aldosterone)	Kidneys	Angiotensin and plasma potassium concentrations; renin	Increase sodium retention and potassium excretion through the kidneys
	Glucocorticoids (cortisol)	Most cells in the body	ACTH	Control metabolism of carbohydrates, fats, and proteins; exert an anti-inflammatory action
	Androgens and estrogens	Ovaries, breasts, and testes	ACTH	Assist in the development of female and male sex characteristics
Pancreas	Insulin	All cells in the body	Plasma glucose and amino acid concentrations	Controls blood glucose levels by lowering glucose levels; increases use of glucose and synthesis of fat
	Glucagon	All cells in the body	Plasma glucose and amino acid concentrations	Increases blood glucose; stimulates the breakdown of protein and fat
	Somatostatin	Islets of Langerhans and intestines	Plasma glucose, insulin, and glucagon concentrations	Depresses the secretion of both insulin and glucagon
Kidney	Renin	Adrenal cortex	Plasma sodium concentrations	Assists in blood pressure control
	Erythropoietin (EPO)	Bone marrow	Low tissue oxygen concentrations	Stimulates erythrocyte production
Testes	Testosterone	Sex organs, muscle	FSH and LH	Promotes development of male sex characteristics, including growth of testes, scrotum, and penis, facial hair, and change in voice; promotes muscle growth
Ovaries	Estrogens and progesterone	Sex organs and adipose tissue	FSH and LH	Promote development of female sex organs and characteristics; increase storage of fat; assist in regulating the menstrual cycle

Table 4.2 Hormone Response to Acute Exercise and Change in Response with Exercise Training

Endocrine gland	Hormone	Response to acute exercise (untrained)	Effect of exercise training
Anterior pituitary	Growth hormone (GH)	Increases with increasing rates of work	Attenuated response at same rate of work
	Thyrotropin (TSH)	Increases with increasing rates of work	No known effect
	Adrenocorticotropin (ACTH)	Increases with increasing rates of work and duration	Attenuated response at same rate of work
	Prolactin	Increases with exercise	No known effect
	Follicle-stimulating hormone (FSH)	Small or no change	No known effect
	Luteinizing hormone (LH)	Small or no change	No known effect
Posterior pituitary	Antidiuretic hormone (ADH or vasopressin)	Increases with increasing rates of work	Attenuated response at same rate of work
	Oxytocin	Unknown	Unknown
Thyroid	Thyroxine (T_4) and triiodothyronine (T_3)	Free T_3 and T_4 increase with increasing rates of work	Increased turnover of T_3 and T_4 at same rate of work
	Calcitonin	Unknown	Unknown
Parathyroid	Parathyroid hormone (PTH or parathormone)	Increases with prolonged exercise	Unknown
Adrenal medulla	Epinephrine	Increases with increasing rates of work, starting at about 75% of $\dot{V}O_{2\,max}$	Attenuated response at same rate of work
	Norepinephrine	Increases with increasing rates of work, starting at about 50% of $\dot{V}O_{2\,max}$	Attenuated response at same rate of work
Adrenal cortex	Aldosterone	Increases with increasing rates of work	Unchanged
	Cortisol	Increases only at high rates of work	Slightly higher values
Pancreas	Insulin	Decreases with increasing rates of work	Attenuated response at same rate of work
	Glucagon	Increases with increasing rates of work	Attenuated response at same rate of work
Kidney	Renin	Increases with increasing rates of work	Unchanged
	Erythropoietin (EPO)	Unknown	Unchanged
Testes	Testosterone	Small increases with exercise	Resting levels decreased in male runners
Ovaries	Estrogens and progesterone	Small increases with exercise	Resting levels might be decreased in highly trained women

3 Hormonal Regulation of Metabolism During Exercise

As noted in Chapter 2, carbohydrate and fat metabolism are responsible for maintaining muscle ATP levels during prolonged exercise. Various hormones work to ensure glucose and free fatty acid (FFA) availability for muscle energy metabolism. In the next sections we examine the major endocrine glands and hormones responsible for metabolic regulation, and how the metabolism of glucose and fat is affected by these hormones during exercise.

3.1 Endocrine Glands Involved in Metabolic Regulation

While many complex systems interact to regulate metabolism at rest and during exercise, the major endocrine glands responsible are the anterior pituitary gland, the thyroid gland, the adrenal glands, and the pancreas.

3.1.1 Anterior Pituitary

The pituitary gland is a marble-sized gland attached to the hypothalamus at the base of the brain. It is composed of three lobes: anterior, intermediate, and posterior. The intermediate lobe is very small and is thought to play little or no role in humans, but both the anterior and posterior lobes serve major endocrine functions. The secretory action of the anterior pituitary is controlled by hormones secreted by the hypothalamus, while the posterior pituitary receives direct nerve signals from neural projections from the hypothalamus. The posterior pituitary is discussed later in the chapter.

The anterior pituitary, also called the adenohypophysis, secretes six hormones in response to releasing factors or inhibiting factors secreted by the hypothalamus. Communication between the hypothalamus and the anterior lobe of the pituitary occurs through a specialized circulatory system. The major functions of each of the anterior pituitary hormones, along with their releasing and inhibiting factors, are listed in Table 4.1. Exercise appears to be a strong stimulus to the hypothalamus because exercise increases the release rate of all six anterior pituitary hormones (see Table 4.2).

Of the six anterior pituitary hormones, four are tropic hormones, meaning they affect the functioning of other endocrine glands. The exceptions are growth hormone and prolactin. Growth hormone (GH) is a potent anabolic agent. It promotes muscle growth and hypertrophy by facilitating amino acid transport into the cells. In addition, GH directly stimulates fat metabolism (lipolysis) by increasing the synthesis of enzymes involved in that process. Growth hormone concentrations are elevated during aerobic exercise in proportion to the exercise intensity and typically remain elevated for some time after exercise.

3.1.2 Thyroid gland

The thyroid gland is located along the midline of the neck, immediately below the larynx. It secretes two important nonsteroid hormones, triiodothyronine (T_3) and thyroxine (T_4) , which regulate metabolism in general, and an additional hormone, calcitonin, which assists in regulating calcium metabolism.

The two metabolic thyroid hormones share similar functions. Triiodothyronine and thyroxine increase the metabolic rate of almost all tissues and can increase the body's basal metabolic rate by as much as 60%–100%. These hormones also

- increase protein synthesis (including enzymes)
- increase the size and number of mitochondria in most cells
- promote rapid cellular uptake of glucose
- enhance glycolysis and gluconeogenesis
- enhance lipid mobilization, increasing FFA availability for oxidation

Release of thyrotropin (thyroid-stimulating hormone, or TSH) from the anterior pituitary increases during exercise. TSH controls the release of triiodothyronine and thyroxine, so exercise increases plasma thyroxine concentrations, but a delay occurs between the increase in TSH concentrations during exercise and the increase in plasma thyroxine concentration. Furthermore, during prolonged submaximal exercise, thyroxine concentrations remain relatively constant after a sharp initial increase as exercise begins, and triiodothyronine concentrations tend to decrease.

3.1.3 Adrenal glands

The adrenal glands are situated directly atop each kidney and are composed of the inner adrenal medulla and the outer adrenal cortex. The hormones secreted by these two parts are quite distinct. The adrenal medulla produces and releases two hormones, epinephrine and norepinephrine, which are collectively referred to as catecholamines. When the adrenal medulla is stimulated by the sympathetic nervous system, approximately 80% of its secretion is epinephrine and 20% is norepinephrine, although these percentages vary with different physiological conditions. These two hormones prepare a person for immediate action, often called the "fight-or-flight response."

Although some of the specific actions of these two hormones differ, the two work together. Their combined effects include

- increased heart rate and force of contraction
- increased metabolic rate
- increased glycogenolysis (breakdown of glycogen to glucose) in the liver and muscle
- increased release of glucose and FFAs into the blood

- redistribution of blood to the skeletal muscles
- increased blood pressure, and
- increased respiration

Release of epinephrine and norepinephrine is affected by a wide variety of factors, including psychological stress and exercise. Plasma concentrations of these hormones increase as individuals gradually increase their exercise intensity. Plasma norepinephrine concentrations increase markedly at work rates above 50% of $\dot{V}O_{2\,max}$, but epinephrine concentrations do not increase significantly until the exercise intensity exceeds 60%–70% of $\dot{V}O_{2\,max}$. During long-duration steady-state activity of moderate intensity, blood concentrations of both hormones increase. When the exercise bout ends, epinephrine returns to resting concentrations within only a few minutes of recovery, but norepinephrine can remain elevated for several hours.

The adrenal cortex secretes more than 30 different steroid hormones, referred to as corticosteroids. These generally are classified into three major types: mineralocorticoids, glucocorticoids, and gonad corticoids (sex hormones). The glucocorticoids are essential to the ability to adapt to exercise and other forms of stress. They also help maintain fairly consistent plasma glucose concentrations even during long periods without ingestion of food. Cortisol, also known as hydrocortisone, is the major corticosteroid. It is responsible for about 95% of all glucocorticoid activity in the body. Cortisol

- stimulates gluconeogenesis to ensure an adequate fuel supply
- increases mobilization of FFAs, making them more available as an energy source
- decreases glucose utilization, sparing it for the brain
- stimulates protein catabolism to release amino acids for use in repair, enzyme synthesis, and energy production
- acts as an anti-inflammatory agent
- depresses immune reactions; and
- increases the vasoconstriction caused by epinephrine

3.1.4 Pancreas

The pancreas is located behind the stomach. Its two major hormones are insulin and glucagon. The balance of these two opposing hormones provides the major control of plasma glucose concentration. When plasma glucose is elevated (hyperglycemia) , as occurs after a meal, the pancreas releases insulin into the blood. Among its actions, insulin

- facilitates glucose transport into the cells, especially muscle fibers
- promotes glycogenesis; and
- inhibits gluconeogenesis

Insulin's main function is to reduce the amount of glucose circulating in the blood. But it is also involved in protein and fat metabolism, promoting cellular uptake of amino acids and enhancing synthesis of protein and fat.

The pancreas secretes glucagon when the plasma glucose concentration falls below normal concentrations (hypoglycemia). Its effects generally oppose those of insulin. Glucagon promotes increased breakdown of liver glycogen to glucose (glycogenolysis) and increased gluconeogenesis, both of which increase plasma glucose levels.

During exercise lasting 30 min or longer, the body attempts to maintain plasma glucose concentrations; however, insulin concentrations tend to decline. The ability of insulin to bind to its receptors on muscle cells increases during exercise, due in large part to increased blood flow to muscle. This increases the body's sensitivity to insulin and reduces the need to maintain high plasma insulin concentrations for transporting glucose into the muscle cells. Plasma glucagon, on the other hand, shows a gradual increase throughout exercise. Glucagon primarily maintains plasma glucose concentrations by stimulating liver glycogenolysis. This increases glucose availability to the cells, maintaining adequate plasma glucose concentrations to meet increased metabolic demands. The responses of these hormones are usually blunted in trained individuals, and those who are well trained are better able to maintain plasma glucose concentrations.

3.2 Regulation of Carbohydrate Metabolism During Exercise

As we learned in Chapter 2, the heightened energy demands of exercise require that more glucose be made available to the muscles. Recall that glucose is stored in the body as glycogen, primarily in the muscles and the liver. Glucose must be freed from its storage form of glycogen, so glycogenolysis must increase. Glucose freed from the liver enters the blood to circulate throughout the body, allowing it access to active tissues. Plasma glucose concentration also can be increased through gluconeogenesis.

3.2.1 Regulation of Plasma Glucose Concentration

The plasma glucose concentration during exercise depends on a balance between glucose uptake by exercising muscles and its release by the liver. Four hormones work to increase the amount of circulating plasma glucose:

- Glucagon
- Epinephrine
- Norepinephrine
- Cortisol

At rest, glucose release from the liver is facilitated by glucagon, which promotes both liver glycogen breakdown and glucose formation from amino acids. During exercise, glucagon secretion increases. Muscular activity also increases the rate of catecholamine release from the adrenal medulla, and these hormones (epinephrine and norepinephrine) work in concert with glucagon to further increase glycogenolysis. After a slight initial drop, cortisol concentration increases during the first 30–45 min of exercise. Cortisol increases protein catabolism, freeing amino acids to be used within the liver for gluconeogenesis. Thus, all four of these hormones can increase plasma glucose by enhancing the processes of glycogenolysis and gluconeogenesis. In addition to the effects of the four major glucose-controlling hormones, growth hormone increases mobilization of FFAs and decreases cellular uptake of glucose, so less glucose is used by the cells and more remains in circulation. The thyroid hormones promote glucose catabolism and fat metabolism.

The amount of glucose released by the liver depends on both exercise intensity and duration. As intensity increases, so does the rate of catecholamine release. This can cause the liver to release more glucose than is being taken up by the active muscles. Consequently, during or shortly after an explosive, short-term sprint, blood glucose concentrations may be 40%–50% above the resting value.

The greater the exercise intensity, the greater the catecholamine release, and thus the rate of glycogenolysis is significantly increased. This process occurs not only in the liver but also in the muscle. The glucose released from the liver enters the blood where it becomes available to the muscle fibers. But the muscle has a more readily available source of glucose: its own glycogen stores. The muscle uses its own glycogen stores before using the plasma glucose during explosive, short-term exercise. Glucose released from the liver is not used as readily, so it remains in the circulation, elevating the plasma glucose. Following exercise, plasma glucose concentration decreases as the glucose enters the muscle to replenish the depleted muscle glycogen stores.

During exercise bouts that last for several hours, the rate of liver glucose release more closely matches the muscles' needs, keeping plasma glucose at or only slightly above the resting concentrations. As muscle uptake of glucose increases, the liver's rate of glucose release also increases. In most cases, plasma glucose does not begin to decline until late in the activity as liver glycogen stores become depleted, at which time the glucagon concentration increases significantly. Glucagon and cortisol together enhance gluconeogenesis, providing more fuel.

Figure 4.4 illustrates the changes in plasma concentrations of epinephrine, norepinephrine, glucagon, cortisol, and glucose during 3 h of cycling. Although the hormonal regulation of glucose remains intact throughout such long-term activities, the liver's glycogen supply may become limiting and the liver's rate of glucose release may be unable to keep pace with the muscles' rate of glucose uptake. Under this condition, plasma glucose may decline despite strong hormonal stimulation. Glucose ingestion during the activity can play a major role in maintaining plasma glucose concentrations.

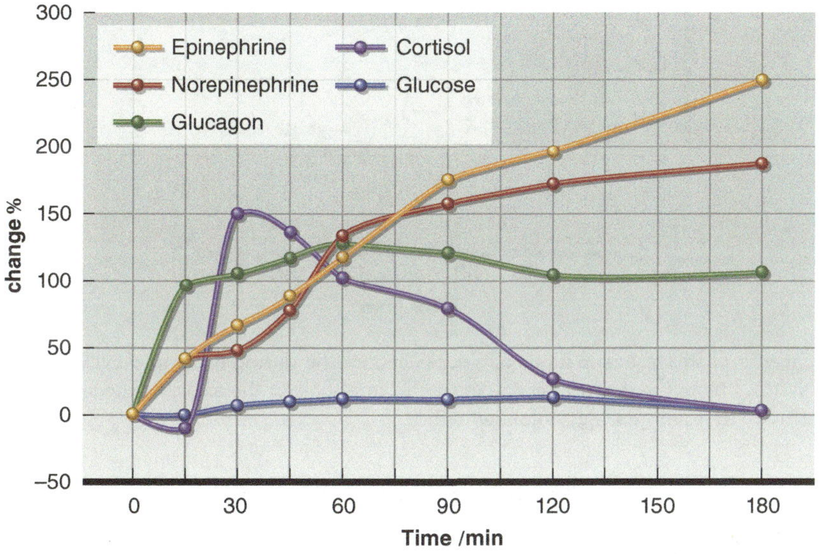

Figure 4.4 Changes (as a percentage of preexercise values) in plasma concentrations of epinephrine, norepinephrine, glucagon, cortisol, and glucose during 3 h of cycling at 65% $\dot{V}O_{2\,max}$.

3.2.2 Glucose Uptake by Muscle

Merely releasing sufficient amounts of glucose into the blood does not ensure that the muscle cells will have enough glucose to meet their energy demands. Not only must the glucose be released and delivered to these cells; it also must be taken up by the cells. Transport of glucose through the cell membranes and into muscle cells is controlled by insulin. Once glucose is delivered to the muscle, insulin facilitates its transport into the fibers.

As seen in Figure 4.5, plasma insulin concentration tends to decrease during prolonged submaximal exercise, despite a slight increase in plasma glucose concentration and glucose uptake by muscle. This apparent contradiction between the plasma insulin concentrations and the muscles' need for glucose serves as a reminder that a hormone's activity is determined not only by its concentration in the blood but also by a cell's sensitivity to that hormone. In this case, the cell's sensitivity to insulin is at least as important as the concentration of circulating hormone. Exercise may enhance insulin's binding to receptors on the muscle fiber, thereby reducing the need for high concentrations of plasma insulin to transport glucose across the muscle cell membrane into the cell. This is important, because during exercise four hormones are working to release glucose from its storage sites and create new glucose. High insulin concentrations would oppose their action, preventing this needed increase in plasma glucose supply.

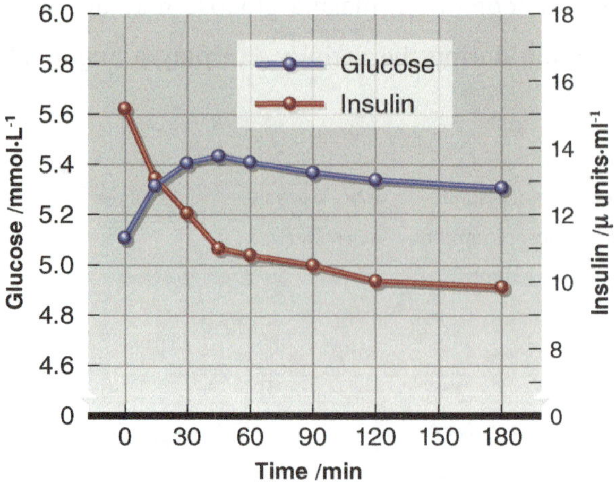

Figure 4.5 Changes in plasma concentrations of glucose and insulin during prolonged cycling at 65%–70% of $\dot{V}O_{2\,max}$. Note the gradual decline in insulin through-out the exercise, suggesting an increased sensitivity to insulin during prolonged effort.

3.3 Regulation of Fat Metabolism During Exercise

Although fat generally contributes less than carbohydrate to muscles' energy needs during exercise, mobilization and oxidation of FFAs are critical to performance in endurance exercise. During such prolonged activity, carbohydrate reserves become depleted, and muscle must rely more heavily on the oxidation of fat for energy production. When plasma glucose and low muscle glycogen are low, the endocrine system can accelerate the oxidation of fats, thus ensuring that muscles' energy needs can be met.

Free fatty acids are stored as triglycerides in adipose tissue and within muscle fibers. Adipose tissue triglycerides, however, must be broken down to release the FFAs, which are then transported to the muscle fibers. The rate of FFA uptake by active muscle correlates highly with the plasma FFA concentration. Increasing this concentration would increase cellular uptake of the FFA. Therefore, the rate of triglyceride breakdown may determine, in part, the rate at which muscles use fat as a fuel source during exercise.

The rate of lipolysis controlled by at least five hormones:

- Insulin
- Epinephrine
- Norepinephrine
- Cortisol
- Growth hormone

The major factor responsible for adipose tissue lipolysis during exercise is a fall in circulating insulin. Lipolysis is also enhanced through the elevation of epinephrine and norepinephrine. In addition to having a role in gluconeogenesis, cortisol accelerates the mobilization and use of FFAs for energy during exercise. Plasma cortisol concentration peaks after 30–45 min of exercise and then decreases to near-normal levels. But the plasma FFA concentration continues to increase throughout the activity, meaning that lipase continues to be activated by other hormones. The hormones that continue this process are the catecholamines and growth hormone. The thyroid hormones also contribute to the mobilization and metabolism of FFAs but to a much lesser degree.

Thus, the endocrine system plays a critical role in regulating ATP production during exercise as well as controlling the balance between carbohydrate and fat metabolism.

4 Hormonal Regulation of Fluid and Electrolytes During Exercise

Fluid balance during exercise is critical for optimal metabolic, cardiovascular, and thermoregulatory function. At the onset of exercise, water is shifted from the plasma volume to the interstitial and intracellular spaces. This water shift is specific to the amount of muscle that is active and the intensity of effort. Metabolic by-products begin to accumulate in and around the muscle fibers, increasing the osmotic pressure there. Water is then drawn into these areas by diffusion. Also, increased muscular activity increases blood pressure, which in turn drives water out of the blood. In addition, sweating increases during exercise. The combined effect of these actions is that plasma volume decreases. For example, prolonged running at approximately 75% of $\dot{V}O_{2\,max}$ decreases plasma volume by 5%–10%. Reduced plasma volume can decrease blood pressure and increase the strain on the heart to pump blood to the working muscles. Both of these effects can impede athletic performance.

4.1 Endocrine Glands Involved in Fluid and Electrolyte Homeostasis

The endocrine system plays a major role in monitoring fluid levels and correcting imbalances, along with regulating electrolyte balance, especially that of sodium. The two major endocrine glands involved in these processes are the posterior pituitary and the adrenal cortex. The kidneys are not only the primary target organ for hormones released by these glands but are also endocrine glands themselves.

4.1.1 Posterior Pituitary

The pituitary's posterior lobe is an outgrowth of neural tissue from the hypothalamus. For this reason, it is also referred to as the neurohypophysis. It secretes two hormones: antidiuretic hormone (ADH; also called vasopressin) and oxytocin. Both of these hormones are actually produced in the hypothalamus. They travel through the neural tissue and are stored in vesicles within nerve endings in the posterior pituitary. These hormones are released into capillaries as needed in response to neural impulses from the hypothalamus.

Of the two posterior pituitary hormones, only ADH is known to play an important role during exercise. Antidiuretic hormone promotes water conservation by increasing water reabsorption by the kidneys. As a result, less water is excreted in the urine, creating an "antidiuresis".

Muscular activity and sweating cause electrolytes to become concentrated in the blood plasma. This is called hemoconcentration, and it increases the plasma osmolality. An increased plasma osmolality is the primary physiological stimulus for ADH release.

The increased osmolality is sensed by osmoreceptors in the hypothalamus. A second and related stimulus for ADH release is a low plasma volume sensed by baroreceptors in the cardiovascular system. In response to either stimulus, the hypothalamus sends neural impulses to the posterior pituitary, stimulating ADH release. The ADH enters the blood, travels to the kidneys, and promotes water retention in an effort to dilute the plasma electrolyte concentration back to normal levels. This hormone's role in conserving body water minimizes the extent of water loss and therefore the risk of severe dehydration during periods of heavy sweating and hard exercise. Figure 4.6 illustrates this process.

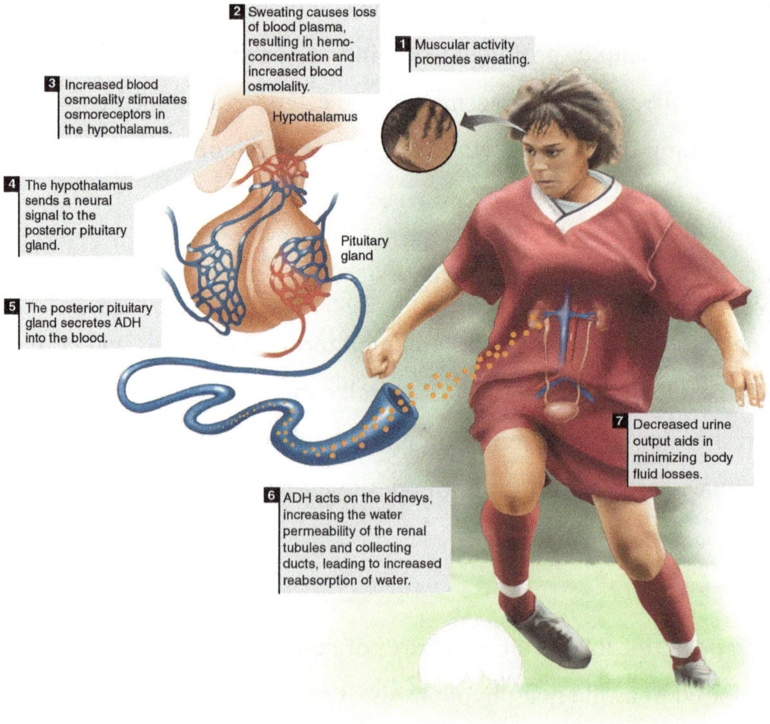

Figure 4.6 The mechanism by which antidiuretic hormone (ADH) helps to conserve body water.

4.1.2 Adrenal Cortex

A group of hormones called mineralocorticoids, secreted from the adrenal cortex, maintain electrolyte balance in the extracellular fluids, especially that of sodium (Na^+) and potassium (K^+). Aldosterone is the major mineralocorticoid, responsible for at least 95% of all mineralocorticoid activity. It works primarily by promoting renal reabsorption of sodium, thus causing the body to retain sodium. When sodium is retained, so is water; thus, aldosterone, like ADH, results in water retention. Sodium retention also enhances potassium excretion, so aldosterone plays a role in potassium balance as well. Aldosterone secretion is stimulated by many factors, including decreased plasma sodium, decreased blood volume, decreased blood pressure, and increased plasma potassium concentration.

4.2 The kidneys as Endocrine Organs

Although the kidneys are not typically considered major endocrine organs, they do release a hormone called erythropoietin. Erythropoietin (EPO) regulates red blood cell (erythrocyte) production by stimulating bone marrow cells. The red blood cells are essential for transporting oxygen to the tissues and removing carbon dioxide, so this hormone is extremely important in our adaptation to training and altitude.

The kidneys also play a role in determining the aldosterone concentration in the blood. While the primary regulator of aldosterone release is plasma potassium and sodium concentrations, a second set of hormones also determines aldosterone concentration and thus helps regulate body fluid balance. In response to a fall in blood pressure or plasma volume, blood flow to the kidneys decreases. Stimulated by activation of the sympathetic nervous system, the kidneys release renin. Renin is an enzyme that is released into the circulation, where it converts a molecule called angiotensinogen to angiotensin I. Angiotensin I is subsequently converted to its active form, angiotonin II, in the lungs with the aid of an enzyme, angiotensin-converting enzyme, or ACE. Angiotonin II stimulates aldosterone release from the adrenal cortex for sodium and water resorption at the kidneys. This process is the renin angiotensin-aldosterone mechanism.

Recall that aldosterone's primary action is to promote sodium reabsorption in the kidneys. Because water follows sodium, this renal conservation of sodium causes the kidneys to also retain water. The net effect is to conserve the body's fluid content, thereby minimizing the loss of plasma volume while keeping blood pressure near normal. Figure 4.7 illustrates the changes in plasma volume and aldosterone concentrations during 2 h of exercise.

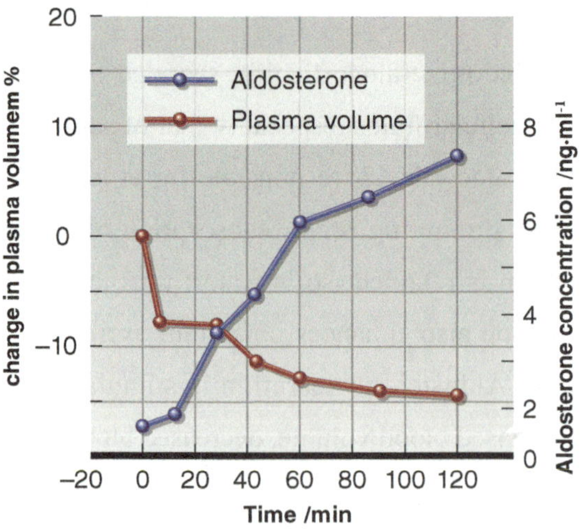

Figure 4.7 Changes in plasma volume and aldosterone concentration during 2 h of cycling exercise. Note that plasma volume declines rapidly during the first few minutes of exercise and then shows a smaller rate of decline despite large sweat losses. Plasma aldosterone concentration increases rather steadily throughout the exercise.

The hormonal influences of ADH and aldosterone persist for up to 12–48 h after exercise, reducing urine production and protecting the body from further dehydration. In fact, aldosterone's prolonged enhancement of Na^+ reabsorption may cause the body's Na^+ concentration to increase above normal following an exercise bout. In an effort to compensate for this elevation in Na^+ concentrations, more of the water ingested shifts into the extracellular compartment.

Most athletes involved in heavy training have an expanded plasma volume. The actual number of proteins and electrolytes within the blood remains unaltered, but the substances are dispersed throughout a greater volume of water, so they are diluted and their concentration decreases. This phenomenon is called hemodilution.

Hemoglobin is one of the substances diluted by plasma expansion. For this reason, some athletes who actually have normal hemoglobin concentrations may appear to be anemic as a consequence of Na^+-induced hemodilution. This condition, not to be confused with true anemia, can be remedied with a few days of rest, allowing time for aldosterone concentrations to return to normal and for the kidneys to unload the extra Na^+ and water.

IN CLOSING

In this chapter, we focused on the role of the endocrine system in regulating some of the many physiological processes that accompany exercise. We discussed the role of hormones in regulating the metabolism of glucose and fat for energy metabolism and the role of other hormones in maintaining fluid balance. We next look at the energy expenditure and fatigue during exercise.

KEY TERMS

antidiuretic hormone; catecholamines; cortisol; cyclic adenosine monophosphate; erythropoietin; glucagon; glucocorticoids; growth hormone; hyperglycemia; insulin; mineralocorticoids; nonsteroid hormones; osmolality; renin; renin-angiotensin-aldosterone mechanism; second messenger; steroid hormones; target cells; thyrotropin; thyroxine; triiodothyronine; upregulation

STUDY QUESTIONS

(1) What is an endocrine gland, and what are the functions of hormones?

(2) Explain the difference between steroid hormones and nonsteroid hormones in terms of their actions at target cells.

(3) How can hormones have very specific functions when they reach nearly all parts of the body through the blood?

(4) How are plasma concentrations of specific hormones controlled?

(5) Define the terms upregulation and downregulation. How do target cells become more or less sensitive to hormones?

(6) What are secondary messengers and what role do they play in hormonal control of cell function?

(7) Briefly outline the major endocrine glands, their hormones, and the specific action of these hormones.

(8) Which of the hormones outlined in Question 7 are of major significance during exercise?

(9) What hormones are involved in the regulation of metabolism during exercise? How do they influence the availability of carbohydrates and fats for energy during exercise lasting for several hours?

(10) Describe the hormonal regulation of fluid balance during exercise.

第四章 运动中的激素调控

在运动中身体需要进行多种生理调节，其中大部分生理调节是由神经系统完成的，但内分泌系统也会影响身体中的每一个细胞、组织和器官。它持续地监测身体的内部环境，注意到发生的所有变化，并迅速释放激素，以确保内稳态不会被严重破坏。在本章中，我们重点介绍运动过程中激素对新陈代谢和体液平衡的调节。

一、内分泌系统

内分泌系统和神经系统通常统称为神经内分泌系统，共同作用以控制所有支持运动的生理过程。神经系统作用迅速而短暂，部位局限；而内分泌系统反应缓慢，但作用更持久。内分泌系统包括能分泌激素的所有组织和腺体。内分泌腺直接将激素分泌到血液中，激素被运送至特定的靶细胞来控制靶组织的活动。有的激素可以影响机体的多种组织，而有的激素则只作用于特定细胞。

（一）激素

激素的作用与运动和身体活动的许多方面有关。本章节主要讨论激素的化学性质及其一般作用机理，以及运动代谢的控制和运动中体液和电解质的调节。

（二）激素的化学分类

激素可分为类固醇激素和非类固醇激素。类固醇激素为脂溶性，很容易穿透细胞膜，其由肾上腺皮质、卵巢、睾丸或胎盘产生。非类固醇激素为非脂溶性，不易穿过细胞膜，其可分为蛋白质或肽类激素、氨基酸类激素。来自甲状腺的激素（甲状腺素和三碘甲腺原氨酸）和来自肾上腺髓质的激素（肾上腺素和去甲肾上腺素）是氨基酸类激素。其他非类固醇激素都是蛋白质或肽类激素。激素的化学结构决定了其对靶细胞和靶组织的作用机制。

（三）激素分泌与血浆浓度

激素的分泌不是匀速的，常常在短时间内有一个分泌高峰期，因此血浆中的激素浓度会在短周期内（一小时或更短）波动。但激素浓度也会在较长的时间内出现波动，可表现出一天甚至一月的周期性变动（如月经周期）。

多数激素的分泌由负反馈系统来调节。机体内特定激素开始或结束分泌是由生理变化决定的。以血糖浓度和胰岛素浓度为例，血糖浓度高时，胰腺就会分泌胰岛素，促进细胞摄取葡萄糖，以降低血糖浓度；当血糖浓度回到正常范围时，胰岛素的释放就会受到抑制，直到血糖水平再度升高，胰岛素的分泌才会再次上升。

特定激素在血浆中的浓度并不能很好地反应激素的活性，因为激素必须与特定的细胞受体结合才能发挥作用。因此，可以改变靶细胞上受体的数量来增加或降低该细胞对激素的敏感性。受体数目减少，结合的激素分子也变少，此过程称为下调，亦称脱敏作用。在少数情况下，细胞长期处于大剂量的激素环境时，可能会通过增加受体数量来增强对激素的反应。此时细胞会对该激素变得更敏感，此过程称为上调。此外，一种激素有时可以作用于另一种激素的受体。

（四）激素的作用

激素随血液流动，其对特定靶组织产生影响是由于靶组织上具有特定的激素受体。每个细胞拥有2 000～10 000个受体。激素与其受体结合称为激素–受体复合物。类固醇激素为脂溶性，从而可以轻易地通过细胞膜，其受体则在细胞质或细胞核中。非类固醇激素不易穿过细胞膜，其受体位于细胞膜上。激素只能对含有特定受体的组织产生效应。一旦与受体结合，激素会通过多种机制控制细胞的活动。

1.类固醇激素

一旦穿过细胞膜并进入细胞内，类固醇激素就会与其特定的受体结合。激素–受体复合物随后进入细胞核，与部分细胞的脱氧核糖核酸（DNA）结合，激活特定的基因。作为对这种激活的反应，信使核糖核酸（mRNA）在细胞核中合成，然后进入细胞质，促进蛋白质合成。这些蛋白质可能是酶、结构蛋白或调节蛋白。

2.非类固醇激素

非类固醇激素只能与细胞膜表面的特异受体结合，激活位于细胞膜上的腺苷酸环化酶。此酶催化三磷酸腺苷转化成环磷酸腺苷（cAMP），cAMP形成后可以产生特定的生理效应，包括激活细胞内的酶，改变细胞膜的通透性，促进蛋白质合成，改变细胞代谢，刺激细胞分泌。除了cAMP，其他重要的第二信使还包括环鸟苷一磷酸（cGMP）、三磷酸肌醇（IP_3）、二酰甘油（DAG）和钙离子（Ca^{2+}）。

二、内分泌腺及其激素概述

将人体的内分泌腺及其分泌的激素归纳为表4.1，该表所列内容主要是与运动相关的腺体和激素。

表4.1　各种内分泌腺及其分泌的激素、作用的靶器官、控制因素以及激素的主要功能

内分泌腺	激素	靶器官	控制因素	主要功能
垂体前叶	生长激素（GH）	全身各部位细胞	下丘脑生长激素释放激素；生长激素抑制激素（生长抑素）	在成年之前促进全身组织生长；增加蛋白质合成；提高脂肪转运速度和脂肪供能比例；降低碳水化合物供能比例
	促甲状腺素（TSH）	甲状腺	下丘脑促甲状腺激素释放激素	控制甲状腺产生和释放的甲状腺素和三碘甲状腺原氨酸（T_3）的量
	促肾上腺皮质激素（ACTH）	肾上腺皮质	下丘脑促肾上腺皮质激素释放激素	控制肾上腺皮质的激素分泌
	催乳素（PRL）	乳腺	催乳激素释放和抑制激素	刺激乳腺分泌乳汁
	促卵泡激素（FSH）	卵巢、睾丸	促性腺激素释放激素	促进卵巢中卵泡的生长；促进卵巢分泌雌激素；促进睾丸中精子的发育
	黄体生成素（LH）	卵巢、睾丸	促性腺激素释放激素	促进雌激素和前列腺素的分泌；促使卵泡破裂，释放卵子；促使睾丸分泌睾酮
垂体后叶	抗利尿激素（ADH或血管升压素）	肾脏	下丘脑分泌神经元	协助肾脏进行水分的排泄；收缩血管以升高血压
	催产素	子宫、乳房	下丘脑分泌神经元	控制子宫收缩；刺激乳汁分泌
甲状腺	四碘甲状腺原氨酸（T_4）和三碘甲状腺原氨酸（T_3）	全身各部位细胞	促甲状腺素，T_3和T_4浓度	增加细胞代谢率；提高心率和心肌收缩力
	降钙素	骨	血钙浓度	控制血液中的钙离子的浓度
甲状旁腺	甲状旁腺激素（PTH或甲状腺旁腺素）	骨、小肠和肾脏	血钙浓度	通过对骨、小肠和肾脏的作用来调控细胞外液的钙离子浓度
肾上腺髓质	肾上腺素	机体的大部分细胞	压力感受器，葡萄糖感受器；脑和脊髓神经中枢	刺激肝糖原和肌糖原水解；加速脂肪分解；增加肌肉血流量；提高心率和心肌收缩力量；增加耗氧量
	去甲肾上腺素	机体的大部分细胞	压力感受器，葡萄糖感受器；脑和脊髓神经中枢	小幅度加速脂肪组织和肌肉内的脂肪分解；通过收缩小动脉与小静脉来提升血压
肾上腺皮质	盐皮质激素（醛固酮）	肾脏	血管紧张素和血钾浓度；肾素	促进肾脏保钠排钾
	糖皮质激素（皮质醇）	机体的大部分细胞	促肾上腺皮质激素	调节糖、脂、蛋白质的代谢；抑制炎症反应
	雌激素和雄激素	卵巢、乳房和睾丸	促肾上腺皮质激素	促进男女性征的发育

续表

内分泌腺	激素	靶器官	控制因素	主要功能
胰腺	胰岛素	全身各部位细胞	血浆葡萄糖和氨基酸浓度	降低血糖；提高葡萄糖的利用率和脂肪合成效率
	胰高血糖素	全身各部位细胞	血浆葡萄糖和氨基酸浓度	提升血糖；刺激蛋白质和脂肪分解
	生长抑素	胰岛和小肠	血糖，胰岛素和胰高血糖素浓度	抑制胰岛素和胰高血糖素的分泌
肾脏	肾素	肾上腺皮质	血钠浓度	协助控制血压
	促红细胞生成素（EPO）	骨髓	较低的组织含氧量	刺激红细胞生成
睾丸	睾酮	性器官、肌肉	促卵泡激素和黄体生成素	促进睾丸、阴囊、阴茎、胡须及变声等男性性征的发育；促进肌肉生长
卵巢	雌激素和黄体激素	性器官、脂肪组织	促卵泡激素和黄体生成素	促进女性性器官和性征的发育；协助调控月经周期

三、运动中代谢的调节

在长时间的运动中，多种激素共同发挥调节作用以确保肌肉对葡萄糖和脂肪酸的需求。主要的内分泌腺是垂体前叶、甲状腺、肾上腺和胰腺。

（一）参与代谢调节的内分泌腺

1.垂体前叶

垂体是位于大脑基底部的弹丸大小的内分泌腺，在解剖结构上分为前叶、中叶和后叶。垂体前叶，也叫作腺垂体，可以分泌六种激素，受下丘脑释放的释放因子和抑制因子的控制。这六种激素中除生长激素和催乳素外，其余四种是促激素。对于下丘脑来说，运动是一种强刺激，它可以促进垂体前叶所有激素的释放。生长激素（GH）是一种强有力的促合成激素，可以通过促进氨基酸进入细胞内而使肌肉体积增长；也可以通过增加脂肪分解所需要的酶的合成，促进脂肪分解代谢。有氧运动期间，生长激素的浓度与运动强度成正比，通常在运动后还会持续升高一段时间。

2.甲状腺

甲状腺位于颈部前正中，喉的下方。它可以分泌两种重要的非类固醇激素：三碘甲状腺原氨酸（T_3）和四碘甲状腺原氨酸（T_4）。T_3和T_4的功能非常相似，它们可以使机体的基础代谢率增加60%~100%。此外，它们还可以促进蛋白质合成（包括酶的合成）；增加绝大部分细胞内线粒体的数量和体积；促进细胞摄取葡萄糖的能力；加强糖酵解和糖异生的速度；加快脂肪动员，增强游离脂肪酸氧化。运动时，垂体前叶释放的促甲状腺激素（TSH）分泌量增加。因此，运动可以增加血浆甲状腺素的浓度，但在运动时TSH浓度增加后，会有一段时间的延迟，甲状腺素的浓度才会增加。

3.肾上腺

肾上腺位于肾脏顶部，由周边的皮质和中央的髓质组成。髓质分泌两种激素：肾上腺素和去甲肾上腺素，二者统称为儿茶酚胺。当交感神经系统兴奋时，肾上腺开始分泌儿茶酚胺，其中肾上腺素约占80%，去甲肾上腺素约占20%。这两种激素可以使机体对外界的刺激做出快速反应，这种现象称之为“急性应激反应”。虽然肾上腺素和去甲肾上腺素的某些具体作用并不相同，但是它们在机体中是协同作用的。它们的主要功能有：增加心率和心肌收缩力量；提高代谢率；提高肝脏和肌肉的糖原分解能力（将糖原分解为葡萄糖）；促进葡萄糖和游离脂肪酸释放入血；促进血液的再分配，使骨骼肌得到更多的血液供应；升高血压；加快呼吸等。肾上腺素和去甲肾上腺素的分泌受到多种因素的影响，包括心理压力和运动等。当机体的运动强度逐渐增加，血浆中这两种激素的浓度也会增加。

肾上腺皮质分泌的激素统称为皮质类固醇激素。这些激素可以分为三大类：盐皮质激素、糖皮质激素和促性腺皮质素（性激素）。糖皮质激素在体内95%的活动是由皮质醇完成的。皮质醇，又称氢化可的松，是主要的一种肾上腺皮质类固醇激素。皮质醇的主要功能包括：加速糖异生，以保证能量供应；促进游离脂肪酸的转移速率，使脂肪供能的效率更高；降低外周器官的葡萄糖利用率，保证脑部的葡萄糖供应；加速蛋白质分解代谢，释放氨基酸，以供组织修复、酶的合成和能量供应；抗炎；降低免疫反应；协同肾上腺素的缩血管作用。

4.胰腺

胰腺位于胃的后下方。胰腺主要分泌两种激素：胰岛素和胰高血糖素。这两种激素的作用相反，共同调控血糖浓度的稳定。餐后人的血糖升高，胰腺分泌胰岛素入血。胰岛素的主要作用是降低血糖浓度，它也可以促使细胞吸收氨基酸，并加强蛋白质和脂肪的合成。当血糖浓度低于正常水平时，胰腺开始分泌胰高血糖素，它的作用与胰岛素相反。胰高血糖素可以促使肝糖原水解为葡萄糖，并能提高糖异生水平，提高血糖浓度。在持续30分钟或者更长时间的运动时，机体会尽量维持血糖浓度不变，但是此时胰岛素浓度开始下降。同时，胰高血糖素的浓度在运动中会逐渐升高。

（二）运动中糖代谢的调节

运动过程中，血糖的浓度取决于运动肌肉对葡萄糖的摄取量和肝脏释放的葡萄糖量之间的平衡。体内升高血糖浓度的激素有四种：胰高血糖素、肾上腺素、去甲肾上腺素和皮质醇。

运动时，胰高血糖素的分泌增加，同时也促进肾上腺髓质释放肾上腺素和去甲肾上腺素，这些激素与胰高血糖素协同作用，进一步增加糖原分解。运动中皮质醇的浓度也有所升高，增加蛋白质的分解代谢，释放氨基酸用于肝脏内糖异生。除了这四种激素外，生长激素促进游离脂肪酸的动员，降低细胞对葡萄糖的摄取，因而减少了细胞对葡萄糖的利用，更多的葡萄糖留在循环血液中。甲状腺激素能促进葡萄糖和脂肪的分解代谢。

在爆发性短距离的运动过程中，肌肉在摄取血糖之前，会优先利用自身所储存的糖原。肝脏释放出来的葡萄糖没有被立即使用，因而保留在循环血液内，升高血糖。运动后，葡萄糖进入肌肉，补充减少了的肌糖原。在持续数小时的运动中，肝脏释放葡萄糖的速率更加接近肌肉对葡萄糖的需求，使得血糖维持或稍高于安静时的浓度。在多数情况下，血糖在长时间运动末期，肝糖原储备耗竭时才开始下降，同时胰高血糖素开始增加。胰高血糖素与皮质醇共同促进糖异生，为肌肉提供更多的能源物质。

当血液中有足量的葡萄糖时，并不能保证肌细胞获取充足的葡萄糖以满足其能量需求。葡萄糖不但要被释放并运输到需要能量的细胞，还必须为这些细胞所利用。胰岛素调控葡萄糖通过细胞膜转运进入肌细胞。细胞对胰岛素的敏感性与循环血液中的激素浓度同样重要。运动能提高胰岛素与肌细胞上的受体结合能力。

（三）运动中脂肪代谢的调节

长时间运动时，糖会逐渐耗尽，肌肉的能量来源将逐渐依赖脂肪的氧化。当低血糖或肝糖原减少时，内分泌系统会促进脂肪氧化，以确保肌肉运动的能量需求。脂肪组织中的甘油三酯分解释放的游离脂肪酸可被转运到肌细胞中进行代谢。运动肌肉对游离脂肪酸摄取的速率与血浆游离脂肪酸浓度紧密相关。在运动中，甘油三酯的分解速率在一定程度上取决于肌肉将其作为能源物质的比例。脂肪分解的速率至少受以下五种激素的调控：胰岛素、肾上腺素、去甲肾上腺素、皮质醇和生长激素。运动中脂肪分解的加快，主要是由于血液中的胰岛素浓度降低所致。肾上腺素和去甲肾上腺素浓度的增加也可促进脂肪分解。皮质醇在运动中可加速游离脂肪酸的动员和利用。

综上所述，内分泌系统在调控运动过程中ATP的产生，以及维持糖与脂肪代谢的平衡中发挥着重要的作用。

四、运动中体液和电解质平衡的激素调节

在运动刚开始时，水会从血浆转移到组织间隙和细胞间隙内。代谢产物会堆积在肌纤维内及肌纤维之间，使此部位的渗透压增加，水分通过扩散方式流入。肌肉活动也可升高血压，导致水分从血液中溢出，此外，运动中的排汗量也是增加的。这些活动的综合效应使血浆量减少导致血压下降，增加心脏向工作肌肉泵血的压力。

（一）内分泌腺参与体液和电解质平衡

内分泌系统在监测体液含量和纠正失衡方面发挥着重要作用，同时也调节电解质平衡，

尤其是钠离子。参与这些过程的两个主要内分泌腺是垂体后叶和肾上腺皮质。

1. 垂体后叶

垂体后叶被称为神经垂体。此处分泌两种激素：抗利尿激素（ADH，也称血管升压素）和催产素。这两种激素都由下丘脑生成，通过神经传递，并在垂体后叶神经末梢的囊泡中储存。这两种激素中，仅抗利尿激素在运动时发挥重要作用，能增加肾脏对水的重吸收，从而使尿液量减少，这就是所谓的“抗利尿”。

促进抗利尿激素释放的主要生理刺激是肌肉活动和排汗引起血浆中电解质逐渐浓缩，血浆渗透压升高。另一个刺激因素是心血管系统压力感受器感受到低的血浆容量。当以上刺激因素形成后，下丘脑向垂体后叶发出神经冲动，促使抗利尿激素释放。随后，抗利尿激素释放入血液，通过血液循环进入到肾脏，促进水的潴留，并使增高的电解质浓度恢复正常水平。抗利尿激素有助于机体留住水分，可以最大限度地减少水分流失，从而降低在大量出汗和剧烈运动期间严重脱水的风险。

2. 肾上腺皮质

由肾上腺皮质分泌的盐皮质激素主要维持细胞外液的电解质平衡，尤其是钠离子和钾离子。醛固酮是主要的盐皮质激素，活性占到所有盐皮质激素的95%以上。它主要通过促进肾脏对钠离子的重吸收，使机体保留钠离子。当机体钠潴留时，水的潴留也随之增加，此功能与抗利尿激素的功能相似。保钠的同时也能促进排钾，因此醛固酮在钾离子平衡中也起着重要的作用。醛固酮的分泌受多种因素影响，如血浆钠离子浓度的降低、血量减少、血压降低及血浆钾离子浓度的增加。

（二）作为内分泌器官的肾脏

肾脏并非一个典型的内分泌器官，但它能分泌一种激素——促红细胞生成素（EPO）。EPO通过刺激骨髓细胞来调节红细胞的生成。因此，其在机体对运动和高原环境的适应中具有非常重要的作用。肾脏也能分泌肾素，它负责调节血压、体液及电解质的平衡。

肾脏在决定血液中醛固酮浓度方面起着重要作用。当血压或血浆容量下降时，流向肾脏的血液减少。此时交感神经系统激活，肾脏释放肾素。肾素是一种释放到循环中的酶，在循环中可将血管紧张素原转化为血管紧张素I。血管紧张素I在血管紧张素转化酶的作用下，在肺部转化为其活性形式血管紧张素II，血管紧张素II刺激肾上腺皮质释放醛固酮，使肾脏吸收钠和水。此过程即肾素-血管紧张素-醛固酮机制。

Chapter 5
Exercise and Oxygen Transport

The cardiovascular system serves a number of important functions in the body. The major cardiovascular functions can be grouped into six categories:

- Delivery of oxygen and other nutrients
- Removal of carbon dioxide and other metabolic waste products
- Transport of hormones and other molecules
- Support of thermoregulation and control of body fluid balance
- Maintenance of acid-base balance
- Regulation of immune function

Obviously, these roles change and become even more critical with the challenges imposed by exercise.

All physiological functions and virtually every cell in the body depend in some way on the cardiovascular system. Any system of circulation requires three components:

- A pump (the heart)
- A system of channels or tubes (the blood vessels)
- A fluid medium (the blood)

In order to keep blood circulating, the heart must generate sufficient pressure to drive blood through the continuous network of blood vessels in a closed-loop system. Thus, the primary goal of the cardiovascular system is to ensure that there is adequate blood flow throughout the circulation to meet the metabolic demands of the tissues. We look first at the heart.

1 The Heart

About the size of a fist and located in the center of the thoracic cavity, the heart is the primary pump that circulates blood through the entire cardiovascular system. As shown in Figure 5.1, the heart has two atria that act as receiving chambers and two ventricles that serve as the pumping units. It is enclosed in a tough membranous sac called the pericardium. The thin cavity between the pericardium and the heart is filled with pericardial fluid, which reduces friction between the sac and the beating heart.

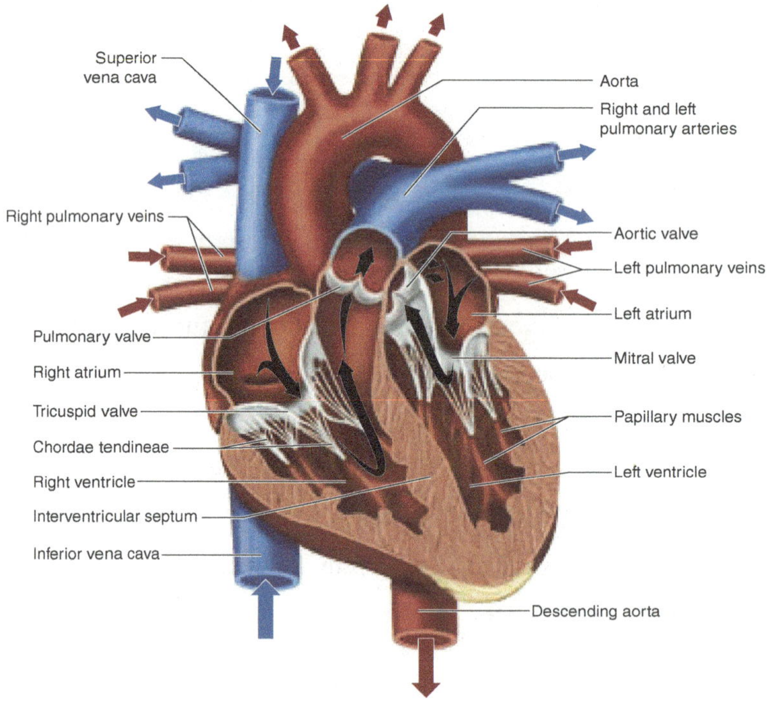

Figure 5.1 An anterior (as if the person is facing you) cross-sectional view of the human heart.

1.1 Myocardium

Cardiac muscle is collectively called the myocardium or myocardial muscle. Myocardial thickness at various locations in the heart varies according to the amount of stress placed on it. The left ventricle is the most powerful pump of the four heart chambers because it must generate sufficient pressure to pump blood through the entire body. When a person is sitting or standing, the left ventricle must contract with enough force to overcome the effect of gravity, which tends to pool blood in the lower extremities.

Because the left ventricle must generate considerable force to pump blood to the systemic circulation, it has the thickest muscular wall compared with the other heart chambers. This hypertrophy is the result of the pressure placed on the left ventricle at rest or under normal conditions of moderate activity. With more vigorous exercise—particularly intense aerobic activity, during which the working muscles' need for blood increases considerably—the demand on the left ventricle to deliver blood to the exercising muscles is higher. In response to both intense aerobic and resistance training, the left ventricle will hypertrophy. In contrast to the positive adaptations that occur as a result of exercise training, cardiac muscle also hypertrophies as a result of several diseases, such as high blood pressure or valvular heart disease. In response to either training or disease, over time the left ventricle adapts by increasing its size and pumping capacity, similar to the way skeletal muscle adapts to physical training. However, the mechanisms for adaptation and cardiac performance with disease are different from those observed with aerobic training.

Although striated in appearance, the myocardium differs from skeletal muscle in several important ways. First, because the myocardium has to contract as if it were a single unit, individual cardiac muscle fibers are anatomically interconnected end to end by dark-staining regions called intercalated disks. These disks have desmosomes, which are structures that anchor the individual cells together so that they do not pull apart during contraction, and gap junctions, which allow rapid transmission of the action potentials that signal the heart to contract as one unit. Secondly, the myocardium contains only one fiber type, similar to type I fibers in skeletal muscle in that it is highly oxidative, has a high capillary density, and has a large number of mitochondria. Figure 5.2 summarizes some of the similarities and differences between cardiac and skeletal muscle.

Muscle type	Location	Appearance	Type of activity	Stimulation
Skeletal ("striated" or "voluntary") muscle 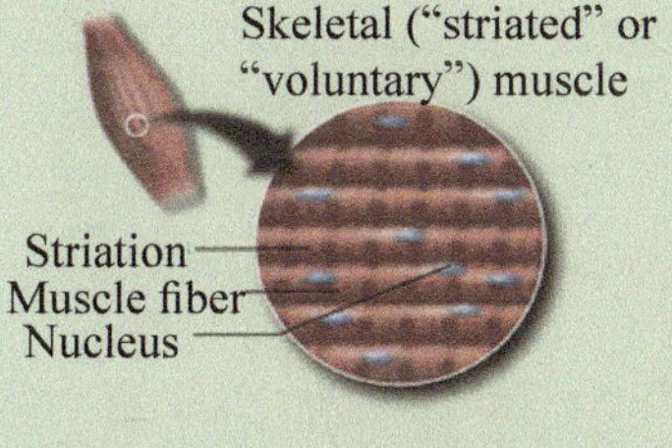	Named muscle (e.g.,the biceps of the arm) attached to the skeleton and fascia of limbs, body wall, and head or neck	Large, long, unbranched, cylindrical fibers with transverse striations (stripes) arranged in parallel bundles; multiple, peripherally located nuclei	Strong, quick intermittent (phasic) contraction above a baseline tonus;acts primarily to produce movement or resist gravity	Voluntary (orreflexive) by the somatic nervous system
Cardiac muscle 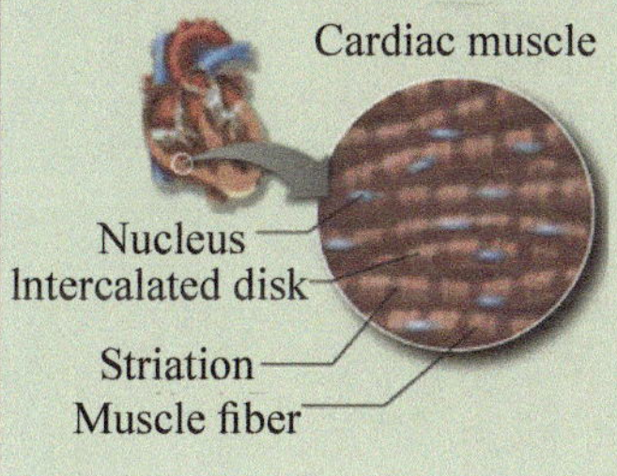	Muscle of heart (myocardium) and adjacent portions of the great vessels (aorta,vena cava)	Branching and anastomosing shorter fibers with transverse striations (stripes) running parallel and connected end to end by complex junctions (intercalated disks); single, central nucleus	Strong, quick continuous rhythmic contraction; pumps blood from the heart	Involuntary; intrinsically (myogenically) stimulated and propagated; rate and strength of contraction modified by the autonomic nervous system

Figure 5.2 Functional and structural characteristics of skeletal and cardiac muscle.

The myocardium, just like skeletal muscle, must have a blood supply to deliver oxygen and nutrients and remove waste products. Although blood courses through each chamber of the heart, little nourishment comes from the blood within the chambers. The primary blood supply to the heart is provided by the coronary arteries.

The coronary arteries are very susceptible to atherosclerosis, or narrowing by the accumulation of plaque and inflammation, leading to coronary artery disease.

Anomalies—shortenings, blockages, or misdirections—sometimes occur in the coronary arteries, and such congenital abnormalities are a common cause of sudden death in athletes.

1.2 Cardiac Conduction System

Cardiac muscle has the unique ability to generate its own electrical signal, called spontaneous rhythmicity, which allows it to contract without any external stimulation. The contraction is rhythmical, in part because of the anatomical coupling of the myocardial cells through gap junctions. Without neural or hormonal stimulation, the intrinsic heart rate (HR) averages ~100 beats (contractions) per minute. This resting heart rate of about 100 beats/min can be observed in patients who have undergone cardiac transplant surgery, because their transplanted hearts lack neural innervation.

Even though all myocardial fibers have inherent rhythmicity, the heart has a series of specialized myocardial cells that function to coordinate the heart's excitation and contraction and maximize the efficient pumping of blood. Figure 5.3 illustrates the four main components of the cardiac conduction system:

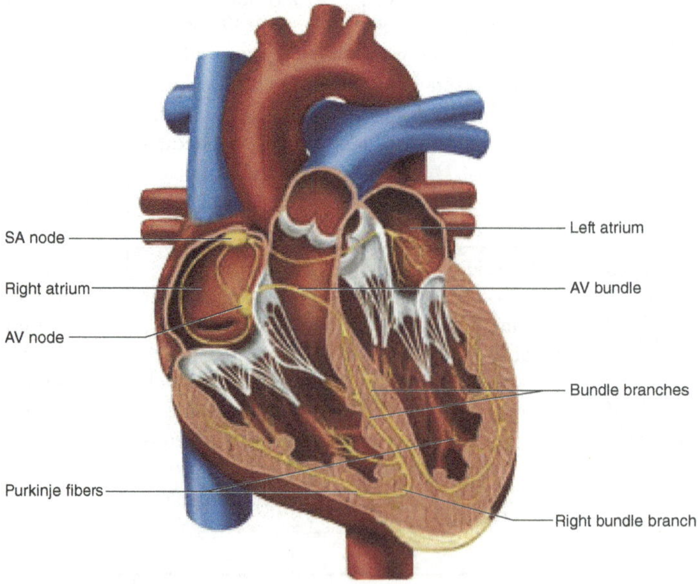

Figure 5.3 The specialized conduction system of the heart.

- Sinoatrial (SA) node
- Atrioventricular (AV) node
- Atrioventricular (AV) bundle (His bundle)
- Purkinje fibers

The impulse for normal heart contractions is initiated in the sinoatrial (SA) node, a group of specialized cardiac muscle fibers located in the upper posterior wall of the right atrium. These specialized cells spontaneously depolarize at a faster rate than other myocardial muscle cells because they are especially leaky to sodium. Because this tissue has the fastest intrinsic firing rate, typically at a frequency of about 100 beats/min, the SA node is known as the heart's pacemaker, and the rhythm it establishes is called the sinus rhythm. The electrical impulse generated by the SA node spreads through both atria and reaches the atrioventricular (AV) node, located in the right atrial wall near the center of the heart. As the electrical impulse spreads through the atria, they are signaled to contract.

The AV node conducts the electrical impulse from the atria into the ventricles. The impulse is delayed by about 0.13 s as it passes through the AV node, and then it enters the AV bundle. This delay is important because it allows blood from the atria to completely empty into the ventricles to maximize ventricular filling before the ventricles contract. While most blood moves passively from the atria to the ventricles, active contraction of the atria (sometimes called the "atrial kick") completes the process. The AV bundle travels along the ventricular septum and then sends right and left bundle branches into both ventricles. These branches send the impulse toward the apex of the heart and then outward. Each bundle branch subdivides into many smaller ones that spread throughout the entire ventricular wall. These terminal branches of the AV bundle are the Purkinje fibers. They transmit the impulse through the ventricles approximately six times faster than through the rest of the cardiac conduction system. This rapid conduction allows all parts of the ventricle to contract at virtually the same time.

1.2.1 Extrinsic Control of Heart Activity

Although the heart initiates its own electrical impulses (intrinsic control) , both the rate and force of contraction can be altered. Under normal conditions, this is accomplished primarily through three extrinsic systems:

- The parasympathetic nervous system
- The sympathetic nervous system
- The endocrine system (hormones)

The parasympathetic nervous system, a branch of the autonomic nervous system, originates centrally in a region of the brain stem called the medulla oblongata and reaches the heart through the vagus nerve (cranial nerve X). The vagus nerve carries impulses to the SA and AV nodes, and when stimulated it releases acetylcholine, which causes hyperpolarization of the conduction cells. The result is a slower spontaneous depolarization and a decrease in heart rate. At rest, parasympathetic system activity predominates and the heart is said to have "vagal tone." Recall that, in the absence of vagal tone, intrinsic heart rate would be approximately 100 beats/min. The vagus nerve has a depressant effect on the heart: It slows impulse generation and conduction and thus decreases the heart rate. Maximal vagal stimulation can decrease the heart rate to as low as 20–30 beats/min. The vagus nerve also decreases the force of cardiac muscle contraction.

The sympathetic nervous system, the other branch of the autonomic system, has opposite effects. Sympathetic stimulation increases the rate of depolarization and conduction speed, and thus heart rate. Maximal sympathetic stimulation can increase the heart rate to 250 beats/min. Sympathetic input also increases the force of contraction of the ventricles. Sympathetic control predominates during times of physical or emotional stress, when the heart rate is greater than 100 beats/min. The parasympathetic system dominates when heart rate is less than 100. Thus, when exercise begins, or if exercise is at a low intensity, heart rate first increases due to withdrawal of vagal tone, with further increases due to sympathetic activation, as shown in Figure 5.4.

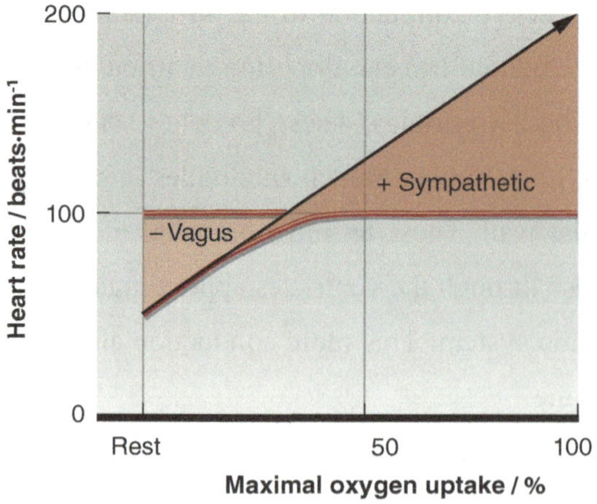

Figure 5.4 Relative contribution of sympathetic and parasympathetic nervous systems to the rise in heart rate during exercise.

The third extrinsic influence, the endocrine system, exerts its effect through two hormones released by the adrenal medulla: norepinephrine and epinephrine. These hormones are also known as catecholamines. Like the norepinephrine released as a neurotransmitter by the sympathetic nervous system, circulating norepinephrine and epinephrine stimulate the heart, increasing its rate and contractility. In fact, release of these hormones from the adrenal medulla is triggered by sympathetic stimulation during times of stress, and their actions prolong the sympathetic response.

Normal resting heart rate (RHR) typically varies between 60 and 100 beats/min. With extended periods of endurance training (months to years) , the RHR can decrease to 35 beats/min or less. A RHR as low as 28 beats/min has been observed in a world-class, long-distance runner. These lower training-induced RHRs result from increased parasympathetic stimulation (vagal tone) , with reduced sympathetic activity playing a lesser role.

1.2.2 Electrocardiogram

The electrical activity of the heart can be recorded (Figure 5.5) to monitor cardiac changes or diagnose potential cardiac problems. Because body fluids contain electrolytes, they are good electrical conductors. Electrical impulses generated in the heart are conducted through body fluids to the skin, where they can be amplified, detected, and printed out on an electrocardiograph. This printout is called an electrocardiogram, or ECG. A standard ECG is recorded from 10 electrodes placed in specific anatomical locations. These 10 electrodes correspond to 12 leads that represent different views of the heart. Three basic components of the ECG represent important aspects of cardiac function (Figure 5.6) :

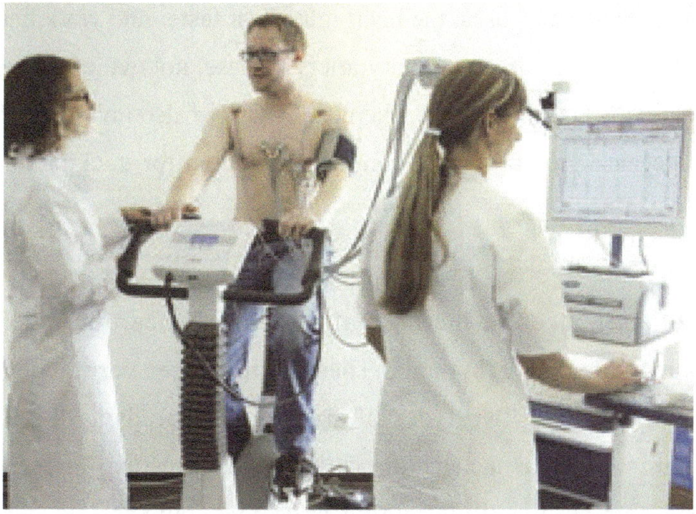

Figure 5.5 Recording an exercise electrocardiogram.

- The P wave
- The QRS complex
- The T wave

The P wave represents atrial depolarization and occurs when the electrical impulse travels from the SA node through the atria to the AV node. The QRS complex represents ventricular depolarization and occurs as the impulse spreads from the AV bundle to the Purkinje fibers and through the ventricles. The T wave represents ventricular repolarization. Atrial repolarization cannot be seen, because it occurs during ventricular depolarization (QRS complex).

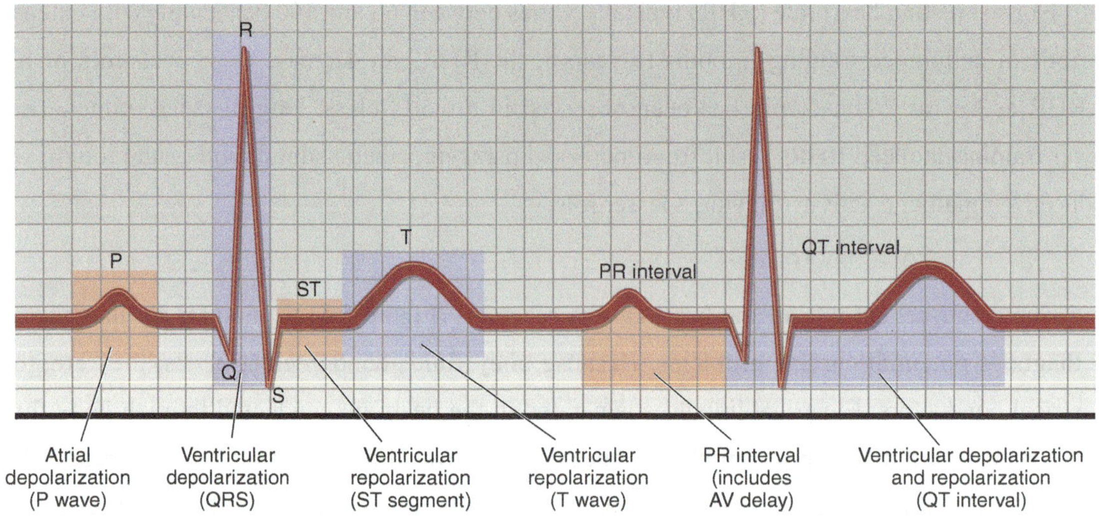

Figure 5.6 A graphic illustration of the various phases of the resting electrocardiogram.

Electrocardiograms are often obtained during exercise as clinical diagnostic tests of cardiac function. As exercise intensity increases, the heart must beat faster and work harder to deliver more blood to active muscles. Indications of coronary artery disease, not evident at rest, may show up on the ECG as the strain on the heart increases. Exercise ECGs are also invaluable tools for research in exercise physiology because they provide a convenient method for tracking heart rate and rhythm changes during acute exercise.

1.2.3 Cardiac Arrhythmias

Occasionally, disturbances in the normal sequence of cardiac events can lead to an irregular heart rhythm, called an arrhythmia. These disturbances vary in degree of seriousness. Bradycardia and tachycardia are two types of arrhythmias. Bradycardia is defined as a RHR lower than 60 beats/min, whereas tachycardia is defined as a resting rate greater than 100 beats/min. With these arrhythmias, the sinus rhythm is normal, but the rate is altered. In extreme cases, bradycardia or tachycardia can affect maintenance of blood pressure. Symptoms of both arrhythmias include fatigue, dizziness, light-headedness, and fainting. Tachycardia can sometimes be sensed as palpitations or a "racing" pulse.

Interestingly, most highly trained endurance athletes develop resting bradycardias, an advantageous adaptation, as a result of training. Also, the heart rate naturally increases during physical activity to meet the increased demands of exercising muscle for blood flow. These adaptations should not be confused with pathological causes of bradycardia or tachycardia, which are abnormal alterations in the RHR that usually indicate underlying disease or dysfunction.

2 Vascular System

The vascular system contains a series of vessels that transport blood from the heart to the tissues and back: the arteries, arterioles, capillaries, venules, and veins.

2.1 Blood Pressure

Blood pressure is the pressure exerted by the blood on the vessel walls, and the term usually refers to arterial blood pressure. It is expressed by two numbers: the systolic blood pressure (SBP) and the diastolic blood pressure (DBP). The higher number is the SBP; it represents the highest pressure in the artery that occurs during ventricular systole. Ventricular contraction pushes the blood through the arteries with tremendous force, and that force exerts high pressure on the arterial walls. The lower number is the DBP and represents the lowest pressure in the artery, corresponding to ventricular diastole when the ventricle is filling.

Mean arterial pressure (MAP) represents the average pressure exerted by the blood as it travels through the arteries. Since diastole takes about twice as long as systole in a normal cardiac cycle, mean arterial pressure can be estimated from the DBP and SBP as follows:

$$\text{MAP} = 2/3\ \text{DBP} + 1/3\ \text{SBP}$$

Alternately,

$$\text{MAP} = \text{DBP} + [0.333\ (\text{SBP} - \text{DBP})]$$

(SBP – DBP) is also called pulse pressure.

To illustrate, with a normal resting blood pressure of 120 mmHg over 80 mmHg, the MAP = 80 + [0.333 × (120 – 80)] = 93 mmHg.

2.2 General Hemodynamics

The cardiovascular system is a continuous closed-loop system. Blood flows through this closed-loop system because of the pressure gradient that exists between the arterial and venous sides of the circulation. To understand regulation of blood flow to the tissues, it is necessary to understand the intricate relationship between pressure, flow, and resistance.

In order for blood to flow in a vessel, there must be a pressure difference from one end of the vessel to the other end. Blood will flow from the region of the vessel with high pressure to the region of the vessel with low pressure. Alternatively, if there is no pressure difference across the vessel, there is no driving force and therefore no blood flow. In the circulatory system, the mean arterial pressure in the aorta is approximately 100 mmHg at rest, and the pressure in the right atrium is very close to 0 mmHg. Therefore, the pressure difference across the entire circulatory system is 100 mmHg − 0 mmHg = 100 mmHg.

The reason for the pressure differential from the arterial to the venous circulation is that the blood vessels themselves provide resistance or impedance to blood flow. The resistance that the vessel provides is largely dictated by the properties of the blood vessels and the blood itself.

Blood flow is proportional to the pressure difference across the system and is inversely proportional to resistance. This relationship can be illustrated by the following equation:

Blood flow = Dpressure / resistance.

Notice that blood flow can increase by either an increase in the pressure difference (D pressure), a decrease in resistance, or a combination of the two. Altering resistance to control blood flow is much more advantageous because very small changes in blood vessel radius equate to large changes in resistance. This is due to the fourth-power mathematical relationship between vascular resistance and vessel radius.

Changes in vascular resistance are largely due to changes in the radius or diameter of the vessels, as the viscosity of the blood and the length of the vessels do not change significantly under normal conditions. Therefore, regulation of blood flow to organs is accomplished by small changes in vessel radius through vasoconstriction and vasodilation. This allows the cardiovascular system to divert blood flow to the areas where it is needed most.

The arterioles are the site of greatest control of the circulation by the sympathetic nervous system, so arterioles are sometimes called resistance vessels. Arterioles are heavily innervated by the sympathetic nervous system and are the main site of control of blood flow to specific tissues. Most resistance to blood flow occurs in the arterioles. Figure 5.7 shows the blood pressure changes across the entire vascular system. The arterioles are responsible for ~70%–80% of the drop in mean arterial pressure across the entire cardiovascular system. This is important because small changes in arteriole radius can greatly affect the regulation of mean arteriole pressure and the local control of blood flow. At the capillary level, changes due to systole and diastole are no longer evident and the flow is smooth (laminar) rather than turbulent.

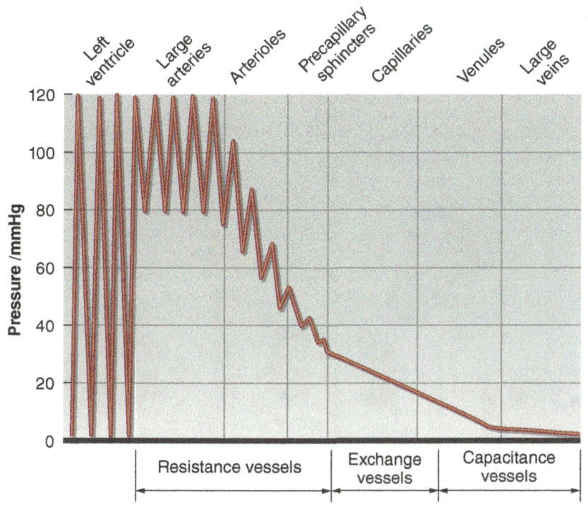

Figure 5.7 Pressure changes across the systemic circulation. Notice the large pressure drop that occurs across the arteriole portion of the system.

2.3 Distribution of Blood

Distribution of blood to the various body tissues varies considerably depending on the immediate needs of a specific tissue compared with those of other areas of the body. As a general rule, the most metabolically active tissues receive the greatest blood supply. At rest under normal conditions, the liver and kidneys combine to receive almost half of the cardiac output, while resting skeletal muscles receive only about 15%–20%.

During heavy endurance exercise, contracting muscles may receive up to 80% or more of the blood flow, and flow to the liver and kidneys decreases. This redistribution, along with increases in cardiac output, allows up to 25 times more blood flow to active muscles (Figure 5.8).

Alternately, after one eats a big meal, the digestive system receives more of the available cardiac output than when the digestive system is empty. Along the same lines, during increasing environmental heat stress, skin blood flow increases to a greater extent as the body attempts to maintain normal temperature. The cardiovascular system responds accordingly to redistribute blood, whether it is to the exercising muscle to match metabolism, for digestion, or to facilitate thermoregulation. These changes in the distribution of cardiac output are controlled by the sympathetic nervous system, primarily by increasing or decreasing arteriolar diameter.

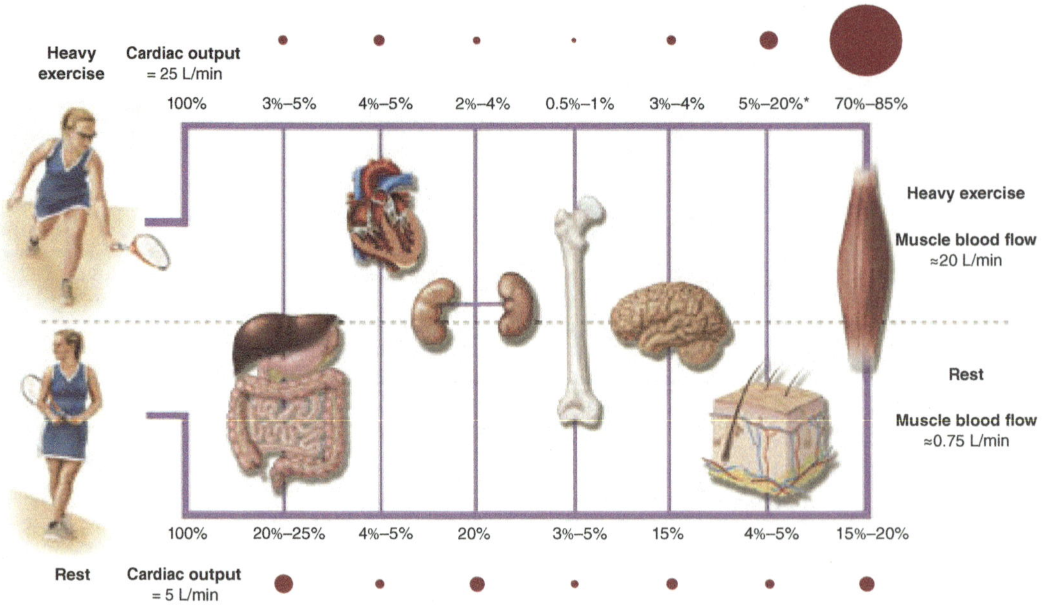

Figure 5.8 Distribution of cardiac output at rest and maximal exercise.
* Depends on ambient and body temperatures

Arterioles have a strong muscular wall that can significantly alter vessel diameter, are highly innervated by sympathetic nerves, and have the capacity to respond to local control mechanisms.

2.3.1 Intrinsic Control of Blood Flow

Intrinsic control of blood distribution refers to the ability of the local tissues to dilate or constrict the arterioles that serve them and alter regional blood flow depending on the immediate needs of those tissues. With exercise and the increased metabolic demand of the exercising skeletal muscles, the arterioles undergo locally mediated vasodilation, opening up to allow more blood to enter that highly active tissue.

There are essentially three types of intrinsic control of blood flow. The strongest stimulus for the release of local vasodilating chemicals is metabolic (such as carbon dioxide, K^+, H^+, lactic acid, inflammatory chemicals, etc.) , in particular an increased oxygen demand. As oxygen uptake by metabolically active tissues increases, available oxygen is diminished. Local arterioles vasodilate to allow more blood to perfuse that area, delivering more oxygen. Other chemical changes that can stimulate increased blood flow are decreases in other nutrients and increases in by-products (carbon dioxide, K^+, H^+, lactic acid) or inflammatory chemicals.

Second, many dilator substances can be produced within the endothelium (inner lining) of arterioles and can initiate vasodilation in the vascular smooth muscle of those arterioles. These substances include nitric oxide (NO) , prostaglandins, and endothelium-derived hyperpolarizing factor (EDHF). These endothelium-derived vasodilators are important regulators of blood flow at rest and during exercise in humans. Third, pressure changes within the vessels themselves can also cause vasodilation and vasoconstriction. This is referred to as the myogenic response. The vascular smooth muscle contracts in response to an increase in pressure across the vessel wall and relaxes in response to a decrease in pressure across the vessel wall. Additionally, acetylcholine and adenosine also have been proposed as potential vasodilators for the increase in muscle blood flow during exercise.

2.3.2 Extrinsic Neural Control

Redistribution at the system or organ level is controlled by neural mechanisms. This is known as extrinsic neural control of blood flow, because the control comes from outside the specific area (extrinsic) instead of from locally inside the tissues (intrinsic).

Blood flow to all body parts is regulated largely by the sympathetic nervous system. The circular layers of smooth muscle within the artery and arteriole walls are abundantly innervated by sympathetic nerves. In most vessels, an increase in sympathetic nerve activity causes these circular smooth muscle cells to contract, constricting blood vessels and thereby decreasing blood flow.

Under normal resting conditions, sympathetic nerves transmit impulses continuously to the blood vessels (in particular, the arterioles) , keeping the vessels moderately constricted to maintain adequate blood pressure. This state of tonic vasoconstriction is referred to as vasomotor tone. When sympathetic stimulation increases, further constriction of the blood vessels in a specific area decreases blood flow into that area and allows more blood to be distributed elsewhere. But if sympathetic stimulation decreases below the level needed to maintain tone, constriction of vessels in the area is lessened, so the vessels passively vasodilate, increasing blood flow into that area. Therefore, sympathetic stimulation will cause vasoconstriction in most vessels. Blood flow can passively be increased through a lowering of the normal tonic level of sympathetic outflow.

2.3.3 Distribution of Venous Blood

While flow to tissues is controlled by changes on the arterial side of the system, most of the blood volume normally resides in the venous side of the system. At rest, the blood volume is distributed among the vasculature as shown in Figure 5.9. The venous system has a great capacity to hold blood volume because veins have little vascular smooth muscle and are very elastic and "balloon-like." Thus, the venous system provides a large reservoir of blood available to be rapidly distributed back to the heart (venous return) and from there, to the arterial circulation. This is accomplished through sympathetic stimulation of the venules and veins, which causes the vessels to constrict (veno-constriction).

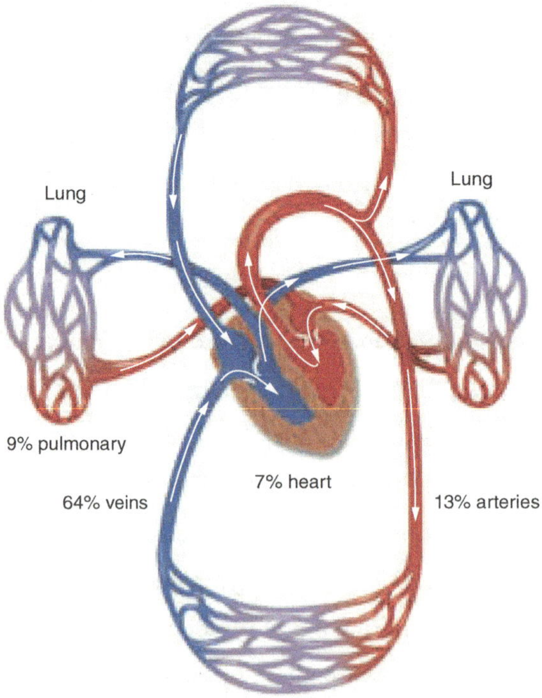

Figure 5.9 Blood volume distribution within the vasculature when the body is at rest.

2.3.4 Integrative Control of Blood Pressure

Blood pressure is normally maintained by reflexes within the autonomic nervous system. Specialized pressure sensors located in the aortic arch and the carotid arteries, called baroreceptors, are sensitive to changes in arterial pressure. When the pressure in these large arteries changes, afferent signals are sent to the cardio-vascular control centers in the brain where autonomic reflexes are initiated, and efferent signals are sent to respond to changes in blood pressure. For example, when blood pressure is elevated, the baroreceptors are stimulated by an increase in stretch. They relay this information to the cardiovascular control center in the brain. In response to the increased pressure there is a reflex increase in vagal tone, to decrease heart rate, and a decrease in sympathetic activity to both the heart and the arterioles, all of which serves to normalize blood pressure. In response to a decrease in blood pressure, less stretch is sensed by the baroreceptors, and the response is to increase heart rate by vagal withdrawal and to increase sympathetic nervous activity, thus correcting the low-pressure signal.

There are also other specialized receptors, called chemoreceptors and mechanoreceptors, that send information about the chemical environment in the muscle and the length and tension of the muscle, respectively, to the cardiovascular control centers. These receptors also modify the blood pressure response and are especially important during exercise.

2.3.5 Return of Blood to the Heart

Because humans spend so much time in an upright position, the cardiovascular system requires mechanical assistance to overcome the force of gravity and assist the return of venous blood from the lower parts of the body to the heart. Three basic mechanisms assist in this process:

- Valves in the veins
- The muscle pumps
- The respiratory pump

The veins contain valves that allow blood to flow in only one direction, thus preventing backflow and further pooling of blood in the lower body. These venous valves also complement the action of the skeletal muscle pump, the rhythmic mechanical compression of the veins that occurs during the rhythmic skeletal muscle contraction accompanying many types of movement and exercise, for example during walking and running (Figure 5.10). The muscle pump pushes blood volume in the veins back toward the heart. Finally, changes in pressure in the abdominal and thoracic cavities during breathing assist blood return to the heart by creating a pressure gradient between the veins and the chest cavity.

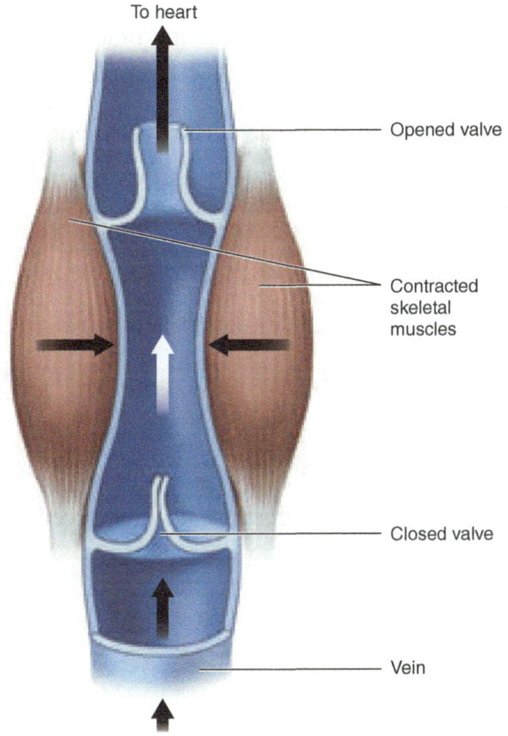

Figure 5.10 The muscle pump. As the skeletal muscles contract, they squeeze the veins in the legs and assist in the return of blood to the heart. Valves within the veins ensure the unidirectional flow of blood back to the heart.

3 Blood

Blood serves many diverse purposes in regulating normal body function. The three functions of primary importance to exercise and sport are:

- Transportation
- Temperature regulation, and
- Acid-base (pH) balance

3.1 Blood Volume and Composition

The total volume of blood in the body varies considerably with an individual's size, body composition, and state of training. Larger blood volumes are associated with greater lean body mass and higher levels of endurance training. The blood volume of people of average body size and normal physical activity generally ranges from 5–6 L in men and 4–5 L in women.

Blood is composed of plasma and formed elements (Figure 5.11). Plasma normally constitutes about 55%–60% of total blood volume. Approximately 90% of the plasma volume is water; 7% consists of plasma proteins; and the remaining 3% includes cellular nutrients, electrolytes, enzymes, hormones, antibodies, and wastes.

The formed elements, which normally constitute the other 40%–45% of total blood volume, are the red blood cells (erythrocytes) , white blood cells (leukocytes) , and platelets (thrombocytes). Red blood cells constitute more than 99% of the formed-element volume; white blood cells and platelets together account for less than 1%. The percentage of the total blood volume composed of cells or formed elements is referred to as the hematocrit. Hematocrit varies among individuals, but a normal range is 41%–50% in adult men and 36%–44% in adult women.

White blood cells protect the body from infection either by directly destroying the invading agents through phagocytosis (ingestion) or by forming anti-bodies to destroy them. Adults have about 7,000 white blood cells per cubic millimeter of blood.

The remaining formed elements are the blood platelets. These are cell fragments that are required for blood coagulation (clotting) , which prevents excessive blood loss.

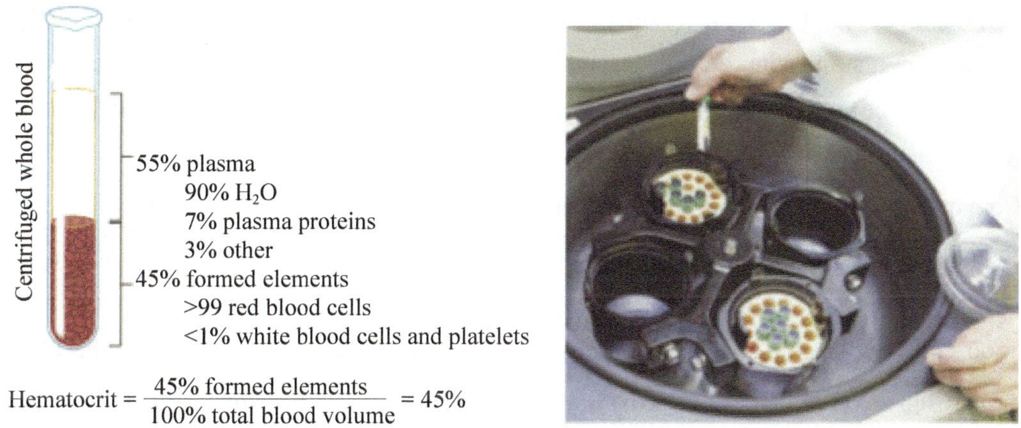

Figure 5.11 The composition of whole blood, illustrating the plasma volume (fluid portion) and the cellular volume (red cells, white cells, and platelets) after the blood sample has been centrifuged. A centrifuge is shown at right.

3.2 Red Blood Cells

Mature red blood cells (erythrocytes) have no nucleus, so they cannot reproduce as other cells can. They must be replaced with new cells on a reoccurring basis, a process called hematopoiesis. The normal life span of a red blood cell is about four months. Thus, these cells are continuously produced and destroyed at equal rates. This balance is very important, because adequate oxygen delivery to tissues depends on having a sufficient number of red blood cells to transport oxygen. Decreases in their number or function can hinder oxygen delivery and thus affect exercise performance. Red blood cells transport oxygen, which is primarily bound to hemoglobin. Hemoglobin is composed of a protein (globin) and a pigment (heme). Heme contains iron, which binds oxygen. Each red blood cell contains approximately 250 million hemoglobin molecules, each able to bind four oxygen molecules—so each red blood cell can bind up to a billion molecules of oxygen! There is an average of 15 g of hemoglobin per 100 ml of whole blood. Each gram of hemoglobin can combine with 1.33 ml of oxygen, so as much as 20 ml of oxygen can be bound for each 100 ml of blood. Therefore, when arterial blood is saturated with oxygen, it has an oxygen-carrying capacity of 20 ml of oxygen per 100 ml of blood.

3.3 Blood Viscosity

Viscosity refers to the thickness of the blood. Recall from our discussion of vascular resistance that the greater the viscosity of a fluid, the greater the resistance to its flow. The viscosity of blood is normally about twice that of water and increases as hematocrit increases.

Because of oxygen transport by the red blood cells, an increase in their number would be expected to maximize oxygen transport. But if an increase in red blood cell count is not accompanied by a similar increase in plasma volume, blood viscosity and vascular resistance will increase, which could result in reduced blood flow. This generally is not a problem unless the hematocrit reaches 60% or more.

Conversely, the combination of a low hematocrit with a high plasma volume, which decreases the blood's viscosity, appears to have certain benefits for the blood's transport function because the blood can flow more easily. Unfortunately, a low hematocrit frequently results from a reduced red blood cell count, as in diseases such as anemia. Under these circumstances, the blood can flow easily, but it contains fewer carriers, so oxygen transport is impeded. For optimal physical performance, a low-normal hematocrit with a normal or slightly elevated number of red blood cells is desirable. This combination facilitates oxygen transport. Many endurance athletes achieve this combination as part of their cardiovascular system's normal adaptation to training.

IN CLOSING

In this chapter, we reviewed the structure and function of the cardiovascular system. We learned how blood flow and blood pressure are regulated to meet the body's needs, and explored the role of the cardiovascular system in transporting and delivering oxygen and nutrients to the body's cells while clearing away metabolic wastes, including carbon dioxide. Knowing how substances are moved within the body, we now look more closely at the movement of oxygen and carbon dioxide. In the next chapter, we explore the role of the respiratory system in delivering oxygen to, and removing carbon dioxide from, the cells of the body.

KEY TERMS

arteries; arterioles; atrioventricular (AV) node; baroreceptor; bradycardia; capillaries; cardiac cycle; cardiac output (Q) ; chemoreceptor; diastolic blood pressure (DBP) ; electrocardiogram (ECG); electrocardiograph; extrinsic neural control; hematocrit; hematopoiesis; hemoglobin; intercalated disks; mean arterial pressure (MAP) ; mechanoreceptors; muscle pump; myocardium; pericardium; ventricular contraction; Purkinje fibers; sinoatrial (SA) node; systolic blood pressure (SBP) ; tachycardia; vasoconstriction; vasodilation; veins; venules

STUDY QUESTIONS

(1) Describe the structure of the heart, the pattern of blood flow through the valves and chambers of the heart, how the heart as a muscle is supplied with blood, and what happens when the resting heart must suddenly supply an exercising body?

(2) What events take place that allow the heart to contract, and how is heart rate controlled?

(3) What is the difference between systole and diastole, and how do they relate to SBP and DBP?

(4) What is the relationship among pressure, flow and resistance?

(5) How is blood flow to the various regions of the body controlled?

(6) Describe the three important mechanisms for returning blood back to the heart when someone is exercising in an upright position.

第五章 运动与氧气运输

心血管系统对机体具有非常重要的功能，主要包括六个方面：运输氧和其他营养物质；排出二氧化碳和其他代谢产物；运送激素和其他分子；调节体温和体液平衡；维持酸碱平衡；调节免疫功能。

心血管系统由以下三个成分组成：泵（心脏）、管道系统（血管）和液体介质（血液）。

一、心脏

1.心肌

心脏的肌肉统称心肌，心肌的厚度会因位置与承受压力程度而有所不同。高强度有氧运动时，肌肉对血量的需求也相应增加，左心室必须供应更多的血液到运动的肌肉中，因此，高强度有氧运动和抗阻训练易引起左心室心肌肥大，这属于积极性适应。疾病也可引发心肌肥大，但疾病和有氧训练所引起的心肌肥大的机制是不同的。

心肌纤维的尾端是由称为闰盘的深染色区域交互联结而成。闰盘上有桥粒，将不同的细胞锚定在一起，使心肌细胞不会因收缩而被拉开。同时，闰盘具有缝隙连接，能让动作电位产生的信号快速传导，使心肌细胞同时收缩。心肌只有一种纤维，与骨骼肌Ⅰ型纤维类似，具有高度的氧化性，富含大量毛细血管和线粒体。

心脏供血主要是由左右冠状动脉承担，冠状动脉出现短小、阻塞或迂回等先天异常，是导致运动员猝死的主要原因。

2.心脏传导系统

心脏传导系统主要包括窦房结、房室结、房室束（希氏束）和浦肯野氏纤维。

（1）心脏活动的外部调节。副交感神经系统一旦受到刺激，会释放乙酰胆碱，导致心率下降。在安静状态下，副交感神经系统的活动占优势。除此之外，迷走神经也可降低心肌收缩力。

交感神经刺激能增加冲动的激发和传导速度，从而增加心率。交感神经也可增加心室的收缩力。当身心处于应激状态时，交感神经系统支配占主导作用，心率会大于100次/分。因此，在运动开始阶段或进行低强度运动时，心率由于迷走神经活动的减弱而增加，随着运动强度的增加，交感神经活动增强，心率会继续增加。

肾上腺髓质释放入血液中的去甲肾上腺素和肾上腺素可刺激心脏，提高心率和心肌的收缩力。刺激交感神经可诱发肾上腺素髓质释放这些激素，这些激素的作用又延长了交感神经的反应。

正常条件下，静息心率的范围为60～100次/分。随着耐力训练时间的延长，静息心率可以降低到35次/分，甚至更低，世界顶级长跑运动员的静息心率可达到28次/分。运动训练导致的静息心率降低是由于副交感神经（迷走紧张）兴奋性提高而交感神经兴奋性降低引起的。

（2）心电图。心电图反映心脏机能的三个基础指标为P波、QRS波群和T波。

运动心电图是评判冠心病的重要方法。

（3）心律不齐。心律不齐分为心动过缓和心动过速两种类型。在心律不齐中，窦性节律是正常的，只是心跳频率上发生了改变。心律不齐的症状有疲劳、头晕目眩、头昏和昏厥等，心动过速有时则表现出心悸或心跳加速。

高水平耐力运动员的静息心率较低，是对训练产生有利适应的结果。但是，有时也会隐藏一些病理性的问题。

二、血管

1.血压

收缩压是心室收缩时动脉的最高压力。舒张压是心室舒张期心室充盈时动脉的压力。平均动脉压反映了血液流经动脉时产生的平均血压。

2.血流动力学

血液是从压力高的部位流向压力低的部位，如果血管内没有压力差，就不会产生血液流动。从动脉至静脉循环产生的压力差是由于血管本身对血流产生阻力造成的。血流与流经系统的压力差呈正相关，与阻力呈负相关，它们之间的关系可以表示为：

血流＝压力差／阻力

如要增加血流量，一方面要增加压力差，另一方面则是降低阻力。因为阻力和血管直径之间是四次幂的关系，血管半径的微小变化就可以较大地改变阻力，进而调节血流量。

交感神经对循环系统控制的主要部位在小动脉，因此小动脉有时被称为阻力血管，大部分的血流阻力产生于小动脉。

3.血流分配

在安静状态下，代谢活跃的组织如肝脏和肾脏所接收的血液几乎占循环血液的一半，而骨骼肌仅接收15%～20%。在高强度耐力训练中，伴随着心输出量的增加，骨骼肌可以接收80%以上，使运动时的骨骼肌获得安静时25倍的血液供应。同样，进食后消化系统会比没有进食时接收更多的血液。当人体受到热刺激时，机体皮肤的血流量会有较大程度的增加。

血液重新分配的变化受交感神经系统的调控，主要通过小动脉半径的增大或减小来实现。

（1）血流的内部调节。小动脉血流的内部调节主要包括三种调节形式。第一，人体的新陈代谢释放一些化学物质，如二氧化碳、K^+、H^+、乳酸或炎症物质等，使局部血管舒张。第二，一些小动脉内皮细胞产生的舒张物质，如一氧化氮、前列腺素、内皮衍生的超极化因子等，可以调控机体的血流，但具体机制尚不明确。第三，血管壁的压力增加使血管平滑肌收缩，血管壁的压力降低使血管平滑肌舒张。此外，乙酰胆碱和腺苷也可以作为潜在的血管舒张剂在运动时增大骨骼肌血流量。

（2）外部神经调节。流经身体各部位的血流大部分受交感神经系统的支配和调节，交感神经活性的增加使大部分血管的平滑肌收缩，从而使血管收缩，血流量降低。但是血管的收缩状态会根据血管收缩因子的多少而不同。

（3）静脉血的分配。静脉血管的平滑肌很少，却富于弹性，可储存大量血液。因此，静脉系统提供了一个巨大的血液储备库，并通过交感神经调节血管收缩来快速实现静脉回流和动脉循环的血液重新分配。

（4）血压的整合调节。当血压升高时，压力感受器会将刺激信号传递给脑内的心血管控制中枢，从而引起迷走神经的反射活动增强，降低心率和交感神经活动，降低血压；当血压降低时，对压力感受器刺激减少，迷走神经活动降低，心率增加，交感神经活动增强，血压升高。同时，化学感受器和张力感受器将骨骼肌中化学环境信息和骨骼肌长度与张力改变的信息传递至心血管控制中枢调节血压。

（5）回心血量。血液从身体各部位回流到心脏，需要机械性的辅助来克服重力，帮助血液回流，包括静脉瓣、肌肉泵和呼吸泵。静脉瓣可以阻止血液逆流或滞留于下肢，使血液向一个方向流动。这些静脉瓣也参与骨骼肌泵的活动，在肌肉有节奏的收缩过程中机械性地挤压静脉，推动静脉血液流至心脏。此外，在呼吸时腹腔和胸腔内的压力改变也可以辅助血液回流到心脏。

三、血液

血液在调控正常身体机能中起到很重要的作用，在运动中的主要作用包括运输、温度调节和酸碱平衡。

1.血流量和血液成分

血液由血浆和有形成分组成。血浆中90%的成分为水，7%为血浆蛋白，还有3%为细胞营养物质、电解质、酶、激素、抗体和代谢产物等。血液的有形成分一般占总血容量的40%～45%，主要为红细胞、白细胞和血小板。

2.红细胞

红细胞的主要作用是运输氧，如果红细胞的数目降低或是机能下降，则会阻碍氧的运输，从而影响运动员的运动成绩。红细胞运输氧主要依靠血红蛋白。每100毫升全血可以与20毫升氧结合。

3.血液黏滞性

氧需红细胞才能运输，如果红细胞与血浆容积的增加比例不一致，那么血液黏滞性和血管阻力也会增加，引起血流减慢。低红细胞压积和高血浆容积，可以降低血液的黏稠度，但是，低红细胞压积势必会减少红细胞数量，也阻碍了氧的运输。最好的情况是红细胞压积降低的同时红细胞的数量正常或较高，才有利于氧的运输，这种情况在耐力运动员中常见。

Chapter 6
Exercise and Respiratory System

The respiratory and cardiovascular systems combine to provide an effective delivery system that carries oxygen to, and removes carbon dioxide from, all tissues of the body.

This transportation involves four separate processes:

- Pulmonary ventilation (breathing): movement of air into and out of the lungs
- Pulmonary diffusion: the exchange of oxygen and carbon dioxide between the lungs and the blood
- Transport of oxygen and carbon dioxide via the blood
- Capillary diffusion: the exchange of oxygen and carbon dioxide between the capillary blood and metabolically active tissues

The first two processes are referred to as external respiration because they involve moving gases from outside the body into the lungs and then the blood. Once the gases are in the blood, they must be transported to the tissues. When blood arrives at the tissues, the fourth step of respiration occurs. This gas exchange between the blood and the tissues is called internal respiration. Thus, external and internal respiration are linked by the circulatory system. The following sections examine all four components of respiration.

1 Pulmonary Ventilation

Pulmonary ventilation, or breathing, is the process by which we move air into and out of the lungs. The anatomy of the respiratory system is illustrated in Figure 6.1. Air is typically drawn into the lungs through the nose, although the mouth must also be used when the demand for air exceeds the amount that can comfortably be brought in through the nose. Nasal breathing is advantageous because the air is warmed and humidified as it swirls through the bony irregular sinus surfaces (turbinates or conchae). Of equal importance, the turbinates churn the inhaled air, causing dust and other particles to contact and adhere to the nasal mucosa. This filters out all but the tiniest particles, minimizing irritation and the threat of respiratory infections. From the nose and mouth, the air travels through the pharynx, larynx, trachea, and bronchial tree.

These anatomical structures serve as the transport zone of the lungs because gas exchange does not occur in these structures. Exchange of oxygen and carbon dioxide occurs when air finally reaches the smallest respiratory units: the respiratory bronchioles and the alveoli. The respiratory bronchioles are primarily transport tubes also but are included in this region because they contain clusters of alveoli. This is known as the respiratory zone because it is the site of gas exchange in the lungs.

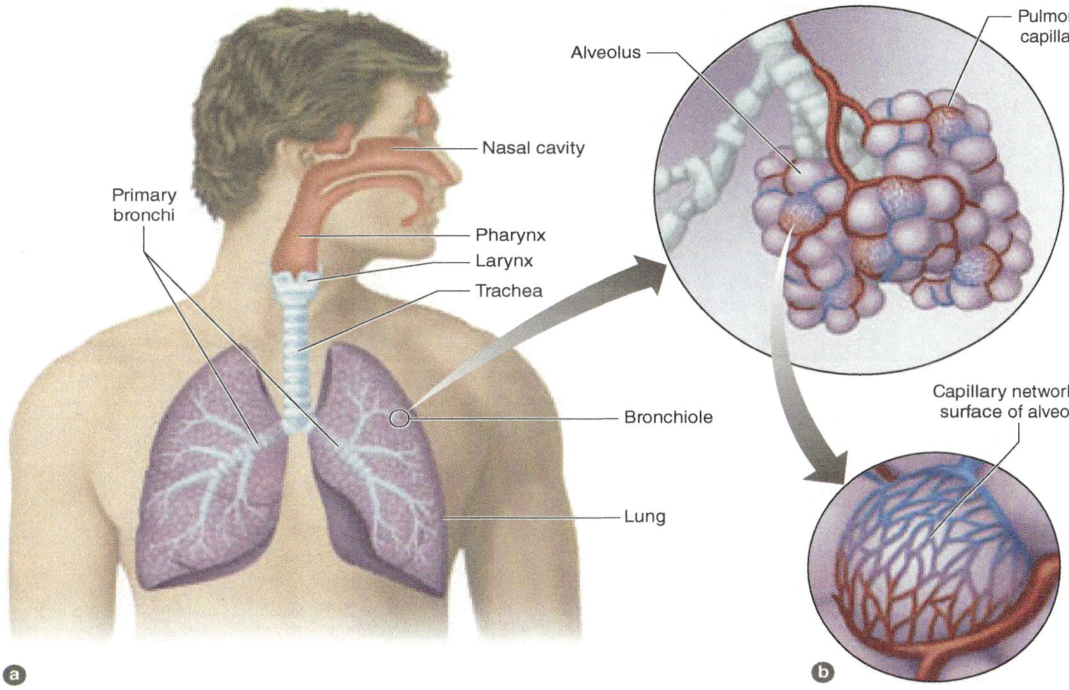

Figure 6.1 (a) The anatomy of the respiratory system, illustrating the respiratory tract (i.e., nasal cavity, pharynx, trachea, and bronchi); (b) The enlarged view of an alveolus shows the regions of gas exchange between the alveolus and pulmonary blood in the capillaries.

1.1 Inspiration

Inspiration is an active process involving the diaphragm and the external intercostal muscles. Figure 6.2a shows the resting positions of the diaphragm and the thoracic cage, or thorax. With inspiration, the ribs and sternum are moved by the external intercostal muscles. The ribs swing up and out and the sternum swings up and forward. At the same time, the diaphragm contracts, flattening down toward the abdomen.

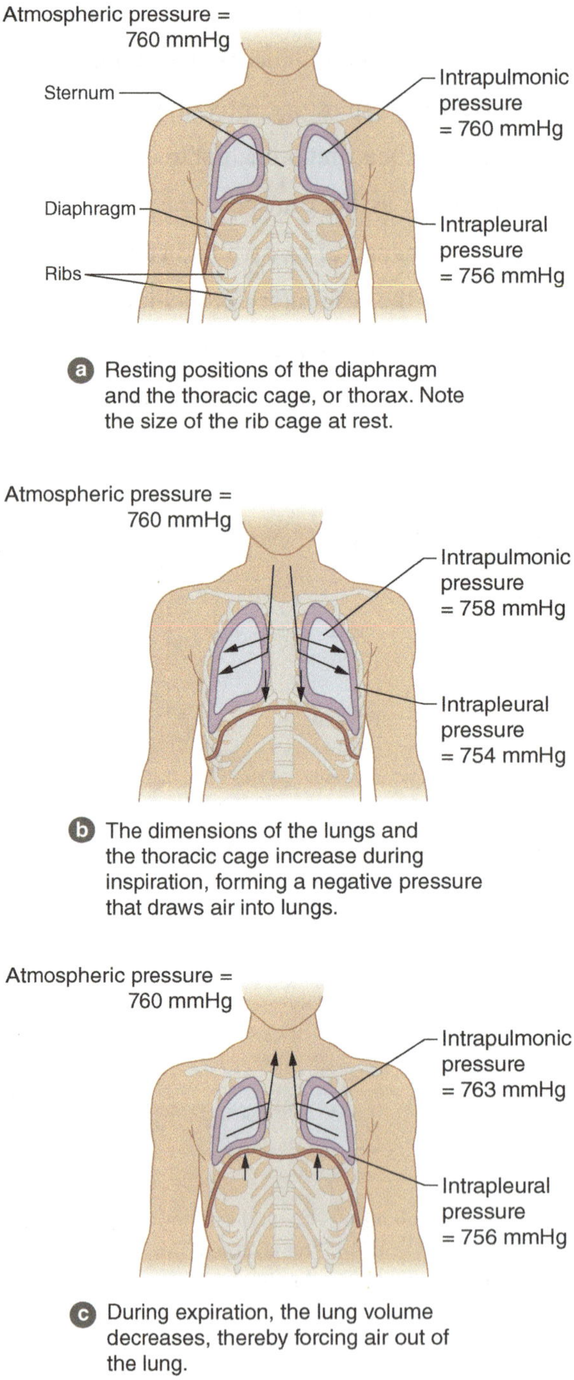

Figure 6.2 The process of inspiration and expiration, showing how movement of the ribs and diaphragm can increase and decrease the size of the thorax.

These actions, illustrated in Figure 6.2b, expand all three dimensions of the thoracic cage, increasing the volume inside the lungs. When the lungs are expanded, they have a greater volume and the air within them has more space to fill. According to Boyle's gas law, which states that pressure × volume is constant (at a constant temperature) , the pressure within the lungs decreases. As a result, the pressure in the lungs (intrapulmonary pressure) is less than the air pressure outside the body. Because the respiratory tract is open to the outside, air rushes into the lungs to reduce this pressure difference.

This is how air moves into the lungs during inspiration.

During forced or labored breathing, as during heavy exercise, inspiration is further assisted by the action of other muscles, such as the scaleni (anterior, middle, and posterior) and sternocleidomastoid in the neck and the pectorals in the chest. These muscles help raise the ribs even more than during regular breathing.

1.2 Expiration

At rest, expiration is a passive process involving relaxation of the inspiratory muscles and elastic recoil of the lung tissue. As the diaphragm relaxes, it returns to its normal upward, arched position. As the external intercostal muscles relax, the ribs and sternum move back into their resting positions (Figure 6.2c). While this happens, the elastic nature of the lung tissue causes it to recoil to its resting size. This increases the pressure in the lungs and causes a proportional decrease in volume in the thorax, and therefore air is forced out of the lungs.

During forced breathing, expiration becomes a more active process. The internal intercostal muscles actively pull the ribs down. This action can be assisted by the latissimus dorsi and quadratus lumborum muscles. Contracting the abdominal muscles increases the intra-abdominal pressure, forcing the abdominal viscera upward against the diaphragm and accelerating its return to the domed position. These muscles also pull the rib cage down and inward.

The changes in intra-abdominal and intrathoracic pressure that accompany forced breathing also help return venous blood back to the heart, working together with the muscle pump in the legs to assist the return of venous volume. As intra-abdominal and intra-thoracic pressure increases, it is transmitted to the great veins—the pulmonary veins and superior and inferior venae cavae—that transport blood back to the heart. When the pressure decreases, the veins return to their original size and fill with blood. The changing pressures within the abdomen and thorax squeeze the blood in the veins, assisting its return through a milking action. This phenomenon is known as the respiratory pump and is essential in maintaining adequate venous return.

2 Pulmonary Volumes

The volume of air in the lungs can be measured with a technique called spirometry. A spirometer measures the volumes of air inspired and expired and therefore changes in lung volume. Although more sophisticated spirometers are used today, a simple spirometer contains a bell filled with air that is partially submerged in water. A tube runs from the subject's mouth under the water and emerges inside the bell, just above the water level. As the person exhales, air flows down the tube and into the bell, causing the bell to rise. The bell is attached to a pen, and its movement is recorded on a simple rotating drum (Figure 6.3).

This technique is used clinically to measure lung volumes, capacities, and flow rates as an aid in diagnosing such respiratory diseases as asthma, chronic obstructive pulmonary disease (COPD) , and emphysema.

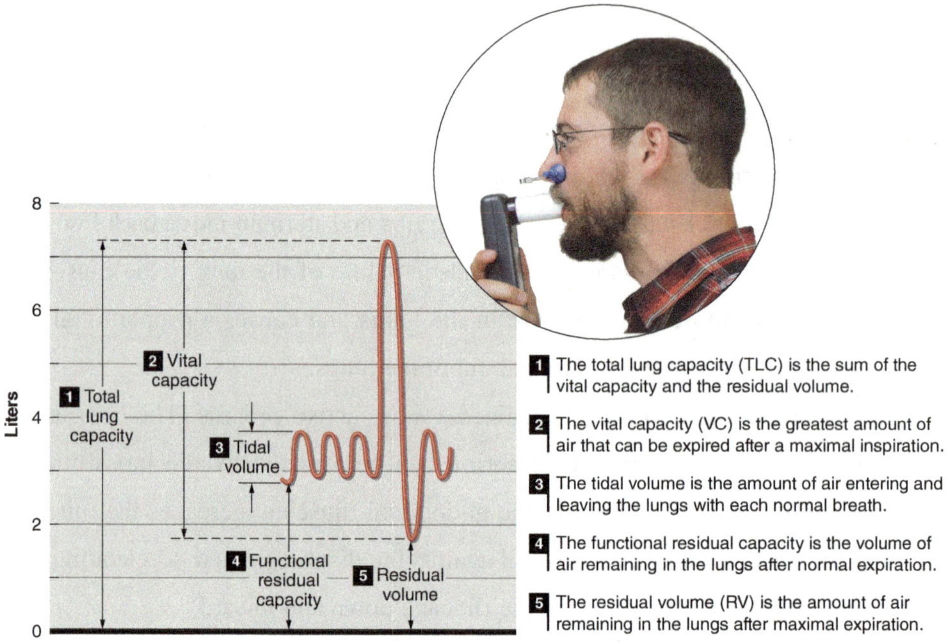

Figure 6.3 A spirometer measures the volumes of air inspired and expired.

The amount of air entering and leaving the lungs with each breath is known as the tidal volume. The vital capacity (VC) is the greatest amount of air that can be expired after a maximal inspiration. Even after a full expiration, some air remains in the lungs. The amount of air remaining in the lungs after a maximal expiration is the residual volume (RV). The residual volume cannot be measured with spirometry. The total lung capacity (TLC) is the sum of the vital capacity and the residual volume.

3 Pulmonary Diffusion

Gas exchange in the lungs between the alveoli and the capillary blood, called pulmonary diffusion, serves two major functions:

- It replenishes the blood's oxygen supply, which is depleted at the tissue level as it is used for oxidative energy production.
- It removes carbon dioxide from returning systemic venous blood.

Air is brought into the lungs during pulmonary ventilation, enabling gas exchange to occur through pulmonary diffusion. Oxygen from the air diffuses from the alveoli into the blood in the pulmonary capillaries, and carbon dioxide diffuses from the blood into the alveoli in the lungs. The alveoli are grapelike clusters, or air sacs, at the ends of the terminal bronchioles.

Blood from the body (except for that returning from the lungs) returns through the vena cava to the right side of the heart. From the right ventricle, this blood is pumped through the pulmonary artery to the lungs, ultimately working its way into the pulmonary capillaries. These capillaries form a dense network around the alveolar sacs. These vessels are so small that the red blood cells must pass through them in single file, such that each cell is exposed to the surrounding lung tissue. This is where pulmonary diffusion occurs.

3.1 Blood Flow to the Lungs at Rest

At rest the lungs receive approximately 4–6L/min of blood flow, depending on body size. Because cardiac output from the right side of the heart approximates cardiac output from the left side of the heart, blood flow to the lungs matches blood flow to the systemic circulation. However, pressure and vascular resistance in the blood vessels in the lungs are different than in the system circulation. The mean pressure in the pulmonary artery is ~15mmHg (systolic pressure is ~25mmHg and diastolic pressure is ~8mmHg) compared to the mean pressure in the aorta of ~95mmHg. The pressure in the left atrium where blood is returning to the heart from the lungs is ~5mmHg; thus there is not a great pressure difference across the pulmonary circulation (15–5mmHg).

Recalling the discussion of blood flow in the cardiovascular system from Chapter 6, pressure = flow × resistance. Since blood flow to the lungs is equal to that of the systemic circulation, and there is a substantially lower change in pressure across the pulmonary vascular system, resistance is proportionally lower compared to that in the systemic circulation. This is reflected in differences in the anatomy of the vessels in the pulmonary versus systemic circulation: The pulmonary blood vessels are thin walled, with relatively little smooth muscle.

3.2 Respiratory Membrane

Gas exchange between the air in the alveoli and the blood in the pulmonary capillaries occurs across the respiratory membrane (also called the alveolar-capillary membrane). This membrane, depicted in Figure 6.4, is composed of

- the alveolar wall
- the capillary wall, and
- their respective basement membranes

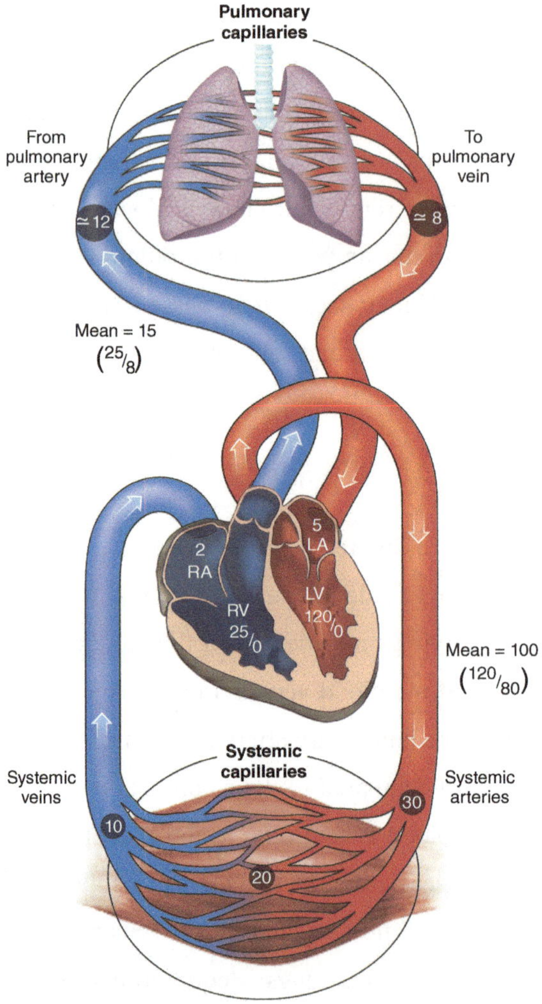

Figure 6.4 Comparison of pressures (mmHg) in the pulmonary and systemic circulations.

The primary function of these membranous surfaces is for gas exchange. The respiratory membrane is very thin, measuring only 0.5–4.0 mm. As a result, the gases in the nearly 300 million alveoli are in close proximity to the blood circulating through the capillaries.

3.3 Gas Exchange in the Alveoli

Differences in the partial pressures of the gases in the alveoli and the gases in the blood create a pressure gradient across the respiratory membrane. This forms the basis of gas exchange during pulmonary diffusion. If the pressures on each side of the membrane were equal, the gases would be at equilibrium and would not move. But the pressures are not equal, so gases move according to partial pressure gradients.

3.3.1 Oxygen Exchange

The PO_2 (partial pressure of oxygen) of air outside the body at standard atmospheric pressure is 159 mmHg. But this pressure decreases to about 105 mmHg when air is inhaled and enters the alveoli, where it is moistened and mixes with the air in the alveoli. The alveolar air is saturated with water vapor (which has its own partial pressure) and contains more carbon dioxide than the inspired air. Both the increased water vapor pressure and increased partial pressure of carbon dioxide contribute to the total pressure in the alveoli. Fresh air that ventilates the lungs is constantly mixed with the air in the alveoli while some of the alveolar gases are exhaled to the environment. As a result, alveolar gas concentrations remain relatively stable.

The blood, stripped of much of its oxygen by the metabolic needs of the tissues, typically enters the pulmonary capillaries with a PO_2 of about 40 mmHg. This is about 60–65 mmHg less than the PO_2 in the alveoli. In other words, the pressure gradient for oxygen across the respiratory membrane is typically about 65 mmHg. As noted earlier, this pressure gradient drives the oxygen from the alveoli into the blood to equilibrate the pressure of the oxygen on each side of the membrane.

Diffusion through tissues is described by Fick's law. Fick's law states that the rate of diffusion through a tissue such as the respiratory membrane is proportional to the surface area and the difference in the partial pressure of gas between the two sides of the tissue. The rate of diffusion is also inversely proportional to the thickness of the tissue in which the gas must diffuse. Additionally, the diffusion constant, which is unique to each gas, influences the rate of diffusion across the tissue.

3.3.2 Carbon Dioxide Exchange

Carbon dioxide, like oxygen, moves along a partial pressure gradient. The blood passing from the right side of the heart through the alveoli has a PCO_2 (partial pressure of carbon dioxide) of about 46 mmHg. Air in the alveoli has a PCO_2 of about 40 mmHg. Although this results in a relatively small pressure gradient of only about 6 mmHg, it is more than adequate to allow for exchange of carbon dioxide. Carbon dioxide's diffusion coefficient is 20 times greater than that of oxygen, so carbon dioxide can diffuse across the respiratory membrane much more rapidly. The partial pressures of gases involved in pulmonary diffusion are summarized in Table 6.1. Note that the total pressure in the venous blood is only 706 mmHg, 54 mmHg lower than the total pressure in dry air and alveolar air. This is the result of a much greater decrease in PO_2 compared with the increase in PCO_2 as the blood goes through the body's tissues.

Table 6.1 Partial Pressures of Respiratory Gases at Sea Level

Gas	% in dry air	Dry air	Alveolar air	Arterial blood	Venous blood	Diffusion gradient
H_2O	0	0	47	47	47	0
O_2	20.93	159.1	105	100	40	60
CO_2	0.03	0.2	40	40	46	6
N_2	79.04	600.7	568	573	573	0
Total	100.00	760	760	760	706*	0

* See text for an explanation of the decresase in total pressune.

4 Transport of Oxygen and Carbon Dioxide in the Blood

We have considered how air moves into and out of the lungs via pulmonary ventilation and how gas exchange occurs via pulmonary diffusion. Next we consider how gases are transported in the blood to deliver oxygen to the tissues and to remove the carbon dioxide that the tissues produce.

4.1 Oxygen Transport

Oxygen is transported by the blood either combined with hemoglobin in the red blood cells (greater than 98%) or dissolved in the blood plasma (less than 2%). Only about 3 ml of oxygen is dissolved in each liter of plasma. Assuming a total plasma volume of 3–5 L, only about 9–15 ml of oxygen can be carried in the dissolved state. This limited amount of oxygen cannot adequately meet the needs of even resting body tissues, which generally require more than 250 ml of oxygen per minute (depending on body size).

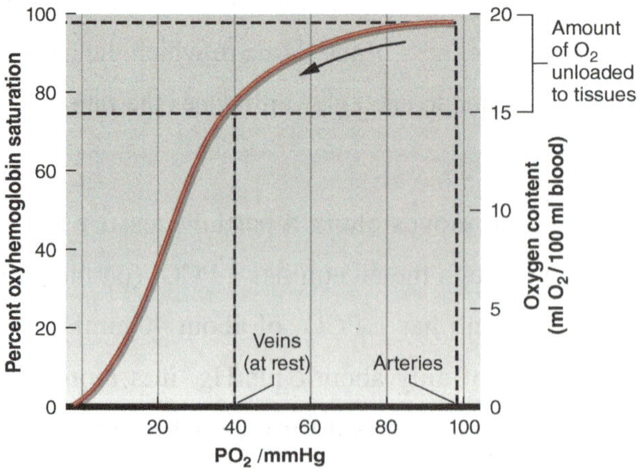

Figure 6.5 Oxyhemoglobin dissociation curve.

4.1.1 Hemoglobin Saturation

As just noted, over 98% of oxygen is transported in the blood bound to hemoglobin. Each molecule of hemoglobin can carry four molecules of oxygen. When oxygen binds to hemoglobin, it forms oxyhemoglobin; hemoglobin that is not bound to oxygen is referred to as deoxyhemoglobin.

The binding of oxygen to hemoglobin depends on the PO_2 in the blood and the bonding strength, or affinity, between hemoglobin and oxygen. The curve in Figure 6.5 is an oxygen-hemoglobin dissociation curve, which shows the amount of hemoglobin saturated with oxygen at different PO_2 values. The shape of the curve is extremely important for its function in the body. The relatively flat upper portion means that, at high PO_2 concentrations such as in the lungs, large drops in PO_2 result in only small changes in hemoglobin saturation. This is called the "loading" portion of the curve. A high blood PO_2 results in almost complete hemoglobin saturation, which means that the maximal amount of oxygen is bound. But as the PO_2 decreases, so does hemoglobin saturation.

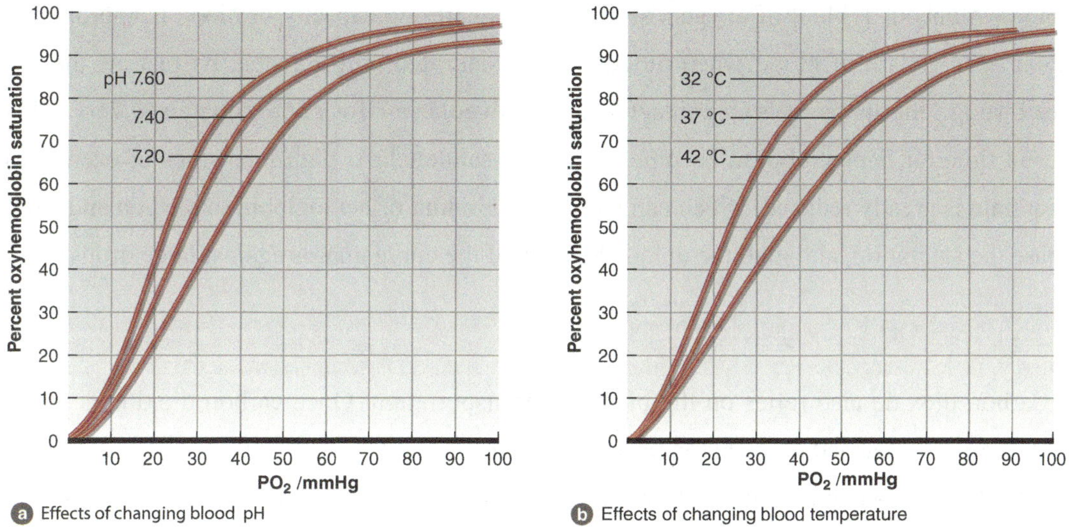

Figure 6.6 The effects of changing blood PH and blood temperature on the oxyhemoglobin dissociation curve.

The steep portion of the curve coincides with PO_2 values typically found in the tissues of the body. Here, relatively small changes in PO_2 result in large changes in saturation. This is also advantageous because this is the "unloading" portion of the curve where hemoglobin loses its oxygen to the tissues.

Many factors determine the hemoglobin saturation. If, for example, the blood becomes more acidic, the dissociation curve shifts to the right. This indicates that more oxygen is being unloaded from the hemoglobin at the tissue level. This rightward shift of the curve (see Figure 6.6a) , attributable to a decline in pH, is referred to as the Bohr effect. The pH in the lungs is generally high, so hemoglobin passing through the lungs has a strong affinity for oxygen, encouraging high saturation.

At the tissue level, especially during exercise, the pH is lower, causing oxygen to dissociate from hemoglobin, thereby supplying oxygen to the tissues. With exercise, the ability to unload oxygen to the muscles increases as the muscle pH decreases.

Blood temperature also affects oxygen dissociation. As shown in Figure 6.6b, increased blood temperature shifts the dissociation curve to the right, indicating that oxygen is unloaded from hemoglobin more readily at higher temperatures. Because of this, the hemoglobin unloads more oxygen when blood circulates through the metabolically heated active muscles.

4.1.2 Blood Oxygen-Carrying Capacity

The oxygen-carrying capacity of blood is the maximal amount of oxygen the blood can transport. It depends primarily on the blood hemoglobin content. Each 100 ml of blood contains an average of 14–18 g of hemoglobin in men and 12–16 g in women. Each gram of hemoglobin can combine with about 1.34 ml of oxygen, so the oxygen-carrying capacity of blood is approximately 16–24 ml per 100 ml of blood when blood is fully saturated with oxygen. At rest, as the blood passes through the lungs, it is in contact with the alveolar air for approximately 0.75 s. This is sufficient time for hemoglobin to become 98%–99% saturated. At high intensities of exercise, the contact time is greatly reduced, which can reduce the binding of hemoglobin to oxygen and slightly decrease the saturation, although the unique S shape of the curve guards against large drops.

4.2 Carbon Dioxide Transport

Carbon dioxide also relies on the blood for transportation. Once carbon dioxide is released from the cells, it is carried in the blood primarily in three forms:

- As bicarbonate ions resulting from the dissociation of carbonic acid;
- Dissolved in plasma;
- Bound to hemoglobin (called carbaminohemoglobin).

4.2.1 Bicarbonate Ion

The majority of carbon dioxide is carried in the form of bicarbonate ion. Bicarbonate accounts for the transport of 60%–70% of the carbon dioxide in the blood. Carbon dioxide and water molecules combine to form carbonic acid (H_2CO_3). This reaction is catalyzed by the enzyme carbonic anhydrase, which is found in red blood cells. Carbonic acid is unstable and quickly dissociates, freeing a hydrogen ion (H^+) and forming a bicarbonate ion (HCO^-) :

$$CO_2 + H_2O \rightarrow H_2CO_3 \rightarrow H^+ + HCO_3^-$$

The H^+ subsequently binds to hemoglobin, and this binding triggers the Bohr effect, mentioned previously, which shifts the oxygen-hemoglobin dissociation curve to the right. The bicarbonate ion diffuses out of the red blood cell and into the plasma. In order to prevent electrical imbalance from the shift of the negatively charged bicarbonate ion into the plasma, a chloride ion diffuses from the plasma into the red blood cell. This is called the chloride shift.

When the blood enters the lungs, where the PCO_2 is lower, the H^+ and bicarbonate ions rejoin to form carbonic acid, which then dissociates into carbon dioxide and water:

$$H^+ + HCO_3^- \rightarrow H_2CO_3 \rightarrow CO_2 + H_2O$$

The carbon dioxide that is thus re-formed can enter the alveoli and be exhaled.

4.2.2 Dissolved Carbon Dioxide

Part of the carbon dioxide released from the tissues is dissolved in plasma; but only a small amount, typically just 7%–10%, is transported this way. This dissolved carbon dioxide comes out of solution where the PCO_2 is low, as in the lungs. There it diffuses from the pulmonary capillaries into the alveoli to be exhaled.

4.2.3 Carbaminohemoglobin

Carbon dioxide transport also can occur when the gas binds with hemoglobin, forming carbaminohemoglobin. The compound is so named because carbon dioxide binds with amino acids in the globin part of the hemoglobin molecule, rather than with the heme group as oxygen does. Because carbon dioxide binding occurs on a different part of the hemoglobin molecule than does oxygen binding, the two processes do not compete. However, carbon dioxide binding varies with the oxygenation of the hemoglobin (deoxyhemoglobin binds carbon dioxide more easily than oxyhemoglobin) and the partial pressure of carbon dioxide. Carbon dioxide is released from hemoglobin when PCO_2 is low as it is in the lungs. Thus, carbon dioxide is readily released from the hemoglobin in the lungs, allowing it to enter the alveoli to be exhaled.

5 Gas Exchange at the Muscles

We have considered how the respiratory and cardiovascular systems bring air into our lungs, exchange oxygen and carbon dioxide in the alveoli, and transport oxygen to the muscles and carbon dioxide to the lungs. We now consider the delivery of oxygen from the capillary blood to the muscle tissue.

5.1 Arterial-Venous Oxygen Difference

At rest, the oxygen content of arterial blood is about 20 ml of oxygen per 100 ml of blood, This value decreases to 15–16 ml of oxygen per 100 ml after the blood has passed through the capillaries into the venous system. This difference in oxygen content between arterial and venous blood is referred to as the arterial-mixed venous oxygen content difference, or Ca -$C_{\bar{v}}$ O_2difference. the rate of oxygen use increases, the Ca -$C_{\bar{v}}$ O_2 difference also increases. The Ca -$C_{\bar{v}}$ O_2 difference increases from a resting value of about 4–5 ml per 100 ml of blood up to values of 15–16 ml per 100 ml of blood during intense exercise. This increase reflects an increased extraction of oxygen from arterial blood by active muscle, thus decreasing the oxygen content of the venous blood. It is important to remember that the blood returning to the right atrium is coming from all parts of the body, active and inactive. Therefore, the mixed venous oxygen content will not decrease to values much lower than 4–5 ml of oxygen per 100 ml of venous blood.

Oxygen is transported in the muscle to the mitochondria by a molecule called myoglobin where it is used in oxidative metabolism. Myoglobin is similar in structure to hemoglobin, but myoglobin has a much greater affinity for oxygen than hemoglobin. This concept is illustrated in Figure 6.7. At PO_2 values less than 20, the myoglobin dissociation curve is much steeper than the dissociation curve for hemoglobin. Myoglobin releases its oxygen content only under conditions in which the PO_2 is very low.

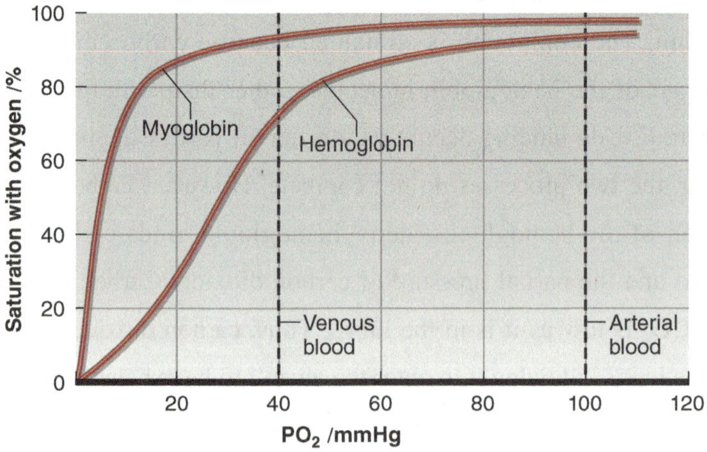

Figure 6.7 A comparison of dissociation curves for myoglobin and hemoglobin.

5.2 Factors Influencing Oxygen Delivery and Uptake

The rates of oxygen delivery and uptake depend on three major variables:

- Oxygen content of blood;
- Blood flow;
- Local conditions (e.g., pH, temperature).

With exercise, each of these variables is adjusted to ensure increased oxygen delivery to active muscle. Under normal circumstances, hemoglobin is about 98% saturated with oxygen. Any reduction in the blood's normal oxygen-carrying capacity would hinder oxygen delivery and reduce cellular uptake of oxygen. Likewise, a reduction in the PO_2 of the arterial blood would lower the partial pressure gradient, limiting the unloading of oxygen at the tissue level. Exercise increases blood flow through the muscles. As more blood carries oxygen through the muscles, less oxygen must be removed from each 100 ml of blood (assuming the demand is unchanged). Thus, increased blood flow improves oxygen delivery.

Many local changes in the muscle during exercise affect oxygen delivery and uptake. For example, muscle activity increases muscle acidity because of lactate production. Also, muscle temperature and carbon dioxide concentration both increase because of increased metabolism. All these changes increase oxygen unloading from the hemoglobin molecule, facilitating oxygen delivery and uptake by the muscles.

5.3 Carbon Dioxide Removal

Carbon dioxide exits the cells by simple diffusion in response to the partial pressure gradient between the tissue and the capillary blood. For example, muscles generate carbon dioxide through oxidative metabolism, so the PCO_2 in muscles is relatively high compared with that in the capillary blood. Consequently, CO_2 diffuses out of the muscles and into the blood to be transported to the lungs.

6 Regulation of Pulmonary Ventilation

Maintaining homeostatic balance in blood PO_2, PCO_2, and pH requires a high degree of coordination between the respiratory and circulatory systems. Much of this coordination is accomplished by involuntary regulation of pulmonary ventilation. This control is not yet fully understood, although many of the intricate neural controls have been identified.

The respiratory muscles are under the direct control of motor neurons, which are in turn regulated by respiratory centers (inspiratory and expiratory) located within the brain stem (in the medulla oblongata and pons). These centers establish the rate and depth of breathing by sending out periodic impulses to the respiratory muscles. The cortex can override these centers if voluntary control of respiration is desired. Additionally, input from other parts of the brain occurs under certain conditions.

The inspiratory area of the brain (dorsal respiratory group) contains cells that intrinsically fire and control the basic rhythm of ventilation. The expiratory area is quiet during normal quiet breathing (recall that expiration is a passive process at rest). However, during forceful breathing such as during exercise, the expiratory area actively sends signals to the muscles of expiration. Two other brain centers aid in the control of respiration. The apneustic area has an excitatory effect on the inspiratory center and results in prolonged firing of the inspiratory neurons. Finally, the pneumotaxic center inhibits or "switches off" inspiration, helping to regulate inspiratory volume.

The respiratory centers do not act alone in controlling breathing. Breathing also is regulated and modified by the changing chemical environment in the body. For example, sensitive areas in the brain respond to changes in carbon dioxide and H^+ levels. The central chemoreceptors in the brain are stimulated by an increase in H^+ ions in the cerebrospinal fluid. The blood-brain barrier is relatively impermeable to H^+ ions or bicarbonate. However, carbon dioxide readily diffuses across the blood-brain barrier and then reacts to increase H^+ ions. This, in turn, stimulates the inspiratory center, which then activates the neural circuitry to increase the rate and depth of respiration. This increase in respiration, in turn, increases the removal of carbon dioxide and H^+.

Chemoreceptors in the aortic arch (the aortic bodies) and in the bifurcation of the common carotid artery (the carotid bodies) are sensitive primarily to blood changes in PO_2, but also respond to changes in H^+ concentration and PCO_2. The carotid chemoreceptors are more sensitive to changes in H^+ concentrations and PCO_2. Overall, PCO_2 appears to be the strongest stimulus for the regulation of breathing. When carbon dioxide levels become too high, carbonic acid forms, then quickly dissociates, giving off H^+. If H^+ accumulates, the blood becomes too acidic (pH decreases). Thus, an increased PCO_2 stimulates the inspiratory center to increase respiration—not to bring in more oxygen but to rid the body of excess carbon dioxide and limit further pH changes.

In addition to the chemoreceptors, other neural mechanisms influence breathing. The pleurae, bronchioles, and alveoli in the lungs contain stretch receptors. When these areas are excessively stretched, that information is relayed to the expiratory center. The expiratory center responds by shortening the duration of an inspiration, which decreases the risk of overinflating the respiratory structures. This response is known as the Hering-Breuer reflex.

Many control mechanisms are involved in the regulation of breathing, as shown in Figure 6.8. Such simple stimuli as emotional distress or an abrupt change in the temperature of the surroundings can affect breathing. But all these control mechanisms are essential. The goal of respiration is to maintain appropriate levels of the blood and tissue gases and to maintain proper pH for normal cellular function. Small changes in any of these, if not carefully controlled, could impair physical activity and jeopardize health.

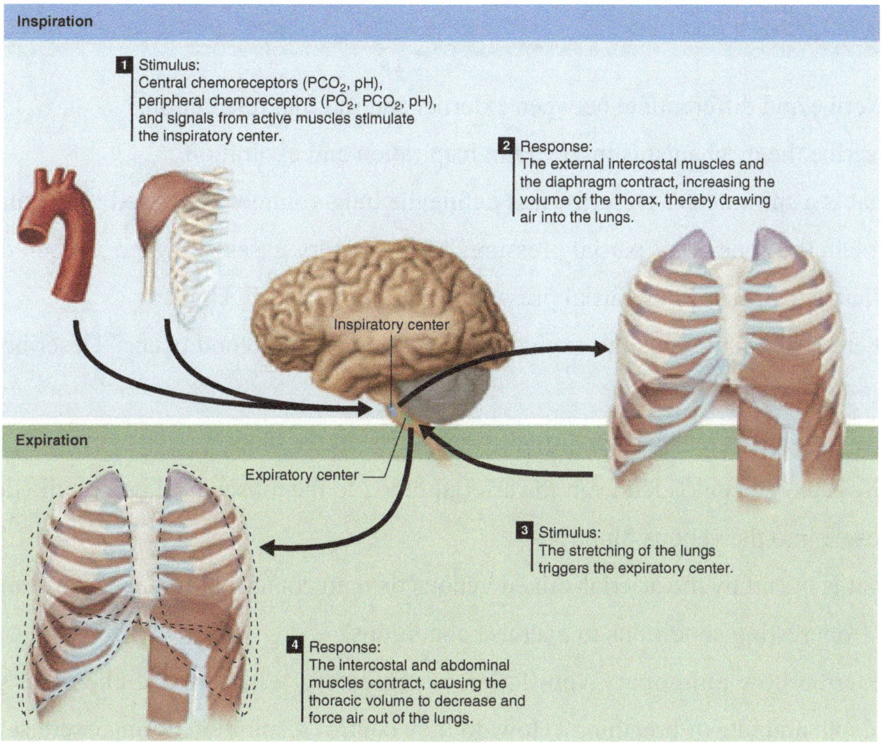

Figure 6.8 An overview of the processes involved in respiratory regulation.

IN CLOSING

In Chapter 5, we discussed the role of the cardiovascular system during exercise. In this chapter we looked at the role played by the respiratory system. In the next chapter, we examine how the cardiovascular and respiratory systems respond to an acute bout of exercise.

KEY TERMS

arterial-mixed venous oxygen content difference; Ca -$C_{\bar{v}}$ O_2 difference; arterial-venous oxygen difference; Boyle's gas law; external respiration; Fick's law; Henry's law; internal respiration; myoglobin; partial pressure; pulmonary diffusion; pulmonary ventilation; residual volume (RV) ; respiratory centers; respiratory membrane; tidal volume; total lung capacity (TLC) ; vital capacity (VC)

STUDY QUESTIONS

(1) Describe and differentiate between external and internal respiration.

(2) Describe the mechanisms involved in inspiration and expiration.

(3) What is a spirometer? Describe and define the lung volumes measured using spirometry.

(4) Explain the concept of partial pressures of respiratory gases—oxygen, carbon dioxide, and nitrogen. What is the role of gas partial pressures in pulmonary diffusion?

(5) Where in the lung does the exchange of gases with the blood occur? Describe the role of the respiratory membrane.

(6) How are oxygen and carbon dioxide transported in the blood?

(7) How is oxygen unloaded from the arterial blood to the muscle and carbon dioxide removed from the muscle into the venous blood?

(8) What is meant by the arterial-mixed venous oxygen content difference? How and why does this change from resting conditions to exercise conditions?

(9) Describe how pulmonary ventilation is regulated. What are the chemical stimuli that control the depth and rate of breathing? How do they control respiration during exercise?

第六章 运动与呼吸系统

整个呼吸过程是由心肺系统将氧运送到组织，并将组织中的二氧化碳排出体外的过程。整个过程包括：肺通气（呼吸）；肺换气；氧和二氧化碳在血液中的运输；氧和二氧化碳在毛细血管和组织之间的交换。其中前两个过程合称为外呼吸，气体在血液和组织之间进行的交换称为内呼吸。

一、肺通气

肺通气是指肺与外界环境之间进行的气体交换，即空气进出肺部的过程。

1.吸气

吸气运动是由膈肌和肋间外肌的收缩引起的，是呼吸的主动过程。吸气时可以扩大胸廓的三维空间，增大肺内容积，降低肺内压，使空气进入肺。深呼吸或用力呼吸时，如剧烈运动时，其他肌肉会协助呼吸，如位于颈部和胸部的三角肌（前部、中部和后部）和胸锁乳突肌等。

2.呼气

呼气运动是由呼吸肌的舒张和肺组织的弹性回缩引起的，是呼吸的被动过程。呼气时，膈肌和肋间外肌舒张，肺组织的弹性部分也回缩至安静状态，胸腔容积减小，肺内压升高，促使气体排出肺部。深呼吸时，呼气成为主动过程，肋间内肌主动收缩，背阔肌和腰方肌作为辅助呼吸肌参与呼气过程。由深呼吸造成的肺内压和胸内压的变化通过挤压方式调节静脉血液，这种现象称为呼吸泵，对维持静脉回流起到重要作用。

二、肺容量

潮气量是指每次平静吸入或呼出的气体量。肺活量是指最大吸气后，再尽力呼气所能呼出的最大气量。余气量是指在最大呼气末仍残留在肺内的气体量，余气量不能直接测定。肺容量是指肺活量和余气量之和。

三、肺换气

肺换气是指在肺内的气体交换。肺通气时气体进入肺，通过肺换气，使气体和血液发生气体交换。肺泡位于细支气管的末端，肺毛细血管包绕着肺泡，氧从肺泡扩散到肺毛细血管中，而二氧化碳从血液扩散到肺泡。

1.安静状态下肺部的血流

右心输出量与左心输出量基本一致，所以肺的血流量与体循环的也一致。然而，肺血管内的压力和阻力与体循环不同。肺动脉中的平均血压大约为15毫米汞柱（收缩压约为25毫米汞柱， 舒张压约8毫米汞柱），左心房内血压大约为5毫米汞柱，肺循环的阻力相对较低。肺血管壁更薄，平滑肌更少。

2.呼吸膜

气体在肺泡和肺毛细血管中的血液之间进行交换必须通过呼吸膜，呼吸膜也称为肺泡-毛细血管膜。呼吸膜非常薄，仅有0.5 ~ 4.0微米。

3.肺泡中的气体交换

肺泡和血液之间的压力差异形成的跨呼吸膜的压力梯度称为气体分压，气体分压是气体交换的基础。如果膜两侧的压力是相等的，则不会发生气体交换。

（1）氧的交换。菲克定律：气体在跨组织扩散时，如跨呼吸膜时，其扩散率与表面积和组织两边分压差成正比，与组织厚度成反比。此外，每种气体都有其恒定的扩散系数，会影响扩散速率。

氧自肺泡扩散至血液的速率称为氧扩散能力，以压力差为1毫米汞柱时，每分钟跨膜扩散的氧量来表示。

（2）二氧化碳的交换。二氧化碳也依靠压力梯度进行扩散。肺动脉血液内二氧化碳分压约为 46毫米汞柱，肺泡中气体的二氧化碳分压约为40毫米汞柱。虽然它们的压力梯度较小，只有6毫米汞柱，但二氧化碳的扩散系数是氧的20倍，因此，二氧化碳能迅速地跨呼吸膜进行扩散。

此外，当血液流经机体组织时，氧分压下降大于二氧化碳分压上升，所以静脉血中气体总压为706毫米汞柱，比干燥空气和肺泡气体的总压低54毫米汞柱。

四、氧和二氧化碳在血液中的运输

1.氧的运输

一般机体每分钟需要大约250毫升的氧，氧在血液中主要与红细胞的血红蛋白结合（98%以上），少量溶解在血浆中（低于2%），每升血浆中仅能溶解大约3毫升的氧。

（1）氧合血红蛋白。氧和血红蛋白的结合依赖于血液中氧分压以及血红蛋白和氧之间的结合力。氧离曲线反映了氧分压与血氧饱和度之间的关系。氧离曲线上段相对平坦，表示肺内氧分压较高时，即使氧分压下降幅度较大，血氧饱和度的变化也很小。曲线中的陡峭阶段表示氧分压的微小变化就会导致血红蛋白饱和度发生巨大变化。

很多因素影响着血氧饱和度。例如，如果血液的酸性增加，氧离曲线右移，促进氧与血红蛋白分离，这被称为波尔效应。肺内血液pH值通常较高，促进了血红蛋白与氧的结合；而在外周组织中，特别是运动状态时，pH值较低，促进了氧与血红蛋白解离，将氧供给组织。温度也会影响氧的解离。温度升高，解离曲线右移，氧更快地从血红蛋白上解离出来。因此，运动时，代谢增强，血液温度升高，利于氧的解离。

（2）血液携氧能力。血液携氧能力主要由血液中血红蛋白的含量决定。在安静状态下，流经肺的血液与肺泡内气体接触的时间大约为0.75秒，足以使血红蛋白的氧饱和度达98%～99%。在高强度运动时，血液与肺泡内气体接触的时间虽然缩短，但是S型曲线（氧离曲线）阻止了氧饱和度的大幅下降。

2.二氧化碳的运输

（1）碳酸氢盐离子。血液中60%～70%的二氧化碳都是以碳酸氢盐的形式运输。二氧化碳和水分子在红细胞中的碳酸酐酶的催化下结合形成碳酸，碳酸不稳定，形成氢离子（H^+）和碳酸氢根离子（HCO_3^-），随后H^+与血红蛋白结合，引起波尔效应，使氧离曲线右移，增加氧释放。通过这样的机制，血红蛋白作为缓冲剂，与H^+中和，防止血液过度酸化。HCO_3^-会扩散到红细胞外，进入血浆。为了防止HCO_3^-进入血浆造成的电子不平衡，血浆中的氯离子就会扩散进入红细胞中。当血液进入二氧化碳分压较低的肺部时，H^+又会和碳酸氢盐离子结合形成碳酸，分解为二氧化碳和水，二氧化碳进入肺泡，通过呼气排出体外。

（2）溶解的二氧化碳。血浆中溶解的二氧化碳数量很少，只有7%～10%。

（3）氨基甲酸血红蛋白。二氧化碳也可与血红蛋白分子的珠蛋白结合，形成氨基甲酸血红蛋白。二氧化碳与血红蛋白分子的结合位点与氧不同，这两个过程不会相互竞争，但是二氧化碳的结合受血红蛋白的氧合水平（脱氧血红蛋白比氧合血红蛋白更易与二氧化碳结合）和二氧化碳分压的影响。因此，二氧化碳可迅速从肺内的血红蛋白中释放出来，经过肺泡后通过呼气排出体外。

五、肌肉内的气体交换

1.动静脉血氧含量差

血液中动脉与静脉之间含氧量的差异称为动脉-混合静脉血氧含量差，或称为动静脉血氧含量差。当氧利用率提高时，动静脉血氧含量差会增大，反映从动脉血释放出的氧量增加，静脉血的含氧量降低。

肌肉中的氧被肌红蛋白运送到线粒体进行氧化代谢。肌红蛋白与血红蛋白的结构相似，但对氧的亲合力比血红蛋白高得多。

2.影响氧运输与利用的因素

氧的运输与利用的速率取决于血液的含氧量、血流量和局部条件（如pH值、温度）。运动时，每个变量都会发生调整，以确保向活跃肌肉输送更多氧气。血液携氧能力降低，氧分压下降，氧分压的梯度减少，限制了组织内氧的释放。运动可增加流经肌肉的血流量，越多的血液通过肌肉，每100毫升血液释放出的氧量就越少（假设需求不变）。因此，增加血流量可以改善氧的运输。运动时肌肉的局部变化也会影响氧的运输与利用。例如，运动时增加的乳酸、肌肉温度与二氧化碳浓度，都会促进血红蛋白分子释放氧。

3. 二氧化碳的排出

肌肉中二氧化碳分压比毛细血管中的高。二氧化碳从肌肉扩散进入血液，并被运送到肺部排出。

六、肺通气的调节

为维持血液中氧分压、二氧化碳分压与pH值的恒定，需要呼吸与循环系统高度配合。

呼吸肌受运动神经元直接调节，而运动神经元受脑干（延髓与脑桥）呼吸中枢调节。呼吸中枢可通过化学感受器感受氧分压、氢离子浓度及二氧化碳分压的变化来调节呼吸，其中，二氧化碳分压是呼吸调节中最重要的刺激源。需要自主控制呼吸时，大脑皮质的调节作用比呼吸中枢更重要。在特定情况下，还有脑部其他区域的调节信息。胸膜、细支气管与肺部的肺泡含有牵张感受器，当这些区域被过度牵拉时，信息传到呼气中枢，从而限制吸气时相，这种反应称为肺牵张反射。此外，情绪变化、压力或环境温度的突然变化等都会影响呼吸。

Chapter 7 Cardiorespiratory Responses to Acute Exercise

After reviewing the basic anatomy and physiology of the cardiovascular and respiratory systems, this chapter looks specifically at how these systems respond to the increased demands placed on the body during acute exercise. With exercise, oxygen demand by the active muscles increases significantly, and more nutrients are used. Metabolic processes speed up, so more waste products are created. During prolonged exercise or exercise in a hot environment, body temperature increases. In intense exercise, H^+ concentration increases in the muscles and blood, lowering their pH.

1 Cardiovascular Responses to Acute Exercise

Numerous interrelated cardiovascular changes occur during dynamic exercise. The primary goal of these adjustments is to increase blood flow to working muscle; however, cardiovascular control of virtually every tissue and organ in the body is also altered. To better understand the changes that occur, we must examine the function of both the heart and the peripheral circulation. In this section we examine changes in all components of the cardiovascular system from rest to acute exercise, looking specifically at the following:

- Heart rate
- Stroke volume

- Cardiac output
- Blood pressure
- Blood flow
- The blood

We then see how these changes are integrated to maintain adequate blood pressure and provide for the exercising body's needs.

1.1 Heart Rate

Heart rate (HR) is one of the simplest physiological responses to measure, and yet one of the most informative in terms of cardiovascular stress and strain. Measuring HR involves simply taking the subject's pulse, usually at the radial or carotid artery. Heart rate is a good indicator of relative exercise intensity.

1.1.1 Resting Heart Rate

Resting heart rate (RHR) averages 60–80 beats/min in most individuals. In highly conditioned, endurance-trained athletes, resting rates as low as 28–40 beats/min have been reported. This is mainly due to an increase in parasympathetic (vagal) tone that accompanies endurance exercise training. Resting heart rate can also be affected by environmental factors; for example, it increases with extremes in temperature and altitude. Just before the start of exercise, preexercise HR usually increases above normal resting values. This is called the anticipatory response. This response is mediated through release of the neurotransmitter norepinephrine from the sympathetic nervous system and the hormone epinephrine from the adrenal medulla. Vagal tone also decreases. Because preexercise HR is elevated, reliable estimates of the true RHR should be made only under conditions of total relaxation, such as early in the morning before the subject rises from a restful night's sleep.

1.1.2 Heart Rate During Exercise

When exercise begins, HR increases directly in proportion to the increase in exercise intensity (Figure 7.1) , until near-maximal exercise is achieved. As maximal exercise intensity is approached, HR begins to plateau even as the exercise workload continues to increase. This indicates that HR is approaching a maximal value. The maximum heart rate (HRmax) is the highest HR value achieved in an all-out effort to the point of volitional fatigue. Once accurately determined, HRmax is a highly reliable value that remains constant from day to day.

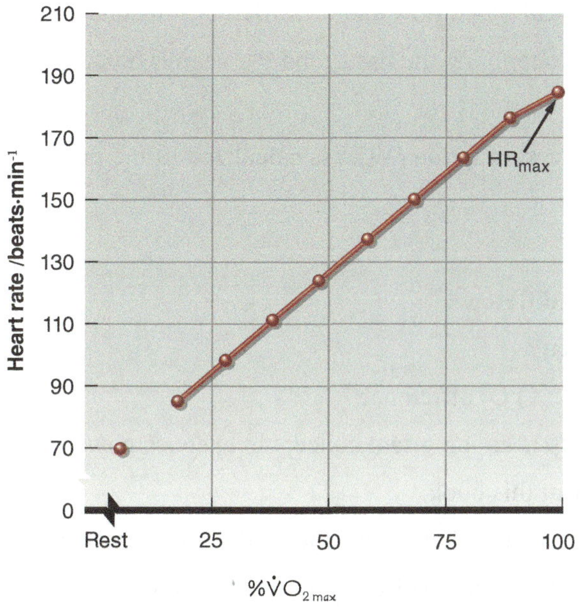

Figure 7.1 Changes in heart rate (HR) as a subject progressively walks, jogs, then run on a treadmill as intensity is increased. Heart rate is plotted against exercise intensity shown as a percent of subject's $\dot{V}O_{2\,max}$, at which point the rise in HR begins to plateau. The HR at this plateau is the subject's maximal HR or HRmax.

However, this value changes slightly from year to year due to a normal age-related decline.

HRmax is often estimated based on age because HRmax shows a slight but steady decrease of about one beat per year beginning at 10–15 years of age. Subtracting one's age from 220 beats/min provides a reasonable approximation of one's predicted HRmax.

A similar but more accurate equation has been developed to estimate HRmax from age. In this equation, HRmax = 208 – (0.7 × age).

When the exercise intensity is held constant at any submaximal workload, HR increases fairly rapidly until it reaches a plateau. This plateau is the steady-state heart rate, and it is the optimal HR for meeting the circulatory demands at that specific rate of work. For each subsequent increase in intensity, HR will reach a new steady-state value within 2–3 min. However, the more intense the exercise, the longer it takes to achieve this steady-state value.

1.2 The Fick Principle and the Fick Equation

In the 1870s, a cardiovascular physiologist by the name of Adolph Fick developed a principle critical to our understanding of the basic relationship between metabolism and cardiovascular function. In its simplest form, the Fick principle states that the oxygen consumption of a tissue is dependent on blood flow to that tissue and the amount of oxygen extracted from the blood by the tissue. This principle can be applied to the whole body or to regional circulations. Oxygen consumption is the product of blood flow and the difference in concentration of oxygen in the blood between the arterial blood supplying the tissue and the venous blood draining out of the tissue—the $Ca\text{-}C_{\bar{v}}\ O_2$ difference.

Whole-body oxygen consumption ($\dot{V}O_2$) is calculated as the product of the cardiac output ($\dot{Q}$) and $Ca\text{-}C_{\bar{v}}\ O_2$ difference.

Fick equation:

$\dot{V}O_2 = \dot{Q} \times (a - \bar{v})\ O_2$ difference

which can be rewritten as

$\dot{V}O_2 = HR \times SV \times (a - \bar{v})\ O_2$ difference

This basic relationship is an important concept in exercise physiology and comes up frequently throughout the remainder of this book.

The concept of steady-state heart rate forms the basis for simple exercise tests that have been developed to estimate cardiorespiratory (aerobic) fitness. In one such test, individuals are placed on an exercise device, such as a cycle ergometer, and then perform exercise at two or three standardized exercise intensities. Those with better cardiorespiratory endurance capacity will have a lower steady-state HR at each exercise intensity than those who are less fit. Thus, a lower steady-state HR at a fixed exercise intensity is a valid predictor of greater cardiorespiratory fitness.

Figure 7.2 illustrates results from a submaximal graded exercise test performed on a cycle ergometer by two different individuals of the same age. Steady-state HR is measured at three or four distinct work-loads, and a line of best fit is drawn through the data points. Because there is a consistent relation between exercise intensity and energy demand, steady-state HR can be plotted against the corresponding energy ($\dot{V}O_2$) required to do work on the cycle ergometer. The resultant line can be extrapolated to the age-predicted HRmax to estimate an individual's maximal exercise capacity. In this Figure, subject A has a higher fitness level than subject B because (1) at any given submaximal intensity, his HR is lower; and (2) extrapolation to age-predicted HRmax yields a higher estimated maximal exercise capacity ($\dot{V}O_{2\,max}$).

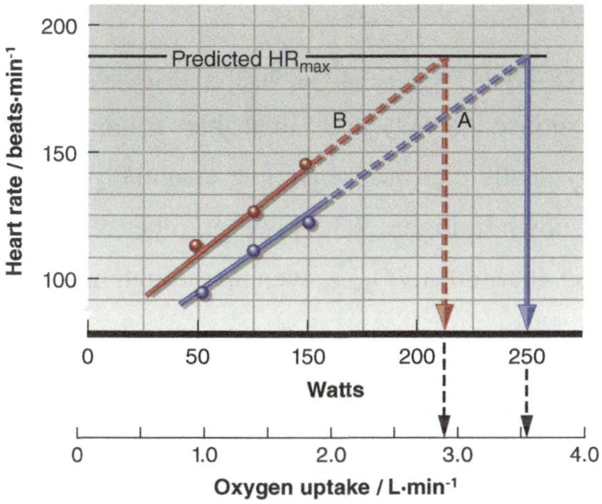

Figure 7.2 The increase in heart rate with inceasing power output on a cycle ergometer and oxygen uptake is linear within a wide range. The predicted maximal oxygen uptake can be extrapolater using the subject's estimated maximum heart rate as demonstrated here for two subjects with similar estimated maximum heart rates but quite different maximal workloads and $\dot{V}O_{2\,max}$ values.

1.3 Stroke Volume

Stroke volume (SV) also changes during acute exercise to allow the heart to meet the demands of exercise. At near-maximal and maximal exercise intensities, as heart rate approaches its maximum, SV is a major determinant of cardiorespiratory endurance capacity.

Stroke volume is determined by four factors:

(1) The volume of venous blood returned to the heart (the heart can only pump what returns) ;

(2) Ventricular distensibility (the capacity to enlarge the ventricle, to allow maximal filling) ;

(3) Ventricular contractility (the inherent capacity of the ventricle to contract forcefully) ;

(4) Aortic or pulmonary artery pressure (the pressure against which the ventricles must contract) .

The first two factors influence the filling capacity of the ventricle, determining how much blood fills the ventricle and the ease with which the ventricle is filled at the available pressure. Together, these factors determine the end-diastolic volume (EDV) , sometimes referred to as the preload. The last two characteristics influence the ventricle's ability to empty during systole, determining the force with which blood is ejected and the pressure against which it must be expelled into the arteries. The latter factor, the aortic mean pressure, which represents resistance to blood being ejected from the left ventricle (and to a less important extent, the pulmonary artery pressure resistance to flow from the right ventricle) , is referred to as the afterload. These four factors combine to determine the SV during acute exercise.

1.3.1 Stroke Volume Increase with Exercise

Stroke volume increases above resting values during exercise. Most researchers agree that SV increases with increasing exercise intensity up to intensities somewhere between 40% and 60% of $\dot{V}O_{2\,max}$. At that point, SV typically plateaus, remaining essentially unchanged up to and including the point of exhaustion as shown in Figure 7.3. However, other researchers have reported that SV continues to increase beyond 40%–60% $\dot{V}O_{2\,max}$, even up through maximal exercise intensities.

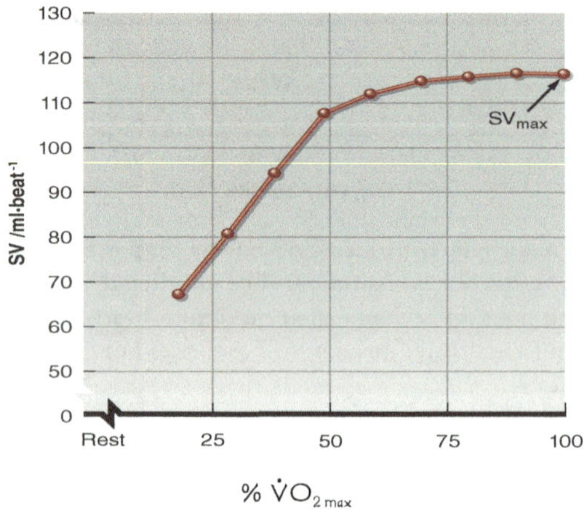

Figure 7.3 Changes in stroke volume (SV) as a subject exercises on a treadmill at increasing intensities. Stroke volume is plotted as a function of percent $\dot{V}O_{2\,max}$. The SV increases with increasing intensity up to approximately 40%–60% of $\dot{V}O_{2\,max}$, before reaching a maximum (SVmax).

When the body is in an upright position, SV can approximately double from resting to maximal values. For example, in active but untrained individuals, SV increases from about 60–70 ml/beat at rest to 110–130 ml/beat during maximal exercise. In highly trained endurance athletes, SV can increase from 80–110 ml/beat at rest to 160–200 ml/beat during maximal exercise. During supine exercise, such as recumbent cycling, SV also increases but usually by only about 20%–40%—not nearly as much as in an upright position. Why does body position make such a difference?

When the body is in the supine position, blood does not pool in the lower extremities. Blood returns more easily to the heart in a supine posture, which means that resting SV values are higher in the supine position than in the upright position. Thus, the increase in SV with maximal exercise is not as great in the supine position as in the upright position because SV starts out higher. The majority of the SV increase during low to moderate intensities of exercise in the upright position appears to be compensating for the force of gravity that causes blood to pool in the extremities.

1.3.2 Explanations for the Stroke Volume Increase

One explanation for the increase in SV with exercise is that the primary factor determining SV is increased preload or the extent to which the ventricle fills with blood and stretches, that is, the EDV. When the ventricle stretches more during filling, it subsequently contracts more forcefully. For example, when a larger volume of blood enters and fills the ventricle during diastole, the ventricular walls stretch to a greater extent. To eject that greater volume of blood, the ventricle responds by contracting more forcefully. This is referred to as the Frank-Starling mechanism. At the level of the muscle fiber, the greater the stretch of the myocardial cells, the more actin-myosin cross-bridges formed, and greater force is developed.

Additionally, SV will increase during exercise if the ventricle's contractility (an inherent property of the ventricle) is enhanced. Contractility can increase by increasing sympathetic nerve stimulation or circulating catecholamines (epinephrine, norepinephrine) , or both. An improved force of contraction can increase SV with or without an increased EDV by increasing the ejection fraction. Finally, when mean arterial blood pressure is low, SV is greater since there is less resistance to outflow into the aorta. These mechanisms all combine to determine the SV at any given intensity of dynamic exercise.

Figure 7.4 illustrates the results of one study of normally active but untrained subjects. In this study, participants were tested during both supine and upright cycle ergometry at rest and at three exercise intensities, which are depicted on the *x*-axis of Figure 7.4.

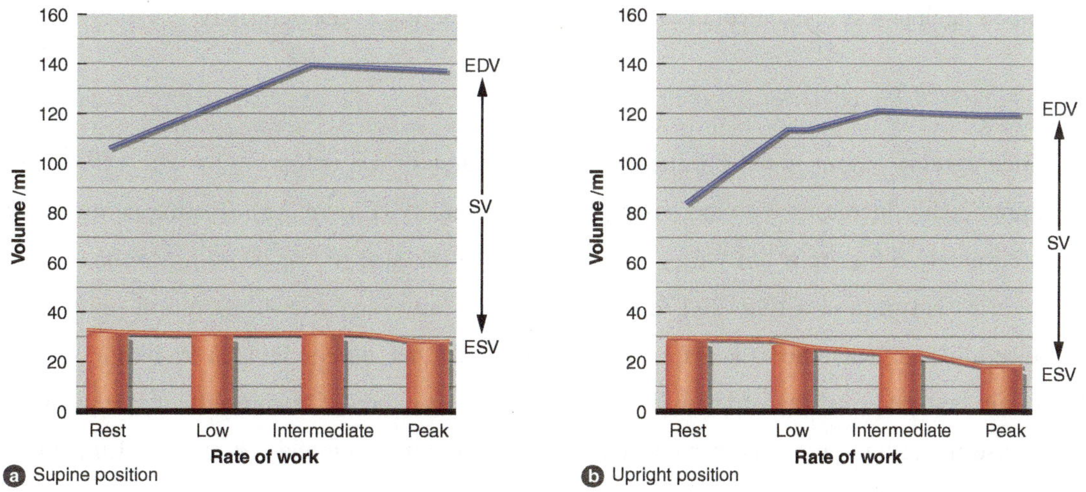

Figure 7.4 Changes in left ventricular end-diastolic volume (EDV) , end-systolic volume (ESV) and stroke volume (SV) at rest and during low-, intermediate-, and peak-intensity exercise when the subject is in the supine and upright positions. Note that SV = EDV − ESV.

Going from resting conditions to exercise of increasing intensity, there is an increase in left ventricular EDV (a greater filling or preload) , which serves to increase SV through the Frank-Starling mechanism. There is also a decrease in the left ventricular end-systolic volume (greater emptying) , indicating an increased force of contraction.

This Figure shows that both the Frank-Starling mechanism and increased contractility are important in increasing SV during exercise. The Frank-Starling mechanism appears to have its greatest influence at lower exercise intensities, and improved contractile force becomes more important at higher exercise intensities.

Recall that HR also increases with exercise intensity. The plateau or small decrease in left ventricular EDV at high exercise intensities could be caused by a reduced ventricular filling time due to the high HR. One study showed that ventricular filling time decreased from about 500–700 ms at rest to about 150 ms at HRs between 150 and 200 beats/min. Therefore, with increasing intensities approaching $\dot{V}O_{2\,max}$ (and HRmax) , the diastolic filling time could be shortened enough to limit filling. As a result, EDV might plateau or even start to decrease.

For the Frank-Starling mechanism to increase SV, left ventricular EDV must increase, necessitating an increased venous return to the heart.

In addition, redistribution of blood flow and volume from inactive tissues such as the splanchnic and renal circulations increases the available central blood volume. The third factor that contributes to the increase in SV during exercise—a decrease in afterload—results from a decrease in total peripheral resistance. Total peripheral resistance decreases because of vasodilation of the blood vessels in exercising skeletal muscle. This decrease in afterload allows the left ventricle to expel blood against less resistance, facilitating greater emptying of the ventricle.

1.4 Cardiac Output

Since cardiac output is the product of heart rate and stroke volume ($\dot{Q}$ = HR × SV, cardiac output predictably increases with increasing exercise intensity (Figure 7.5). Resting cardiac output is approximately 5.0 L/ min but varies in proportion to the size of the person. Maximal cardiac output varies between less than 20 L/min in sedentary individuals to 40 or moreL/min in elite endurance athletes. Maximal $\dot{Q}$ is a function of both body size and endurance training. The linear relationship between cardiac output and exercise intensity is expected because the major purpose of the increase in cardiac output is to meet the muscles' increased demand for oxygen. Like $\dot{V}O_{2\,max}$, when cardiac output approaches maximal exercise intensity it may. reach a plateau (Figure 7.5). In fact, it is likely that $\dot{V}O_{2\,max}$ is ultimately limited by the inability of cardiac output to increase further.

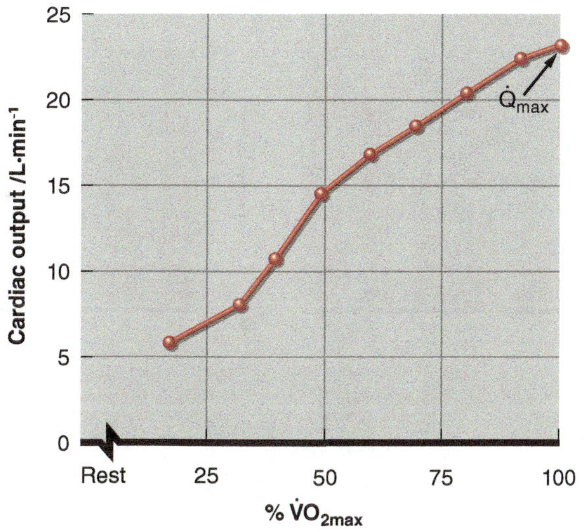

% $\dot{V}O_{2\,max}$

Figure 7.5 The cardiac output ($\dot{Q}$) response to walking/running on a treadmill at increasing intensities plotted as a function of percent $\dot{V}O_{2\,max}$. Cardiac output increases in direct proportion to increasing intensity, eventually reaching a maximum ($\dot{Q}max$).

1.5 The Integrated Cardiac Response to Exercise

To see how HR, SV, and $\dot{Q}$ vary under various conditions of rest and exercise, consider the following example. An individual first moves from a reclining position to a seated posture and then to standing. Next the person begins walking, then jogging, and finally breaks into a fast-paced run. How does the heart respond?

In a reclining position, HR is ~50 beats/min; it increases to about 55 beats/min during sitting and to about 60 beats/min during standing. When the body shifts from a reclining to a sitting position and then to a standing position, gravity causes blood to pool in the legs, which reduces the volume of blood returning to the heart and thus decreases SV. To compensate for the reduction in SV, HR Increases in order to maintain cardiac output; that is, $\dot{Q} = HR \times SV$.

During the transition from rest to walking, HR increases from about 60–about 90 beats/min. Heart rate increases to 140 beats/min with moderate-paced jogging and can reach 180 beats/min or more with a fast-paced run. The initial increase in HR—up to about 100 beats/min—is mediated by a withdrawal of parasympathetic (vagal) tone. Further increases in HR are mediated by increased activation of the sympathetic nervous system. Stroke volume also increases with exercise, further increasing cardiac output. These relationships are illustrated in Figure 7.6.

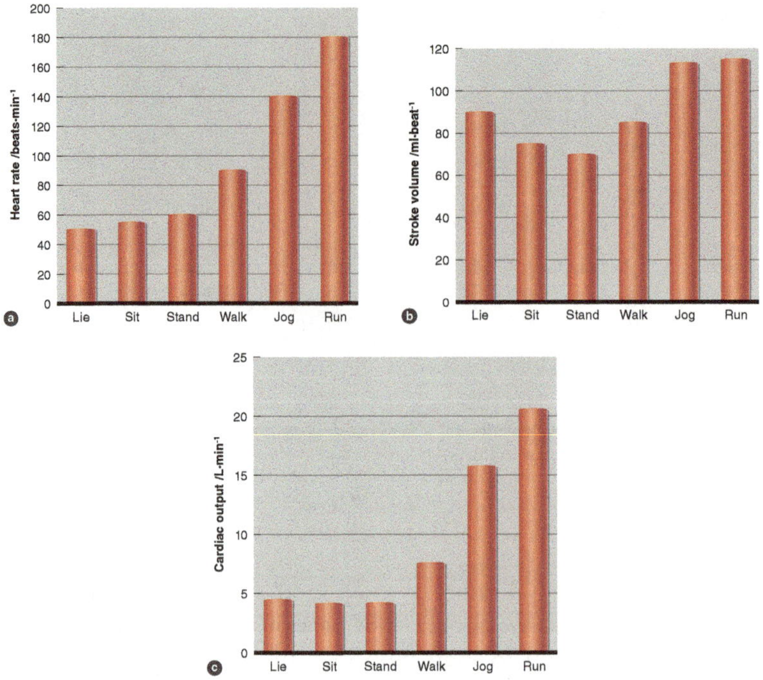

Figure 7.6 Changes in (a) heart rate, (b) stroke volume, and (c) cardiac output with changes in posture (lying supine, siting, and standing upright) and with exercise (walking at 5 km/h), jogging at 11 km/h, and running at 16 km/h) .

During the initial stages of exercise in untrained individuals, increased cardiac output is caused by an increase in both HR and SV. When the level of exercise exceeds 40%–60% of the individual's maximal exercise capacity, SV either plateaus or continues to increase at a much slower rate. Thus, further increases in cardiac output are largely the result of increases in HR. Further stroke volume increases contribute more to the rise in cardiac output at high intensities of exercise in highly trained athletes.

1.6 Blood Pressure

During endurance exercise, systolic blood pressure increases in direct proportion to the increase in exercise intensity. However, diastolic pressure does not change significantly and may even decrease. As a result of the increased systolic pressure, mean arterial blood pressure increases. A systolic pressure that starts out at 120 mmHg in a normal healthy person at rest can exceed 200 mmHg at maximal exercise. Systolic pressures of 240–250 mmHg have been reported in normal, healthy, highly trained athletes at maximal intensities of aerobic exercise.

Increased systolic blood pressure results from the increased cardiac output ($\dot{Q}$) that accompanies increasing rates of work. This increase in pressure helps facilitate the increase in blood flow through the vasculature. Also, blood pressure (that is, hydrostatic pressure) in large part determines how much plasma leaves the capillaries, entering the tissues and carrying needed supplies. Thus increased systolic pressure aids substrate delivery to working muscles.

After increasing initially, mean arterial pressure reaches a steady state during submaximal steady-state endurance exercise. As work intensity increases, so prolonged, the systolic pressure might start to decrease gradually, but diastolic pressure remains constant. The slight decrease in systolic blood pressure, if it occurs, is a normal response and simply reflects increased vasodilation in the active muscles, which decreases the total peripheral resistance, or TPR (since mean arterial pressure = cardiac output × total peripheral resistance).

Diastolic blood pressure changes little during submaximal dynamic exercise; however, at maximal exercise intensities, diastolic blood pressure may increase slightly. Remember that diastolic pressure reflects the pressure in the arteries when the heart is at rest (diastole). With dynamic exercise there is an overall increase in sympathetic tone to the vasculature, causing overall vasoconstriction. However, this vasoconstriction is blunted in the exercising muscles by the release of local vasodilators, a phenomenon called sympatholysis. Thus, because there is a balance between vasoconstriction to inactive regional circulations and vasodilation in active skeletal muscle, diastolic pressure does not change substantially. However, in some cases of cardio-vascular disease, increases in diastolic pressure of 15 mmHg or more occur in response to exercise and are one of several indications for immediately stopping a diagnostic exercise test.

Periodic blood pressure increases during resistance exercise, such as weightlifting, can be extreme. With high-intensity resistance training, blood pressure can briefly reach 480/350 mmHg. Very high pressures like these are more commonly seen when the exerciser performs a Valsalva maneuver to aid heavy lifts. This maneuver occurs when a person tries to exhale while the mouth, nose, and glottis are closed. This action causes an enormous increase in intrathoracic pressure. Much of the subsequent blood pressure increase results from the body's effort to overcome the high internal pressures created during the Valsalva maneuver.

1.7 Blood Flow

Acute increases in cardiac output and blood pressure during exercise allow for increased total blood flow to the body. These responses facilitate increased blood to areas where it is needed, primarily the exercising muscles. Additionally, sympathetic control of the cardiovascular system redistributes blood so that areas with the greatest metabolic need receive more blood than areas with low demands.

1.7.1 Redistribution of Blood During Exercise

Blood flow patterns change markedly in the transition from rest to exercise. Through the vasoconstrictor action of the sympathetic nervous system on local arterioles, blood flow is redirected away from areas where elevated flow is not essential to those areas that are active during exercise (Figure 7.7). Only 15%–20% of the resting cardiac output goes to muscle, but during high-intensity exercise, the muscles may receive 80%–85% of the cardiac output. This shift in blood flow to the muscles is accomplished primarily by reducing blood flow to the kidneys and the so-called splanchnic circulation (which includes the liver, stomach, pancreas, and intestines).

As exercise begins, active skeletal muscles rapidly require increased oxygen delivery. This need is partially met through sympathetic stimulation of vessels in those areas to which blood flow is to be reduced (e.g., the splanchnic and renal circulations).

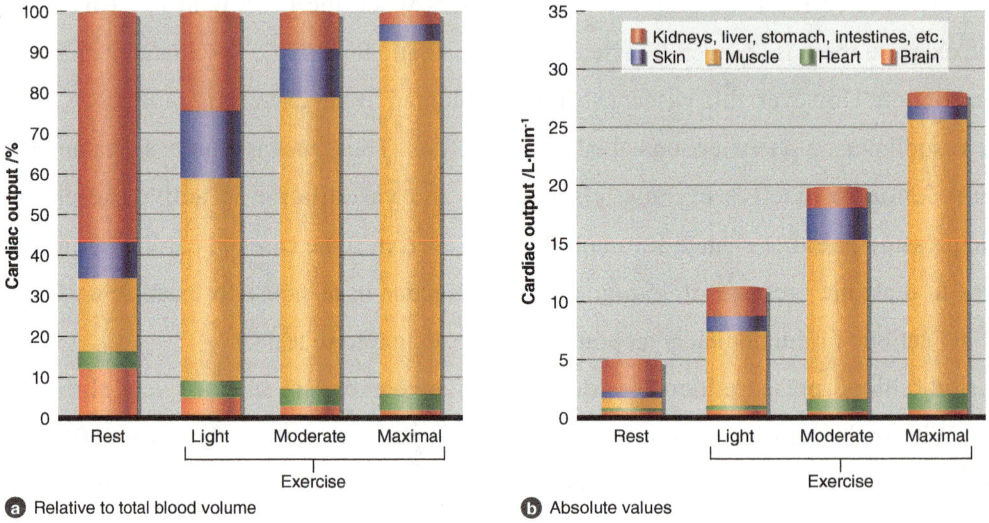

Figure 7.7 The distribution of cardiac output at rest and during exercise.

The resulting vasoconstriction in those areas allows for more of the (increased) cardiac output to be distributed to the exercising skeletal muscles. In the skeletal muscles, sympathetic stimulation to the constrictor fibers in the arteriolar walls also increases; however, local vasodilating substances are released from the exercising muscle and overcome sympathetic vasoconstriction, producing an overall vasodilation in the muscle (sympatholysis). Many local vasodilating substances are released in exercising skeletal muscle. As the metabolic rate of the muscle tissue increases during exercise, metabolic waste products begin to accumulate. Increased metabolism causes an increase in acidity (increased hydrogen ions and lower pH) , carbon dioxide, and temperature in the muscle tissue. These are some of the local changes that trigger vasodilation of, and increasing blood flow through, the arterioles feeding local capillaries. Local vasodilation is also triggered by the low partial pressure of oxygen in the tissue or a reduction in oxygen bound to hemoglobin (increased oxygen demand) , the act of muscle contraction, and possibly other vasoactive substances (including adenosine) released as a result of skeletal muscle contraction.

When exercise is performed in a hot environment, there is also an increase in blood flow to the skin to help dissipate the body heat. The sympathetic control of skin blood flow is unique in that there are sympathetic vasoconstrictor fibers (similar to skeletal muscle) and sympathetic active vasodilator fibers interacting over most of the skin surface area. During dynamic exercise, as body core temperature rises, there is initially a reduction in sympathetic vasoconstriction, causing a passive vasodilation. Once a specific body core temperature threshold is reached, skin blood flow begins to dramatically increase by activation of the sympathetic active vasodilator system. The increase in skin blood flow during exercise promotes heat loss, because metabolic heat from deep in the body can be released only when blood moves close to the skin. This limits the rate of rise in body temperature.

1.7.2 Cardiovascular Drift

With prolonged aerobic exercise or aerobic exercise in a hot environment at a steady-state intensity, SV gradually decreases and HR increases. Cardiac output is well maintained, but arterial blood pressure also declines. These alterations, illustrated in Figure 7.8, have been referred to collectively as cardiovascular drift, and they are generally associated with increasing body temperature and dehydration. Cardiovascular drift is associated with a progressive increase in the fraction of cardiac output directed to the vasodilated skin to facilitate heat loss and attenuate the increase in body core temperature. With more blood in the skin for the purpose of cooling the body, less blood is available to return to the heart, thus decreasing preload. There is also a small decrease in blood volume resulting from sweating and from a generalized shift of plasma across the capillary membrane into the surrounding tissues. These factors combine to decrease ventricular filling pressure, which decreases venous return to the heart and reduces the EDV. With the reduction in EDV, SV is reduced (SV = EDV−ESV). In order to maintain cardiac output ($\dot{Q} = HR \times SV$) , HR increases to compensate for the decrease in SV.

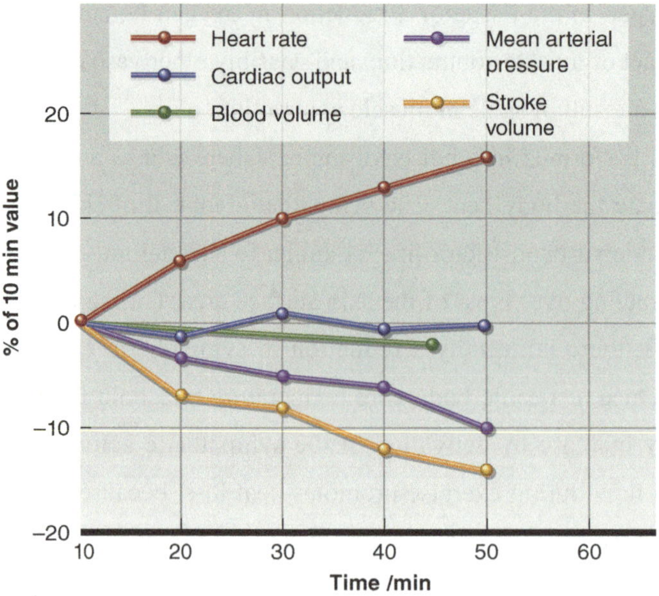

Figure 7.8 Circulatory responses to prolonged, moderately intense exercise in the upright posture in a thermoneutral 20 ℃ environment, illustrating cardiovascular drift. Values are expressed as the percentage of change from the values measured at the 10 min point of the exchange.

1.7.3 Competition for Blood Supply

When the demands of exercise are added to blood flow demands for all other systems of the body, competition for a limited available cardiac output can occur.

For example, there may be competition for available blood flow between active skeletal muscle and the gastrointestinal system following a meal. McKirnan and coworkers studied the effects of feeding versus fasting on the distribution of blood flow during exercise in miniature pigs. The pigs were divided into two groups. One group fasted for 14–17 h before exercise. The other group ate their morning ration in two feedings: Half the ration was fed 90–120 min before exercise and the other half 30–45 min before exercise. Both groups of pigs then ran at approximately 65% of their $\dot{V}O_{2\,max}$.

Blood flow to the hindlimb muscles during exercise was 18% lower, and gastrointestinal blood flow was 23% higher, in the fed group than in the fasted group. Similar results in humans suggest that the redistribution of gastrointestinal blood flow to the working muscles is attenuated after a meal. As a practical application, these findings suggest that athletes should be cautious in timing their meals before competition to maximize blood flow to the active muscles during exercise.

1.8 Blood

As metabolism increases during exercise, several aspects of the blood itself become increasingly critical for optimal performance.

1.8.1 Oxygen Content

At rest, the blood's oxygen content varies from 20 ml of oxygen per 100 ml of arterial blood to 14 ml of oxygen per 100 ml of venous blood returning to the right atrium. The difference between these two values (20 ml–14 ml = 6 ml) is referred to as the arterial-mixed venous oxygen difference, or Ca -$C_{\bar{v}}$ O_2 difference. This value represents the extent to which oxygen is extracted, or removed, from the blood as it passes through the body.

With increasing exercise intensity, the Ca -$C_{\bar{v}}$ O_2 difference increases progressively and can almost triple from rest to maximal exercise intensities. This increased difference really reflects a decreasing venous oxygen content, because arterial oxygen content changes little from rest up to maximal exertion. With exercise, more oxygen is required by the active muscles; therefore more oxygen is extracted from the blood. The venous oxygen content decreases, approaching zero in the active muscles. However, mixed venous blood in the right atrium of the heart rarely decreases below 4 ml of oxygen per 100 ml of blood because the blood returning from the active tissues is mixed with blood from inactive tissues as it returns to the heart. Oxygen extraction by the inactive tissues is far lower than in the active muscles.

1.8.2 Plasma Volume

Approximately a 10%–15% reduction in plasma volume can occur with prolonged exercise, with the largest falls occurring during the first few minutes. During resistance training, the plasma volume loss is proportional to the intensity of the effort, with similar transient losses of fluid from the vascular space of 10%–15%.

If exercise intensity or environmental conditions cause sweating, additional plasma volume losses may occur. Although the major source of fluid for sweat formation is the interstitial fluid, this fluid space will be diminished as sweating continues. This increases the oncotic (since proteins do not move with the fluid) and osmotic (since sweat has fewer electrolytes than interstitial fluid) pressures in the interstitial space, causing even more plasma to move out of the vascular compartment into the interstitial space. Intracellular fluid volume is impossible to measure directly and accurately, but research suggests that fluid is also lost from the intracellular compartment during prolonged exercise and even from the red blood cells, which may shrink in size.

A reduction in plasma volume can impair performance. For long-duration activities in which dehydration occurs and heat loss is a problem, blood flow to active tissues may be reduced to allow increasingly more blood to be diverted to the skin in an attempt to lose body heat. Note that a decrease in muscle blood flow occurs only in conditions of dehydration and only at high intensities. Severely reduced plasma volume also increases blood viscosity, which can impede blood flow and thus limit oxygen transport, especially if the hematocrit exceeds 60%.

In activities that last a few minutes or less, body fluid shifts are of little practical importance. As exercise duration increases, however, body fluid changes and temperature regulation become important for performance. For the football player, the Tour de France cyclist, or the marathon runner, these processes are crucial, not only for competition but also for survival. Deaths have occurred from dehydration and hyperthermia during, or as a result of, various sport activities.

1.8.3 Hemoconcentration

When plasma volume is reduced, hemoconcentration occurs. When the fluid portion of the blood is reduced, the cellular and protein portions represent a larger fraction of the total blood volume; that is, they become more concentrated in the blood. This hemoconcentration increases red blood cell concentration substantially—by up to 20% or 25%. Hematocrit can increase from 40%–50%. However, the total number and volume of red blood cells do not change substantially. As the red blood cell concentration increases, so does the blood's per unit hemoglobin content. This substantially increases the blood's oxygen-carrying capacity, which is advantageous during exercise and provides a distinct advantage at altitude.

1.9 Integration of the Exercise Response

As is evident from all of the changes in cardiovascular function that take place during exercise, the cardiovascular system is extremely complex but responds exquisitely to deliver oxygen to meet the demands of exercising muscle. Figure 7.9 is a simplified flow diagram that illustrates how the body integrates all these cardiovascular responses to provide for its needs during exercise. Key areas and responses are labeled and summarized to help illustrate how these complex control mechanisms are coordinated. It is important to note that although the body attempts to meet the blood flow needs of the muscle, it can do so only if blood pressure is not compromised. Maintenance of arterial blood pressure appears to be the highest priority of the cardiovascular system, irrespective of exercise, the environment, and other competing needs.

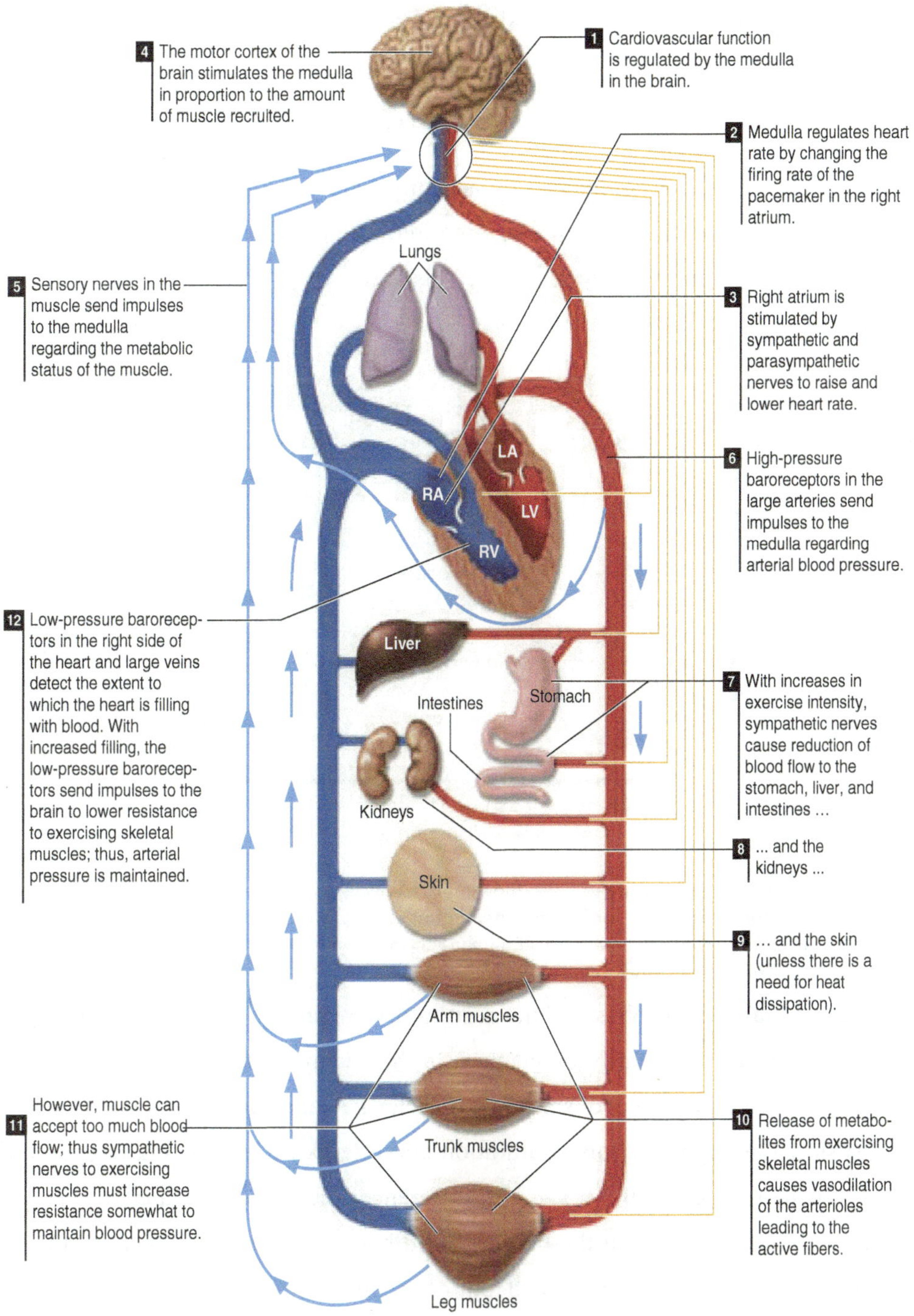

Figure 7.9 Integration of the cardiovascular system's response to exercise.

2 Respiratory Responses to Acute Exercise

2.1 Pulmonary Ventilation During Dynamic Exercise

The onset of exercise is accompanied by an immediate increase in ventilation. In fact, like the HR response, the marked increase in breathing may occur even before the onset of muscular contractions, that is, be an anticipatory response. This is shown in Figure 7.10 for light, moderate, and heavy exercise.

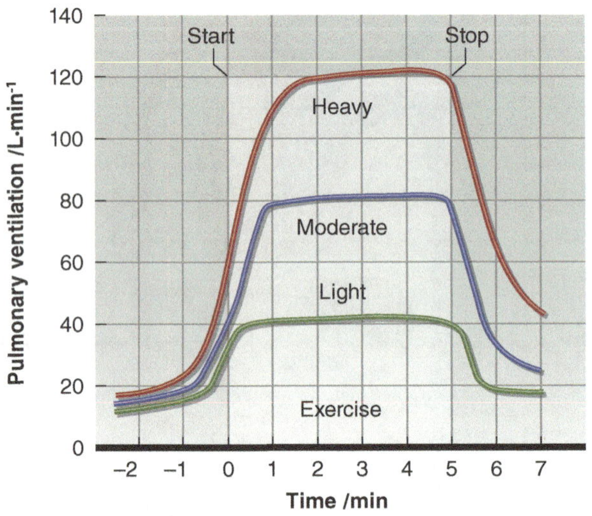

Figure 7.10 The ventilatory response to light, moderate and heavy exercise. The subject exercised at each of the three intensities for 5 min. After an initial steep increase, the ventilation rate tended to plateau at a steady-state value at the light and moderate intensities but continued to increase somewhat at the heavy intensity.

The more gradual second phase of the respiratory increase shown during heavy exercise in Figure 7.10 is controlled primarily by changes in the chemical status of the arterial blood. As exercise progresses, increased metabolism in the muscles generates more CO_2 and H^+. Recall that these changes shift the oxyhemoglobin saturation curve leftward, enhancing oxygen unloading in the muscles, which increases the Ca -$C_{\bar{v}}$ O_2 difference. Increased CO_2 and H^+ are sensed by chemoreceptors primarily located in the brain, carotid bodies, and lungs, which in turn stimulate the inspiratory center, increasing rate and depth of respiration. Chemoreceptors in the muscles themselves might also be involved. In addition, receptors in the right ventricle of the heart send information to the inspiratory center so that increases in cardiac output can stimulate breathing during the early minutes of exercise. The influences of CO_2 and H^+ concentrations in the blood on breathing rate and pattern serve to fine-tune the neutrally mediated respiratory response to exercise in order to precisely match oxygen delivery with aerobic demands without overtaxing respiratory muscles.

At the end of exercise, the muscles' energy demands decrease almost immediately to resting levels. But pulmonary ventilation returns to normal at a slower rate. If the rate of breathing perfectly matched the metabolic demands of the tissues, respiration would decrease to the resting level within seconds after exercise. But respiratory recovery takes several minutes, which suggests that postexercise breathing is regulated primarily by acid-base balance, the partial pressure of dissolved carbon dioxide (PCO_2) , and blood temperature.

2.2 Breathing Irregularities During Exercise

Ideally, breathing during exercise is regulated in a way that maximizes aerobic performance. However, respiratory dysfunction during exercise can hinder performance.

2.2.1 Dyspnea

The sensation of dyspnea (shortness of breath) during exercise is common among individuals with poor aerobic fitness levels who attempt to exercise at intensities that significantly elevate arterial CO_2 and H^+ concentrations. As discussed in Chapter 6, both stimuli send strong signals to the inspiratory center to increase the rate and depth of ventilation. Although exercise-induced dyspnea is sensed as an inability to breathe, the underlying cause is an inability to adjust breathing to blood PCO_2 and H^+.

Failure to reduce these stimuli during exercise appears to be related to poor conditioning of respiratory muscles. Despite a strong neural drive to ventilate the lungs, the respiratory muscles fatigue easily and are unable to reestablish normal homeostasis.

2.2.2 Hyperventilation

The anticipation of or anxiety about exercise, as well as some respiratory disorders, can cause an increase in ventilation in excess of that needed to support exercise. Such over breathing is termed hyperventilation. At rest, hyperventilation can decrease the normal PCO_2 of 40 mmHg in the alveoli and arterial blood to about 15 mmHg. As arterial CO_2 concentrations decrease, blood pH increases. These effects combine to reduce the ventilatory drive. Because the blood leaving the lungs is almost always about 98% saturated with oxygen, an increase in the alveolar PO_2 does not increase the oxygen content of the blood. Consequently, the reduced drive to breathe—along with the improved ability to hold one's breath after hyperventilating—results from carbon dioxide unloading rather than increased blood oxygen. This is sometimes referred to as "blowing off CO_2." Even when performed for only a few seconds, such deep, rapid breathing can lead to light-headedness and even loss of consciousness. This phenomenon reveals the sensitivity of the respiratory system's regulation by carbon dioxide and pH.

2.2.3 Valsalva Maneuver

The Valsalva maneuver is a potentially dangerous respiratory procedure that frequently accompanies certain types of exercise, in particular the lifting of heavy objects. This occurs when the individual

- closes the glottis (the opening between the vocal cords)
- increases the intra-abdominal pressure by forcibly contracting the diaphragm and the abdominal muscles, and
- increases the intrathoracic pressure by forcibly contracting the respiratory muscles

As a result of these actions, air is trapped and pressurized in the lungs. The high intra-abdominal and intra-thoracic pressures restrict venous return by collapsing the great veins. This maneuver, if held for an extended period of time, can greatly reduce the volume of blood returning to the heart, decreasing cardiac output and lowering arterial blood pressure. Although the Valsalva maneuver can be helpful in certain circumstances, this maneuver can be dangerous and should be avoided.

2.3 Ventilation and Energy Metabolism

During long periods of mild steady-state activity, ventilation matches the rate of energy metabolism, varying in proportion to the volume of oxygen consumed and the volume of carbon dioxide produced (O_2 and CO_2, respectively) by the body.

2.3.1 Ventilatory Equivalent for Oxygen

The ratio between the volume of air expired or ventilated ($\dot{V}_E$) and the amount of oxygen consumed by the tissues ($\dot{V}O_2$) in a given amount of time is referred to as the ventilatory equivalent for oxygen, or $\dot{V}_E/\dot{V}O_2$. It is typically measured in liters of air breathed per liter of oxygen consumed per minute.

At rest, the $\dot{V}_E/\dot{V}O_2$ can range from 23–28 L of air per liter of oxygen. This value changes very little during mild exercise, such as walking. But when exercise intensity increases to near-maximal levels, the $\dot{V}_E/\dot{V}O_2$ can be greater than 30 L of air per liter of oxygen consumed. In general, however, the $\dot{V}_E/\dot{V}O_2$ remains relatively constant over a wide range of exercise intensities, indicating that the control of breathing is properly matched to the body's demand for oxygen.

2.3.2 Ventilatory Threshold

As exercise intensity increases, at some point ventilation increases disproportionately to oxygen consumption.

The point at which this occurs, typically between ~55%–70% of $\dot{V}O_{2max}$, is called the ventilatory threshold, illustrated in Figure 7.11. At approximately the same intensity as the ventilatory threshold, more lactate starts to appear in the blood. This may result from greater production of lactate or less clearance of lactate or both. This lactic acid combines with sodium bicarbonate (which buffers acid) and forms sodium lactate, water, and carbon dioxide. As we know, the increase in carbon dioxide stimulates chemoreceptors that signal the inspiratory center to increase ventilation. Thus, the ventilatory threshold reflects the respiratory response to increased carbon dioxide levels. Ventilation increases dramatically beyond the ventilatory threshold, as seen in Figure 7.11.

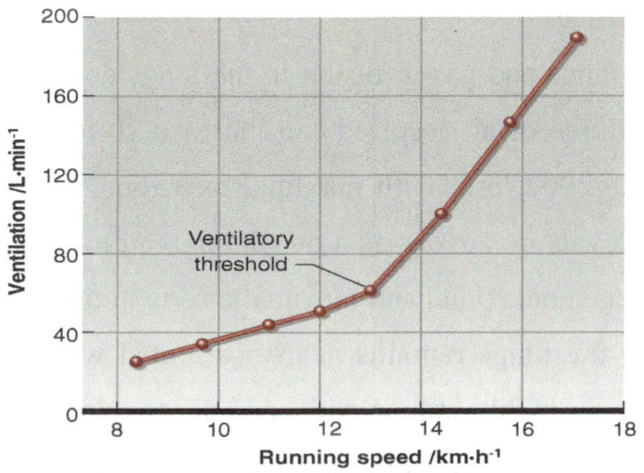

Figure 7.11 Changes in pulmonary ventilation ($\dot{V}_E$) during running at increasing velocities, illustrating the concept of ventilatory threshold.

2.4 Respiratory Limitations to Performance

Like all tissue activity, respiration requires energy. Most of this energy is used by the respiratory muscles during pulmonary ventilation. At rest, the respiratory muscles account for only about 2% of the total oxygen uptake. As the rate and depth of ventilation increase, so does the energy cost of respiration. The diaphragm, the intercostal muscles, and the abdominal muscles can account for up to 11% of the total oxygen consumed during heavy exercise and can receive up to 15% of the cardiac output. During recovery from dynamic exercise, sustained elevations in ventilation continue to demand increased energy, accounting for 9%–12% of the total oxygen consumed postexercise.

Although the muscles of respiration are heavily taxed during exercise, ventilation is sufficient to prevent an increase in alveolar PCO_2 or a decline in alveolar PO_2 during activities lasting only a few minutes. Even during maximal effort, ventilation usually is not pushed to its maximal capacity to voluntarily move air in and out of the lungs. This capacity is called the maximal voluntary ventilation and is significantly greater than ventilation at maximal exercise. However, considerable evidence suggests that pulmonary ventilation might be a limiting factor during very high intensity (95%–100% $\dot{V}O_{2\,max}$) exercise in highly trained subjects.

Can heavy breathing for several hours (such as during marathon running) cause glycogen depletion and fatigue of the respiratory muscles? Animal studies have shown a substantial sparing of their respiratory muscle glycogen compared with muscle glycogen in exercising muscles. Although similar data are not available for humans, our respiratory muscles are better designed for long-term activity than are the muscles in our extremities. The diaphragm, for example, has two to three times more oxidative capacity (oxidative enzymes and mitochondria) and capillary density than other skeletal muscle. Consequently, the diaphragm can obtain more energy from oxidative sources than can skeletal muscles.

Similarly, airway resistance and gas diffusion in the lungs do not limit exercise in a normal, healthy individual. The volume of air inspired can increase 20-to 40-fold with exercise—from ~5 L/min at rest up to 100–200 L/min with maximal exertion. Airway resistance, however, is maintained at near-resting levels by airway dilation (through an increase in the laryngeal aperture and bronchodilation). During submaximal and maximal efforts in untrained and moderately trained individuals, blood leaving the lungs remains nearly saturated with oxygen (~98%). However, with maximal exercise in some highly trained elite endurance athletes, there is too large a demand on lung gas exchange, resulting in a decline in arterial PO_2 and arterial oxygen saturation (i.e., exercise-induced arterial hypoxemia, or EIAH). Approximately 40%–50% of elite endurance athletes experience a significant reduction in arterial oxygenation during exercise approaching exhaustion. Arterial hypoxemia at maximal exercise is likely the result of a mismatch between ventilation and perfusion of the lung. Since cardiac output is extremely high in elite athletes, blood is flowing through the lungs at a high rate and thus there may not be sufficient time for that blood to become saturated with oxygen. Thus, in healthy individuals, the respiratory system is well designed to accommodate the demands of heavy breathing during short- and long-term physical effort.

However, some highly trained individuals who consume unusually large amounts of oxygen during exhaustive exercise can face respiratory limitations.

2.5 Respiratory Regulation of Acid-Base Balance

As noted earlier, high-intensity exercise results in the production and accumulation of lactate and H^+. Although regulation of acid-base balance involves more than control of respiration, it is discussed here because the respiratory system plays such a crucial role in rapid adjustment of the body's acid-base status during and immediately after exercise.

Acids, such as lactic acid and carbonic acid, release hydrogen ions (H^+). As noted in Chapter 2, the metabolism of carbohydrate, fat, or protein produces inorganic acids that dissociate, increasing the H^+ concentration in body fluids, thus lowering the pH. To minimize the effects of free H^+, the blood and muscles contain base substances that combine with, and thus buffer or neutralize, the H^+:

H^+ + buffer → H-buffer.

Under resting conditions, body fluids have more bases (such as bicarbonate, phosphate, and proteins) than acids, resulting in a slightly alkaline tissue pH that ranges from 7.1 in muscle to 7.4 in arterial blood. The tolerable limits for arterial blood pH extend from 6.9–7.5, although the extremes of this range can be tolerated only for a few minutes. An H^+ concentration above normal (low pH) is referred to as acidosis, whereas a decrease in H^+ below the normal concentration (high pH) is termed alkalosis.

The pH of intracellular and extracellular body fluids is kept within a relatively narrow range by

- chemical buffers in the blood,
- pulmonary ventilation, and
- kidney function.

The three major chemical buffers in the body are bicarbonate (HCO_3^-) , inorganic phosphates (Pi) , and proteins. In addition to these, hemoglobin in the red blood cells is also a major buffer. Table 7.1 illustrates the relative contributions of these buffers in handling acids in the blood.

Table 7.1 Buffering Capacity of Blood Components

Buffer	Slykes*	%
Bicarbonate	18.0	64
Hemoglobin	8.0	29
Proteins	1.7	6
Phosphates	0.3	1
Total	28.0	100

*Milliequivalents of hydrogen ions taken up by each liter of blood from pH 7.4–7.0.

The amount of bicarbonate that combines with H^+ equals the amount of acid buffered. When lactic acid decreases the pH from 7.4–7.0, more than 60% of the bicarbonate initially present in the blood has been used. Even under resting conditions, the acid produced by the end products of metabolism would use up a major portion of the bicarbonate from the blood if there were no other way of removing H^+ from the body. Blood and chemical buffers are required only to transport metabolic acids from their sites of production (the muscles) to the lungs or kidneys, where they can be removed. Once H^+ is transported and removed, the buffer molecules can be reused.

In the muscle fibers and the kidney tubules, H^+ is primarily buffered by phosphates, such as phosphoric acid and sodium phosphate.

As noted earlier, any increase in free H^+ in the blood stimulates the respiratory center to increase ventilation. This facilitates the binding of H^+ to bicarbonate and the removal of carbon dioxide. The end result is a decrease in free H^+ and an increase in blood pH. Thus, both the chemical buffers and the respiratory system provide short-term means of neutralizing the acute effects of exercise acidosis. To maintain a constant buffer reserve, the accumulated H^+ is removed from the body via excretion by the kidneys and eliminated in urine. The kidneys filter H^+ from the blood along with other waste products. This provides a way to eliminate H^+ from the body while maintaining the concentration of extracellular bicarbonate.

During sprint exercise, muscle glycolysis generates a large amount of lactate and H^+, which lowers the muscle pH from a resting level of 7.1–less than 6.7. As shown in Table 7.2, an all-out 400 m sprint decreases leg muscle pH to 6.63 and increases muscle lactate from a resting value of 1.2 mmol/kg to almost 20 mmol/kg of muscle. Such disturbances in acid-base balance can impair muscle contractility and its capacity to generate adenosine triphosphate (ATP). Lactate and H^+ accumulate in the muscle, in part because they do not freely diffuse across the skeletal muscle fiber membranes. Despite the great production of lactate and H^+ during the ~60s required to run 400 m, these by-products diffuse throughout the body fluids and reach equilibrium after only about 5–10 min of recovery. Five minutes after the exercise, the runners described in Table 7.2 had blood pH values of 7.10 and blood lactate concentrations of 12.3 mmol/L, compared with a resting pH of 7.40 and a resting lactate level of 1.5 mmol/L.

Table 7.2 Blood and Muscle pH and Lactate Concentration 5 min After a 400 m Run

Runner	Time /s	MUSCLE		BLOOD	
		pH	Lactate /mmol · kg^{-1}	pH	Lactate /mmol · kg^{-1}
1	61.0	6.68	19.7	7.12	12.6
2	57.1	6.59	20.5	7.14	13..4
3	65.0	6.59	20.5	7.02	13.1
4	58.5	6.68	18.2	7.10	10.1
Average	60.4	6.64	19.7	7.10	12..3

Reestablishing normal resting concentrations of blood and muscle lactate after such an exhaustive exercise bout is a relatively slow process, often requiring 1–2 h. As shown in Figure 7.12, recovery of blood lactate to the resting level is facilitated by continued lower-intensity exercise, called active recovery. After a series of exhaustive sprint bouts, the participants in this study either sat quietly (passive recovery) or exercised at an intensity of 50% $\dot{V}O_{2\,max}$. Blood lactate is removed more quickly during active recovery because the activity maintains elevated blood flow through the active muscles, which in turn enhances both lactate diffusion out of the muscles and lactate oxidation.

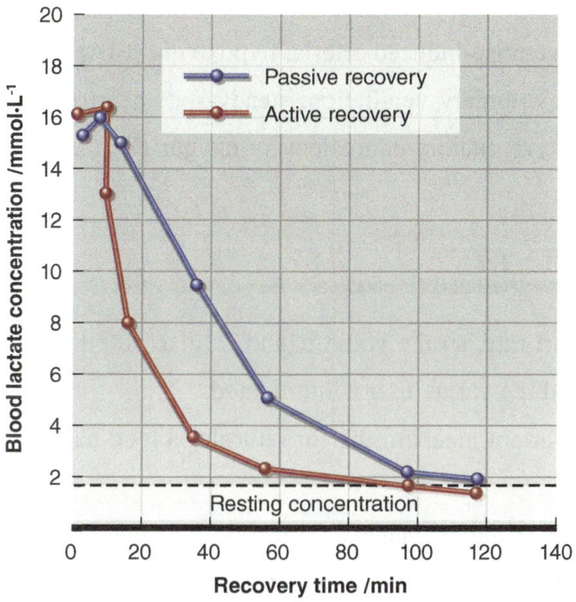

Figure 7.12 Effects of active and passive recovery on blood lactate levels after a series of exhaustive sprint bouts. Note that the blood lactate removal rate is faster when the subjects perform exercise during recovery than when they rest during recovery.

Although blood lactate remains elevated for 1–2 h after highly anaerobic exercise, blood and muscle H^+ concentrations return to normal within 30–40 min of recovery. Chemical buffering, principally by bicarbonate, and respiratory removal of excess carbon dioxide are responsible for this relatively rapid return to normal acid-base homeostasis.

IN CLOSING

In this chapter, we discussed the responses of the cardiovascular and respiratory systems to exercise. We also considered the limitations that these systems can impose on abilities to perform sustained aerobic exercise. The next chapter presents basic principles of exercise training, allowing us to better understand in the subsequent chapters how the body adapts to resistance training as well as aerobic and anaerobic training.

KEY TERMS

cardiovascular drift; exercise-induced arterial hypoxemia (EIAH) ; Frank-Starling mechanism; hyperventilation; maximal voluntary ventilation; steady-state heart rate; total peripheral resistance (TPR) ; Valsalva maneuver; ventilatory equivalent for oxygen ($\dot{V}_E$ / $\dot{V}O_2$) ; ventilatory threshold

STUDY QUESTIONS

(1) Describe how heart rate, stroke volume, and cardiac output respond to increasing rates of work. Illustrate how these three variables are interrelated.

(2) Describe two important mechanisms for returning blood back to the heart during exercise in an upright position.

(3) Define the Frank-Starling mechanism. How does this work during exercise?

(4) How does blood pressure respond to exercise?

(5) What are the major cardiovascular adjustments that the body makes when someone is overheated during exercise?

(6) How does pulmonary ventilation respond to increasing intensities of exercise?

第七章
一次性运动的心肺功能反应

一、一次性运动的心血管反应

运动时心血管系统会发生许多变化，以满足运动时身体各部分需求的增加。本章将介绍心血管系统各组成部分的变化，特别是心率、每搏输出量、心输出量、血压、血流量和血液的变化，以及这些变化如何彼此协调满足运动时机体的需要。

1.心率

（1）安静心率。大部分人的安静心率为60～80次/分，耐力项目运动员的安静心率可以降到28～40次/分，这主要是迷走神经兴奋性增强所致。安静心率也会受环境因素影响，必须在完全放松的状态下，如经过充足睡眠后，清晨醒来时测定。

（2）运动时心率。运动开始时，心率会随着运动强度的增大成比例增加。当接近最高运动强度时，心率出现平台期，不会随着运动强度的增大而继续增加，意味着心率已接近最大值。最大心率（HRmax）相对可靠，不易发生变化。最大心率会随着年龄增加而逐渐降低。最大心率可以用“220－年龄”进行估算，但个体间存在显著差异。较为准确的公式为：HRmax = 208 －（0.7 × 年龄）。当以次最高强度恒定速率运动时，心率迅速升高，并达到平台期，称为稳定状态心率（steady-state heart rate），随着运动强度继续增加，心率在2～3分钟内达到新的稳定状态。运动强度越大，达到稳定状态的时间就越长。稳定状态心率可作为评定身体能力的基础指标，较低的稳定状态心率表示心肺机能较好。

2. 菲克定律和菲克公式

菲克定律是理解人体代谢和心血管功能基本关系的关键。它认为一个组织的氧气消耗量依赖于该组织的血流量以及从血液中摄取的氧量。耗氧量是血流量和动-静脉氧之差的乘积。

菲克公式：$\dot{V}O_2 = \dot{Q} \times (a - \bar{v})\ O_2$ difference

$\dot{V}O_2 = HR \times SV \times (a - \bar{v})\ O_2$ difference

3. 每搏输出量

运动时每搏输出量（SV）会发生变化以适应运动的需求，在接近或达到最高强度运动时，每搏输出量是心肺耐力的主要决定因素。每搏输出量由以下四个因素决定：

- 从静脉回流到心脏的血流量（心脏只能泵出回流到心脏的血液）；
- 心室的扩张力（心室扩张时能够充盈血液的能力）；
- 心室的收缩力（心室收缩的内在能力）；
- 主动脉或肺动脉压（心室收缩泵出血液时的阻力）。

前两个因素影响心室的充盈能力和心脏舒张末期的容积，决定能够进入心室的血流量，以及在一定压力下心室充盈的难易程度，称为前负荷（preload）。后两个因素影响心室排空血液的能力，决定血液从心室射入动脉的力量和对动脉产生的压力，称为后负荷（afterload）。

（1）运动时每搏输出量的增加。大多数研究者认为当运动强度在最高运动强度的40%～60%时，每搏输出量随运动强度的增加而增长。超过此范围后，每搏输出量到达平台期，并且在力竭之前，每搏输出量不会发生变化。

以直立位进行中低强度运动时，每搏输出量的增加主要是补充由于重力引起血液滞留下肢的现象。在直立位进行最高强度运动时，每搏输出量大约是安静时的2倍。当机体处于仰卧位运动时，血液不会聚集在下肢，容易回流到心脏，安静时的每搏输出量水平基线大于直立位，因此仰卧位运动每搏输出量只会提高安静时的20%～40%。

（2）每搏输出量增加的原因。在心室舒张期，大量的血液进入心室，心室舒张得越充分，心室产生的收缩力越大，这一现象称为Frank-Starling调节。此外，运动时交感神经兴奋性增高，血液中儿茶酚胺（肾上腺素和去甲肾上腺素）释放量增加，使得心室收缩力度增强。Frank-Starling调节对低强度运动时每搏输出量的影响较为明显，而心室收缩力增加则在较高强度运动时影响较大。

在中低强度运动时，左心室舒张末期容积增加（前负荷较大），而在高强度运动时，由于心室血液充盈时间缩短，心室舒张末期容积会出现平台期或小幅下降。此时，交感神经调节肾脏等腹腔区域动脉收缩，完成血液再分配；同时，肌肉和呼吸泵也会辅助增加静脉回流量。此外，由于运动肌肉的血管舒张，外周总血管阻力减小，使心脏的后负荷降低，左心室排空血液的阻力减小，促进腔室血液的排空。

4. 心输出量

心输出量等于心率乘以每搏输出量（$\dot{Q} = HR \times SV$）。安静时人体的心输出量大约为5.0 升/分，不同体型的人之间存在差异。心输出量与运动强度之间存在一定的线性关系。与最大摄氧量（$\dot{V}O_{2max}$）一样，在接近最高运动强度运动时，心输出量会出现平台期，心输出量的水平可能限制了最大摄氧量的增加。

5.心脏对运动的整体反应

在安静和运动等不同状态下，心率、每搏输出量和心输出量都会发生变化。

人体从斜躺到直立的过程中，血液由于重力滞留在下肢，回心血流量减少，每搏输出量也减少。为了弥补每搏输出量的下降，心率增加，以维持心输出量的稳定。

从安静状态到行走，心率最初的增加主要是由迷走神经调节减弱所致，而后续心率持续增加是由交感神经调节增强所引起的。随着运动的继续，每搏输出量和心输出量持续增加。

未经训练的人在运动的起始阶段，心率和每搏输出量都同时增加。当运动强度超过40%～60% $\dot{V}O_{2max}$时，每搏输出量出现平台期或是小幅增加，此时，心输出量依赖心率的增加而增大。对于高水平运动员而言，在进行较高强度运动时，心输出量大部分是依赖每搏输出量的增加而增大的。

6.血压

运动时，平均动脉压升高，收缩压和舒张压的增长幅度不同。在全身性耐力运动时，收缩压随运动强度的增高而明显升高，而舒张压不会显著增加，甚至会略有下降。

运动强度增加，心输出量增大，从而导致收缩压升高。血压升高，血管中血流量增加，使更多的血浆（流体静压）流出毛细血管进入组织。因此，收缩压的升高有助于将物质运送到工作肌肉。

在进行次最高强度耐力运动时，血压保持相对恒定。当运动强度增高时，收缩压也会随之升高。当运动强度保持恒定时，由于活跃的肌肉内小动脉扩张增大，总外周血管阻力（TPR）下降（血压 = 心输出量 × 总外周血管阻力），收缩压可能会缓慢下降，但舒张压保持恒定。在进行最高强度运动时，舒张压会缓慢升高。运动时，交感神经作用增加，血管收缩，但在运动肌肉中，局部舒张因子的释放会阻碍血管的收缩，使舒张压基本不变。

在训练中常会发生瓦尔沙瓦现象（Valsalva maneuver），是指人体在口、鼻及声门关闭时还努力呼气，导致胸腔内压急速增加，从而机体的血压升高以克服胸内压增大引起的静脉血液回流受阻。

7.血流量

运动时，全身血流量上升，并且交感神经会对心血管系统进行调节，使代谢需求高的组织接收更多血液。

（1）运动时血液的重新分配。当运动开始时，活跃的骨骼肌对氧气的需求快速增加。在交感神经的调节下，内脏血管收缩；但肌肉中，释放的舒张因子能克服交感神经引起的小动脉收缩，产生总的扩张效应，使更多的血液被输送到运动的肌肉中。

皮肤血流的交感神经调节较为特殊，包括了交感缩血管纤维和交感舒血管纤维的作用。在运动过程中，皮肤的血流量最初因交感神经兴奋刺激血管收缩而暂时降低；随着机体核心温度升高，交感神经缩血管作用减弱，交感舒血管纤维兴奋，血管舒张，皮肤血流量显著增加，促进散热。

（2）心血管的变化。长时间或热环境下进行恒定强度的有氧运动时，每搏输出量逐渐下降，心率逐渐升高，心输出量维持不变，而动脉血压则会降低，这些现象与体温升高和机体脱水有直接的关系。在整个变化过程中，心输出量增加，一部分会直接流入扩张的皮肤，用于散热和降低核心体温。皮肤血流量增加，回心血量减少，从而降低前负荷。此外，由于排汗和血浆经毛细血管渗出到周围组织中，血流量降低，使得回心血量减少，舒张末期心室容积下降，心室充盈压降低，从而引起每搏输出量下降。为了维持心输出量，心率必须上升以弥补每搏输出量的不足。

（3）血液供应的竞争。当运动强度增加时，身体各系统对血液的需求增加，相互间产生竞争。进食后再做运动，本该流向运动肌的血液量被分配到了肠胃。因此，运动员在比赛前必须注意用餐时间，保证骨骼肌在运动时可以得到最大血流供应。

8. 血液

血液对运动能力的影响很大。

（1）氧含量。动脉血含氧量在安静和运动时差异并不大，但运动时，肌肉需要较多的氧，血液耗氧量增加，静脉血含氧量减少，动脉–混合静脉血氧含量差增大。

（2）血容量。长时间运动或出汗时，血浆量会减少，甚至连红细胞中的水分也会丢失，发生皱缩。血浆量的减少，会引起皮肤血流减少，散热困难，血流变慢，血液黏稠度增加，肌肉血流减少，运动能力下降，严重时甚至危及生命。

（3）血液浓缩。血浆量下降，血液变浓稠，但血红蛋白的数目和细胞体积实质上并没有变化。

9. 运动时心血管的整体反应

心血管系统输送氧的方式是复杂且精细的。需要注意的是，无论是运动还是环境等其他所需，心血管系统的第一要务是维持动脉血压，机体只在血压没有降低的状况下才会尽可能供应肌肉所需的血流。

二、一次性运动的呼吸反应

1.运动时的肺通气

运动开始的第一阶段，肺通气量会迅速增加，到第二阶段，位于脑、颈动脉体和肺的化学感受器感受血液中化学成分变化，刺激呼吸中枢，增加呼吸频率与幅度。有研究表明，骨骼肌中的化学感受器也可能参与调节。此外，右心室受体把心输出量增加的信息发送到呼吸中枢，能在运动开始时促使呼吸加强。体液对呼吸深浅和频率产生的精细调节，使氧的运送与有氧代谢的需求相匹配，避免呼吸肌过度工作。

运动结束时，肌肉对于能量的需求下降至接近安静水平，但肺通气量恢复到安静水平的速率较慢，通常需要几分钟后才会恢复到安静水平。这表明运动后的呼吸反应主要受到酸碱平衡、二氧化碳分压和血液温度的影响。

2.运动时的呼吸异常

（1）呼吸困难。呼吸肌功能不足时，即使呼吸中枢传来增加呼吸的指令，但因为呼吸肌疲劳，无法调整收缩来调节体内二氧化碳和氢离子的浓度，常出现呼吸困难。

（2）过度换气。肺通气量超过身体代谢所需的状况称为过度换气（hyperventilation）。因为动脉血氧饱和浓度超过98%，所以过度换气不会增加血液含氧量。但过度换气使肺泡和动脉血液二氧化碳分压从40 毫米汞柱下降到15 毫米汞柱左右，血液二氧化碳浓度下降，导致血液pH值上升，反而会抑制呼吸。过度换气常会引起头晕甚至失去意识，说明呼吸调节系统对血液二氧化碳和pH值的变化相当敏感。

（3）瓦尔沙瓦现象。在进行某些特定运动，如举重物时，运动员常关闭声门，并剧烈收缩膈肌、腹肌和呼吸肌，引起空气滞留，肺部压力、腹内压和胸腔内压都增加，大静脉被压迫，静脉血液不容易流回心脏。若闭气用力过久，回心血量大幅减少，随之，心输出量减少，动脉血压改变。虽然闭气式呼吸有时对克服负荷会有帮助，但有潜在的危险，最好避免。

3.肺通气和能量代谢

（1）氧通气当量。单位时间内呼出气体量或是通气量（$\dot{V}_E$）和组织耗氧量（$\dot{V}O_2$）的比率称为氧通气当量（Ventilatory Equivalent for Oxygen），表示为$\dot{V}_E / \dot{V}O_2$，用每分钟每消耗一升氧气所需要呼吸的气体量来表示。通常，在较大范围的运动强度内，呼吸的调节能满足机体对氧的需求，$\dot{V}_E / \dot{V}O_2$都会维持相对恒定水平。

（2）通气阈。随着运动强度的增高，通气量会在某一点突然增加，与耗氧量的增长不成比例，这个拐点称为通气阈。这个拐点一般也对应着血乳酸浓度变化的拐点。血乳酸与碳酸钠结合，生成乳酸钠、水和二氧化碳，而二氧化碳的增加可以刺激化学感受器，增加肺通气。因此，通气阈反映呼吸对二氧化碳水平升高的反应。

4.限制运动能力的呼吸因素

呼吸过程所消耗的能量大部分用于肺通气时呼吸肌的收缩。无论是安静状态还是高强度运动状态，呼吸肌消耗占总摄氧量的比例很低。呼吸肌的氧化能力和毛细血管密度比骨骼肌高，可以从氧化反应中获得更多的能量，因此比骨骼肌更能承受长时间的运动。

运动过程中，气道阻力不会限制健康人的运动能力，而肺通气量却达不到最大能力水平，不能使空气随意进出肺部。肺通气水平可能是高水平运动员进行高强度运动的一个限制因素。高水平耐力运动员在进行最高强度运动时，肺部气体交换的需求量极大，而心输出量水平较高，血流流经肺部时速度较快，通气/血流比不匹配，造成动脉氧饱和度降低，动脉血含氧量下降。因此，健康者的呼吸系统功能足以应付短时间或长时间运动通气所需，反而是一些高度训练的运动员在进行力竭运动时，因为氧消耗量大，面临肺通气功能的限制。

5.呼吸对酸碱平衡的调节

通过血液中的缓冲物质、肺通气和肾脏三个调节途径，细胞内外液的pH值变动范围很小。代谢反应所产生的大部分酸可以利用血液中的碳酸氢盐离子来缓冲；在肌纤维和肾小管中，主要是利用磷酸盐，如磷酸钾或磷酸钠来缓冲H^+。H^+的增加可以刺激呼吸中枢，促进二氧化碳的排出。因此，化学缓冲和呼吸系统都可以减轻运动引起的酸中毒；同时，过多的H^+及其他代谢产物也会经尿液排出体外。

力竭运动后，血液和肌肉中乳酸浓度恢复到安静状态是一个比较缓慢的过程。如果运动后继续进行一段低强度运动，会让血液维持较高的流量，反而有助于乳酸从肌肉中移出并被氧化代谢。

虽然高强度无氧运动后1～2个小时血乳酸的水平仍然较高，但是血液和肌肉中H^+只需30～40分钟就能恢复到正常值。碳酸氢盐等物质的缓冲和呼吸排出二氧化碳，对酸碱平衡的快速恢复发挥了重要作用。

Chapter 8
Principles of Exercise Training

When one performs regular exercise over a period of days, weeks, and months, a variety of physiological adaptations occur. The positive adaptations that accompany proper training principles lead to improvement in both exercise capacity and sport performance. With resistance training, muscles become stronger. With aerobic training, the heart and lungs become more efficient at oxygen delivery, and exercise endurance increases. With high-intensity anaerobic training, the neuromuscular, metabolic, and cardiovascular systems adapt to generate more adenosine triphosphate (ATP) per unit of time, thus increasing muscular endurance and speed of movement over short periods of time. These adaptations are highly specific to the type of training performed.

1 General Principles of Training

Some specific physiological adaptations result from resistance training, aerobic training, and anaerobic training. Several principles, however, apply to all forms of exercise training.

1.1 Principle of Individuality

Individuals do not all possess the same inherent ability to respond to an acute exercise bout or the same capacity to adapt to exercise training. Heredity plays a major role in determining the body's response to a single bout of exercise, as well as the chronic changes that result from a training program. This is the principle of individuality. Except for identical twins, no two people have exactly the same genetic characteristics, so individuals are unlikely to exhibit the same responses. Variations in cellular growth rates, metabolism, cardiovascular and respiratory regulation, and neural and endocrine regulation lead to tremendous individual variation. Such individual variation likely explains why some people show great improvement after participating in a given program (high responders) whereas others experience little or no change after following the same program (low responders). For these reasons, any training program must take into account the specific needs and abilities of the individuals for whom it is designed. Do not expect all individuals to have exactly the same degree of improvement, even when they train exactly the same.

1.2 Principle of Specificity

Training adaptations are highly specific to the type of activity being performed and to the volume and intensity of the exercise. To improve muscular power, for example, a shot-putter would not emphasize distance running or slow, low-intensity resistance training. The shot-putter needs to develop explosive power. Similarly, the marathon runner would not focus on sprint training.

This is likely the reason that athletes who train for strength and power, such as weightlifters, often have great strength but don't have highly developed aerobic endurance when compared to untrained people. According to the principle of specificity, exercise adaptations are specific to the mode, intensity, and duration of training, and the training program must stress the physiological systems that are critical for optimal performance in a given sport in order to achieve specific training adaptations and goals.

1.3 Principle of Reversibility

Resistance training improves muscle strength and the capacity to resist fatigue. Likewise, endurance training improves the ability to perform aerobic exercise at higher intensities and for longer periods. But if training is decreased or stopped (detraining) , the physiological adaptations that caused those improvements in performance will be reversed. Any gains achieved with training will eventually be lost. The principle of reversibility lends scientific support to the saying "Use it or lose it." All effective training programs must include a maintenance plan that sustains the physiological adaptations gained by training.

1.4 Principle of Progressive Overload

Two important concepts, overload and progressive training, form the foundation of all training programs. According to the principle of progressive overload, systematically increasing the demands on the body is necessary for continued improvement. For example, when undergoing a strength training program, in order to gain strength the muscles must be overloaded, which means they must be loaded beyond the point to which they are normally loaded. Progressive resistance training implies that as the muscles become stronger, either increased resistance or increased repetitions or both are required to stimulate further strength increases.

As an example, consider a young woman who can perform only 10 repetitions of a bench press before reaching fatigue, using 30 kg of weight. With a week or two of resistance training, she should be able to increase to 14 or 15 repetitions with the same weight. She then adds 2.3 kg to the bar, and her repetitions decrease to 8 or 10. As she continues to train, the repetitions continue to increase, and within another week or two, she is ready to add another 2.3 kg of weight. Thus, improvement depends on a progressive increase in the amount of weight lifted. In a similar way, training volume (intensity and duration) must be increased progressively with anaerobic and aerobic training for further improvements to occur.

1.5 Principle of Variation

The principle of variation, also called the principle of periodization, first proposed in the 1960s, has become very popular in the area of resistance training. Periodization is the systematic process of changing one or more variables in the training program—mode, volume, or intensity—over time to allow for the training stimulus to remain challenging and effective. Training intensity and volume of training are the most commonly manipulated aspects of training to achieve peak levels of fitness for competition. Classical periodization involves high initial training volume with low intensity; then, as training progresses, volume decreases and intensity gradually increases. Undulating periodization uses more frequent variation within a training cycle.

For sport-specific training, the volume and intensity of training are varied over a macrocycle, which is generally up to a year of training. A macrocycle is composed of two or more mesocycles that are dictated by the dates of major competitions. Each mesocycle is subdivided into periods of preparation, competition, and transition.

2 Resistance Training Programs

Over the past 75 years, research has provided a substantial knowledge base concerning resistance training and its application to health and sport. This section concerns primarily the use of resistance training for sport.

2.1 Recommendations for Resistance Training Programs

Resistance training programs can be designed and prescribed in terms of

- the exercises that will be performed;
- the order in which they will be performed;
- the number of sets for each exercise;
- the rest periods between sets and between exercises; and
- the amount of resistance, the number of repetitions, and the velocity of movement to be used.

In 2009, the American College of Sports Medicine (ACSM) revised its position stand on progressive resistance training for healthy adults (Table 8.1). Previous statements specified, for all adults, a minimum of one set of 8–12 reps for each of 8–10 different exercises that together involve all of the major muscle groups. The new position stand recommends resistance training models specific to desired outcomes, that is, improvements in strength, muscle hypertrophy, power, local muscular endurance, or gross motor performance.

Resistance programs aimed at improving strength should involve repetitions with both concentric (muscle shortening) and eccentric (muscle lengthening) actions. Isometric contractions play a beneficial, but secondary, role and may be included as well. Concentric strength improvement is greatest when eccentric exercises are included, and eccentric training has been shown to produce specific benefits for those action-specific movements. Large muscle groups should be stressed before smaller groups, multiple-joint exercises before single-joint exercises, and higherintensity efforts before those of lower intensity. Table 8.1 provides a summary of the ACSM recommendations on loading, volume (sets and reps) , velocity of movements, and frequency of training.

It is recommended that rest periods of 2–3 min or more be used between heavy loads for novice and intermediate lifters; for advanced lifters, 1 or 2 min may suffice. Once an individual can perform the current workload at or above the desired number of reps for two consecutive training sessions, a 2%–10% increase in load should be applied. While both machine-based exercises and free weights can be used for novice and intermediate lifters, for advanced lifters, the emphasis should be placed on free weights.

When muscle hypertrophy (in bodybuilders, for example) or development of muscular power is the goal, recommendations for sequencing, rest periods, and so on are the same as those for strength development. However, as shown in Table 8.1, other aspects of the program differ.

Table 8.1 American College of Sports Medicine's Recommendations for Resistance Training Program[a]

Primary goal of resistance training program	Training level	Loading	Volume	Velocity	Frequency (times per week)
Strength development	Novice	60%–70% 1RM	1–3 sets, 8–12 reps	Slow, moderate	2–3
	Intermediate	70%–80% 1RM	Multiple sets, 6–12 repss	Moderate	3–4
	Advanced	80%–100%1RM	Multiple sets, 1–12 repss	Unintentionally slow to fast	4–6
Muscle hypertrophy	Novice	70%–85% 1RM	1–3 sets, 8–12 reps	Slow, moderate	2–3
	Intermediate	70%–85% 1RM	1–3 sets, 6–12 reps	Slow, moderate	4
	Advanced	70%–100% 1RM; emphasis on 70–85%	3–6 sets, 1–12 reps	Slow, moderate, fast	4–6
Development of muscle power	Novice	0%–60% 1RM–lower body; 30%–60% 1RM–upper body	1–3 sets, 3–6 reps	Moderate	2–3
	Intermediate	0%–60% 1RM–lower body; 30%–60% 1RM–upper body	1–3 sets, 3–6 reps	Fast	3–4
	Advanced	85%–100%1RM	3–6 sets, 1–6 reps, various strategies[b]	Fast	4–5
Increased local muscular endurance	Novice	Light	1–3 sets, 10–15 reps	Slow–moderate reps; Moderate–high reps	2–3
	Intermediate	Light	1–3 sets, 10–15 reps	Slow–moderate reps; Moderate–high reps	3–4
	Advanced	30%–80% 1RM	Various strategies[b], 10–25 reps or more	Slow–moderate reps; Moderate–high reps	4–6

a These recommendations also include the type of muscle action (eccentric and concentric) , single-joint versus multiple-joint exercises, order or sequence of exercises, and the rest intervals. See text for further information.

b Periodized—see text for explanation of periodization.

2.2 Types of Resistance Training

Resistance training can use static contractions, dynamic contractions, or both. Dynamic contractions can include concentric or eccentric contractions, or both. Typical resistance training can be performed using free weights, variable-resistance devices, isokinetic devices, and plyometrics.

2.2.1 Static-Contraction Resistance Training

Static-contraction resistance training, also called isometric training, gained great popularity in the mid-1950s as a result of research by several German scientists. These studies indicated that static resistance training caused tremendous strength gains and that those gains exceeded the gains resulting from dynamic-contraction procedures. Subsequent studies were unable to reproduce the original studies' results, and training programs based heavily on isometric contractions have generally fallen out of favor. However, static contractions remain an important form of training, particularly for core stabilization (discussed later in the chapter) and for enhancing grip strength. Additionally, in postsurgical rehabilitation when a limb is immobilized and thus incapable of dynamic contractions, static contractions facilitate recovery and reduce muscle atrophy and strength loss.

2.2.2 Free Weights Versus Machines

With free weights, such as barbells and dumbbells, the resistance or weight lifted remains constant throughout the dynamic range of movement. If a 50 kg weight is lifted, it will always weigh 50 kg. In contrast, a variable-resistance contraction involves varying the resistance to try to match it to the strength curve. Figure 8.1 illustrates how strength varies throughout the range of motion in a two-arm curl. Maximal strength production by the elbow flexors occurs at approximately 100° in the range of movement. These muscles are weakest at 60° (elbows fully flexed) and at 180° (elbows fully extended). In these positions, one is able to generate only 67% and 71%, respectively, of the maximal force-producing capabilities at the optimal angle of 100°.

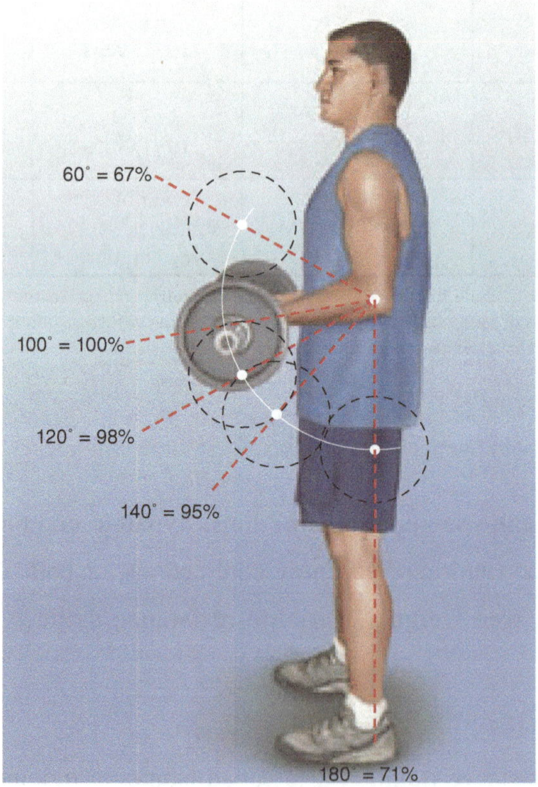

Figure 8.1 The variation in strength relative to the angle of the elbow during the two-arm curl. Strength is optimized at an angle of 100°. The maximal force-development capacity of the muscle group at a given angle is given as a percentage of the capacity at the optimal angle of 100°.

Starting in the 1970s, a number of resistance training machines or devices were introduced that used stacked weights, variable-resistance, and isokinetic techniques.

Variable-resistance machines use cams, pulleys, and levers to vary the weight throughout the range of movement. Such machines have been regarded as safer; they are easy to use and allow performance of some exercises that are difficult to do with free weights. Machines help stabilize the body, especially for novice lifters, and limit the muscle action to that desired without extraneous muscle groups firing.

On the other hand, free weights offer some advantages that resistance machines do not provide. The lifter must control the weight being lifted. A lifter must recruit more motor units—not only in the muscles being trained but also in supporting muscles—to gain control of the bar, stabilize the weight lifted, and maintain body balance. The lifter must both balance and stabilize the weight. In that regard, when an athlete is training for a sport such as football, the experience with free weights more closely resembles actions associated with actual sport competition. Also, because free weights do not limit the range of motion of a particular exercise, optimal training specificity can be achieved. Whereas a bicep curl on a machine may be done only in the vertical plane, an athlete using free weights can perform the curl in any plane, choosing one, for example, that reflects a sport-specific motion. And finally, data show that if significant strength gains are to be achieved over a shortened training period, free weights may provide greater strength gains than many types of weight machines.

Both machine-based resistance programs and free weight training programs result in measurable gains in strength, hypertrophy, and power. Free-weight programs result in greater improvements in free-weight tests, and machine training results in greater gains in machine-based tests. The choice to use weight machines versus free weights depends on the experience of the lifter and the desired outcomes.

2.2.3 Eccentric Training

Another form of dynamic-contraction resistance training, called eccentric training, emphasizes the eccentric phase. With eccentric contractions, the muscle's ability to resist force is considerably greater than with concentric contractions (see Chapter1). Subjecting the muscle to this greater training stimulus theoretically produces greater strength gains. A number of studies have shown the importance of including the eccentric phase of muscle contraction along with the concentric phase to maximize gains in muscle strength and size. Further, eccentric contraction is important to stimulate muscle hypertrophy, as discussed in the next chapter.

2.2.4 Variable-Resistance Training

With a variable-resistance device, the resistance is decreased at the weakest points in the range of movement and increased at the strongest points. Variable-resistance training is the basis for several popular resistance training machines. The underlying theory is that the muscle can be more fully trained if it is forced to act at higher constant percentages of its capacity throughout each point in its range of movement. Figure 8.2 illustrates a variable-resistance device in which a cam alters the resistance through the range of motion. As noted earlier, there are advantages and disadvantages to training using such machines.

Figure 8.2 A variable-resistance training device that uses a cam to alter the resistance through the range of motion.

2.2.5 Isokinetic Training

Isokinetic training is conducted with equipment that keeps movement speed constant. Whether one applies very light force or an all-out maximal muscle contraction, the speed of movement does not vary. Using electronics, air, or hydraulics, the device can be preset to control the speed of movement (angular velocity) from 0 °/s (static contraction) to 300 °/s or higher. Theoretically, if properly motivated, the individual can contract the muscles at maximal force at all points in the range of motion.

2.2.6 Plyometrics

Plyometrics, or stretch-shortening cycle exercise, became popular during the late 1970s and early 1980s, primarily for improving jumping ability. As an example, to develop knee extensor muscle strength and power, a person goes from standing upright to a deep squat position (eccentric contraction) and then jumps up onto a box (concentric contraction) , landing in a squat position on top of the box. The person then jumps off the box onto the ground, landing in a squat position, and repeats the sequence with the next box (Figure 8.3).

Proposed to bridge the gap between speed and strength training, plyometrics uses the stretch reflex to facilitate recruitment of motor units. It also stores energy in the elastic and contractile components of muscle during the eccentric contraction (stretch) that can be recovered during the concentric contraction.

Figure 8.3 Plyometric box jumping.

2.2.7 Electrical Stimulation

One can stimulate a muscle by passing an electric current directly across it or its motor nerve. This technique, called electrical stimulation, has proven effective in clinical settings to reduce the loss of strength and muscle size during periods of immobilization and to restore strength and size during rehabilitation. Electrical stimulation training also has been used experimentally in healthy subjects (including athletes). Athletes have used this technique to supplement their regular training programs, but no evidence shows any additional gains in strength, power, or performance from this supplementation.

2.2.8 Core Training

In recent years, a significant emphasis has been placed on core stability and strengthening exercises. While there are varying opinions on what anatomical features constitute the core, the general consensus is that the core is the group of trunk muscles that surround the spine and abdominal viscera and include the abdominal, gluteal, hip girdle, paraspinal, and other accessory muscles.

Initially, this type of core-specific exercise training was explored in rehabilitation settings, specifically for the treatment of lower back pain, but its benefits have also been recognized in sport performance. Theoretically, greater core stability could benefit sport performance by providing a foundation for greater force production and force transfer to the extremities. For example, having the core stabilized and engaged in the simple action of throwing a ball allows for greater biomechanical efficiency in the limb transmitting the force to throw the ball and for the activation of stabilizing muscles in the contralateral arm. The principle of core stabilization promotes proximal stability for distal mobility.

There has been little definitive research on the benefits of core stability and core strengthening for athletic performance. One reason is that there are no standardized tests for evaluating core strength and stability. Further, the studies that have been done have been mainly with injured populations and not specific to athletic performance. However, the limited research does show that this type of training decreases the likelihood of injury, especially in the lower back and the lower extremities, during sport performance. The physiological explanation for this finding is that core stability training increases the sensitivity of the muscle spindles, thereby permitting a greater state of readiness for loading joints during movement and protecting the body from injury.

The many different types of core stability and strengthening training include balance and instability resistance (e.g., physio ball). It is thought that because the core is composed mainly of type I muscle fibers, the core musculature may respond well to multiple sets of exercises with high repetitions. Yoga, Pilates, tai chi, and the physio ball are commonly incorporated into athletes' training programs to promote core stability and strength. Further research is needed to determine the benefits of core training and the underlying mechanisms.

3 Anaerobic and Aerobic Power Training Programs

Anaerobic and aerobic power training programs, while quite different at the extremes (e.g., training for the 100 m dash versus the 42.195 km full marathon) , are designed along a continuum. Table 8.2 illustrates how training requirements vary in competitive running events as one goes from short sprints to long distances. With this table serving as an example that can be applied to all sports, Anaerobic power is represented by the ATP-PCr and anaerobic glycolytic systems, while aerobic power is represented by the oxidative system. Note, however, that even at the extremes, more than one energy system must be trained. Different types of training programs can be used to meet the specific training requirements of each event, such as in running and swimming, and each sport. This section describes some of the more popular types of training programs and how they are used to improve the specific energy systems.

Table 8.2 Percentage of Emphasis on the Three Metabolic Energy Systems in Training for Various Running Events

Running event	Anaerobic speed (ATP−PCr system)	Anaerobic endurance (anaerobic glycolytic system)	Aerobic endurance (oxidative system)
100 m	95	3	2
200 m	95	2	3
400 m	80	15	5
800 m	30	65	5
1,500 m	20	55	25
3,000 m	20	40	40
5,000 m	10	20	70
10,000 m	5	15	80
Marathon (42.195km)	5	5	90

3.1 Interval Training

Interval training consists of repeated bouts of high to moderate intensity exercise interspersed with periods of rest or reduced-intensity exercise. Research has shown that athletes can perform a considerably greater total volume of exercise by breaking the overall exercise period into shorter, more intense bouts, with rest or active recovery intervals inserted between the intense bouts.

The vocabulary used to describe an interval training program is similar to that used in resistance training and includes the terms sets, repetitions, training time, training distance and frequency, exercise interval, and rest or active recovery interval. Interval training is frequently prescribed in these terms, as illustrated in the following example for a middle-distance runner:

- Set 1: 6 × 400 m at 75 s (90s slow jog)
- Set 2: 6 × 800 m at 180s (200s jog-walk)

For the first set, the athlete would run six repetitions of 400 m each, completing the exercise interval in 75 s and recovering for 90s between exercise intervals with slow jogging. The second set consists of running six repetitions of 800 m each, completing the exercise interval in 180s, and recovering for 200s with walking-jogging.

While interval training is traditionally associated with track, cross country running, and swimming, it is appropriate for all sports and activities. One can adapt interval training procedures for each sport or event by first selecting the form or mode of training and then manipulating the following primary variables to fit the sport and athlete:

- Rate of the exercise interval;
- Distance of the exercise interval;
- Number of repetitions and sets during each training session;

- Duration of the rest or active recovery interval;
- Type of activity during the active recovery interval;
- Frequency of training per week.

3.1.1 Exercise Interval Intensity

One can determine the intensity of the exercise interval either by establishing a specific duration for a set distance, as illustrated in our previous example for set 1 (i.e., 75 s for 400 m) , or by using a fixed percentage of the athlete's maximal heart rate (HRmax). Setting a specific duration is more practical, particularly for short sprints. One typically determines this by using the athlete's best time for the set distance and then adjusting the duration according to the relative intensity that the athlete wants to achieve, with 100% equal to the athlete's best time. As an example, to develop the ATP-PCr system, the intensity should be near maximal (e.g., 90%–98%) ; to develop the anaerobic glycolytic system, it should be high (e.g., 80%–95%) ; and to develop the aerobic system, it should be moderate to high (e.g., 75%–85%). These estimated percentages are only approximations and are dependent on the athlete's genetic potential and fitness level, duration of the interval (e.g., 10s versus 10 min) , number of repetitions and sets, and duration of the active recovery interval.

Using a fixed percentage of the athlete's HRmax might provide a better index of the physiological stress experienced by the athlete. Heart rate monitors are now readily available and relatively inexpensive (Figure 8.4). HRmax can be determined during a maximal exercise test in the laboratory or during an all-out run on the track using the heart rate monitor. Training the ATP-PCr system requires training at very high percentages of the athlete's HRmax (e.g., 90%–100%) , as does training to develop the anaerobic glycolytic system (e.g., 85%–100% HRmax). To develop the aerobic system, the intensity should be moderate to high (e.g., 70%–90% HRmax).

Figure 8.5 illustrates changes in blood lactate concentration in a runner using interval training at three different intensities corresponding to those intensities needed to train the ATP-PCr system, the glycolytic system, and the oxidative system. The runner performed a single set consisting of five repetitions at each intensity on different days, and the lactate concentrations were obtained from a blood sample taken after the last repetition of each intensity. Monitoring blood lactate concentrations can verify the energy system that is primarily being trained.

Figure 8.4 A runner outfitted with a heart rate monitor

The receiving unit, attached to the chest strap, picks up and transmits electrical impulses from the heart to the digital monitor and memory device worn on the wrist. After the workout, the contents of the memory device can be downloaded to a computer.

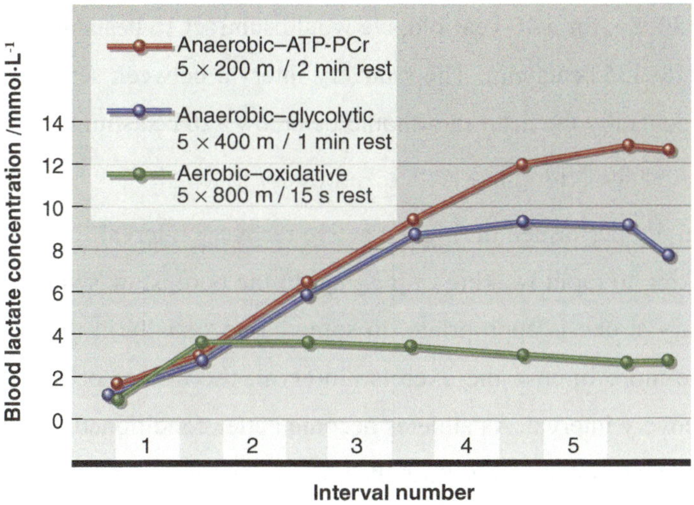

Figure 8.5 Blood lactate concentrations in a single runner following a set of five repetitions of interval training at three different paces, each on different days, corresponding to the appropriate pace for training each energy system.

3.1.2 Distance of the Exercise Interval

The distance of the exercise interval is determined by the requirements of the event, sport, or activity. Athletes who run or sprint short distances, such as track sprinters, basketball players, and soccer players, use short intervals of 30–200 m, although a 200 m sprinter frequently runs over distances of 300–400 m. A 1,500 m runner may run intervals as short as 200 m to increase speed, but most of this athlete's training would be at distances of 400–1,500 m, or even longer distances, to increase endurance and decrease fatigue or exhaustion in the race.

3.1.3 Number of Repetitions and Sets During Each Training Session

The number of repetitions and sets is also largely determined by the needs of the sport, event, or activity. Generally, the shorter and more intense the interval, the greater the number of repetitions and sets should be. As the training interval is lengthened in both distance and duration, the number of repetitions and sets is correspondingly reduced.

3.1.4 Duration of the Rest or Active Recovery Interval

The duration of the rest or active recovery interval depends on how rapidly the athlete recovers from the exercise interval. The extent of recovery is best determined by the reduction of the athlete's heart rate to a predetermined level during the rest or active recovery period. For younger athletes (30 years of age or younger) , heart rate is generally allowed to drop to between 130 and 150 beats/min before the next exercise interval begins. For those over 30 years, since HRmax decreases ~1beat/min per year, we subtract the difference between the athlete's age and 30 years from both 130 and 150. So, for a 45-year-old, we would subtract 15 beats/min to obtain the athlete's recovery range of 115–135 beats/min. The recovery interval between sets can be established in a similar manner, but generally the heart rate should be below 120 beats/min.

3.1.5 Type of Activity During the Active Recovery Interval

The type of activity performed during the active recovery interval for land-based training can vary from slow walking to rapid walking or jogging. In the pool, slow swimming using alternative strokes or the primary stroke is appropriate. In some cases, usually in the pool, total rest can be used. Generally, the more intense the exercise interval, the lighter or less intense the activity performed in the recovery interval. As athletes become better conditioned, they are able to increase the intensity of the exercise interval, decrease the duration of the rest interval, or both.

3.1.6 Frequency of Training per Week

The frequency of training depends largely on the purpose of the interval training. A world-class sprinter or middle-distance runner typically works out five to seven days a week, although not every workout will include interval training. Swimmers use interval training almost exclusively. Team sport athletes can benefit from two to four days of interval training per week when interval training is used only as a supplement to a general conditioning program.

3.2 Continuous Training

Continuous training involves continuous activity without rest intervals. This can vary from long, slow distance (LSD) training to high-intensity endurance training. Continuous training is structured primarily to affect the oxidative and glycolytic energy systems. High-intensity continuous activity is usually performed at intensities representing 85%–95% of the athlete's HRmax. For swimmers and track and cross-country athletes, this could be above, at, or near race pace. This pace would likely match or exceed the pace associated with the athlete's lactate threshold. Scientific evidence has clearly demonstrated that marathon runners typically race at, or very close to, their lactate threshold.

Long, slow distance training is probably the most popular and safest form of aerobic endurance conditioning for the nonathlete who just wants to get into shape and stay in shape for health-related purposes. More vigorous or burst types of activity generally are not encouraged in older, sedentary people. Long, slow distance is also a good training program for athletes in team sports for maintaining aerobic endurance during the season as well as the off-season.

Fartlek training, or speed play, is another form of continuous exercise that has some components of interval training. This form of training was developed in Sweden in the 1930s and is used primarily by distance runners. The athlete varies the pace from high speed to jogging speed at his or her discretion. This is a free form of training in which fun is the primary goal, and distance and time are not even considered. Fartlek training is normally performed in the countryside where there are hills of various inclines. Many coaches have used Fartlek training to supplement either high-intensity continuous training or interval training, since it provides variety to the normal training routine.

3.3 Interval-Circuit Training

Introduced in the Scandinavian countries in the 1960s and 1970s, interval-circuit training combines interval and circuit training into one workout. The circuit may be 3,000–10,000 m in length, with stations every 400–1,600 m. The athlete jogs, runs, or sprints the distance between stations; stops at each station to perform a strength, flexibility, or muscular endurance exercise in a manner similar to that in actual circuit training; and continues on jogging, running, or sprinting to the next station. These courses are typically located in parks or in the country where there are many trees and hills. Such a training regimen can benefit almost any type of athlete and provide diversity to what might be an otherwise monotonous training regimen.

3.4 High-Intensity Interval Training (HIIT)

Traditionally, exercise physiologists have recommended one of three regimens to improve aerobic power: continuous exercise at a moderate to high intensity; long, slow (low-intensity) exercise; or interval training. However, a growing body of research suggests that high intensity interval training (HIIT) is a time-efficient way to induce many adaptations normally associated with traditional endurance training. Scientists at McMaster University in Canada have studied the effects of training using short bursts of very intense cycling, interspersed with up to a few minutes of rest or low-intensity cycling for recovery. A common training mode employed is based on the Wingate test, a test that consists of 30s of all-out cycling and generally produces mean power outputs that are two to three times higher than what subjects typically generate during a maximal oxygen uptake test.

A typical HIIT workout consists of four to six bouts of 30s all-out cycling separated by a few minutes of recovery. Therefore, the total exercise time is as little as 2 min spread over a 20 min total time period. Several studies have now confirmed that performing six or so sessions of this type of interval training over a 2-week span can dramatically improve aerobic capacity in previously untrained individuals. The best feature of this type of training for busy exercisers is that such a regimen involves only 15 min total of all-out cycling within a total time commitment of 2.5 h !

Tabata, named for Dr. Izumi Tabata from Ritsumeikan University in Japan, is a high-intensity interval training (HIIT) protocol that incorporates brief, supramaximal (170% of $\dot{V}O_{2\,max}$) 20s intervals followed by 10s of rest into a 4 min exercise bout. In 1996, Dr. Tabata published the results of a study that found that—although just 4 min in duration—subjects who followed this HIIT protocol four days a week showed notable improvements in aerobic and anaerobic fitness, higher than those observed in subjects who performed classical endurance training (70% of $\dot{V}O_{2\,max}$) for 60 min a day. Subsequent research has shown that Tabata and other HIIT programs can be effectively used to increase aerobic and anaerobic fitness, promote fat loss, and improve health outcomes in a relatively short period of time.

In addition to improving $\dot{V}O_{2\,max}$, HIIT has been proven to have additional health benefits. Similar to continuous aerobic training programs, HIIT improves glucose control and insulin sensitivity, especially in individuals with (or at risk for) type 2 diabetes. HIIT has also been shown to improve vascular endothelial function, a measure of blood vessel health. In fact, studies have demonstrated that HIIT may be more effective than continuous, long-duration training in promoting metabolic and cardiovascular adaptations.

IN CLOSING

In this chapter, we reviewed general principles of training and the terminology used to describe these principles. We then learned the essential ingredients of successful resistance training and anaerobic and aerobic power training programs. With this background, we can now focus on how the body adapts to these different types of training programs. In the next chapter, we will see how the body responds to resistance training.

KEY TERMS

1-repetition maximum (1RM); long, slow distance (LSD) training; aerobic power; muscular endurance; anaerobic power; plyometrics; continuous training; power; eccentric training; principle of individuality; electrical stimulation; principle of periodization; Fartlek training; principle of progressive overload; free weights; principle of reversibility; high-intensity interval training (HIIT) ; principle of specificity; hypertrophy; principle of variation; interval-circuit training; static-contraction resistance training; interval training; strength; isokinetic training; variable-resistance training; isometric training

STUDY QUESTIONS

(1) Describe and provide examples for the principles of individuality, specificity, reversibility, progressive overload, and variation.

(2) What would be the appropriate range for resistance and repetitions when one is designing a resistance training program targeted to develop strength? Muscular endurance? Muscular power? Hypertrophy?

(3) Describe the various types of resistance training, and explain the advantages and disadvantages of each.

(4) What type of training program would likely provide the greatest improvement for sprinters? Marathon runners? Football players?

(5) High-intensity interval training has been shown to cause beneficial adaptations leading to improved performance. Describe those physiological adaptations.

第八章 运动训练原则

一个人如果在几天、几周、几个月的时间里进行有规律的锻炼，就会产生各种各样的生理适应。适度训练带来的积极适应可以提高运动能力和运动表现。肌肉可以通过抗阻训练变得更强壮；心肺运输氧的效率以及运动耐力可以通过有氧训练得到提高；通过高强度无氧训练，神经、肌肉、代谢和心血管系统的适应使单位时间生成更多的三磷酸腺苷（ATP），从而在短时间内增加肌肉的耐力和运动速度。这些运动适应因运动类型而有所不同。

一、运动训练的一般原则

抗阻训练、有氧训练和无氧训练可以产生一些特定的生理适应。

1.个性化原则

每个人应对急性运动的能力不同，对运动训练产生的适应性也不同。遗传对急性运动产生的反应以及在运动训练中的适应起到重要的作用，这就是个性化原则的理论依据。细胞生长速率、新陈代谢、心血管和呼吸调节、神经和内分泌调节的变化导致巨大的个体差异，任何训练计划都需要根据个人的需求和能力进行设计。

2.特异性原则

训练产生的适应因运动类型、运动量、运动强度而有所不同。例如，为了提高肌肉的爆发力，铅球运动员不会重点练习长跑或进行低强度、慢速的抗阻训练。因为铅球运动员需要增强的是爆发力。同样，马拉松运动员也不会专注于短跑训练。为了达到某种运动适应或目标，训练计划中要着重加强对最佳运动表现起关键作用的生理系统。

3.可逆性原则

抗阻训练可以提高肌肉力量和抗疲劳能力。同样，耐力训练可以提高长时间高强度有氧运动的能力。但是，如果训练减少或停止（脱训练），那么引起这些能力提高的生理适应也将被逆转。有效的训练计划应包括一个保持计划，用于维持通过训练获得的生理适应。

4.渐进负荷原则

超负荷训练和渐进式训练是所有训练计划的基础。在进行力量训练时，为了获得力量，肌肉必须超负荷。渐进式抗阻训练表示当肌肉变得更强壮时，要么增加阻力，要么增加重复次数，或者两者都增加，以刺激肌肉力量的进一步增强。

5.多样化原则

多样化原则，也称为周期性原则，是一个系统的过程。改变训练计划中的一个或多个变量（训练方式、训练量或训练强度），随着时间的推移，使训练刺激保持挑战性和有效性。经典训练周期是，初期高训练量、低强度训练，随着训练的进行，训练量逐渐减少，强度逐渐增加。

对于体育专项训练来说，训练量和训练强度在一个大周期内会有所不同，通常最多要训练一年。一个大周期是由两个或两个以上的中周期组成，这些中周期主要由竞赛的日期决定。每个中周期又细分为准备阶段、比赛阶段和过渡阶段。

二、抗阻训练计划

过去的研究已经为抗阻训练及其在健康和运动方面的应用提供了大量知识基础。本节主要讨论运动中抗阻训练的使用。

1.抗阻训练计划建议

抗阻训练计划可以根据将要进行运动的内容、顺序、组数、间歇时间、阻力大小及重复次数、练习速度等几个方面进行设计和指导。旨在提高力量的抗阻训练应该包括多次的向心收缩（肌肉缩短）和离心收缩（肌肉拉长）动作的结合。大肌群运动应先于小肌群运动，多关节运动先于单关节运动，高强度运动先于低强度运动。

建议初学者和中级举重运动员在高负重练习间最少休息2～3分钟；对于高级举重运动员，休息1或2分钟就足够。一旦个人可以连续两次训练达到或超过预期次数的运动量，则应增加2%~10%的负荷。初学者和中级举重运动员可以通过器械训练或自由重量进行练习，高级举重运动员应以自由重量训练为主。

2.抗阻训练的类型

抗阻训练可以使用静力性收缩或动力性收缩，或两者兼而有之。动力性收缩可以包括向心收缩或离心收缩，或两者兼而有之。典型的抗阻训练通过使用杠铃、变阻装置、等速装置和超等长训练来进行。

（1）静力性收缩抗阻训练，又称静力性训练。静力性收缩抗阻训练是一种重要的训练形式，特别适用于提高核心稳定性和增长握力。此外，在手术后的康复中，当肢体活动受限而无法进行动力性收缩时，静力性收缩有助于恢复，并减少肌肉萎缩和力量损失。

（2）自由重量训练与器械训练。对于杠铃和哑铃这样的自由重量，阻力或重量在整个动态运动范围内保持不变；而变阻收缩需要改变阻力使其与强度曲线相匹配。

可变阻力机械通过凸轮、滑轮和杠杆在整个运动范围内改变重量。这种器械被认为相对安全，因为它们易于使用，并且可以完成一些自由重量训练难以完成的运动。器械有助于稳定身体，尤其对于举重新手而言，它可以将肌肉的运动限制在所需的范围内，而不会刺激其他不相关的肌肉。

自由重量训练具有一些抗阻器械所没有的优势。举重运动员必须控制举起的重量，同时募集更多的运动单元用于控制杠铃，以稳定举起的重量并保持身体平衡。自由举重的练习更接近于与实际运动竞赛相关的动作，可以在较短的训练期间内获得显著的力量增长。

（3）离心训练。离心训练是另一种形式的动力性收缩抗阻训练，强调在离心阶段用力。离心收缩时，肌肉的抗阻能力要比向心收缩时大得多，可以让肌肉受到更大的训练刺激，从而获得更大的力量提升。

（4）变阻训练。运用变阻设备，阻力在运动范围内肌肉力量最小处减小，而在肌肉力量最强点增大。肌肉在其活动范围内的每一点都以其能力的更高百分比来活动，则可以得到更充分的训练。

（5）等动训练。等动训练要在使运动速度保持恒定的设备上进行。可以使用电子设备、空气或液压装置对设备进行预设，将移动速度（角速度）从0度/秒（静态收缩）控制到300度/秒或更高。个体可以在整个运动范围内所有的点上都以最大力量收缩肌肉。

（6）超等长训练，又称拉伸–缩短循环训练。超等长训练弥补了速度和力量训练之间的差距，它利用牵张反射来促进运动单位的募集。

（7）电刺激。人们可以通过电流直接作用于肌肉或运动神经来刺激肌肉。它可以在肢体固定期间减少肌肉力量和体积的损失，并在康复期间恢复其力量和体积。

（8）核心训练。尽管教练员对于构成核心的解剖结构有不同的看法，但普遍的共识是，核心是围绕脊柱和腹部脏器的一组躯干肌肉，包括腹部肌、臀肌、腰束肌、椎旁肌和其他辅助肌肉。从理论上讲，更大的核心稳定性可以为更大的力量产生和力量转移到四肢提供基础，从而有利于运动表现。核心稳定性训练降低了运动损伤的风险，特别是下背部和下肢损伤风险。

三、无氧和有氧功率训练计划

虽然无氧和有氧功率训练计划在极端情况下有很大的不同（例如100米跑和全程马拉松的训练），但它们都是能量供给的连续统一体。无氧功率以ATP-CP和酵解能系统为代表，有氧功率则以氧化能系统为代表。

本节介绍了一些较流行的训练计划类型，以及如何将其用于改善特定的能源系统。

1.间歇训练

间歇训练是指包括从高强度到中等强度的多重复次数训练，中间穿插休息或低强度的训练。研究表明，运动员可以通过将整个训练课次分解为更短、更剧烈的间歇性运动，并在间歇运动之间穿插休息或小运动量的练习，以完成相当大的运动量。

用于描述间歇训练计划的元素与抗阻训练相似，包括组数、次数、训练时间、训练距离和频率、训练间歇，以及休息或主动恢复间歇。通常用这些术语来描述间歇训练。以中距离跑运动员训练为例：

第一组：6×400米，每组75秒，组间90秒慢跑。

第二组：6×800米，每组180秒，组间200秒走跑。

虽然间歇训练适用于所有的运动，但根据运动类型和运动员情况，为每项运动调整间歇训练计划时，应首先选择训练的形式，其次控制相应的强度、组数、次数、间歇时间、训练频次等运动变量。

2.持续训练

持续训练是没有休息间歇的连续性训练。持续训练主要是为了影响氧化能系统和酵解能系统。高强度持续训练的强度通常相当于运动员最大心率的85%～95%。马拉松运动员通常以其乳酸阈水平或非常接近其乳酸阈水平进行比赛。

法特莱克训练是另一种形式的持续训练，它包含间歇性训练的部分内容。这种训练方式是一种以乐趣为主要目标的训练，为常规训练提供了多样性。

3.间歇性循环训练

间歇性循环训练将间歇训练和循环训练结合在一起。循环赛道可以长3 000～10 000米，每400～1 600米设置一个站。运动员在站与站之间进行慢跑、跑步或冲刺；在每个站点停留，进行力量、柔韧性或肌肉耐力的锻炼，其方式类似于实际的循环训练。

4.高强度间歇训练

高强度间歇训练（HIIT）是一种高效率的运动方式，可以激发许多与传统耐力训练有关的适应。加拿大麦克马斯特大学的科学家们研究了短时间内进行高强度自行车运动的训练效果，其中穿插了几分钟的休息或低强度骑行。常用的训练模式以温盖特（Wingate）试验为基础，该试验包括30秒的全力骑行，通常产生的平均输出功率是最大摄氧量测试中产生的

2~3倍。

Tabata，是一种HIIT方案。该方案要求练习者在20秒内完成最高强度（170%最大摄氧量）的训练，休息10秒钟，如此循环，总时间为4分钟。Tabata和其他HIIT方案可在相对较短的时间内有效提高有氧和无氧适应能力，促进脂肪的减少，并在相对较短的时间内达到改善健康的效果。

Chapter 9
Adaptations to Resistance Training

With any type of effective chronic exercise, multiple adaptations occur in the neuromuscular system. The type and extent of the adaptations depend on the type of training: aerobic training, such as running, cycling, or swimming, results in little gain in muscle size and strength, but major neuromuscular adaptations occur with resistance training.

Resistance training was once considered inappropriate for athletes except those in competitive weightlifting, throwing events in track and field, and wrestling and boxing. Women typically avoided the weight room for fear of becoming masculine looking! But in the late 1960s and early 1970s, coaches and researchers discovered that strength and power training are beneficial for almost all sports and activities, and for women as well as men. It was not until the late 1980s and early 1990s that health professionals began to recognize the importance of resistance training to overall health, fitness, and rehabilitation.

Most athletes now include resistance training as an important component of their overall training program. Much of this attitude change is attributable to research that has proven the performance benefits of resistance training and to innovations in training techniques and equipment. Resistance training is now an important part of the exercise prescription for all those who seek the health-related benefits of exercise.

1 Resistance Training and Gains in Muscular Fitness

The neuromuscular system is one of the most responsive systems in the body to the repeated stimulation of training. Resistance training programs can produce substantial strength gains. In three to six months, one can see from 25%–100% improvement, sometimes even more. These estimates of percentage gains in strength are, however, somewhat misleading. Most subjects in strength training research studies have never lifted weights or participated in any other form of resistance training. Most of their early gains in strength are the result of learning how to more effectively produce force and produce a true maximal movement, such as moving a barbell from the chest to a fully extended position in the bench press. This learning effect can account for as much as 50% of the early strength gains.

Muscle is very plastic, increasing in size and strength with training and decreasing in size and strength when immobilized. The remainder of this chapter details the physiological adaptations that allow people to become stronger.

2 Mechanisms of Gains in Muscle Strength

For many years, strength gains were assumed to result directly from increases in muscle size (hypertrophy). This assumption was logical because many people who regularly strength trained developed visually larger muscles. Also, muscles associated with a limb immobilized in a cast for weeks or months start to decrease in size (atrophy) and lose strength almost immediately. Gains in muscle size are generally paralleled by gains in strength, and losses in muscle size correlate highly with losses in strength. Thus, it is tempting to conclude that a direct cause-and-effect relationship exists between muscle size and muscle strength. While there is an association between size and strength, muscle strength involves far more than mere muscle size.

This does not mean that muscle size is unimportant in the ultimate strength potential of the muscle. The ability to generate force depends on the number of cross-bridges within sarcomeres, which in turn depends on the amount of actin and myosin. Size is extremely important, as revealed by the existing men's and women's world records for competitive weightlifting. As weight classification increases (implying increased muscle mass) , so does the record for the total weight lifted. However, the mechanisms associated with strength gains are more complex. What, in addition to increased size of the muscle, explains strength gains with training? Let's first consider the strong evidence that neural control of the muscle is altered with resistance training, allowing for a greater force production.

2.1 Neural Control of Strength Gains

An important component of the strength gains that result from resistance training, especially in the early stages, are neural adaptations. Enoka has made a convincing argument that strength gains can be achieved without structural changes in muscle but not without neural adaptations. Thus, strength is not solely a property of muscle but rather a property of the neuromotor system. Motor unit recruitment, frequency of motor nerve firing rates, better synchronization of motor units during a particular movement, and other neural factors are important to strength gains. Removal of neural inhibition may also play a role. These neural factors may well explain most, if not all, strength gains that occur in the absence of hypertrophy, as well as episodic superhuman feats of strength.

2.1.1 Synchronization and Recruitment of Additional Motor Units

Motor units are generally recruited asynchronously; they are not all engaged at the same instant. They are controlled by a number of different neurons that can transmit either excitatory or inhibitory impulses. Whether the muscle fibers contract or stay relaxed depends on the summation of the many impulses received by the given motor unit at any one time. The motor unit is activated and its muscle fibers contract only when the incoming excitatory impulses exceed the inhibitory impulses and the threshold is met or exceeded.

Strength gains may result from changes in the connections between motor neurons located in the spinal cord, allowing motor units to act more synchronously. This increased synchronicity means that a greater number of motor units will be firing at any one time, facilitating contraction and increasing the muscle's ability to generate force. There is good evidence to support increased motor unit synchronization with resistance training, but controversy still exists as to whether synchronization of motor unit activation produces a more forceful contraction. It is clear, however, that synchronization does improve the rate of force development and the capability to exert steady forces.

2.1.2 Increased Rate Coding of Motor Units

The increase in neural drive of α-motor neurons could also increase the frequency of discharge, or rate coding, of their motor units. Recall from Chapter 1 that as the frequency of stimulation of a given motor unit increases, the muscle eventually reaches a state of tetanus, producing the absolute peak force or tension of the muscle fiber or motor unit. There is limited evidence that rate coding is increased with resistance training. Rapid movement or ballistic-type training appears to be particularly effective in stimulating increases in rate coding.

2.1.3 Increased Neural Drive

Neural drive refers to the combination of motor unit recruitment and rate coding of the units. Neural drive starts in the central nervous system and is spread to muscle fibers through peripheral nerves. Electromyography (EMG) using surface electrodes over the muscle measures the total activity within the nerve and muscle and therefore is a good measure of neural drive.

An alternate explanation for neutrally mediated strength gains is simply that more motor units are recruited to perform the given task, independent of whether these motor units act in unison. Such improvement in recruitment patterns could result from an increase in neural drive to the α-motor neurons during maximal contraction. Trained muscles generate a given amount of submaximal force with less EMG activity, suggesting a more efficient motor unit recruitment pattern. This increase in neural drive could increase the frequency of discharge (rate coding) of the motor units or reduce inhibitory impulses, allowing more motor units to be activated or to be activated at a higher frequency. Additionally, maximal neural drive appears to increase with resistance training.

2.1.4 Autogenic Inhibition

Inhibitory mechanisms in the neuromuscular system, such as the Golgi tendon organs, might be necessary to prevent the muscles from exerting more force than the bones and connective tissues can tolerate. This control is referred to as autogenic inhibition. However, under extreme situations when larger forces are sometimes produced, significant damage can occur to these structures, suggesting that the protective inhibitory mechanisms can be overridden.

The function of Golgitendon organs is discussed in Chapter 3. When the tension on a muscle's tendons and internal connective tissue structures exceeds the threshold of the embedded Golgi tendon organs, motor neurons to that muscle are inhibited; that is, autogenic inhibition occurs. Both the reticular formation in the brain stem and the cerebral cortex function to initiate and propagate inhibitory impulses.

Resistance training can gradually reduce or counteract these inhibitory impulses, allowing the muscle to achieve a greater force production independent of increases in muscle mass. Thus, strength gains may be achieved by reduced neurological inhibition. This theory is attractive because it can at least partially explain superhuman feats of strength and strength gains in the absence of hypertrophy.

2.1.5 Other Neural Factors

In addition to increasing motor unit recruitment or decreasing neurological inhibition, other neural factors can contribute to strength gains with resistance training. One of these is referred to as coactivation of agonist and antagonist muscles (the agonist muscles are the primary movers, and the antagonist muscles act to impede the agonists). If we use forearm flexor concentric contraction as an example, the biceps is the primary agonist and the triceps is the antagonist. If the two were contracting with equal force development, no movement would occur. Thus, to maximize the force generated by an agonist, it is necessary to minimize the amount of coactivation. Reduction in coactivation could explain a portion of strength gains attributed to neural factors, but its contribution likely would be small. Changes also have been noted in the morphology of the neuromuscular junction, with both increased and decreased activity levels that might be directly related to the muscle's force-producing capacity.

2.2 Muscle Hypertrophy

How does a muscle's size increase? Two types of hypertrophy can occur: transient and chronic. Transient hypertrophy is the increased muscle size that develops during and immediately following a single exercise bout. This results mainly from fluid accumulation (edema) in the interstitial and intracellular spaces of the muscle that comes from the blood plasma. Transient hypertrophy, as its name implies, lasts only for a short time. The fluid returns to the blood within hours after exercise.

Chronic hypertrophy refers to the increase in muscle size that occurs with long-term resistance training. This reflects actual structural changes in the muscle that can result from an increase in the size of existing individual muscle fibers (fiber hypertrophy) , in the number of muscle fibers (fiber hyperplasia) , or in both. Controversy surrounds the theories that attempt to explain the underlying cause of this phenomenon. Of importance, however, is the finding that the eccentric component of training is important in maximizing increases in muscle fiber cross-sectional area. A number of studies have shown greater hypertrophy and strength resulting solely from eccentric contraction training as compared to concentric contraction or combined eccentric and concentric contraction training. Further, higher-velocity eccentric training appears to result in greater hypertrophy and strength gains than slower-velocity training. These greater increases appear to be related to disruptions in the sarcomere Z-lines. This disruption was originally labeled muscle damage but is now thought to represent fiber protein remodeling. Thus, training with only concentric actions could limit muscle hypertrophy and increases in muscle strength.

2.2.1 Intensity and Hypertrophy

With traditional training methods, the prevailing opinion has been that an intensity of 60%–85% of 1RM or higher is needed to achieve substantial increases in muscle size.

More recently, however, research has suggested that low-intensity exercise at <50% of 1RM can lead to gains in muscle size equal to those seen at high intensities, provided that the training is performed to volitional muscle fatigue. This theory holds that fatiguing contractions at light loads lead to metabolic stimuli that result in maximal muscle fiber recruitment.

Is there a minimal intensity for resistance training that will lead to muscle hypertrophy, provided that resistance exercises are performed to volitional fatigue? It has been reported that from intensities as low as 30% and as high as 90% of 1RM, load played a minimal role in stimulating muscle protein synthesis, muscle hypertrophy, and strength gains in novice exercisers. High-repetition (HR) and low-repetition (LR) —low and high load, respectively—training caused similar increases in skeletal muscle mass when resistance exercise was performed until volitional failure. Increases in lean body mass, as an indirect measure of muscle mass, and muscle fiber CSA, a direct measure of muscle area, occurred in both LR and HR groups with no differences between groups. There was a significant increase in 1RM strength for the leg press, knee extension, and shoulder press exercises, again with no differences between groups. These effects do not seem to depend on training status because similar results occurred in men with previous strength-training experience.

The following section examines the two postulated mechanisms for increasing muscle size with resistance training: fiber hypertrophy and fiber hyperplasia.

2.2.2 Fiber Hypertrophy

Early research suggested that the number of muscle fibers in each of a person's muscles was established by birth or shortly thereafter and that this number remained fixed throughout life. If this were true, then whole-muscle hypertrophy could result only from individual muscle fiber hypertrophy. This could be explained by

- more myofibrils,
- more actin and myosin filaments,
- more sarcoplasm,
- more connective tissue, or
- any combination of these.

As seen in the micrographs in Figure 9.1, effective resistance training can significantly increase the cross-sectional area of muscle fibers. Such dramatic enlargement of muscle fibers does not occur, however, in all cases of muscle hypertrophy.

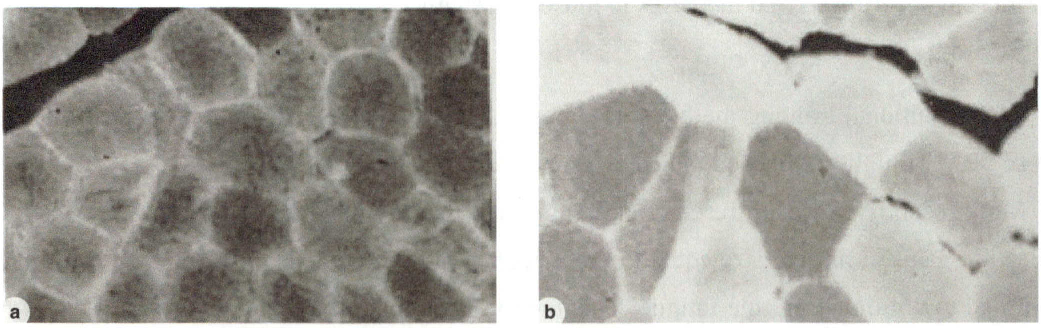

Figure 9.1 Microscopic views of muscle cross sections taken from the leg muscle of a man who had not trained during the previous two years (a) before he resumed training and (b) after he completed six months of dynamic strength training. Note the significantly lager fibers (hypertrophy) after training.

Muscle fiber hypertrophy is probably caused by increased numbers of myofibrils and actin and myosin filaments, which would provide more cross-bridges for force production during maximal contraction. The size of existing myofibrils does not appear to change. The increase in muscle cross-sectional area results from adding new sarcomeres in parallel to each other.

Individual muscle fiber hypertrophy from resistance training appears to result from a net increase in muscle protein synthesis. The muscle's protein content is in a continual state of flux. Protein is always being synthesized and degraded. But the rates of these processes vary with the demands placed on the body. During exercise, protein synthesis decreases, while protein degradation increases. After exercise, although protein degradation continues, protein synthesis increases three-to five-fold more, leading to a net synthesis of myofibrillar (myosin and actin) protein. A single bout of resistance exercise can elevate net protein synthesis for up to 24 h .

2.2.3 Hormones and Hypertrophy

The prevailing perspective in muscle physiology is that the hormone changes induced by resistance exercise facilitate increases in muscle mass that in turn increase muscular strength. The hormones that are typically associated with this response include the anabolic hormones testosterone, growth hormone (GH) , and insulin-like growth factor 1 (IGF-1). The hormone testosterone has traditionally been thought to be at least partly responsible for these changes because one of its primary functions is promoting muscle growth. Testosterone is a steroidal hormone with major anabolic functions, and men experience a significantly greater increase in muscle growth starting at puberty, which is largely due to a 10-fold increase in testosterone production. Furthermore, it has been well established that massive doses of anabolic steroids coupled with resistance training markedly increase muscle mass and strength.

While it is true that acute resistance training transiently increases the concentrations of these hormones, it has been shown experimentally that acute increases in these hormones are not required for increases in muscle mass or strength. Researchers at McMaster University designed a series of studies to examine whether exercise-induced elevations in testosterone, GH, and IGF-1 were necessary for, or could enhance, muscle anabolism. They examined the elbow flexor muscles when exposed (1) to low hormone concentrations during a small muscle mass exercise consisting of isolated arm curls and (2) to high circulating hormone concentrations induced by an intense lower body exercise routine in addition to arm curls. In the low hormone trials, myofibrillar protein synthesis was elevated after acute exercise bouts, and there were gains in strength and hypertrophy after trainingeven though testosterone, GH, and IGF-1 all remained near baseline concentrations. This implies that postexercise increases in these hormones are not necessary to stimulate muscle anabolism. Furthermore, when these hormones were elevated postexercise, there was no further enhancement in myofibrillar protein synthesis or gain in strength and hypertrophy with training.

In addition to these studies, researchers have compared men's and women's responses to resistance training. Women have a 45-fold lower postexercise testosterone response compared to men even after their 20-fold lower baseline testosterone concentration is accounted for. Despite having drastically lower postexercise increases in testosterone, the women were able to robustly increase rates of myofibrillar protein synthesis. Moreover, as in most exercise training studies, the men and women trained in this study had variable individual responses in terms of muscle hypertrophy. Despite these variable responses, there was no relation between each subject's exercise-induced increases in testosterone, GH, and IGF-1 and his or her muscle growth or strength gains.

These new data provide strong new evidence that postexercise elevations in testosterone, GH, and IGF-1 are not required to increase muscle anabolism and strength. An alternate hypothesis is that the muscle hypertrophy and strength gains occurring with resistance training are mediated by changes in intrinsic intramuscular properties.

2.2.4 Fiber Hyperplasia

Research on animals suggests that hyperplasia, an increase in the total number of fibers within a muscle, may also be a factor in the hypertrophy of whole muscles. Studies on cats provide fairly clear evidence that fiber splitting occurs with extremely heavy weight training. Cats were trained to move a heavy weight with a forepaw to get their food (Figure 9.2). With the use of food as a powerful incentive, they learned to generate considerable force. With this intense strength training, selected muscle fibers appeared to actually split in half, and each half then increased to the size of the parent fiber.

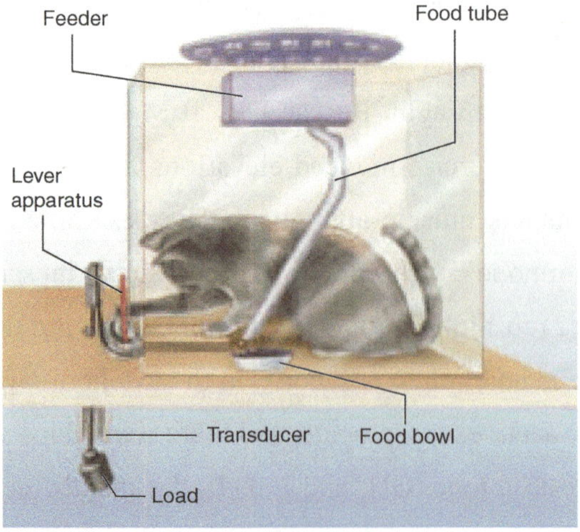

Figure 9.2 Heavy resistance training in cats.

Subsequent studies, however, demonstrated that hypertrophy of selected muscles in chickens, rats, and mice resulting from chronic exercise overload was attributable solely to hypertrophy of existing fibers, not hyperplasia. In these studies, each fiber in the whole muscle was actually counted. These direct fiber counts revealed no change in fiber number.

This finding led the scientists who performed the initial cat experiments to conduct an additional resistance training study with cats. This time they used actual fiber counts to determine if total muscle hypertrophy resulted from hyperplasia or fiber hypertrophy. Following a resistance training program of 101 weeks, the cats were able to perform one-leg lifts of an average of 57% of their body weight, resulting in an 11% increase in muscle weight. Most important, the researchers found a 9% increase in the total number of muscle fibers, confirming that muscle fiber hyperplasia did occur.

The difference in results between the cat studies and those with rats and mice most likely is attributable to differences in the manner in which the animals were trained. The cats were trained with a pure form of resistance training: high resistance and low repetitions. The other animals were trained with more endurance-type activity: low resistance and high repetitions.

One additional animal model has been used to stimulate muscle hypertrophy associated with hyperplasia. Scientists have placed the anterior latissimus dorsi muscle of chickens in a state of chronic stretch by attaching weights to it, with the other wing serving as the normal control condition. In many of the studies that have used this model, the chronic stretch has resulted in substantial hypertrophy and hyperplasia.

Researchers are still uncertain about the roles played by hyperplasia and individual fiber hypertrophy in increasing human muscle size with resistance training. Most evidence indicates that individual fiber hypertrophy accounts for most whole-muscle hypertrophy. However, results from selected studies indicate that hyperplasia is possible in humans. It is possible that only very high intensity in resistance training can result in fiber hyperplasia, and even then, the percentage of the total muscle size increase due to this phenomenon is small, perhaps 5%–10%. Whether strength training results in muscle fiber hyperplasia in humans remains unresolved.

In a cadaver study of seven previously healthy young men who had suffered sudden accidental death, the investigators compared cross sections of autopsied right and left tibialis anterior muscles (lower leg). Right-hand dominance is known to lead to greater hypertrophy of the left leg. In fact, the average cross-sectional area of the left muscle was 7.5% larger than that of the right. This was associated with a 10% greater number of fibers in the left muscle. There was no difference in mean fiber size.

The differences between these studies might be explained by the nature of the training load or stimulus. Training at high intensities or high resistances is thought to cause greater fiber hypertrophy, particularly of the type II (fast-twitch) fibers, than training at lower intensities or resistances.

Only one longitudinal study demonstrated the possibility of hyperplasia in men who had previous recreational resistance training experience. Following 12 weeks of intensified resistance training, the muscle fiber number in the biceps brachii of several of the 12 subjects appeared to increase significantly. It appears from this study that hyperplasia can occur in humans but possibly only in certain subjects or under certain training conditions.

From the preceding information, it appears that fiber hyperplasia can occur in animals and possibly in humans. How are these new cells formed? It is postulated that individual muscle fibers have the capacity to divide and split into two daughter cells, each of which can then develop into a functional muscle fiber. Importantly, satellite cells, which are the myogenic stem cells involved in skeletal muscle regeneration, are likely involved in the generation of new muscle fibers. These cells are typically activated by muscle stretching and injury; as we see later in this chapter, muscle injury results from intense training, particularly eccentric-action training. Muscle injury can lead to a cascade of responses in which satellite cells become activated and proliferate, migrate to the damaged region, and fuse to existing myofibers or combine and fuse to produce new myofibers. This is illustrated in Figure 9.3.

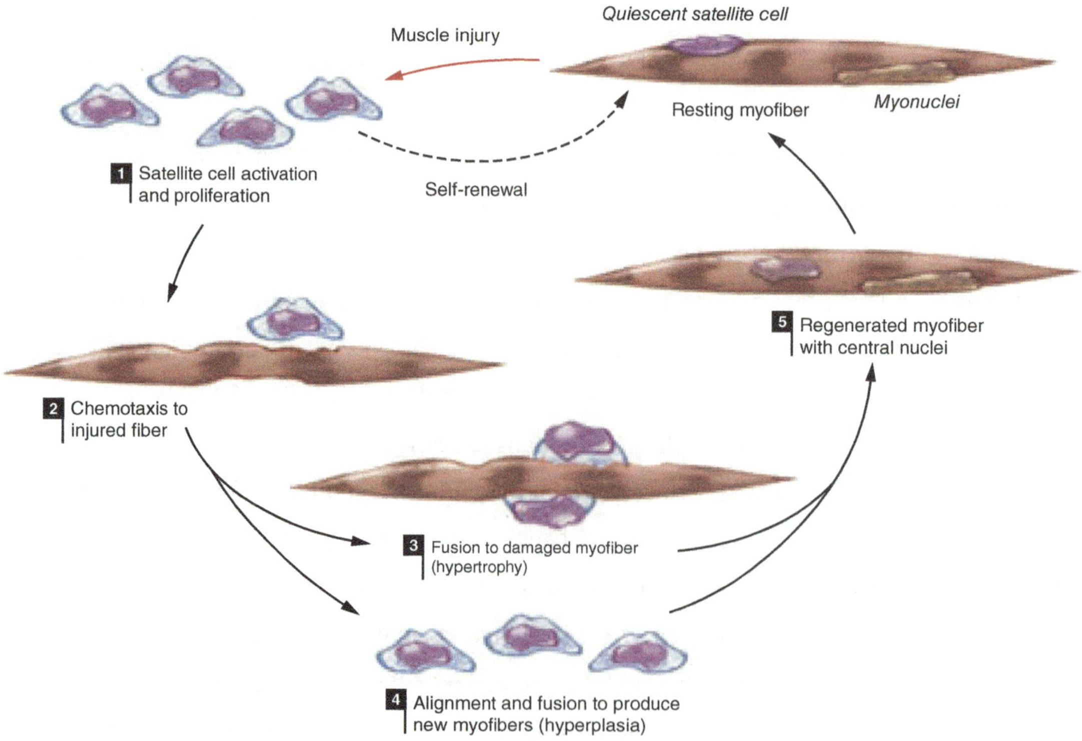

Figure 9.3 The satellite cell response to muscle injury.

Satellite cells provide additional nuclei within muscle fibers. The added genetic machinery (DNA) is necessary to provide the increased muscle protein content and related materials to facilitate hypertrophy (and theoretically, hyperplasia).

2.3 Integration of Neural Activation and Fiber Hypertrophy

Research on resistance training adaptations indicates that early increases in voluntary strength, or maximal force production, are associated primarily with neural adaptations resulting in increased voluntary activation of muscle. This was clearly demonstrated in a study of both men and women who participated in an eight-week, high-intensity resistance training program, training twice per week. Muscle biopsies were obtained at the beginning of the study and every two weeks during the training period. Strength, measured according to the 1RM, increased substantially over the eight weeks of training, with the greatest gains coming after the second week. Muscle biopsies, however, revealed only a small, insignificant increase in muscle fiber cross-sectional area by the end of the eight weeks of training. Thus, the strength gains were largely the result of increased neural activation.

Long-term increases in strength generally result from hypertrophy of the trained muscle. However, because it takes time to build protein through a decrease in protein degradation, an increase in protein synthesis, or both, early strength gains are typically due to changes in the pattern by which nerves activate the muscle fibers. Most research shows that neural factors contribute prominently to strength gains during the first eight to ten weeks of training. Hypertrophy contributes little during these initial weeks of training but progressively increases its contribution, becoming the major contributor after ten weeks of training. However, not all studies concur with this pattern of strength development. One six-month study of strength-trained athletes showed that neural activation explained most of the strength gains during the most intensive training months and that hypertrophy was not a major factor.

2.4 Muscle Atrophy and Decreased Strength with Inactivity

When a normally active or highly trained person reduces his or her level of activity or ceases training altogether, changes occur in both muscle structure and function. This is illustrated by the results of two types of studies: studies in which entire limbs have been immobilized and studies in which highly trained people stop training—so-called detraining.

2.4.1 Immobilization

When a trained muscle suddenly becomes inactive through immobilization, major changes are initiated within that muscle in a matter of hours. During the first 6 h of immobilization, the rate of protein synthesis starts to decrease. This decrease likely initiates muscular atrophy, which is the wasting away or decrease in the size of muscle tissue. Atrophy results from lack of muscle use and the consequent loss of muscle protein that accompanies the inactivity. Strength decreases are most dramatic during the first week of immobilization, averaging 3%–4% per day. This is associated not only with the atrophy but also with decreased neuromuscular activity of the immobilized muscle.

Immobilization appears to affect both type I and type II fibers. From various studies, researchers have observed disintegrated myofibrils, streaming Z-disks (discontinuity of Z-disks and fusion of the myofibrils) , and mitochondrial damage. When muscle atrophies, the cross-sectional fiber area decreases. Several studies have shown the effect to be greater in type I fibers, including a decrease in the percentage of type I fibers, thereby increasing the relative percentage of type II fibers.

Muscles can and often do recover from immobilization when activity is resumed. The recovery period is substantially longer than the period of immobilization.

2.4.2 Cessation of Training

Similarly, significant muscle alterations can occur when people stop training. In one study, women resistance trained for 20 weeks and then stopped training for 30–32 weeks. The training program focused on the lower extremity, using a full squat, leg press, and leg extension. Finally, the participants retrained for six weeks. Strength increases were dramatic, as seen in Figure 9.4. Compare the women's strength after their initial training period (post-20) with their strength after detraining (pre-6). This represents the strength loss they experienced with cessation of training.

To prevent losses in the strength gained through resistance training, basic maintenance programs must be established once the desired goals for strength development have been achieved. Maintenance programs are designed to provide sufficient stress to the muscles to maintain existing levels of strength while allowing a reduction in intensity, duration, or frequency of training.

In one study, men and women resistance trained with knee extensions for either 10 or 18 weeks and then spent an additional 12 weeks with either no training or reduced training. Knee extension strength increased 21.4% during the training period. Subjects who then stopped training lost 68% of their strength gains during the weeks they didn't train. But subjects who reduced their training (from three days per week to two, or from two to one) did not lose strength. Thus, it appears that strength can be maintained for at least up to 12 weeks with reduced training frequency.

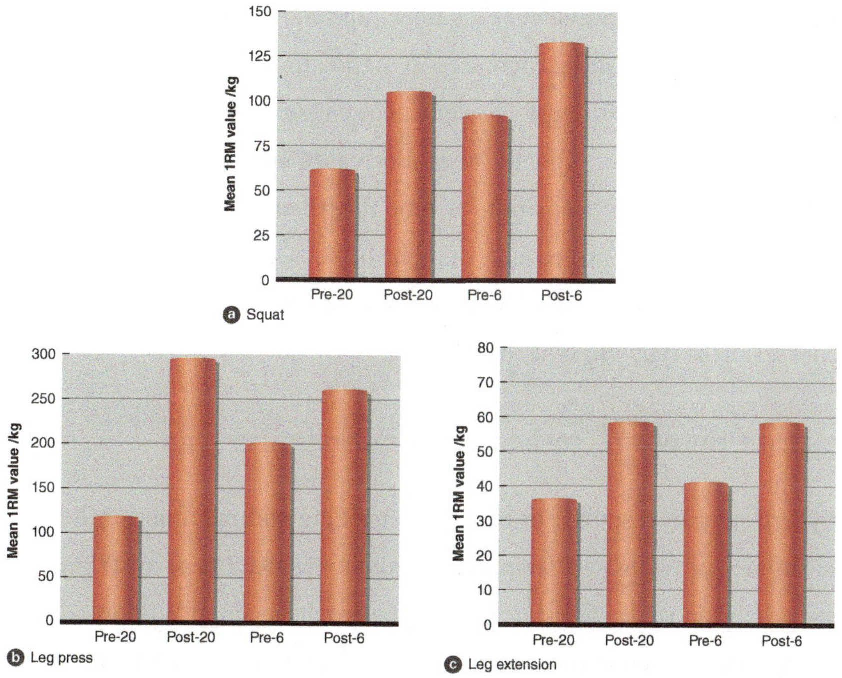

Figure 9.4 Changes in muscle strength for three different resistance exercises, (a) squat, (b) leg press, and (c) leg extension with resistance training in women. Pre-20 values indicate strength before starting training, post-20 values indicate the changes following 20 weeks of training, pre-6 values indicate the changes following 30–32 weeks of detraining, and post-6 values indicate the changes following 6 weeks of retraining.

2.5 Fiber Type Alterations

Can muscle fibers change from one type to another through resistance training? The earliest research concluded that neither speed (anaerobic) nor endurance (aerobic) training could alter the basic fiber type, specifically from type I to type II or from type II to type I. These early studies did show, however, that fibers began to take on certain characteristics of the opposite fiber type if the training was of the opposite kind (e.g., type II fibers might become more oxidative with aerobic training).

Research using animal models has shown that fiber type conversion is indeed possible under conditions of cross-innervation, in which a type II motor unit is experimentally innervated by a type I motor neuron or a type I motor unit is experimentally innervated by a type II motor neuron. Also, chronic, low-frequency nerve stimulation transforms type II motor units into type I motor units within a matter of weeks. Muscle fiber types in rats have changed in response to 15 weeks of high-intensity treadmill training, resulting in an increase in type I and type Ⅱa fibers and a decrease in type Ⅱx fibers. The transition of fibers from type Ⅱx to type Ⅱa and from type Ⅱa to type I was confirmed by several different histochemical techniques.

Staron and coworkers found evidence of fiber type transformation in women as a result of heavy resistance training. Substantial increases in static strength and in the cross-sectional area of all fiber types were noted following a 20-week heavy resistance training program for the lower extremity. The mean percentage of type Ⅱx fibers decreased significantly, but the mean percentage of type Ⅱa fibers increased. The transition of type Ⅱx fibers to type Ⅱa fibers with resistance training has been consistently reported in a number of subsequent studies. Further, other studies demonstrate that a combination of high-intensity resistance training and short-interval speed work can lead to a conversion of type I to type Ⅱa fibers.

3 Interaction Between Resistance Training and Diet

Muscle hypertrophy in response to resistance training can be either limited or enhanced by nutrition. As mentioned previously, a net positive protein balance (more synthesis than breakdown) is the necessary condition under which muscle hypertrophy occurs. Without adequate protein in the diet, protein synthesis is compromised and muscles cannot increase their protein content and hypertrophy. Ingesting protein within a few hours after a bout of resistance exercise increases the rate of protein synthesis and thus adds to the net positive protein balance. Increased protein intake over the subsequent 24 h period will continue to support muscle anabolism. Therefore, nutrition and exercise are powerful stimulators of skeletal muscle protein synthesis.

An international group of researchers recently performed a systematic analysis of 49 published studies (1,863 subjects) to determine if dietary protein supplementation enhances the gains in muscle mass and strength with resistance training. They surveyed randomized controlled trials in which subjects performed resistance training for at least six weeks and took various amounts of dietary protein supplementation. Their analysis of this large sample showed that dietary protein supplementation significantly enhanced changes in strength as measured by 1-repetition maximum tests and muscle size (fiber cross-sectional area and whole-muscle cross-sectional area). However, protein intakes greater than ~1.6 g/kg of body weight per day did not further contribute to these gains. So, although the current U.S. Dietary Reference Intake (DRI) for protein for people over 18 years of age, regardless of physical activity status, is 0.8 g/kg per day, athletes engaged in resistance training may require protein intakes in the diet as high as 1.7 g/kg per day. Although ingestion of relatively small amounts of protein (5–10 g) can stimulate muscle protein synthesis in young men and women, to make muscles larger, one should consume larger amounts of protein, on the order of 20–25 g, immediately after resistance exercise.

What type of protein should be ingested and how much? The best forms of protein for muscle hypertrophy are easily and rapidly digested and rich in essential amino acids, especially leucine. Whey protein found in milk is one source that meets both of these goals. In practice, after resistance training, athletes should consume a small amount of high-quality protein along with adequate carbohydrate in order to stimulate muscle proteins and replenish muscle glycogen stores after exercise. This can be accomplished with either a recovery beverage or foods such as milk or yogurt, a small sandwich, or a protein-rich energy bar. Adding carbohydrate to postexercise protein ingestion does not markedly affect muscle protein balance but does have other benefits, including aiding in the resynthesis of muscle glycogen.

Ingesting repeated small doses of protein during recovery from resistance training may be more effective in increasing muscle hypertrophy than eating just one large meal. However, elevated muscle protein synthesis rates are not totally limited to the few hours of acute postexercise recovery. The so-called window of opportunity lasts from just before the start of resistance exercise to several hours postexercise. Providing protein before or during exercise can enhance muscle protein synthesis during exercise and is a good strategy for prolonged or repeated workouts.

4 Resistance Training for Special Populations

Until the 1970s, resistance training was widely regarded as appropriate only for young, healthy male athletes. This narrow concept led many people to overlook the benefits of resistance training when planning their own activities. In recent years, considerable interest has focused on training for women, children, and people who are elderly. As mentioned earlier in this chapter, the widespread use of resistance training by women, either for sport or for health-related benefits, is rather recent. Substantial knowledge has developed since the early 1970s revealing that women and men have the same ability to develop strength but that, on average, women may not be able to achieve peak values as high as those attained by men. This difference in strength is attributable primarily to muscle size differences related to sex differences in anabolic hormones. Resistance training techniques developed for and applied to men's training seem equally appropriate for women's training. In this section, we first consider age, and then we summarize the importance of this form of training for all athletes, regardless of their sex, age, or sport.

Relative gains in strength appear to be similar when we compare women to men, children to adults, and elderly people to young and middle-aged adults when these gains are expressed as a percentage of their initial strength. However, the increase in the absolute weight lifted is generally greater in men compared to women, in adults compared to children, and in young adults compared to older adults. For example, after 20 weeks of resistance training, assume that a 12-year-old boy and a 25-year-old man each improves his bench press strength by 50%. If the man's initial bench press strength (1-repetition maximum, 1RM) were 50 kg, he would have improved by 25 kg to a new 1RM of 75 kg. If the boy's initial 1RM were 25 kg, he would have improved by 12.5 kg to a new 1RM of 37.5 kg.

4.1 Resistance Exercise for Older Adults

Interest in resistance training for elderly people has increased since the 1980s. A substantial loss of fat-free body mass accompanies aging, a condition known as sarcopenia. This loss reflects mainly the loss of muscle mass, largely because most people become less active as they age. When a muscle isn't used regularly, it loses function, with predictable atrophy and loss of strength. Can resistance training in elderly people prevent or reverse this process, and does nutrition play the same role in older people as it does in young individuals? Elderly exercisers can indeed gain strength and muscle mass in response to resistance training. This fact has important implications for both their health and quality of life. One of the important benefits is that, with maintained or improved strength, they are less likely to fall. This is significant because falls are a major source of injury and debilitation for elderly people and often lead to death.

Under basal conditions, fractional protein synthesis and breakdown are not much different between young and aged people. Rather, sarcopenia results from aged muscle's inability to respond appropriately to anabolic stimuli. An acute bout of resistance exercise does not appear to elicit the same hypertrophic response in skeletal muscles of older individuals. This anabolic resistance has been attributed to the inability of resistance exercise to appropriately increase mTOR (mammalian target of rapamycin) signaling in the elderly. Resistance training is certainly capable of increasing strength and muscle mass in elderly persons; the response is simply blunted. With resistance training, large increases in strength are often accompanied by only small increases in myofibrillar protein and muscle size. In this age group, strength increases depend significantly on neural adaptations.

The impact of protein intake on muscle hypertrophy in the elderly is likewise blunted. Whereas as little as 5 g of protein in combination with resistance training stimulates skeletal muscle protein synthesis in young individuals, larger amounts must be ingested to cause the same effect in the elderly. This may be attributable to changes in the sensitivity of aged muscle to branched-chain amino acids. Studies indicate that ingestion of 25–30 g of high-quality protein or greater than 2 g of leucine is necessary to stimulate aged muscle protein synthesis to a similar degree as in young muscle. Aging is also associated with a resistance of skeletal muscle to the influence of insulin on protein synthesis, which could be a key factor in the etiology of sarcopenia.

In human aging, there is significant variation in regional body composition, and age-associated dysfunction and disability have been associated with sex and race. For example, women have greater muscle fat infiltration and higher subcutaneous fat and lower limb mass compared to men, and African Americans exhibit greater limb muscle mass that is accompanied by greater subcutaneous fat and intermuscular and intramuscular fat than Caucasians of the same sex.

4.2 Resistance Training for Children

The wisdom of resistance training for children and adolescents has long been debated. The potential for injury, particularly growth plate injuries from the use of free weights, has caused much concern. Many people once believed that children would not benefit from resistance training, based on the assumption that the hormonal changes associated with puberty are necessary for gaining muscle strength and mass. We now know that children and adolescents can train safely with minimal risk of injury if appropriate safeguards are implemented. Furthermore, they can indeed gain both muscular strength and muscle mass.

Resistance training programs for children should be prescribed in much the same way as for adults, but with a special emphasis on teaching proper lifting technique. Specific guidelines have been established by a number of professional organizations, including the American Orthopedic Society for Sports Medicine, the American Academy of Pediatrics, the American College of Sports Medicine, the National Athletic Trainers' Association, the National Strength and Conditioning Association, the President's Council on Physical Fitness and Sports, and the U.S. Olympic Committee. Basic guidelines for the progression of resistance exercise in children are presented in Table 9.1.

Table 9.1 Basic Guidelines for Resistance Exercise Progression in Children

Age	Considerations
7 years or younger	Introduce child to basic exercises using little or no weight; develop the concept of a training session; teach exercise technique; progress from body weight calisthenics, partner exercises, and lightly resisted exercises; keep volume low
8–10 years	Gradually increase the number of exercises; practice exercise technique in all lifts; start gradual progressive loading of exercises; keep exercises simple; gradually increase training volume; carefully monitor tolerance of the exercise stress
11–13 years	Teach all basic exercise techniques; continue progressive loading of each exercise; emphasize exercise techniques; introduce more advanced exercises with little or no resistance. Progress to more advanced youth programs in resistance exercise; add sport–specific components; emphasize exercise techniques; increase volume
14–15 years	Progress to more advanced youth programs in resistance exercise; add sport–specific components; emphasize exercise techniques; increase volume
16 years or older	Move child to entry–level adult programs after all background knowledge has been mastered and a basic level of training experience has been gained

4.3 Resistance Training for Athletes

Gaining strength, power, or muscular endurance simply for the sake of being stronger, being more powerful, or having greater muscular endurance is of relatively little importance to athletes unless it also improves their athletic performance. Resistance training by field-event athletes and competitive weightlifters makes intuitive sense. The need for resistance training by the gymnast distance runner, baseball player, high jumper, or ballet dancer is less obvious.

We do not have extensive research to document the specific benefits of resistance training for every sport or for every event within a sport. But clearly, each has basic strength, power, and muscular endurance requirements that must be met to achieve optimal performance. Training beyond these requirements, however, may be unnecessary.

Training is costly in terms of time, and athletes can't afford to waste time on activities that won't result in better athletic performances. Thus, some performance measurement is imperative to evaluate any resistance training program's efficacy. To resistance train solely to become stronger, with no associated improvement in performance, is of questionable value. However, it should also be recognized that resistance training to improve muscular endurance can reduce the risk of injury for most sports because fatigued individuals are at an increased risk of injury.

IN CLOSING

In this chapter, we have considered the role of resistance training in increasing muscular strength and improving performance. We have examined how muscle strength is gained through both muscular and neural adaptations, the importance of dietary protein intake in muscle hypertrophy, how resistance training can slow the impact of sarcopenia in the elderly, and how resistance training is of importance for both health and sport, regardless of age or sex. In the next chapter, we turn our attention away from resistance training and begin exploring how the body adapts to aerobic and anaerobic training.

KEY TERMS

atrophy; autogenic inhibition; chronic hypertrophy; fiber hyperplasia; fiber hypertrophy; resistance training; sarcopenia; transient hypertrophy

STUDY QUESTIONS

(1) What is a reasonable expectation for percentage strength gains following a six-month resistance training program? How do these percentage gains differ by age, sex, and previous resistance training experience?

(2) What is the suggested minimal intensity for resistance training that will lead to muscle hypertrophy when the exercises are performed to volitional fatigue?

(3) Discuss the different theories that have attempted to explain how muscles gain strength with training.

(4) What is autogenic inhibition? How might it be important to resistance training?

(5) Differentiate between transient and chronic muscle hypertrophy.

(6) What is fiber hyperplasia? How might it occur? How might it be related to gains in size and muscle strength with resistance training?

(7) What is the physiological basis for hypertrophy?

(8) Describe the respective effects of intensity and circulating hormones on muscle adaptation to fatiguing resistance training.

(9) What is the physiological response to muscle immobilization?

(10) To support protein synthesis during resistance training, what type of protein should be ingested and how much?

(11) Is there an optimal timing of protein ingestion when an individual is trying to optimize the hypertrophic response to successive exercise sessions?

第九章
机体对抗阻训练的适应

长期运动会使神经肌肉系统产生多种适应性变化。其适应程度取决于训练的类型，如慢跑、骑自行车或游泳等有氧运动仅引起肌肉体积和力量的轻微增长，主要的神经肌肉适应发生在抗阻训练中。

除了竞技性举重、田径运动中的投掷及一定水平的足球、摔跤和拳击项目，抗阻训练一度被认为是不适合其他项目运动员采用的方法。从20世纪60年代末到70年代初，教练员和研究人员发现力量和爆发力训练几乎对所有的体育运动和身体活动都有利，对男性和女性都是如此。直到20世纪80年代末至90年代初，健康专家们才开始意识到抗阻训练对机体全面的健康及康复的重要性。

现在大多数运动员都将抗阻训练作为他们整体训练计划的一个重要组成部分。这种态度的转变很大程度上是因为研究证实了抗阻训练能够提高运动员的运动表现。对于那些想从运动中获得健康益处的人来说，抗阻训练是其运动处方的重要部分。

一、抗阻训练与肌肉机能的提高

神经肌肉系统是机体在训练的重复刺激后反应最灵敏的系统之一。抗阻训练能够引起肌肉力量的实质性增长，在3~6个月肌肉力量可提高25%~100%，有时甚至更多。但对力量增长百分比的预估可能有误导作用。其实大多数抗阻训练研究中的受试者都从来没有进行过举重或参与其他任何形式的抗阻训练。他们早期的力量增长大部分是因为掌握了合理的动作模式，如卧推时将杠铃由胸部推至完全伸展的位置。这种动作模式的学习效果占早期力量增长的50%。

二、肌肉力量增长的机制

虽然肌肉体积与肌肉力量之间确实存在一定关系，但肌肉力量绝不只取决于肌肉的体积。当然，这并不意味着肌肉体积对于肌肉的极限力量潜能不重要。产生力量的能力取决于肌节内的横桥数量，而横桥的数量又取决于肌动蛋白和肌球蛋白的数量。目前，男子和女子举重世界纪录都表明肌肉体积是极为重要的。随着体重级别的增加（肌肉质量的增加），运动员举起的总重量也会增加。然而，导致肌肉力量增加的相关机制非常复杂且目前尚未完全明确。除了肌肉体积的增加，还有什么可以解释训练所导致的肌肉力量增长呢？首先让我们考虑一个有力的证据，即抗阻训练会改变肌肉的神经控制，使其产生更大的力量。

1.肌肉力量增长的神经控制

抗阻训练是导致力量增长的重要因素，尤其在早期，是神经适应的结果。伊诺卡的实验证实，在没有肌肉结构变化的条件下可以实现肌肉力量增长，但没有神经适应则不可能发生。因此，力量并不仅是肌肉独有的特性，更确切地说，力量也是神经运动系统的一种特性。运动单位的募集、运动神经放电频率、特定运动中运动单位的同步性以及其他神经因素对力量的增长都很重要。消除神经抑制也能起到力量增长的作用。这些神经因素可以在很大程度上解释不发生肌肉肥大时的肌肉力量增长以及偶尔发生的超常力量现象。

（1）更多运动单位的同步化与募集。运动单位通常不是同时募集的，即它们并不在同一时刻被动员。它们被许多能够传导兴奋性和抑制性冲动的不同神经元控制。肌纤维是收缩还是舒张，取决于同一时间内运动单位所接受到的大量脉冲的总和。只有在传入的兴奋性冲动超过抑制性冲动达到阈值时，运动单位才被激活，其支配的肌纤维才会发生收缩。

肌肉力量增长可能是由脊髓中运动神经元之间联系的变化引起的，这种变化使得运动单位的活动更加同步化，收缩更加容易且肌肉产生力量的能力更强。证据显示，抗阻训练会导致运动单位同步化增强，但至于运动单位活化的同步究竟是否能够引起更强有力的收缩仍有争议。不过很明显，运动单元同步化确实提高了力量增长的程度和发挥稳定力量的能力。

（2）运动单位编码频率的增加。α运动神经元神经冲动的增加也能够增加相应运动单位的放电频率或编码频率。当一个运动单位的刺激频率持续增加时，肌肉最终会处于一个强直收缩状态，此时的肌纤维或运动单位产生绝对最大力量和张力峰值。目前，能证明编码频率随抗阻训练而增加的研究较少。快速运动或弹道式训练对于刺激编码频率特别有效。

（3）神经驱动的增强。神经驱动是指运动单位募集与编码频率的结合，它起始于中枢神经系统，通过周围神经扩散到肌纤维。肌电图是通过表面电极测量神经和肌肉活动的，是一种很好的测量神经驱动的方法。

（4）自发性抑制。神经肌肉系统的抑制性机制是必需的，如高尔基腱器官可防止肌肉产生大于骨与结缔组织所能承受的力量，这一机制被称为自发性抑制。然而，在发挥超常力量的过程中，主要损伤常发生于这些结构，提示保护性抑制机制受到了限制。抗阻训练可逐渐减少或对抗这些抑制性神经冲动，让肌肉产生更大的力，而不受肌肉质量增加的影响。因此，力量增长可通过降低神经抑制而实现。这一理论极具吸引力，因为它能够部分解释在不发生肌肉肥大时的超常力量和力量增长现象。

（5）其他神经因素。除了增加运动单位募集和自发性抑制减弱外，其他神经因素也可以有助于抗阻训练中肌肉力量的增加。如主动肌和对抗肌的共激活。如上臂弯举动作，肱二头肌是主动肌，肱三头肌是对抗肌，当两者同时收缩且力量相等时，关节不会运动。因此，为了使主动肌的力量最大，必须使共激活程度最小化。另外神经肌接头形态学的改变也会增加肌肉力量。

2. 肌肉肥大

肌肉的体积是如何增长的呢？我们知道肌肉肥大可分为暂时性和长期性两种。暂时性肌肉肥大是指一次运动中或运动结束后即刻产生的肌肉体积增大，这主要是血浆中体液聚集（水肿）于细胞间质和细胞内引起的。暂时性肥大，顾名思义，其持续时间很短，因为体液将在运动后数小时内重新回到血液中去。长期性肌肉肥大是指长期进行抗阻训练所引起的肌肉体积增大，它反映了现有单根肌纤维体积的增大（肌纤维肥大）、纤维数量的增多或两者共同引起的肌肉结构变化。

（1）训练强度和肌纤维肥大。传统的训练方法普遍认为要实现肌肉体积的大幅增加，需要达到1RM强度的60%~85%或更高。然而，最新研究表明，如果抗阻训练达到肌肉疲劳，50%的低强度运动可以诱导与高强度运动相同的肌肉体积增加。这一理论认为，轻负荷时的疲劳收缩引起代谢刺激，从而导致肌纤维大量募集。

（2）肌纤维肥大。早期研究认为每个人肌肉中的肌纤维数量早在出生时或此后不久就已经确定，且此数量将保持一生不变。如果这是真的，那么整体肌肉肥大只可能是由单根肌纤维肥大引起的。可能发生如下变化：

- 更多的肌原纤维；
- 更多的肌动蛋白和肌球蛋白；
- 更多的肌浆；
- 更多结缔组织或上述因素的综合效应。

（3）激素和肌纤维肥大。肌肉生理学的主流观点是，抗阻训练诱导的激素变化促进了肌肉质量的增加，促使肌肉力量增长。通常与这种反应相关的激素包括合成代谢激素睾酮、生长激素（GH）和胰岛素样生长因子1（IGF-1）。睾酮一直被认为参与这些变化，因为它的主要功能之一就是促进肌肉生长。睾酮是甾类激素，其主要发挥合成代谢功能。男性在青春期肌肉明显增长，主要原因是体内睾酮增加了近10倍。此外，大量的合成代谢类固醇及抗阻训练也可显著增加肌肉质量和力量，这一点已经得到了充分的证实。

（4）肌纤维数量增生。动物研究表明，肌纤维总数量的增加也可能是导致整个肌肉肥大的一个因素。对猫的研究提供了相当明确的证据，证明在极大负荷运动训练中会发生肌纤维分裂。

3.神经活化与肌纤维肥大的整合

对抗阻训练产生适应的研究表明，自主力量早期增长或最大力量产生首先与神经适应有关，这一适应会导致肌肉的自主活化增加。力量的长期增加通常与训练肌的肥大有关。然而，减少蛋白质降解、增加蛋白质合成或两者协同发生需要一定的时间，因此，最初的力量增加往往是神经肌肉激活的改变。大多数研究者发现，神经因素显著影响力量增长是在前8～10周训练期间，肌肉肥大在前期对于力量增长的贡献很小，蛋白质经过一定时间的构建积累，在10周训练后成为影响力量增长的主要因素。但也并非所有的研究都赞同这种力量发展模式。一项为期6个月的针对运动员力量训练的研究显示，神经激活作用可以解释为什么训练强度最大的几个月中肌肉力量增长最多，但肌肉的肥大并不是主要原因。

4. 废用性肌萎缩与肌力下降

当一个体力活动正常的人减少其活动水平或一个训练有素的人停止训练，其肌肉结构和功能都会发生变化。这一现象可分为两类：一类是整个肢体都被固定；另一类是经常训练的人突然停训。

（1）固定。当运动员某一训练肌突然因为制动而不能活动，则几小时内肌肉就开始发生变化。在固定的最初6小时内，蛋白质合成率开始下降，这种下降很可能导致肌肉开始萎缩，即肌肉组织体积减小。肌肉缺乏使用导致萎缩发生和肌蛋白丢失，固定的第1周内力量下降最为明显，日平均下降可达3%～4%。这一现象与被制动肌肉的萎缩和神经肌肉活动下降均有关。

（2）停训。当运动员停止训练时也会发生类似的显著性肌肉变化。在一项研究中，女性受试者经过20周的抗阻训练后停训30～32周，随后又重新进行6周训练。此训练计划目标在下肢肌群，采用深蹲、腿举及腿部伸展进行训练。将训练期刚结束时（20周训练后）女性受试者的肌肉力量和停训后（6周恢复训练前）的肌肉力量进行比较，发现其肌肉力量显著增加。

5. 纤维类型改变

抗阻训练是否能够使肌纤维从一种类型转变为另一种类型呢？最初的研究认为，无论是速度（无氧）训练还是耐力（有氧）训练均不能改变基本的肌纤维类型，尤其是从Ⅰ型肌纤维变为Ⅱ型肌纤维或从Ⅱ型肌纤维变为Ⅰ型肌纤维。但这些研究也认为，如果采用的训练方式与肌纤维类型相反，则该类型肌纤维也会表现出某些相反类型的特点（如有氧训练可能使Ⅱ型肌纤维变得更具氧化性）。

三、抗阻训练和饮食的相互作用

抗阻训练引起的肌肉肥大可以通过营养来限制或增强。如前所述，净正蛋白质平衡（合成大于分解）是肌肉肥大发生的必要条件。如果饮食中没有足够的蛋白质，蛋白质合成就会受到影响，导致肌肉不能增加蛋白质含量而产生肥大。一次抗阻运动后的几个小时内摄入蛋白质会提高蛋白质合成的速度，从而增加净正蛋白质平衡。随后24小时内蛋白质摄入量的增加将继续促进肌肉合成代谢。因此，营养和运动是骨骼肌蛋白质合成的有力促进剂。

蛋白质摄入量建议。一个国际研究小组最近对已发表的49项研究（1 863名研究对象）进行了系统分析，以确定膳食蛋白质补充是否能通过抗阻训练提高肌肉质量和力量。他们调查了随机对照试验，在这些试验中，受试者进行了至少6周的抗阻训练，并服用了不同剂量的膳食蛋白质补充剂。分析表明，膳食蛋白质补充可显著增强1RM力量及肌肉围度（肌纤维横截面积和肌肉整体横截面积）。然而，每天摄入的蛋白质超过1.6 克/千克体重，并没有进一步起到促进作用。因此，美国目前18岁以上人群的蛋白质参考摄入量（DRI）无论身体活动状况如何，都是每天0.8 克/千克体重，但从事抗阻训练的运动员每天可能需要从饮食中摄取高达1.7 克/千克体重的蛋白质。虽然摄入相对少量的蛋白质（5～10 克）也可以促进年轻男性和女性的肌肉蛋白合成，但要使肌肉肥大，应在抗阻运动后即刻摄入20～25 克的蛋白质。

四、特殊人群的抗阻训练

总的来说，对于绝对举重重量的增幅，男性要大于女性，成年人要大于儿童，年轻人要大于老年人。例如，经过20周的抗阻训练，假设一个12岁的男孩和一个25岁的成年男性各自提高了50%的卧推力量，如果这个成年男性最初的1RM卧推力量是50千克，他将1RM提高了25千克从而达到75千克；如果这个男孩最初的1RM是25千克，他将1RM提高了12.5千克从而达到37.5千克。

1.老年人的抗阻训练

老年人确实能够通过抗阻训练获得力量和肌肉质量的增长，而且，这对老年人的健康以及生活质量都有着重要意义。通过力量的维持或提高，他们就不容易跌倒。一般情况下，年轻人、老年人体内蛋白合成与分解并无太大差异。当然，老年肌少症状态下对合成代谢刺激的反应会下降。老年人进行一次性抗阻运动并不会引起骨骼肌肥大应答，其原因主要是老年人在抗阻训练后并不能有效激活mTOR信号通路。抗阻训练确实能够增强老年人的力量和肌肉质量，但是这种应答相对迟缓，通常表现为抗阻训练后力量增加但是肌肉围度却增加很小。老年人力量的增长主要依赖于神经适应。

2.儿童和青少年的抗阻训练

儿童和青少年进行抗阻训练是否明智一直是争论的焦点。使用自由杠铃可能造成的损伤，特别是生长板的损伤，已经引起了广泛关注。许多人曾认为，儿童和青少年不会从抗阻训练中受益，因为与青春期相关的激素变化是肌肉力量和质量增长的必要条件。我们现在知道，如果实施适当的安全措施，儿童和青少年可以在最低的受伤风险下安全地训练。此外，他们确实可以获得肌肉力量和质量的提升。

3.运动员的抗阻训练

如果增长力量、爆发力及肌肉耐力仅仅为了变得更强壮、更有冲击力或具备更好的肌肉耐力，这对运动员的意义并不大除非能帮助他们提高运动表现。田赛项目和举重运动员的抗阻训练有着直观的意义，而体操、长跑、棒球、跳高运动员对抗阻训练的需求就不那么明显了。我们没有广泛的研究来证明抗阻训练对每项运动或一项运动中每个小项的具体益处，但很明显，每项运动都有基本的力量、爆发力和肌肉耐力要求，这些是达到最佳运动表现所必须的。

Chapter 10 Adaptations to Aerobic and Anaerobic Training

During a single bout of aerobic exercise, the human body precisely adjusts its cardiovascular and respiratory function to meet the energy and oxygen demands of actively contracting muscle. When these systems are challenged repeatedly, as happens with regular exercise training, they adapt in ways that allow the body to improve $\dot{V}O_{2\,max}$ and overall endurance performance. Aerobic training, or cardiorespiratory endurance training, improves cardiac function and peripheral blood flow and enhances the capacity of the muscle fibers to generate greater amounts of adenosine triphosphate (ATP). Anaerobic training improves anaerobic metabolism; short-term, high-intensity exercise capacity; tolerance for acid-base imbalances; and in some cases, muscle strength. Both aerobic and anaerobic training induce a variety of adaptations that benefit exercise and sport performance.

The effects of training on cardiovascular and respiratory, or aerobic, endurance is well known to endurance athletes like distance runners, cyclists, cross-country skiers, and swimmers but are often ignored by other types of athletes. Training programs for many nonendurance athletes often ignore the aerobic endurance component. This is understandable, because for maximum improvement in performance, training should be highly specific to the particular sport or activity in which the athlete participates, and endurance is frequently not recognized as important to nonendurance activities. The reasoning is, why waste valuable training time if the result is not improved performance?

The problem with this reasoning is that most nonendurance sports do indeed have an endurance, or aerobic, component. For example, in football, players and coaches might fail to recognize the importance of cardiorespiratory endurance as part of the total training program. From all outward appearances, American football is an anaerobic, or burst-type, activity consisting of repeated bouts of high-intensity work of short duration. Seldom does a run exceed 40–60 yd (about 37~55 m) , and even this is usually followed by a substantial rest interval. The need for endurance may not be readily apparent. What athletes and coaches might fail to consider is that this burst-type activity must be repeated many times during the game. With a higher aerobic endurance capacity, an athlete could maintain the quality of each burst activity throughout the game and would still be relatively fresh (less drop-off in performance, fewer feelings of fatigue) during the all-important closing minutes of the game.

1 Adaptations to Aerobic Training

Improvements in endurance that accompany regular (e.g., daily, every other day) aerobic training, such as running, cycling, or swimming, result from multiple adaptations to the training stimuli. Some adaptations occur in the cardiovascular system, improving circulation to and within the muscles. Still other important changes occur within the muscles themselves, promoting more efficient utilization of oxygen and fuel substrates.

1.1 Muscular Versus Cardiorespiratory Endurance

Endurance is a term that refers to two separate but related concepts: muscular endurance and cardiorespiratory endurance. Each makes a unique contribution to athletic performance, and each differs in its importance to different athletes.

For sprinters, endurance is the quality that allows them to sustain a high speed over the full distance of, for example, a 100 m or 200 m dash. This component of fitness is termed muscular endurance, the ability of a single muscle or muscle group to maintain high-intensity, repetitive, or static contractions. This type of endurance is also exemplified by a weightlifter doing multiple repetitions, a boxer, or a wrestler. The exercise or activity can be rhythmic and repetitive in nature, such as multiple repetitions of the bench press for the weightlifter and jabbing for the boxer. Or the activity can be more static, such as a sustained muscle action when a wrestler attempts to pin an opponent. In either case, the resulting fatigue is confined to a specific muscle group, and the activity's duration is usually no more than 2 min. Muscular endurance is highly related to muscular strength and to anaerobic power development.

While muscular endurance is specific to individual muscles or muscle groups, cardiorespiratory endurance relates to the ability to sustain prolonged, dynamic whole-body exercise using large muscle groups. Cardiorespiratory endurance is related to the development of the cardiorespiratory systems' ability to maintain oxygen delivery to working muscles during prolonged exercise, as well as the muscles' ability to use energy aerobically. This is why the terms cardiorespiratory endurance and aerobic endurance are sometimes used synonymously.

1.2 Evaluating Cardiorespiratory Endurance Capacity

Studying the effects of training on endurance requires an objective, repeatable means of measuring an individual's cardiorespiratory endurance capacity.

1.2.1 Maximal Endurance Capacity: $\dot{V}O_{2\,max}$

Most exercise scientists regard $\dot{V}O_{2\,max}$, sometimes called maximal aerobic power or maximal aerobic capacity, as the best objective laboratory measure of cardiorespiratory endurance. $\dot{V}O_{2\,max}$ is defined as the highest rate of oxygen consumption attainable during maximal or exhaustive exercise. $\dot{V}O_{2\,max}$ as defined by the Fick equation is determined by maximal cardiac output (delivery of oxygen and blood flow to working muscles) and the maximal $Ca\text{-}C_{\bar{v}}O_2$ difference (the ability of the active muscles to extract and use the oxygen).

As exercise intensity increases, oxygen consumption eventually either plateaus or decreases slightly, even with further increases in workload, indicating that a true maximal $\dot{V}O_2$ has been achieved.

With endurance training, more oxygen can be delivered to, and used by, active muscles than in an untrained state. Previously untrained subjects demonstrate average increases in $\dot{V}O_{2\,max}$ of 15%–20% after a 20-week training program. These improvements allow individuals to perform endurance activities at a higher intensity, improving their performance potential. Figure 10.1 illustrates the increase in $\dot{V}O_{2\,max}$ after 12 months of aerobic training in a previously untrained individual. In this example, $\dot{V}O_{2\,max}$ increased by about 30%. Note that the $\dot{V}O_2$ cost of running at a certain submaximal intensity (referred to as running economy) did not change, but higher running speeds could be attained after training.

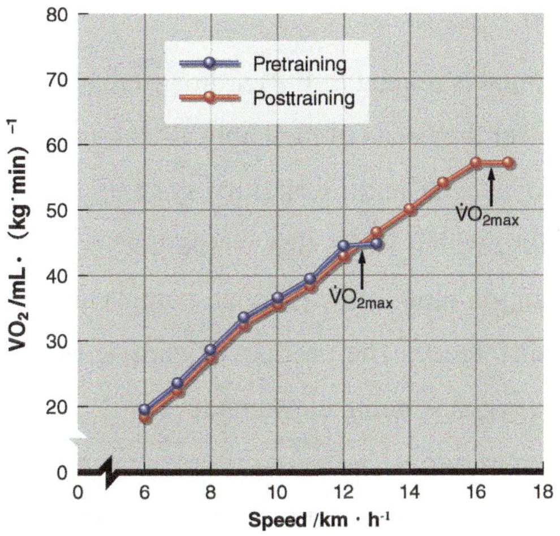

Figure 10.1 Changes in $\dot{V}O_2$ with 12 months of endurance training. $\dot{V}O_2$ increased from 44–57 ml · kg^{-1} · min^{-1}, a 30% increase. Peak speed during the treadmill test increased from 13 km/h to 16 km/h.

1.2.2 Submaximal Endurance

In addition to increasing maximal endurance capacity, endurance training also increases submaximal endurance, which is more difficult to evaluate. A lower steady-state heart rate at the same submaximal exercise intensity is one physiological variable that can be used to objectively quantify the effect of training. Additionally, one could measure the average peak absolute power output a person can maintain over a fixed period of time on a cycle ergometer. For running, the average peak speed or velocity a person can maintain for a set period of time would be a similar test of submaximal endurance. Generally, these tests last 30 min to an hour. Submaximal endurance, like critical power, is more closely related to actual competitive endurance performance than $\dot{V}O_{2\,max}$. With endurance training, submaximal endurance increases.

1.3 Cardiovascular Adaptations to Training

Multiple cardiovascular adaptations occur in response to exercise training, including changes in the following:

- Heart size;
- Stroke volume;
- Heart rate;
- Cardiac output;
- Blood flow;
- Blood and red cell volumes.

1.3.1 Oxygen Transport System

Cardiorespiratory endurance is related to the cardiovascular and respiratory systems' ability to deliver sufficient oxygen to meet the needs of metabolically active tissues.

The ability of the cardiovascular and respiratory systems to deliver oxygen to active tissues is defined by the Fick equation, which states that whole-body oxygen consumption is determined by both the delivery of oxygen via blood flow (cardiac output) and the amount of oxygen extracted by the tissues, the $Ca\text{-}C_{\bar{v}}O_2$ difference. The product of cardiac output and the $Ca\text{-}C_{\bar{v}}O_2$ difference determines the rate at which oxygen is being consumed:

$\dot{V}O_2$ = stroke volume × heart rate × $Ca\text{-}C_{\bar{v}}O_{22}$ difference and

$\dot{V}O_{2\,max}$ = maximal stroke volume × maximal heart rate × maximal $Ca\text{-}C_{\bar{v}}O_2$ difference

Because maximal heart rate (HRmax) either stays the same or decreases slightly with training, increases in $\dot{V}O_{2\,max}$ depend on adaptations in maximal stroke volume and maximal $Ca\text{-}C_{\bar{v}}O_2$difference.

The oxygen demand of exercising muscles increases with increasing exercise intensity. Aerobic endurance depends on the cardiorespiratory system's ability to deliver sufficient oxygen to these active tissues to meet their heightened demands for oxygen for oxidative metabolism. As maximal levels of exercise are achieved, heart size, blood flow, blood pressure, and blood volume can all potentially limit the maximal ability to transport oxygen. Endurance training elicits numerous changes in these components of the oxygen transport system that enable it to function more effectively.

1.3.2 Heart Size

As an adaptation to the increased work demand, cardiac muscle mass and ventricular volume increase with training. Cardiac muscle, like skeletal muscle, undergoes morphological adaptations as a result of chronic endurance training. At one time, cardiac hypertrophy induced by exercise—athlete's heart, as it was called, was viewed with concern because experts incorrectly believed that enlargement of the heart always reflected a pathological state, as sometimes occurs with severe hypertension. Training-induced cardiac hypertrophy, on the other hand, is now recognized as a normal adaptation to chronic endurance training.

The left ventricle does the most work and thus undergoes the greatest adaptation in response to endurance training. The type of ventricular adaptation depends on the type of exercise training performed. For example, during resistance training, the left ventricle must contract against increased afterload from the systemic circulation. We learned that blood pressure during resistance exercise can exceed 480/350 mmHg. This presents a considerable resistance that must be overcome by the left ventricle. To overcome this high afterload, the heart muscle compensates by increasing left ventricular wall thickness, thereby increasing its contractility. Thus, the increase in its muscle mass is in direct response to repeated exposure to the increased afterload with resistance training. However, there is little change in ventricular volume.

With endurance training, left ventricular chamber size increases. This allows for increased left ventricular filling and consequently an increase in stroke volume. The increase in left ventricular dimensions is largely attributable to a training-induced increase in plasma volume that increases left ventricular end-diastolic volume (increased preload). In concert with this, a decrease in heart rate at rest caused by increased parasympathetic tone, and during exercise at the same rate of work, allows a longer diastolic filling period. The increases in plasma volume and diastolic filling time increase left ventricular chamber size at the end of diastole. This effect of endurance training on the left ventricle is often called a volume loading effect.

It was originally hypothesized that this increase in left ventricular dimensions was the only change in the left ventricle caused by endurance training. Additional research has revealed that, similar to what happens in resistance training, myocardial wall thickness increases with endurance training. Highly trained endurance athletes (competitive cross-country skiers, endurance cyclists, and long-distance runners) have greater left ventricular masses than non-endurance-trained men and women. Furthermore, left ventricular mass is highly correlated with $\dot{V}O_{2\,max}$.

1.3.3 Stroke Volume

Stroke volume at rest is substantially higher after an endurance training program than it is before training. This endurance training-induced increase is also seen at a given submaximal exercise intensity and at maximal exercise. This increase is illustrated in Figure 10.2, which shows the changes in stroke volume of a subject who exercised at increasing intensities up to a maximal intensity before and after a six-month endurance training program. Typical values for stroke volume at rest and during maximal exercise in untrained, trained, and highly trained athletes are listed in Table 10.1. The wide range of stroke volume values for any given cell within this table is largely attributable to differences in body size. Larger people typically have larger hearts and a greater blood volume, and thus higher stroke volumes—an important point when one is comparing stroke volumes of different people.

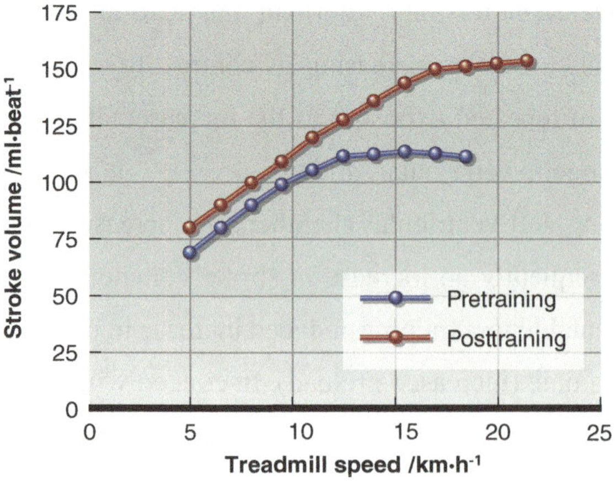

Figure 10.2 Changes in stroke volume with endurance training during walking, jogging, and running on a treadmill at increasing velocities.

Table 10.1 Stroke VOlumes at Rest (SV_{rest}) and During Maximal Exercise (SV_{max}) for Different States of Training

Subjects	SV_{rest} /ml · $beat^{-1}$	SV_{max} /ml · $beat^{-1}$
Untrained	50–70	80–110
Trained	70–90	110–150
Highly trained	90–110	150–220 +

After aerobic training, the left ventricle fills more completely during diastole. Plasma volume expands with training, which allows for more blood to enter the ventricle during diastole, increasing end-diastolic volume (EDV). The heart rate of a trained heart is also lower at rest and at the same absolute exercise intensity than that of an untrained heart, allowing more time for the increased diastolic filling. More blood entering the ventricle increases the stretch on the ventricular walls; by the Frank-Starling mechanism, this results in an increased force of contraction.

The thickness of the posterior and septal walls of the left ventricle also increases slightly with endurance training. Increased ventricular muscle mass results in increased contractile force, in turn causing a lower end-systolic volume (ESV).

The decrease in ESV is facilitated by the decrease in peripheral resistance that occurs with training. Increased contractility resulting from an increase in left ventricular thickness and greater diastolic filling (Frank-Starling mechanism) , coupled with the reduction in systemic peripheral resistance, increases the ejection fraction [equal to (EDV – ESV) / EDV] in the trained heart. More blood enters the left ventricle, and a greater percentage of what enters is forced out with each contraction, resulting in an increase in stroke volume.

To summarize, increased left ventricular dimensions, reduced systemic peripheral resistance, and a greater blood volume account for the increases in resting, submaximal, and maximal stroke volume after an endurance training program.

1.3.4 Heart Rate

Aerobic training has a major impact on heart rate at rest, during submaximal exercise, and during the postexercise recovery period. The effect of aerobic training on maximal heart rate is rather negligible.

(1) Resting Heart Rate

Resting heart rate decreases markedly as a result of endurance training. Some studies have shown that a sedentary individual with an initial resting heart rate of 80 beats/min can decrease resting heart rate by approximately 1beat/min with each week of aerobic training, at least for the first few weeks. After 10 weeks of moderate endurance training, resting heart rate can decrease from 80–70 beats/min or lower. On the other hand, well-controlled studies with large numbers of subjects have shown much smaller decreases in resting heart rate, that is, fewer than 5 beats/min following up to 20 weeks of aerobic training.

Bradycardia is a term indicating a heart rate of fewer than 60 beats/min. In untrained individuals, bradycardia can be the result of abnormal cardiac function or heart disease. However, highly conditioned endurance athletes often have resting heart rates lower than 40 beats/min, and some have values lower than 30 beats/min. Therefore, it is necessary to differentiate between training-induced bradycardia, which is a normal response to endurance training, and pathological bradycardia, which can be cause for concern.

The low resting heart rate (HR) of well-trained endurance athletes is most often attributed to an elevated parasympathetic (vagal) tone. However, a 2013 review of the available evidence casts doubt on this mechanism. The two alternative explanations for the resting bradycardia of athletes are a diminished sympathetic tone and a lower intrinsic heart rate. The intrinsic heart rate is the rate of sinoatrial (SA) node firing in the absence of any neural or hormonal input. In studies that have blocked parasympathetic activity to the heart using the drug atropine, there is still a significant resting bradycardia in athletes. In fact, the difference in HR after parasympathetic blockade is greater than the difference in the normal HR, suggesting that the bradycardia is not the result of elevated vagal tone.

Other studies have blocked both branches of the autonomic nervous system, that is, used a complete autonomic blockade. The HR after complete autonomic blockade is a measure of the intrinsic HR. In studies showing a lowered resting HR after endurance training, the bradycardia persists after complete autonomic blockade. Thus, the resting bradycardia seen in athletes is at least partially, and perhaps completely, the result of a decreased intrinsic HR.

A decreased intrinsic HR can result from a remodeling of the SA node. The SA node serves as the pacemaker of the heart due to properties of ion channels and Ca^{2+}-handling proteins in the SA node cells. Changes in these properties cause the well-known bradycardias associated with SA node disease, heart failure, atrial fibrillation, and even aging itself. In fact, the age-associated decrease in resting HR has been attributed to a downregulation of ryanodine receptors that are involved in Ca^{2+} flux. If these mechanisms are involved in bradycardias associated with these other processes and diseases, it is likely that they are involved in training-induced bradycardia as well.

(2) Submaximal Heart Rate

During submaximal exercise, aerobic training results in a lower heart rate at any given absolute exercise intensity. This is illustrated in Figure 10.3, which shows the heart rate of an individual exercising on a treadmill before and after training. At each walking or running speed, the post training heart rate is lower than the heart rate before training. The training-induced decrease in heart rate is typically greater at higher intensities.

While maintaining a cardiac output appropriate to meet the needs of working muscle, a trained heart performs less work (lower heart rate, higher stroke volume) than an untrained heart at the same absolute workload.

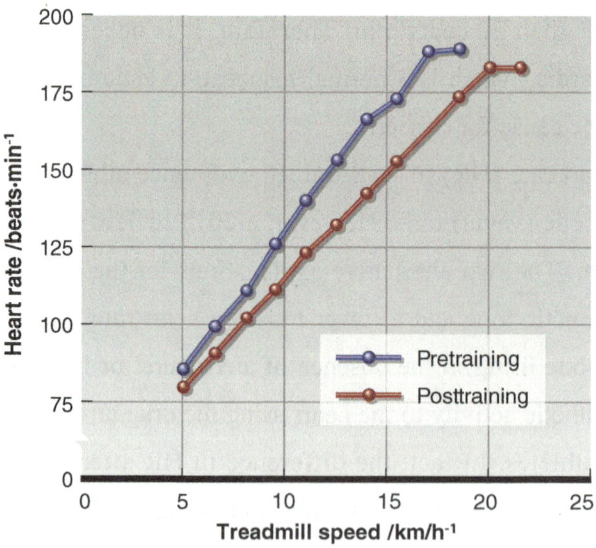

Figure 10.3 Endurance training-induced changes in heart rate during progressive walking, jogging and running on a treadmill at increasing speeds.

(3) Maximum Heart Rate

A person's maximal heart rate (HRmax) tends to be stable and typically remains relatively unchanged after endurance training. However, several studies have suggested that for people whose untrained HRmax values exceed 180 beats/min, HRmax might be slightly lower after training. Also, highly conditioned endurance athletes often have lower HRmax values than untrained individuals of the same age, although this is not always the case. Athletes over 60 years old sometimes have higher HRmax values than untrained people of the same age.

(4) Heart Rate Recovery

During exercise, heart rate must increase to increase cardiac output to meet the blood flow demands of active muscles. When the exercise bout is finished, heart rate does not instantly return to its resting level. Instead, it remains elevated for a while, slowly returning to its resting rate. The time it takes for heart rate to return to its resting rate is called the heart rate recovery period.

After endurance training, as shown in Figure 10.4, heart rate returns to its resting level much more quickly after an exercise bout than it does before training. This is true after both submaximal and maximal exercise.

Because the heart rate recovery period is shorter after endurance training, this measurement has been proposed as an indirect index of cardiorespiratory fitness. In general, a more fit person recovers faster after a standardized rate of work than a less fit person, so this measure may have some utility in field settings when more direct measures of endurance capacity are not possible or feasible. However, factors other than training can also affect heart rate recovery time. For example, an elevated core temperature or an enhanced sympathetic nervous system response can prolong heart rate elevation. The heart rate recovery curve is a useful tool for tracking a person's progress during a training program. But because of the potential influence of other factors, it should not be used to compare individuals.

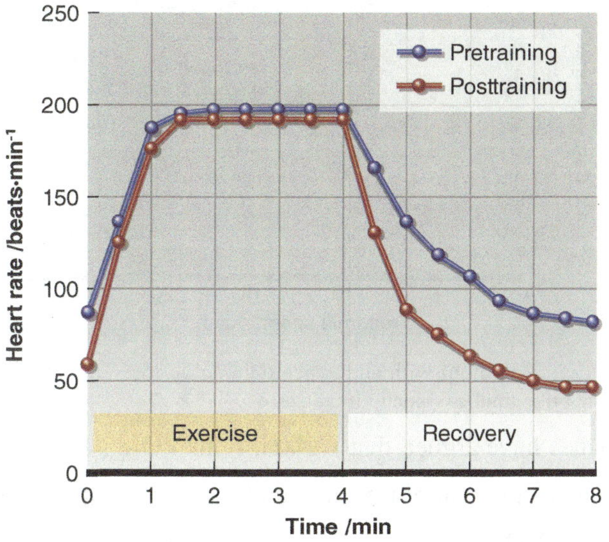

Figure 10.4 Changes in heart rate during recovery after a 4 min, all-out bout of exercise before and after endurance training.

1.3.5 Cardiac Output

We have looked at the effects of training on the two components of cardiac output: stroke volume and heart rate. While stroke volume increases with training, heart rate generally decreases at rest and during exercise at a given absolute intensity.

Because the magnitude of these reciprocal changes is similar, cardiac output at rest and during submaximal exercise at a given exercise intensity does not change much following endurance training. In fact, cardiac output can decrease slightly. This is likely the result of an increase in the $Ca\text{-}C_{\bar{v}}O_2$ difference (reflecting greater oxygen extraction by the tissues) or a decrease in the rate of oxygen consumption (reflecting an increased mechanical efficiency). Generally, cardiac output matches the oxygen consumption required for any given intensity of effort.

Maximal cardiac output, however, increases considerably in response to aerobic training, as seen in Figure 10.5, and is largely responsible for the increase in $\dot{V}O_{2\,max}$. This increase in cardiac output must result from an increase in maximal stroke volume, because HRmax changes little, if any. Maximal cardiac output ranges from 14–20 L/min in untrained individuals and from 25–35 L/min in trained individuals, and can be 40 L/min or more in highly conditioned endurance athletes. These absolute values, however, are greatly influenced by body size.

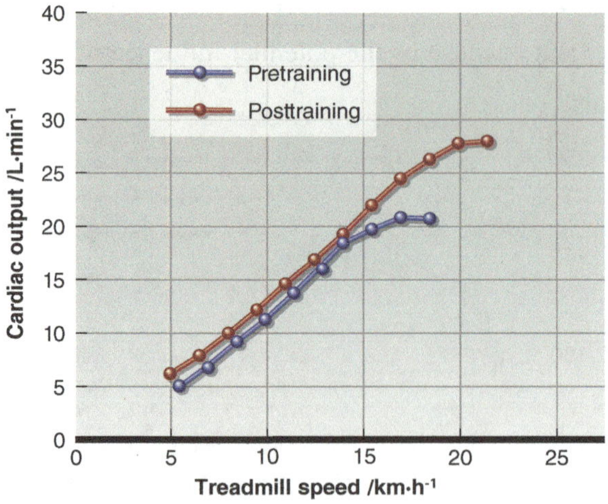

Figure 10.5 Changes in cardiac output with endurance training during walking, then jogging, and finally running on a treadmill as velocity increases.

Lundby and colleagues have argued that variability in $\dot{V}O_{2\,max}$ among individuals is primarily determined by differences in two variables: maximal cardiac output and red blood cell volume. Therefore, the response of $\dot{V}O_{2\,max}$ to endurance training reflects relative changes in these two important determinants.

1.3.6 Blood Flow

Active muscles need substantially more oxygen and fuel substrates than inactive ones. To meet these increased needs, more blood must be delivered to these muscles during exercise. With endurance training, the cardiovascular system adapts to increase blood flow to exercising muscles to meet their higher demand for oxygen and metabolic substrates. In addition to changes in the heart that allow for better pumping and increased stroke volume, four factors account for this enhanced blood flow to muscle following training:

- Increased capillarization;
- Greater recruitment of existing capillaries;
- More effective blood flow redistribution away from inactive regions;
- Increased total blood volume.

To permit increased blood flow, new capillaries develop in trained muscles. This allows the blood flowing into skeletal muscle from arterioles to more fully perfuse the active fibers. This increase in capillaries usually is expressed as an increase in the number of capillaries per muscle fiber, or the capillary-to-fiber ratio. Table 10.2 illustrates the differences in capillary-to-fiber ratios between well-trained and untrained men, both before and after exercise.

Table 10.2 Muscle Fiber Capillarization in Well-Trained and Untrained Men

Stage	Capillaries per mm^2	Muscle fibers per mm^2	Capillary-to-fiber ratio	Diffusion distance/μm
Well-trained				
Preexercise	640	440	1.5	20.1
Postexercise	611	414	1.6	20.3
Untrained				
Preexercise	600	557	1.1	20.3
Postexercise	599	579	1.1	20.6

Note. This table illustrates the larger size of the muscle fibers in the well-trained men in that they had fewer fibers for a given area (fibers per mm^2). They also had an approximately 50% higher capillary-to-fiber ratio than the untrained men.
*Diffusion distance is expressed as the average half-distance between capillaries on the cross-sectional view expressed in micrometers.

In all tissues, including muscle, not all capillaries are open at any given time. In addition to new capillary formation, existing capillaries in trained muscles can be recruited and open to flow, which also increases blood flow to muscle fibers. The increase in new capillaries with endurance training and increased capillary recruitment combine to increase the overall area for diffusion of oxygen between the vascular system and the metabolically active muscle fibers.

A more effective redistribution of cardiac output also can increase blood flow to the active muscles. Blood flow is directed to the active musculature and shunted away from areas that do not need high flow. Blood flow can increase to the more active fibers even within a specific muscle group. Armstrong and Laughlin first demonstrated that endurance-trained rats could redistribute blood flow to their most active tissues during exercise better than untrained rats could. The total blood flow to the exercising hindlimbs did not differ between the trained and untrained rats. However, the trained rats distributed more of their blood to the most oxidative muscle fibers, effectively redistributing the blood flow away from the glycolytic muscle fibers. These findings are difficult to replicate in humans because of measurement challenges, as well as the fact that human skeletal muscle is a mosaic with mixed fiber types among individual muscles.

Finally, the body's total blood volume increases with endurance training, providing more blood to meet the body's many blood flow needs during endurance activity without compromising venous return, as discussed next in this chapter.

1.3.7 Blood Volume

Endurance training increases total blood volume, and this effect is larger with higher training intensities. Furthermore, the effect occurs rapidly. This increased blood volume results primarily from an increase in plasma volume, but there is also an increase in the volume of red blood cells. The time course and mechanism for the increase of each of these components of blood are quite different.

(1) Plasma Volume

The increase in plasma volume with training is thought to result from two mechanisms. The first mechanism, which has two phases, results in increases in plasma proteins, particularly albumin. Plasma proteins are the major driver of oncotic pressure in the vasculature. As plasma protein concentration increases, so does oncotic pressure, and fluid is reabsorbed from the interstitial fluid into the blood vessels. During an intense bout of exercise, proteins leave the vascular space and move into the interstitial space. They are then returned in greater amounts through the lymph system. It is likely that the first phase of rapid plasma volume increase is the result of the increased plasma albumin, which is noted within the first hour of recovery from the first training bout. In the second phase, protein synthesis is turned on (upregulated) by repeated exercise, and new proteins are formed. With the second mechanism, exercise increases the release of antidiuretic hormone and aldosterone, hormones that cause reabsorption of water and sodium in the kidneys, which increases blood plasma. That increased fluid is kept in the vascular space by the oncotic pressure exerted by the proteins. Nearly all of the increase in blood volume during the first two weeks of training can be explained by the increase in plasma volume. This early blood volume expansion allows stroke volume to increase despite the fact that changes in the structure and function of the heart itself take longer to develop.

(2) Red Blood Cells

An increase in red blood cell volume with endurance training also contributes to the overall increase in blood volume, but this is an inconsistent finding. Although the actual number of red blood cells may increase, the hematocrit (the ratio of the red blood cell volume to the total blood volume) may actually decrease. Figure 10.6 illustrates this apparent paradox. Notice that the hematocrit is reduced even though there has been a slight increase in red blood cells. A trained athlete's hematocrit can decrease to such an extent that the athlete appears to be anemic on the basis of a relatively low concentration of red cells and hemoglobin ("pseudoanemia").

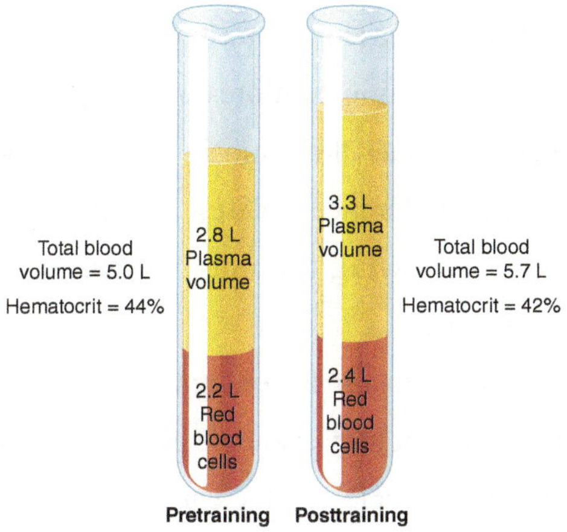

Figure 10.6 Increases in total blood volume and plasma volume occur with endurance training. Note that although the hematocrit (percentage of red blood cells) decreased from 44%–42%, the total volume of red blood cells increased by 10%.

The increased ratio of plasma to cells resulting from a greater increase in the fluid portion reduces the blood's viscosity, or thickness. Reduced viscosity may aid the smooth flow of blood through the blood vessels, particularly through the smaller vessels such as the capillaries. One of the physiological benefits of decreasing blood viscosity is that it enhances oxygen delivery to the active muscle mass.

Both the total amount (absolute values) of hemoglobin and the total number of red blood cells are typically elevated in highly trained athletes. This ensures that the blood has more than adequate oxygen-carrying capacity; that is, the blood's ability to deliver oxygen to exercising muscle is not a limiting factor in exercise. The turnover rate of red blood cells also may be higher with intense training.

1.4 Respiratory Adaptations to Training

No matter how proficient the cardiovascular system is at supplying blood to exercising muscle, endurance would be hindered if the respiratory system were not able to deliver enough oxygen to fully oxygenate red blood cells. Respiratory system function does not usually limit performance because ventilation can be increased to a much greater extent than cardiovascular function. But, as with the cardiovascular system, the respiratory system undergoes specific adaptations to endurance training to maximize its efficiency.

1.4.1 Pulmonary Ventilation

After training, pulmonary ventilation is essentially unchanged at rest. Although endurance training does not change the structure or basic physiology of the lung, it does decrease ventilation during submaximal exercise by as much as 30% at a given submaximal intensity. Maximal pulmonary ventilation is substantially increased from a rate of about 100–120 L/min in untrained sedentary individuals to about 130–150 L/min or more following endurance training. Pulmonary ventilation rates typically increase to about 180 L/min in highly trained athletes and can exceed 200 L/min in very large, highly trained endurance athletes. Two factors can account for the increase in maximal pulmonary ventilation following training: increased tidal volume and increased respiratory frequency at maximal exercise.

Ventilation is not usually a limiting factor for endurance exercise performance. However, in some very highly trained athletes, the pulmonary system's capacity for oxygen transport may not be able to meet the demands of exercising muscle and the cardiovascular system. This results in what has been termed exercise-induced arterial hypoxemia, in which arterial oxygen saturation decreases below 96%. This desaturation in highly trained elite athletes likely results from the large right heart cardiac output directed to the lung during exercise and consequently a decrease in the time the blood spends in the lung.

1.4.2 Pulmonary Diffusion

Pulmonary diffusion, or gas exchange occurring in the alveoli, is unaltered at rest and during submaximal exercise following training. However, it increases at maximal exercise intensity. Pulmonary blood flow (blood coming from the right side of the heart to the lungs) increases following training, particularly flow to the upper regions of the lungs when a person is sitting or standing. This increases lung perfusion. More blood is brought into the lungs for gas exchange, and at the same time ventilation increases so that more air is brought into the lungs. This means that more alveoli will be involved in pulmonary diffusion. The net result is that pulmonary diffusion increases.

1.4.3 Arterial-Venous Oxygen Difference

It is clear that stroke volume adapts with endurance training, but peripheral adaptations also contribute to the increase in $\dot{V}O_{2\,max}$. The oxygen content of arterial blood changes very little with endurance training. Even though total hemoglobin is increased, the amount of hemoglobin per unit of blood is the same or even slightly reduced. The $Ca\text{-}C_{\bar{v}}O_2$ difference, however, does increase with training, particularly at submaximal exercise intensities. This increase results from a lower mixed venous oxygen content, reflecting both greater oxygen extraction by active tissues and a more effective distribution of blood flow to active tissues. The increased extraction results in part from an increase in oxidative capacity of active muscle fibers.

While most studies have shown an increase in maximal $Ca\text{-}C_{\bar{v}}O_2$ difference after aerobic training, a 2015 analysis of the literature challenged this long-held notion. That study reported that, based on a survey of 13 studies that measured both cardiac output and $Ca\text{-}C_{\bar{v}}O_2$ difference before and after training, improvements in $\dot{V}O_{2\,max}$ following 5–13 weeks of training were associated with increases in cardiac output, but not in $Ca\text{-}C_{\bar{v}}O_2$ difference. That an increase in maximal cardiac output is the predominant factor associated with increases in $\dot{V}O_{2\,max}$ is not surprising, given the close relation between these variables. However, the training period in the studies analyzed was relatively short, so training adaptations may not have been complete. In longer term endurance training studies, maximal $Ca\text{-}C_{\bar{v}}O_2$ differences were enhanced by 1%–29%.

In summary, the respiratory system is quite adept at bringing adequate oxygen into the body. For this reason, the respiratory system seldom limits endurance performance. Not surprisingly, the major training adaptations noted in the respiratory system are apparent mainly during maximal exercise, when all systems are being maximally stressed.

1.5 Adaptations in Muscle

Repeated excitation and contraction of muscle fibers during endurance training stimulate changes in their structure and function. Our main interest here is in aerobic training and the changes it produces in muscle fiber type, mitochondrial function, and oxidative enzymes.

1.5.1 Muscle Fiber Type

Low-to moderate-intensity aerobic activities rely extensively on type I (slow-twitch) fibers. In response to aerobic training, type I fibers become larger. More specifically, they develop a larger cross-sectional area, although the magnitude of change depends on the intensity and duration of each training bout and the length of the training program. Increases in cross-sectional area of up to 25% have been reported. Fast-twitch (type II) fibers, because they are not being recruited to the same extent during endurance exercise, generally do not increase cross-sectional area.

Most early studies showed no change in the percentage of type I versus type II fibers following aerobic training, but subtle changes were noted among the different type II fiber subtypes. Type Ⅱx fibers have a low oxidative capacity and are recruited less often than type Ⅱa fibers during aerobic exercise. However, during long-duration exercise, these fibers may eventually be recruited to perform in a manner resembling type Ⅱa fibers. This can cause some type Ⅱx fibers to take on the characteristics of the more oxidative type Ⅱa fibers. Recent evidence suggests that not only is there a transition of type Ⅱx to Ⅱa fibers but also there can be a transition of type II to type I fibers. The magnitude of change is generally small, not more than a few percent. As an example, in the HERITAGE Family Study, a 20-week program of aerobic training increased type I fibers from 43% pretraining to almost 47% posttraining and decreased type Ⅱx fibers from 20%–15%, with type Ⅱa remaining essentially unchanged. These more recent studies have included larger numbers of subjects and have taken advantage of improved measurement technology; both might explain why fiber type composition changes within a muscle are now recognized.

1.5.2 Capillary Supply

One of the most important adaptations to aerobic training is an increase in the number of capillaries surrounding each muscle fiber. Endurance-trained men have considerably more capillaries in their leg muscles than sedentary individuals. With long periods of aerobic training, the number of capillaries may increase by more than 15%. Having more capillaries allows for greater exchange of gases, heat, nutrients, and metabolic by-products between the blood and contracting muscle fibers. In fact, the increase in capillary density (i.e., increase in capillaries per muscle fiber) is potentially one of the most important alterations in response to training that causes the increase in $\dot{V}O_{2\,max}$. It is now clear that the diffusion of oxygen from the capillary to the mitochondria is a major factor limiting the maximal rate of oxygen consumption by the muscle. Increasing capillary density facilitates this diffusion, thus maintaining an environment well suited to energy production and repeated muscle contractions.

1.5.3 Myoglobin Content

When oxygen enters the muscle fiber, it binds to myoglobin, a molecule similar to hemoglobin. This iron-containing molecule shuttles the oxygen molecules from the cell membrane to the mitochondria. Type I fibers contain large quantities of myoglobin, which gives these fibers their red appearance (myoglobin is a pigment that turns red when bound to oxygen). Type II fibers, on the other hand, are highly glycolytic, so they contain (and require) little myoglobin—hence their whiter appearance. More important, their limited myoglobin supply limits their oxidative capacity, resulting in poor endurance for these fibers.

Myoglobin transports oxygen and releases it to the mitochondria when oxygen becomes limited during muscle action. This oxygen reserve is used during the transition from rest to exercise, providing oxygen to the mitochondria during the lag between the beginning of exercise and the increased cardiovascular delivery of oxygen. Endurance training has been shown to increase muscle myoglobin content by 75%–80%. This adaptation clearly supports a muscle's increased capacity for oxidative metabolism after training.

1.5.4 Mitochondrial Function

Oxidative energy production takes place in the mitochondria. Not surprisingly, aerobic training also induces changes in mitochondrial function that improve the muscle fibers' capacity to produce ATP. The ability to use oxygen and produce ATP via oxidation depends on the number and size of the muscle mitochondria. Both increase with aerobic training.

During one study that involved endurance training in rats, the number of mitochondria increased approximately 15% during 27 weeks of exercise.16 Average mitochondrial size also increased by about 35% over that training period. As with other training-induced adaptations, the magnitude of change depends on training volume.

1.5.5 Oxidative Enzymes

Regular endurance exercise has been shown to induce major adaptations in skeletal muscle, including an increase in the number and size of the muscle fiber mitochondria as just discussed. These changes are further enhanced by an increase in mitochondrial capacity. The oxidative breakdown of fuels and the ultimate production of ATP depend on the action of mitochondrial oxidative enzymes, the specialized proteins that catalyze (i.e., speed up) the breakdown of nutrients to form ATP. Aerobic training increases the activity of these important enzymes.

In summary, endurance exercise training causes a wide variety of phenotypic adaptations in skeletal muscle, including angiogenesis (creation of new capillaries) , transformation of fiber types from glycolytic to oxidative, increased ability to mobilize and use fats as a substrate, and increased glucose uptake by muscle fibers, which increases the number of mitochondria and improves the overall quality of the existing mitochondrial pool.

1.6 Metabolic Adaptations to Training

Now that we have discussed training changes in both the cardiovascular and respiratory systems, as well as skeletal muscle adaptations, we are ready to examine how these integrated adaptations are reflected by changes in three important physiological variables related to metabolism:

- Lactate threshold

- Respiratory exchange ratio
- Oxygen consumption

1.6.1 Lactate Threshold

Lactate threshold is a physiological marker that is closely associated with endurance performance-the higher the lactate threshold, the better the performance capacity. Figure 10.7a illustrates the difference in lactate threshold between an endurance-trained individual and an untrained individual. This Figure also accurately represents the changes in lactate threshold that would occur following a 6-month to 12-month program of endurance training. In either case, in the trained state, one can exercise at a higher percentage of one's $\dot{V}O_{2\,max}$ before lactate begins to accumulate in the blood. In this example, the trained runner could sustain a race pace of 70%–75% of $\dot{V}O_{2\,max}$, an intensity that would result in continued lactate accumulation in the blood of the untrained runner. This translates into a much faster race pace (Figure 10.7b). Above the lactate threshold, the lower lactate at a given rate of work is likely attributable to a combination of reduced lactate production and increased lactate clearance. As athletes become better trained, their postexercise blood lactate concentrations are lower for a given rate of work.

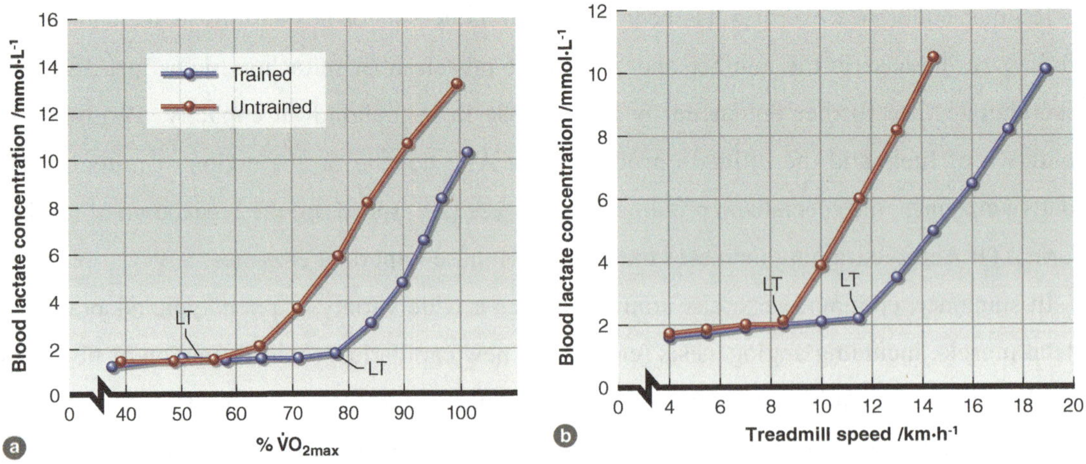

Figure 10.7 Changes in lactate threshold (LT) with training expressed as (a) a percentage of maximal oxygen uptake (% $\dot{V}O_{2\,max}$) and (b) an increase in speed on the treadmill. Lactate threshold occurs at a speed of 8.4 km/h in the untrained state and at 11.6 km/h in the trained state.

1.6.2 Respiratory Exchange Ratio

The respiratory exchange ratio (RER) is the ratio of carbon dioxide released to oxygen consumed during metabolism. The RER reflects the composition of the mixture of substrates being used as an energy source, with a lower RER reflecting an increased reliance on fats for energy production and a higher RER reflecting a higher contribution of carbohydrates.

After training, the RER decreases at both absolute and relative submaximal exercise intensities. These changes are attributable to a greater utilization of free fatty acids instead of carbohydrate at these work rates following training.

1.6.3 Resting and Submaximal Oxygen Consumption

Oxygen consumption ($\dot{V}O_2$) at rest is unchanged following endurance training. While a few cross-sectional comparisons have suggested that training elevates resting $\dot{V}O_2$, the HERITAGE Family Study with a large number of subjects and with duplicate measures of resting metabolic rate both before and after 20 weeks of training showed no evidence of an increased resting metabolic rate after training.

During submaximal exercise at a given intensity, $\dot{V}O_2$ is either unchanged or slightly reduced following training. In the HERITAGE Family Study, training reduced submaximal $\dot{V}O_2$ by 3.5% at a work rate of 50 W. There was a corresponding reduction in cardiac output at 50W reinforcing the strong interrelationship between $\dot{V}O_2$ and cardiac output. This small decrease in $\dot{V}O_2$ during submaximal exercise, not seen in many studies, could have resulted from an increase in exercise economy (performing the same exercise intensity with less extraneous movement).

1.6.4 Maximal Oxygen Consumption

$\dot{V}O_{2\,max}$ is the best indicator of cardiorespiratory endurance capacity and increases substantially in response to endurance training. While small and very large increases have been reported, an increase of 15%–20% is typical for a previously sedentary person who trains at 50%–85% of his or her $\dot{V}O_{2\,max}$ three to five times per week, 20–60 min per day, for six months. For example, the $\dot{V}O_{2\,max}$ of a sedentary individual could reasonably increase from 35 ml · (kg · min)$^{-1}$ to 42 ml · (kg · min)$^{-1}$ as a result of such a program. This is far below the values we see in world-class endurance athletes; whose values generally range from 70–94 ml · kg^{-1} · min^{-1}.

1.7 What Limits Aerobic Power and Endurance Performance?

A number of years ago, exercise scientists were divided on what major physiological factor or factors actually limit $\dot{V}O_{2\,max}$. Two contrasting theories had been proposed.

One theory held that endurance performance was limited by the lack of sufficient concentrations of oxidative enzymes in the mitochondria. Endurance training programs substantially increase these oxidative enzymes, allowing active tissue to use more of the available oxygen, resulting in a higher $\dot{V}O_{2\,max}$. In addition, endurance training increases both the size and number of muscle mitochondria. Thus, this theory argued, the main limitation of maximal oxygen consumption is the inability of the existing mitochondria to use the available oxygen beyond a certain rate. This theory was referred to as the utilization theory.

The second theory proposed that central and peripheral cardiovascular factors limit endurance capacity. These circulatory influences would preclude delivery of sufficient amounts of oxygen to the active tissues. Taking into account the observation that improvement in $\dot{V}O_{2\,max}$ following endurance training results from increased blood volume, increased cardiac output (via stroke volume) , and a better perfusion of active muscle with blood, this theory proposed that these cardiovascular factors are the limiting factor for $\dot{V}O_{2\,max}$.

Evidence strongly supports the latter theory. In one study, subjects breathed a mixture of carbon monoxide (which irreversibly binds to hemoglobin, limiting hemoglobin's oxygen-carrying capacity) and air during exercise to exhaustion. $\dot{V}O_{2\,max}$ decreased in direct proportion to the percentage of carbon monoxide breathed. The carbon monoxide molecules bonded to approximately 15% of the total hemoglobin; this percentage agreed with the percentage reduction in $\dot{V}O_{2\,max}$. In another study, approximately 15%–20% of each subject's total blood volume was removed. $\dot{V}O_{2\,max}$ decreased by approximately the same relative amount. Reinfusion of the subjects' packed red blood cells approximately four weeks later increased $\dot{V}O_{2\,max}$ well above baseline or control conditions. In both studies, the reduction in the oxygen-carrying capacity of the blood—via either blocking hemoglobin or removing whole blood—resulted in the delivery of less oxygen to the active tissues and a corresponding reduction in $\dot{V}O_{2\,max}$. Similarly, studies have shown that breathing oxygen-enriched mixtures, in which the partial pressure of oxygen in the inspired air is substantially increased, increases endurance capacity.

These and subsequent studies indicated that the available oxygen supply is the major limiter of endurance performance. Oxygen transport to the working muscles, not the available mitochondria and oxidative enzymes, limits $\dot{V}O_{2\,max}$. The argument was that increases in $\dot{V}O_{2\,max}$ with training are largely attributable to increased maximal blood flow and increased muscle capillary density in the active tissues. Skeletal muscle adaptations (including increased mitochondrial content and respiratory capacity of the muscle fibers) contribute importantly to the ability to perform prolonged, high-intensity, submaximal exercise.

1.8 Long-Term Improvement in Aerobic Power and Cardiorespiratory Endurance

Although an individual's highest attainable $\dot{V}O_{2\,max}$ is usually achieved within 12–18 months of intense endurance training, endurance performance can continue to improve. Improvement in endurance performance without improvement in $\dot{V}O_{2\,max}$ is likely attributable to improvements in the ability to perform at increasingly higher percentages of $\dot{V}O_{2\,max}$ for extended periods. Consider, for example, a young male runner who starts training with an initial $\dot{V}O_{2\,max}$ of 52.0 ml · (kg · min)$^{-1}$.

He reaches his genetically determined peak $\dot{V}O_{2\,max}$ of 71.0 ml・(kg・min)$^{-1}$after two years of intense training, after which no further increases occur, even with more frequent or more intense workouts. At this point, the young runner is able to run at 75% of his $\dot{V}O_{2\,max}$〔$0.75 \times 71.0 = 53.3$ ml・(kg・min)$^{-1}$〕in a 10 km race. After an additional two years of intensive training, his $\dot{V}O_{2\,max}$ is unchanged, but he is now able to compete at 88% of his $\dot{V}O_{2\,max}$〔$0.88 \times 71.0 = 62.5$ ml・(kg・min)$^{-1}$〕. Obviously, by being able to sustain an oxygen uptake of 62.5 ml・(kg・min)$^{-1}$, he is able to run at a much faster race pace.

This ability to sustain exercise at a higher percentage of $\dot{V}O_{2\,max}$ is partly the result of an increase in the ability to buffer lactate, because race pace is directly related to the $\dot{V}O_2$ value at which lactate begins to accumulate.

1.9 Factors Affecting an Individual's Response to Aerobic Training

We have discussed general trends in adaptations that occur in response to endurance training. However, we must always remember that we are talking about adaptations in individuals and that everyone does not respond in the same manner. Several factors that can affect individual response to aerobic training must be considered.

1.9.1 Training Status and $\dot{V}O_{2\,max}$

The higher the initial state of conditioning, the smaller the relative improvement for the same volume of training. For example, if two people, one sedentary and the other partially trained, undergo the same endurance training program, the sedentary person will show the greatest relative (%) improvement.

In fully mature athletes, the highest attainable $\dot{V}O_{2\,max}$ is reached within 8–18 months of intense endurance training, indicating that each athlete has a finite maximal attainable level of oxygen consumption. This finite range is genetically determined but may potentially be influenced by training in early childhood during the development of the cardiovascular system.

1.9.2 Heredity

The ability to increase maximal oxygen consumption levels is genetically limited. This does not mean that each individual has a preprogrammed $\dot{V}O_{2\,max}$ that cannot be exceeded. Rather, a range of $\dot{V}O_{2\,max}$ values seems to be predetermined by an individual's genetic makeup, with that individual's highest attainable $\dot{V}O_{2\,max}$ somewhere in that range. Each individual is born into a predetermined genetic window, and the person can shift up or down within that window with exercise training or detraining, respectively.

Bouchard and colleagues concluded that heredity accounts for between 25% and 50% of the variance in $\dot{V}O_{2\,max}$ values. This means that of all factors influencing $\dot{V}O_{2\,max}$, heredity alone is responsible for one-quarter to one-half of the total influence. World-class athletes who have stopped endurance training continue for many years to have high $\dot{V}O_{2\,max}$ values in their sedentary, deconditioned state. Their $\dot{V}O_{2\,max}$ values may decrease from 85–65 ml · kg^{-1} · min^{-1}, but this deconditioned value is still very high compared with that of the general population. Heredity also potentially explains the fact that some people have relatively high $\dot{V}O_{2\,max}$ values yet have no history of endurance training. In a study that compared untrained men who had $\dot{V}O_{2\,max}$ values below 49 ml · kg^{-1} · min^{-1} with untrained men who had $\dot{V}O_{2\,max}$ values above 62.5 ml · kg^{-1} · min^{-1}, those with high values were distinguished by having higher blood volumes, which contributed to higher stroke volumes and cardiac outputs at maximal intensities. The higher blood volumes in the high $\dot{V}O_{2\,max}$ group were most likely genetically determined.

Thus, both genetic and environmental factors influence $\dot{V}O_{2\,max}$ values. The genetic factors probably establish the boundaries for the athlete, but endurance training can push $\dot{V}O_{2\,max}$ to the upper limit of these boundaries. Dr. Per-Olof Åstrand, one of the most highly recognized exercise physiologists during the second half of the 20th century, stated on numerous occasions that the best way to become a champion Olympic athlete is to be selective when choosing one's parents!

1.9.3 Sex

Healthy untrained girls and women have significantly lower $\dot{V}O_{2\,max}$ values (20%–25% lower) than healthy untrained boys and men. Highly conditioned female endurance athletes have values much closer to those of highly trained male endurance athletes (i.e., only about 10% lower).

1.9.4 High Responders and Low Responders

For years, researchers have found wide variations in the amount of improvement in $\dot{V}O_{2\,max}$ with endurance training. Studies have demonstrated individual improvements in $\dot{V}O_{2\,max}$ ranging from 0%–50% or more, even in similarly fit subjects completing exactly the same training program.

In the past, exercise physiologists have assumed that these variations result from differing degrees of compliance with the training program. People who comply with the program should, and do, have the highest percentage of improvement, and poor compliers should show little or no improvement. However, given the same training stimulus and full compliance with the program, substantial variations still occur in the percent improvement in $\dot{V}O_{2\,max}$ for different people.

It is now evident that some of the response to a training program is also genetically determined. This is illustrated in Figure 10.8. Ten pairs of identical twins completed a 20-week endurance training program; the improvements in $\dot{V}O_{2\,max}$, expressed as percentages, are plotted for each twin pair—twin A on the x-axis and twin B on the y-axis. Notice the similarity in response of each twin pair. Yet across twin pairs, improvement in $\dot{V}O_{2\,max}$ varied from 0%–40%. These results, and those from other studies, indicate that there will be high responders (showing large improvement) and low responders (showing little or no improvement) among groups of people who participate in identical training programs. However, while genetic variants may be involved, such variants appear to be associated with the physiological mechanisms (increased cardiac output, expanded blood volume, improved muscle oxygen extraction) that underpin such differences.

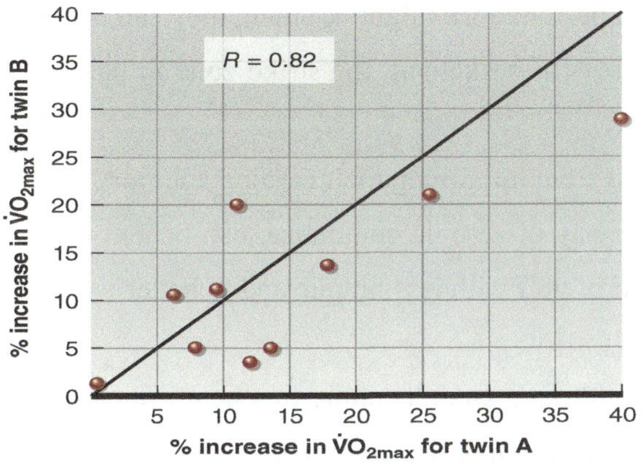

Figure 10.8 Variations in the percentage increase in $\dot{V}O_{2\,max}$ for identical twins undergoing the same 20-week training program.

Results from the HERITAGE Family Study also support a strong genetic component in the magnitude of increase in $\dot{V}O_{2\,max}$ with endurance training. Families, including the biological mother and father and three or more of their children, trained three days a week for 20 weeks, initially exercising at a heart rate equal to 55% of their $\dot{V}O_{2\,max}$ for 35 min per day and progressing to a heart rate equal to 75% of their $\dot{V}O_{2\,max}$ for 50 min per day by the end of the 14th week, which they maintained for the last six weeks. The average increase in $\dot{V}O_{2\,max}$ was about 17% but varied from 0% to more than 50%.

It is clear that this is a genetic phenomenon, not a result of compliance or noncompliance. One must consider this important point when conducting training studies and designing training programs. Individual differences must always be accounted for.

1.10 Cardiorespiratory Endurance in Nonendurance Sports

Many people regard cardiorespiratory endurance as the most important component of physical fitness. Low endurance capacity leads to fatigue, even in activities that are not aerobic. For any athlete, regardless of the sport or activity, fatigue represents a major deterrent to optimal performance. Even minor fatigue can hinder the athlete's total performance:

- Muscular strength is decreased

- Reaction and movement times are prolonged
- Agility and neuromuscular coordination are reduced
- Whole-body movement speed is slowed
- Concentration and alertness are reduced

The decline in concentration and alertness associated with fatigue is particularly important. The athlete can become careless and more prone to serious injury, especially in contact sports. Even though these decrements in performance might be small, they can be just enough to cause an athlete to miss the critical free throw in basketball, the strike zone in baseball, or the 20 ft (6 m) putt in golf.

All athletes can benefit from improving their cardiorespiratory endurance. Even golfers, whose sport demands little in the way of aerobic endurance, can benefit. Improved endurance can allow golfers to complete a round of golf with less fatigue and to better withstand long periods of walking and standing.

For the sedentary, middle-aged adult, numerous health factors indicate that cardiovascular endurance should be the primary emphasis of training.

The extent of endurance training needed varies considerably from one sport to the next and from one athlete to the next. It depends on the athlete's current endurance capacity and the endurance demands of the chosen activity. However, adequate cardiovascular conditioning must be the foundation of any athlete's general conditioning program.

2 Adaptations to Anaerobic Training

In muscular activities that require near-maximal force production for relatively short periods of time, such as sprinting, much of the energy needs are met by the ATP-phosphocreatine (PCr) system and the anaerobic breakdown of muscle glycogen (glycolysis). The following sections focus on the trainability of these two systems.

2.1 Changes in Anaerobic Power and Anaerobic Capacity

Exercise scientists have had difficulty agreeing on an appropriate laboratory or field test to measure anaerobic power. Unlike the situation with aerobic power, for which $\dot{V}O_{2\,max}$ is generally agreed to be the gold standard measurement, no single test adequately measures anaerobic power. Most research has been conducted through use of three different tests of either anaerobic power, anaerobic capacity, or both: the Wingate anaerobic test, the critical power test, and the maximal accumulated oxygen deficit test. Of these three, the Wingate test has been the most widely used.

Despite the limitations inherent in each of these methods, they remain our only indirect indicators of the metabolic potential of anaerobic capacity.

The Wingate anaerobic test is commonly used to measure anaerobic power. Peak power output, the highest mechanical power achieved during the first 5–10s, is considered an index of anaerobic power. The mean power output is computed as the average power output over the total 30s period, and one obtains total work simply by multiplying the mean power output by 30s. Mean power output and total work have both been used as indexes of anaerobic capacity.

With anaerobic training, such as sprint training on the track or on a cycle ergometer, there are increases in both peak anaerobic power and anaerobic capacity. However, results have varied widely across studies, from those that showed only minimal increases to those showing increases of up to 25%.

2.2 Adaptations in Muscle with Anaerobic Training

With anaerobic training, which includes sprint training and resistance training, there are changes in skeletal muscle that specifically reflect muscle fiber recruitment for these types of activities. At higher intensities, type II muscle fibers are recruited to a greater extent, but not exclusively, because type I fibers continue to be recruited. Overall, sprint and resistance activities use the type II muscle fibers significantly more than do aerobic activities. Consequently, both type Ⅱa and type Ⅱx muscle fibers undergo an increase in their cross-sectional areas. The cross-sectional area of type I fibers also is increased but usually to a lesser extent. Furthermore, with sprint training there appears to be a reduction in the percentage of type I fibers and an increase in the percentage of type II fibers, with the greatest change in type Ⅱa fibers. In two of these studies, in which subjects performed 15–30s all-out sprints, the type I percentage decreased from 57%–48% and type Ⅱa increased from 32%–38%. This shift of type I to type II fibers is not typically seen with resistance training.

2.3 Adaptations in the Energy Systems

Just as aerobic training produces changes in the aerobic energy system, anaerobic training alters the ATP-PCr and anaerobic glycolytic energy systems. These changes are not as obvious or predictable as those that result from endurance training, but they do improve performance in anaerobic activities.

2.3.1Adaptations in the ATP-PCr System

Activities that emphasize maximal muscle force production, such as sprinting and weightlifting events, rely most heavily on the ATP-PCr system for energy. Maximal effort lasting less than about

6 s places the greatest demands on the breakdown and resynthesis of ATP and PCr. Costill and coworkers reported their findings from a study of resistance training and its effects on the ATP-PCr system. Their participants trained by performing maximal knee extensions. One leg was trained using 6 s maximal work bouts that were repeated 10 times. This type of training preferentially stressed the ATP-PCr energy system. The other leg was trained with repeated 30s maximal bouts, which instead preferentially stressed the glycolytic system.

The two forms of training produced the same muscular strength gains (about 14%) and the same resistance to fatigue. The activities of the anaerobic muscle enzymes creatine kinase and myokinase increased as a result of the 30s training bouts but were almost unchanged in the leg trained with repeated 6 s maximal efforts. This finding leads us to conclude that maximal sprint bouts (6 s) might improve muscular strength but contribute little to the mechanisms responsible for ATP and PCr breakdown. Data have been published, however, that show improvements in ATP-PCr enzyme activities with training bouts lasting only 5 s.

Regardless of the conflicting results, these studies suggest that the major value of training bouts that last only a few seconds (sprints) is the development of muscular strength. Such strength gains enable the individual to perform a given task with less effort, which reduces the risk of fatigue. Whether these changes allow the muscle to perform more anaerobic work remains unanswered, although a 60s sprint-fatigue test suggests that short sprint-type anaerobic training does not enhance anaerobic endurance.

2.3.2 Adaptations in the Glycolytic System

Anaerobic training (30s bouts) increases the activities of several key glycolytic enzymes. The most frequently studied glycolytic enzymes are phosphorylase, phosphofructokinase (PFK) , and lactate dehydrogenase (LDH). The activities of these three enzymes increased 10%–25% with repeated 30s training bouts but changed little with short (6 s) bouts that stress primarily the ATP-PCr system. In another study, 30s maximal all-out sprints significantly increased hexokinase (56%) and PFK (49%) but not total phosphorylase activity or LDH.

Because both PFK and phosphorylase are essential to the anaerobic yield of ATP, such training might enhance glycolytic capacity and allow the muscle to develop greater tension for a longer period of time. However, this conclusion is not supported by results of a 60s sprint performance test, in which the subjects performed maximal knee extension and flexion. Power output and the rate of fatigue (shown by a decrease in power production) were affected to the same degree after sprint training with either 6 s or 30s training bouts. Thus, we must conclude that performance gains with these forms of training result from improvements in strength rather than improvements in the anaerobic yield of ATP.

3 Adaptations to HIIT

We introduced a special form of training using short bursts of very intense cycling, interspersed with up to a few minutes of rest or low-intensity cycling for recovery. High-intensity interval training (HIIT) is a time-efficient way to induce many aerobic training benefits normally associated with continuous running, cycling, or swimming.

Adaptations to HIIT mirror those associated with more traditional aerobic training. In one study, untrained young subjects performed four to six 30s sprints separated by 4 min of recovery, three times a week. These men showed the same beneficial changes in their heart, blood vessels, and muscles as another group who underwent a traditional training program involving up to an hour of continuous cycling, five days per week. Improvements in exercise performance—whether measured as cycling time to exhaustion at a fixed work intensity or in time trials that more closely resemble normal athletic competition—were comparable between groups, despite considerable differences in training time commitment. High-intensity interval training appears to stimulate some of the same molecular signaling pathways that regulate skeletal muscle remodeling in response to endurance training, including mitochondrial biogenesis and changes in the capacity for carbohydrate and fat transport and oxidation.

4 Specificity of Training and Cross-Training

Physiological adaptations in response to physical training are highly specific to the nature of the training activity. Furthermore, the more specific the training program is to a given sport or activity, the greater the improvement in performance in that sport or activity.

This concept is also important in testing of athletes. As an example, to accurately measure endurance improvements, athletes should be tested while engaged in an activity similar to the sport or activity in which they usually participate. Consider one study of highly trained rowers, cyclists, and cross-country skiers. Their $\dot{V}O_{2max}$ was measured while they performed two types of work: uphill running on a treadmill and maximal performance of their sport-specific activity. A key finding was that the $\dot{V}O_{2max}$ attained by all the athletes during their sport-specific activity was as high as or higher than the values obtained on the treadmill. For many of these athletes, $\dot{V}O_{2max}$ was substantially higher during their sport-specific activity.

A highly creative design for studying the concept of specificity of training involves one-legged exercise training, with the untrained opposite leg used as the control. In one study, subjects were placed into three groups: a group that sprint trained one leg and endurance trained the other, a group that sprint trained one leg and did not train the other, and a group that endurance trained one leg and did not train the other. Improvement in $\dot{V}O_{2\,max}$ and lowered heart rate and blood lactate response at submaximal work rates were found only when exercise was performed with the endurance-trained leg.

Cross-training refers to training for more than one sport at the same time or training several different fitness components (such as endurance, strength, and flexibility) at one time. The athlete who trains by swimming, running, and cycling in preparation for competing in a triathlon is an example of the former, and the athlete involved in heavy resistance training and high-intensity cardiorespiratory training at the same time is an example of the latter.

For the athlete training for cardiorespiratory endurance and strength at the same time, the studies conducted to date indicate that gains in strength, power, and endurance can result. However, the gains in muscular strength and power are less when strength training is combined with endurance training than when strength training alone is done. The opposite does not appear to be true: Improvement of aerobic power with endurance training does not appear to be attenuated by inclusion of a resistance training program. In fact, short-term endurance can be increased with resistance training. Although earlier studies supported the conclusion that concurrent strength and endurance training limits gains in strength and power, McCarthy and colleagues reported similar gains in strength, muscle hypertrophy, and neural activation in a group of previously untrained subjects who underwent concurrent high-intensity strength training and cycle endurance training compared with a group who performed only high-intensity strength training.

IN CLOSING

In this chapter, we examined how the cardiovascular, respiratory, and metabolic systems adapt to aerobic and anaerobic training, as well as HIIT training. The focus was on how these adaptations can improve both aerobic and anaerobic performance. This chapter concludes our review of how body systems respond to both acute and chronic exercise. Now that we have completed our examination of how the body responds to internal challenges induced by various types, durations, and intensities of exercise, we turn our attention to the external environment. In the next part of the book, we focus on the body's adaptations to varying environmental conditions.

KEY TERMS

aerobic training; cross-training; mitochondrial; oxidative enzymes; anaerobic training; Fick equation; oxygen transport system; athlete's heart; specificity of training; capillary-to-fiber ratio; high responders; submaximal; endurance; cardiac hypertrophy

STUDY QUESTIONS

(1) Differentiate between muscular endurance and cardiovascular endurance.

(2) What is maximal oxygen uptake ($\dot{V}O_{2\,max}$) ? How is it defined physiologically, and what determines its limits?

(3) Of what importance is $\dot{V}O_{2\,max}$ to endurance performance? Why does the competitor with the highest $\dot{V}O_{2\,max}$ not always win?

(4) Describe the changes in the oxygen transport system that occur with endurance training.

(5) What is possibly the most important adaptation that the body makes in response to endurance training, which allows for an increase in both $\dot{V}O_{2\,max}$ and performance? Through what mechanisms do these changes occur?

(6) What are the theoretical reasons given for the resting bradycardia that accompanies endurance exercise training?

(7) What metabolic adaptations occur in response to endurance training?

(8) Explain the two theories that have been proposed to account for limitations to aerobic performance that may be altered by endurance training. Which of these has the greatest validity today?

(9) How important is genetic potential in a developing young athlete?

(10) What adaptations have been shown to occur in muscle fibers with anaerobic training?

(11) Discuss specificity of anaerobic training with respect to enzyme changes in muscle.

(12) Can athletes who already train vigorously still improve performance by integrating HIIT into their training regimens? In what way are adaptive mechanisms different from those seen in untrained individuals who undergo HIIT?

(13) Why is cross-training beneficial to endurance athletes? How does it benefit sprint and power athletes?

第十章
机体对有氧训练和无氧训练的适应

机体在单次有氧运动中，能通过对心血管和呼吸机能的精确调节来满足肌肉在收缩活动中对能量和氧气的需求。当这些系统在受到多次有规律的运动训练后，会以不同方式进行适应，从而提高机体的最大摄氧量和全身的耐力运动水平。有氧或心肺耐力训练可提高心脏功能和外周血流量，并且提高肌纤维产生更多三磷酸腺苷（ATP）的能力。无氧训练可提高无氧代谢能力，短时间、高强度的运动能力，酸碱失衡的耐受能力并增加肌肉力量。有氧训练和无氧训练所致的一系列适应有利于运动表现。

对心血管、呼吸或者有氧耐力的训练已经被耐力运动员如长跑、自行车、越野滑雪、游泳运动员所熟知，而其他项目的运动员常常忽视这种训练。很多非耐力专项运动员为了最大限度地提高运动表现，常常更加关注专项化训练而忽视有氧耐力训练。但是大部分非耐力运动项目都包含有耐力或有氧成分，需要运动员进行适当的有氧耐力训练。

一、有氧训练的适应

有规律的有氧训练可以提高耐力水平，机体可因训练刺激产生多种适应现象。心血管系统对有氧训练的适应性变化可以提高循环系统运输氧气到骨骼肌的能力；骨骼肌系统对有氧训练的适应性变化可以提高肌肉利用氧气和能源底物的能力。

1.肌肉耐力与心肺耐力

耐力包括肌肉耐力和心肺耐力，每种耐力对不同运动员的运动表现都有其特有的贡献。对于短跑运动员，耐力能够使其在整个跑步过程中保持高速度运动。肌肉耐力是指单块肌肉或者肌群维持高强度的反复运动或静态收缩的能力。举重运动员、拳击运动员和摔跤运动员都可以证明这种耐力。这种类型的运动本质上具有节奏感和反复性，如举重运动员的多次反复卧推杠铃、拳击运动员的反复出拳等。这种运动也可以是静态的，如摔跤运动员将对手压在垫子上维持肌肉用力的动作。无论在哪种情况下，由特定肌群用力至疲劳的持续动作时间一般不会超过2分钟。肌肉耐力和肌肉力量与无氧功率发展的关系甚为密切。心肺耐力与维持长时间、全身大肌群动力性运动的能力有关，与心肺系统运输氧到工作肌的能力有关，也与肌肉利用氧气产生能量的能力有关。

2.心肺耐力的评定

（1）最大耐力能力。最大摄氧量（maximal oxygen consumption，$\dot{V}O_{2\,max}$），指在最高运动强度或者力竭性运动中可达到的氧消耗的最大速率，是评定心肺耐力最客观的实验室测试方法。根据菲克（fick）方程，$\dot{V}O_{2\,max}$取决于最大心输出量（向工作肌肉运输氧气和血流的能力）和最大动静脉血氧含量差（活动肌肉摄取和利用氧气的能力）。随着运动强度的增加，耗氧量最终出现平台或者略微下降，此时即使运动强度进一步增加，摄氧量也不会继续增加。

经过耐力训练后，活动的肌肉可以输送和消耗更多的氧气。没有训练经历的受试者在经过20周训练后最大摄氧量平均增加了15%～20%。但是，训练后在次最高运动强度下跑步时的耗氧量并没有改变，但可以提高跑步速度。

（2）次最大耐力能力。耐力训练还可以提高次最大耐力能力，但是次最大耐力能力很难评估。在同一个次最高运动强度下达到的稳态心率较低，可以作为客观量化评估训练效果的生理学指标。通常这种测试将持续30~60分钟。次最大耐力能力和临界功率一样，比最大摄氧量更能真实反映实际比赛的耐力运动表现。进行长期的耐力训练会使次最大耐力能力提高。

3.心血管对运动训练的适应

心血管系统对运动训练会产生很多适应，表现在氧运输系统、心脏大小、每搏输出量、心率、心输出量、血流、血容量等方面。

（1）氧运输系统。心肺耐力与心血管和呼吸系统运输足够氧气到活动组织并满足其代谢需要的能力有关，由菲克方程来决定。

摄氧量 = 每搏输出量 × 心率 × 动静脉血氧含量差

最大摄氧量 = 最大每搏输出量 × 最大心率 × 最大动静脉血氧含量差

最大摄氧量的增加依赖于对最大每搏输出量和最大动静脉血氧含量差的适应，最大心率保持不变或轻微下降。当运动达到最高水平时，心脏大小、血流、血压和血容量都有可能限制氧气运输的最大能力。

（2）心脏大小。为了适应运动负荷增长的需求，心脏的重量和心室容积会随着训练而增加。心肌像骨骼肌一样，可通过长期的耐力训练促进形态学适应，训练导致的心脏肥大已经被视为长期耐力训练的正常适应。

心室适应的类型取决于运动训练类型，如抗阻训练时左心室必须对抗体循环后负荷的增加，心脏通过增加左心室壁厚度来增强心肌组织，从而增加其收缩性。但是，心室容积大小很少改变。随着耐力训练的持续进行，左心室腔会增大，这将增加左心室充盈量，从而增加每搏输出量。左心室容积的增大多因耐力训练引起的血浆容量的增加（增大前负荷）导致。同时，由于副交感神经兴奋性的提高导致安静时心率降低，在同样工作强度下降低的心率有利于更长的心室舒张充盈期。血浆量和心舒张充盈时间增加，可增加心舒张末期容积（EDV）。

（3）每搏输出量。每搏输出量在安静时、次最高强度运动和最高强度运动中，都显著高于训练前水平。在比较不同受试者每搏输出量大小时，体型也非常关键。体型比较大的受试者通常有更大的心脏和更多的血容量，因此具有较高的每搏输出量。

有氧训练后，血容量增加，心率下降致心室充盈时间延长，这些都会使心舒张末期容积增加。根据Frank-Starling机制，更多的血液进入心室增加了心室壁的伸展性，从而增加心肌收缩力。左心室的后壁及室间隔厚度也会随着耐力训练而稍微增加，心室肌肉重量的增加也会导致收缩力量增大，引起心收缩末期容积（ESV）的下降，从而心脏的射血分数也会增加。

（4）心率。有氧训练对安静时、次最高强度运动和运动后恢复阶段的心率有较大影响，而有氧训练对最高心率的影响目前还不明确。

①安静心率：有氧训练会导致安静心率下降，出现运动性心动徐缓。心动徐缓指每分钟心跳低于60次。未经训练者出现心动徐缓，往往是由于心功能异常或者心脏病导致的。高水平耐力运动员安静时心率常低于40次/分。因此，有必要区分运动性心动徐缓（耐力训练后的正常反应）和病理性心动徐缓（可能需要关注）。受到良好耐力训练的运动员安静心率较低，以往认为是副交感神经的兴奋性增高导致，但也有人认为是固有心率的降低（如，窦房结的重塑）导致。

②次最大心率：在进行次最高强度运动，且绝对运动强度一定时，有氧训练可以降低心率。为了满足工作肌肉的需求，必须维持合适的心输出量。同样的绝对运动负荷，运动心脏比非运动心脏做更少的功（较低的心率，较高的每搏输出量）。

③最大心率：耐力训练是否能改变最大心率还无定论，但训练后最大心率通常更趋向稳定且不易受到影响。

④心率恢复：耐力训练后心率恢复期缩短，所以对心率恢复期的测量常用作评估心肺功能的间接指标。

（5）心输出量。运动训练对心输出量的两个组成部分即每搏输出量和心率，且这两部分对心输出量都有影响。运动训练后，在安静状态和相对强度的运动中，每搏输出量增加，而心率下降。但是心输出量变化不大，心输出量也可能会略微下降，或许是动静脉血氧含量差增加（组织摄取更多的氧）或氧气消耗率降低（机械效率的增加）的结果。经过一段时间的有氧训练后，最大心输出量有较大程度的增加，并且保证了最大摄氧量的增加。心输出量的增加是最大每搏输出量增加的结果，但最大心率变化不大。

（6）血流。肌肉在运动情况下需要更多的氧和能源底物，为了满足需求的增加，活动的肌肉会有更多的血流。耐力训练后，心血管系统会增加活动肌肉的血流，以提供更多的氧气和能源底物。除了心脏能更好地泵血和增加每搏输出量外，还有以下四个因素会增加肌肉的血流：增加训练肌肉中的毛细血管；增加训练肌肉已存在毛细血管的募集；从不活动部位进行更有效的血液再分配；增加血液总量。

（7）血容量。耐力训练会增加血容量，这种效果会随着训练强度的增大而更加明显。血容量增加的主要原因是血浆容量的增加，但有时红细胞容量也会增多。每一种血液成分增加的时相和机制是不一样的。

①血浆容量：训练导致血浆容量增加通过两种机制来实现。第一种机制分为两个阶段：第一阶段，增加血浆蛋白，特别是白蛋白；第二阶段，长期运动训练引起新蛋白质合成。在第二种机制中，运动增加抗利尿激素与醛固酮的分泌，这些激素能增加肾脏内水和钠的重吸收而增加血浆。增加血液储备，是受到蛋白质胶体渗透压的影响。在训练的前两周，几乎所有增加的血容量都可以用血浆容量增加来解释。

②红细胞容量：随着耐力训练的持续，红细胞容量的增加也是影响总体血容量增加的因素，并且红细胞容量和心输出量一样，与最大摄氧量相关。虽然红细胞的数量可能会增加，但是红细胞比容可能会降低，出现假性贫血现象。大量增加体液比例导致血浆对血细胞的比值增高，会降低血液黏滞性或浓度。高水平耐力训练运动员的血红蛋白总量（绝对值）和红细胞总数都会升高，从而保证血液具有充足携带氧气的能力。在强化训练后，红细胞周转率也会提高。

4. 呼吸对训练的适应

有氧运动的运动表现与呼吸系统密切相关。但呼吸系统功能通常不会限制运动表现，因为相较于心血管功能，通气能力可以在更大程度上增加。与心血管系统一样，耐力训练可以导致呼吸系统出现特定适应，以最大化提高呼吸效率。

（1）肺通气。运动训练后，在安静状态下肺通气量不会改变。虽然耐力训练不会改变肺部的结构或基本生理功能，但是会减少次最高强度运动下的通气量，减少量高达30%。训练后使最大肺通气量增加的因素有两个：最高强度运动时的潮气量和呼吸频率的增加。

（2）肺换气。训练后，在安静状态和次最高强度运动下肺扩散能力都不会发生变化，然而在最高强度运动下却会增加。

（3）动静脉血氧含量差。耐力训练后动脉含氧量的改变非常小，即使血红蛋白总量增加，单位血液内的血红蛋白含量仍然相同，甚至可能会稍微减少。然而，动静脉血氧含量差会随着训练而增加，尤其是在进行次最高强度运动时。这一增加是由于混合静脉血含氧量较低，反映了活跃组织摄取了更多的氧气，以及血流更有效地被分配到活跃组织中。

总之，呼吸系统能很有效地携带充足氧气进入机体。所以，呼吸系统很少会限制耐力运动表现。但在最高强度运动中，当所有系统都承受最大压力时，呼吸系统才会出现训练适应。

5.骨骼肌对训练的适应

（1）肌纤维类型。低至中等强度的有氧运动主要依赖Ⅰ型（慢肌）肌纤维。有氧训练使Ⅰ型肌纤维肥大，也就是增加了Ⅰ型肌纤维横断面积。但是，肌纤维的改变取决于每次训练的强度、持续时间以及训练计划的长短。

（2）毛细血管网发达。有氧训练最重要的适应之一是增加肌纤维周围的毛细血管数量。经过耐力训练的人，其腿部肌肉的毛细血管数量多于久坐不动者。较多的毛细血管可以增加血流和肌纤维之间气体、热量、营养物质与代谢废物的交换。事实上，毛细血管密度增大是训练提高最大摄氧量最重要的改变之一。

（3）肌红蛋白量。氧气进入肌纤维会与类似血红蛋白分子的肌红蛋白结合。这种含铁的分子将氧分子从细胞膜转运到线粒体。已有研究表明，耐力训练可以使肌肉中肌红蛋白含量增加75%～80%。这种训练适应能够明显提升肌肉的氧化代谢能力。

（4）线粒体功能对训练的适应。有氧训练也会导致线粒体功能改变，增强肌纤维产生ATP的能力。这种通过氧化产生ATP的能力，取决于肌肉线粒体的数量与体积。

（5）氧化酶。能源物质的氧化分解与最终ATP的生成都要依靠线粒体氧化酶的活性。氧化酶是一种特殊蛋白质，可以催化能源物质的分解并形成ATP，有氧训练可以提高这些重要酶的活性。

6.代谢对训练的适应

（1）乳酸阈。乳酸阈是与耐力运动表现密切相关的生理指标。乳酸阈值越高，有氧能力就越好。运动员在持续6～12个月的耐力训练后乳酸阈就会出现明显提高。

（2）呼吸交换率。呼吸交换率（RER）是指机体在代谢过程中二氧化碳排出与氧气消耗之比，呼吸交换率能反映能量来源底物的组成比。较低的呼吸交换率反映机体主要以脂肪氧化能量，而较高的呼吸交换率反映碳水化合物贡献较大。训练后的呼吸交换率在绝对和相对次最高强度运动时会降低，这是训练后在某一运动强度下，游离脂肪酸参与供能逐渐取代碳水化合物的结果。

（3）安静和次最高强度运动的摄氧量。耐力训练后，安静时和次最高强度运动下的摄氧量不会改变或略微下降。次最高强度运动时的摄氧量小范围降低是运动经济性提高的结果。

（4）最大摄氧量。最大摄氧量是反映心肺耐力的最佳指标，它随耐力训练的持续而提高。

7. 最大摄氧量的限制因素

多年前，运动科学家曾提出限制最大摄氧量最重要的生理学因素的两种对立理论，现在大多数证据支持第二种理论。

第一种理论认为，限制耐力运动表现的原因是线粒体内缺乏足够浓度的氧化酶。耐力训练可以增加这些氧化酶，让活动组织有更多可利用的氧，导致较高的最大摄氧量。另外，耐力训练也会增加肌肉线粒体的体积与数量。因此，该理论认为，最大摄氧量的主要限制因素是线粒体无法以特定的高速率使用氧气。此理论被认为是利用理论。

第二种理论认为，中枢和外周的循环因素限制了耐力能力。这些循环因素阻止充足的氧气被运送到活动组织。根据此理论，耐力训练后最大摄氧量会提高是血量增加、心输出量增加（通过增加每搏输出量）和较好的活动肌肉血流灌流所致。这一理论认为心血管因素是最大摄氧量的限制因素。

8.长期训练提高有氧功率和心肺耐力

运动员经过12～18个月的强化耐力训练后，机体的最大摄氧量可达到最高值，但耐力运动表现还可以继续得到提高。在没有提高最大摄氧量的情况下，耐力运动表现获得改善，可能是因为以较高最大摄氧量百分比进行长时间运动的能力获得提高。这种能力的提高部分是因为乳酸缓冲能力得到提高，因为跑步速度直接与乳酸开始累积时的摄氧量有关。

9.影响个体有氧训练反应的因素

（1）训练水平和最大摄氧量。同样的训练负荷量，最初体能水平越高，有氧耐力提高幅度则相对较小。每一位运动员都可获得有限的最大摄氧量水平，这个有限的范围由遗传决定，但也受到儿童早期训练对心血管系统发育的影响。

（2）遗传。提高最大摄氧量水平的能力受到遗传的限制。布沙尔等人认为，遗传可决定最大摄氧量25%～50%的变化。遗传可以解释为什么有些人即使没有经过耐力训练，也有很高的最大摄氧量值。具备较高最大摄氧量的人群也有较高的血容量，而这可能是由遗传所决定的。因此，遗传和环境因素都会影响最大摄氧量。遗传因子可能决定了运动员最大摄氧量的边界，但是耐力训练可以将最大摄氧量推进到这些边界的最上限。

（3）性别。无训练经历的健康女性最大摄氧量显著低于同年龄段无训练经历的健康男性（低20%～25%）。高训练水平的女性耐力运动员最大摄氧量接近高训练水平的男性耐力运动员（只低约10%）。

（4）高反应者和低反应者。目前证据表明，对训练计划的反应也由遗传决定。有研究表明，不同群体参与完全相同的训练计划，可能会出现高反应者（提高较大）和低反应者（很少或没有提高）两种现象。这些训练差异与基因变异和生理学机制有关（增加心输出量，扩张血容量，提高肌肉氧气摄取能力）。家庭遗传研究结果也证实了耐力训练对最大摄氧量的提高幅度受遗传成分的影响。在进行训练研究和训练计划设计时要考虑遗传因素对最大摄氧量的影响，制定个性化运动方案。

10.非耐力项目运动员的心肺耐力

许多人把心肺耐力作为体适能最重要的组成部分。即便是在非有氧的运动中，耐力水平低也易导致疲劳。对运动员而言，疲劳是发挥出最佳运动表现的主要障碍。即使轻微疲劳也会阻碍运动员的整体表现：肌力下降、反应与动作时间延长、灵敏和神经肌肉协调下降、全身移动速度减慢、注意力和警觉性降低。

所有运动员都能从提升的心肺耐力中获得益处。每一个运动员的耐力训练内容都不一样，这取决于运动员当前的耐力水平和运动项目对耐力的要求。但是，强大的心血管机能是任何一个运动员一般体能训练计划的基础。

二、无氧训练的适应

无氧工作能力指ATP-CP系统和无氧糖酵解产生ATP供能的能力。

1.无氧功率和无氧工作能力的改变

无氧工作能力的测试有温盖特无氧功率测试、临界功率测试和最大氧亏积累测试。这三种测试方法中，温盖特无氧功率测试应用最为广泛。

2.无氧训练对肌肉的适应

无氧训练，如冲刺训练和抗阻训练都可诱导骨骼肌的变化，主要反映了与这种活动形式相关的肌纤维募集。整体而言，冲刺训练和抗阻训练比有氧运动使用更多的Ⅱ型肌纤维。因此，Ⅱa型肌纤维和Ⅱx型肌纤维的横断面积都有所增加；Ⅰ型肌纤维的横断面积也会增加，但是通常范围比较小。另外，冲刺训练时募集的Ⅰ型肌纤维百分比下降，而Ⅱ型肌纤维百分比增加，尤其Ⅱa型肌纤维变化更为明显。

3.能量系统的适应

（1）ATP-CP系统的适应。短跑和举重项目强调最大肌肉力量输出，主要依赖ATP-CP系统提供能量。持续时间小于6秒的最高强度运动对ATP与CP的分解与重新合成有最大需求。研究结果显示，最大冲刺训练（6秒）或许可以提高肌力，但对ATP-CP分解供能的机制贡献不大。

（2）糖酵解系统的适应。无氧训练（30秒）可提高几个关键酵解酶的活性。最常被研究的酵解酶包括磷酸激酶、磷酸果糖激酶和乳酸脱氢酶。多次反复30秒的无氧训练会使三种酵解酶的活性增加10%～25%。但是在以ATP-CP系统为主的短时间（6秒）反复冲刺训练中，三种酶的活性变化不大。另一项研究表明，30秒全力冲刺训练可以显著提高机体己糖激酶（56%）和磷酸果糖激酶（49%）的活性，但没有增加总的磷酸激酶或乳酸脱氢酶的活性。

三、高强度间歇训练的适应

高强度间歇训练的适应与传统有氧训练很相似。在一项研究中，一组是无训练经历的年轻受试者完成4～6次的30秒冲刺训练，中间恢复4分钟，每周3次；另一组受试者从事传统训练，如持续1小时的自行车运动，每周5次。两组受试者在心脏、血管、肌肉等方面表现出一样的有利变化，且运动表现的改善情况差不多。高强度间歇训练能够刺激一些与耐力训练相同的分子信号通路，调节骨骼肌重塑，包括线粒体生物合成以及糖和脂肪运输和氧化能力的改变。

四、训练的专项性和交叉训练

运动训练产生的生理学适应具有高度专项性。要准确评估耐力水平的提高，应以运动员平时参与的相似运动方式进行测试。

交叉训练是指在同一时间内进行多种运动训练，或是同时进行不同体能要素（如耐力、力量和柔韧性）的训练。运动员可以在同一时间训练心肺耐力和力量。目前研究认为力量、爆发力和耐力在训练中可同时获得。然而，当力量训练合并耐力训练时，与单独的力量训练相比，所获得的肌肉力量和爆发力会差些。然而，相反情况并没有出现，如随耐力训练而提升的有氧功率并没有因抗阻训练的加入而出现效果减弱的现象。事实上，短期的耐力水平可随抗阻训练的加入而提高。

Chapter 11
Exercise at Altitude

The reduced barometric pressure at altitude is referred to as a hypobaric environment or simply hypobaria (low atmospheric pressure). The lower atmospheric pressure also means a lower PO_2 in the inspired air, which limits pulmonary diffusion of oxygen from the lungs and oxygen transport to the tissues. The low PO_2 in the air is termed hypoxia (low oxygen) , while the resulting low PO_2 in the blood is called hypoxemia.

In this chapter, we examine the unique characteristics of hypobaric, hypoxic environments and how these conditions alter physiological responses at rest and during physical activity, training, and sport performance. We cover these changes upon acute ascent to altitude, the ways in which these responses change as humans acclimate to high altitude, and specialized training strategies used by athletes to improve performance at altitude. We also examine several specific health risks associated with hypoxic environments.

1 Environmental Conditions at Altitude

Based on the effects of altitude on performance, the following definitions are useful:

- Near sea level (below 500 m): There are no effects of altitude on well-being or exercise performance.
- Low altitude (500–2,000 m): There are no effects on well-being but performance may be diminished, especially in athletes performing above 1,500 m. These performance decrements may be overcome with acclimation.
- Moderate altitude (2,000–3,000 m): Effects on well-being in unacclimated individuals and

decreased maximal aerobic capacity and performance are likely. Optimal performance may or may not be restored with acclimation.

- High altitude (3,000–5,500 m): There are adverse health effects (including acute mountain sickness, discussed later in this chapter) in a large percentage of individuals and significant performance decrements, even after full acclimation.
- Extreme altitude (above 5,500 m): Severe hypoxic effects are experienced. The highest permanent human settlements are at 5,200–5,800 m).

For our discussion, the term altitude refers to elevations above 1,500 m, because few negative physiological effects on exercise or sport performance are seen below that altitude.

While the major impact of altitude on exercise physiology is attributable to the low PO_2 that ultimately limits oxygen availability to the tissues, the atmosphere at altitude also differs in other ways from sea-level conditions.

1.1 Atmospheric Pressure at Altitude

At sea level, the air extending to the outermost reaches of the earth's atmosphere (approximately 38.6 km) exerts a pressure equal to 760 mmHg. At the summit of Mount Qomolangma, the highest point on earth (8,848 m) , the pressure exerted by the air above is only about 250 mmHg. These and related altitude differences are depicted in Figure 11.1.

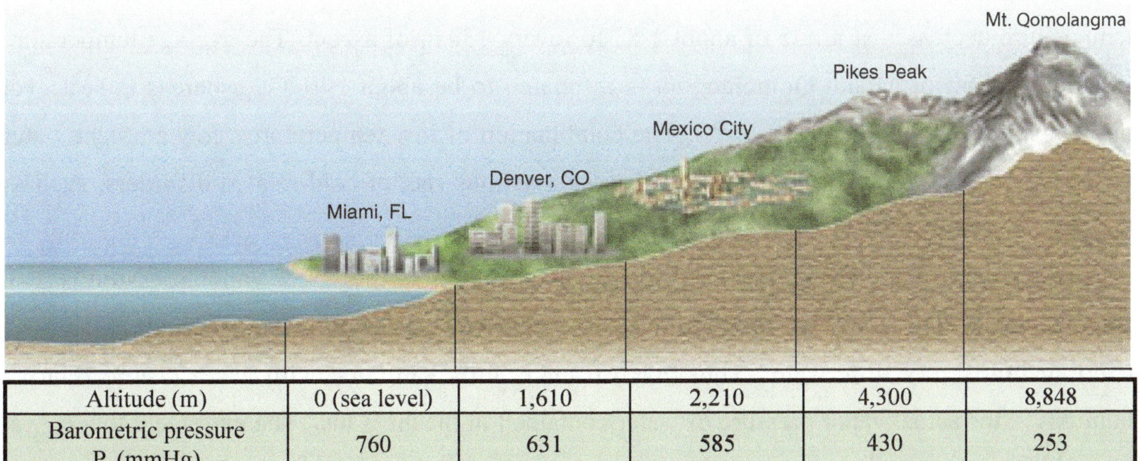

Altitude (m)	0 (sea level)	1,610	2,210	4,300	8,848
Barometric pressure P_b (mmHg)	760	631	585	430	253
% O_2 in the air	20.93	20.93	20.93	20.93	20.93
Partial pressure of oxygen PO_2 (mmHg) in the air	159	132	122	90	53
Typical temperature (℃) (°F)	15 59	9 47	2 36	−11 12	−43 −46

Figure 11.1 Differences in atmospheric conditions at sea level as altitude increases and barometric pressure falls accordingly. Note that the partial pressure of oxygen in the air decreases from 159 mmHg at sea level to only 53 mmHg at the summit of Mount Qomolangma.

The barometric pressure on earth does not remain constant. Rather, it varies somewhat with changes in climatic conditions, time of year, and the specific site at which the measurement is taken. On Mount Qomolangma, for example, the mean barometric pressure varies from 243 mmHg in January to nearly 255 mmHg in June and July. These minor variations are of little interest at sea level, except to meteorologists because of their effect on weather patterns, but are of considerable physiological importance for a climber attempting to ascend Mount Qomolangma without supplemental oxygen.

Although barometric pressure varies, the percentages of gases in the air that we breathe remain unchanged from sea level to high altitude. At any elevation, the air always contains 20.93% oxygen, 0.03% carbon dioxide, and 79.04% nitrogen. Only the partial pressures of these gases change. As shown in Figure 11.1, the pressure that oxygen molecules in the air exert at various altitudes drops proportionally with decreases in the barometric pressure. The consequent changes in PO_2 have significant effects on the partial pressure of oxygen that reaches the lungs, as well as the gradients between the alveoli of the lungs and the blood (where oxygen is loaded) and between the blood and the tissues (where oxygen is unloaded). These effects are discussed in detail later in this chapter.

1.2 Air Temperature and Humidity at Altitude

Clearly, the low PO_2 at altitude has the greatest impact on exercise physiology. However, other environmental factors contribute to the ability to perform exercise as well. For example, air temperature decreases at a rate of about 1 ℃ for every 150 m of ascent. The average temperature near the summit of Mount Qomolangma is estimated to be about −40 ℃ , whereas at sea level the temperature would be about 15 ℃. The combination of low temperatures, low ambient water vapor pressure, and high winds at altitude poses a serious risk of cold-related disorders, such as hypothermia, frostbite, and nonfreezing cold injuries.

Water vapor has its own partial pressure, also known as the water vapor pressure (P_{H_2O}). Because of the cold temperatures at altitude, the water vapor pressure in the air is extremely low. Cold air holds very little water. Thus, even if air is fully saturated with water (100% relative humidity) , the actual vapor pressure of water contained in the air is low. The extremely low P_{H_2O} at high altitude promotes evaporation of moisture from the skin (or clothing) surface, because of the high gradient between skin and air, and can lead quickly to dehydration. In addition, a large volume of water is lost through respiratory evaporation due to a combination of (a) a large vapor pressure gradient between warmed air leaving the mouth and nose and the dry air in the environment and (b) an increased respiration rate (discussed later) experienced at altitude.

1.3 Solar Radiation at Altitude

The intensity of solar radiation increases at high altitude for two reasons. First, at high altitudes, light travels through less of the atmosphere before reaching the earth. For this reason, less of the sun's radiation, especially ultraviolet rays, is absorbed by the atmosphere at higher altitudes. Second, because atmospheric water normally absorbs a substantial amount of the sun's radiation, the low water vapor in the air at altitude also increases radiant exposure. Solar radiation may further amplified by reflective light from snow, which is usually found at higher elevations.

2 Physiological Responses to Acute Altitude Exposure

This section deals with how the human body responds to acute altitude exposure, emphasizing responses that can affect exercise and sport performance. The main concerns are respiratory, cardiovascular, and metabolic responses. Most physiological studies have been performed on healthy, fit young men; unfortunately, few studies on the effects of altitude have included women, children, or the elderly—populations whose responses to the conditions of altitude might differ from those described here.

2.1 Respiratory Responses to Altitude

Adequate oxygen supply to exercising muscles is essential to physical performance and, depends on an adequate supply of oxygen being brought into the body, moved from the lungs to the blood, transported to the muscles, and adequately taken up into the muscles. A limitation in any of these steps can impair performance.

2.1.1 Pulmonary Ventilation

The sequence of steps leading to the transport of oxygen to working muscle begins with pulmonary ventilation, the active movement of gas molecules into the alveoli of the lungs (breathing). Ventilation increases within seconds of exposure to high altitude, both at rest and during exercise, because chemoreceptors in the aortic arch and carotid arteries are stimulated by the low PO_2 and signals are sent to the brain to increase breathing. The increased ventilation is primarily associated with an increased tidal volume and an even greater increase in respiratory rate. Over the next several hours and days, ventilation remains elevated to a level proportional to the altitude.

Increased ventilation acts much the same as hyperventilation at sea level. The amount of carbon dioxide in the alveoli is reduced. Carbon dioxide follows the pressure gradient, so more diffuses out of the blood, where its pressure is relatively high, and into the lungs to be exhaled. This "blowing off" of CO_2 causes blood PCO_2 to fall and blood pH to increase, a condition known as respiratory alkalosis. This alkalosis has two effects. First, it causes the oxyhemoglobin saturation curve to shift to the left. Second, it helps keep the rise in ventilation caused by the hypoxic (low PO_2) drive from increasing even further. At a given submaximal exercise intensity, ventilation is higher at altitude than at sea level, but maximal exercise ventilation is similar.

In an effort to offset respiratory alkalosis, the kidneys excrete more bicarbonate ion, the ions that buffer the carbonic acid formed from carbon dioxide. Thus, a reduction in bicarbonate ion concentration reduces the blood's buffering capacity. More acid remains in the blood, and the alkalosis is minimized.

2.1.2 Pulmonary Diffusion

Under resting conditions, pulmonary diffusion (diffusion of O_2 from the alveoli to the arterial blood) does not limit the exchange of gases between the alveoli and the blood. If gas exchange were limited or impaired at altitude, less oxygen would enter the blood, so the arterial PO_2 would be much lower than the alveolar PO_2. Instead, these two values are almost equal. Therefore, the low arterial blood PO_2, or hypoxemia, is a direct reflection of the low alveolar PO_2 and not a limitation of oxygen diffusion from the alveoli to the arterial blood.

2.1.3 Gas Exchange at the Muscles

Arterial PO_2 at sea level is about 100 mmHg, and the PO_2 in body tissues is consistently about 40 mmHg at rest; so the difference, or the pressure gradient, between the arterial PO_2 and the tissue PO_2 at sea level is about 60 mmHg. However, when one moves to an elevation of 4,300 m, arterial PO_2 decreases to about 42 mmHg and the tissue PO_2 drops to 27 mmHg. Thus, the pressure gradient decreases from 60 mmHg at sea level to only 15 mmHg at the higher altitude. This represents a 75% reduction in the diffusion gradient. At 5,800 m, the gradient shrinks to only 10 mmHg. Because the diffusion gradient is responsible for driving the oxygen from the hemoglobin in the blood into the tissues, this change in arterial PO_2 at altitude is a much greater consideration for exercise performance than the small reduction in hemoglobin saturation that occurs in the lungs.

2.2 Cardiovascular Responses to Altitude

As the respiratory system becomes increasingly limiting at altitude, the cardiovascular system likewise undergoes substantial changes to attempt to compensate for the decrease in arterial PO_2 that accompanies hypoxia.

2.2.1 Blood Volume

Within the first few hours of arrival at altitude, plasma volume begins to progressively decrease, and the decline reaches a plateau by the end of the first few weeks. This decrease in plasma volume is the result of both respiratory water loss and increased urine production. This combination of respiratory water loss and the excretion of fluid can reduce total plasma volume by up to 25%. Initially, the result of the plasma loss is an increase in the hematocrit, the percentage of the blood volume composed of red blood cells (containing hemoglobin). This adaptation—more red blood cells for a given blood flow—allows more oxygen to be delivered to the muscles for a given cardiac output. Over a period of weeks at altitude, this diminished plasma volume eventually returns to normal if adequate fluids are ingested.

Continued exposure to high altitude triggers the release of erythropoietin (EPO) from the kidneys; this is the hormone responsible for stimulating erythrocyte (red blood cell) production. This increases the total number of red blood cells and creates a greater total blood volume, which allows the person to partially compensate for the lower PO_2 experienced at altitude. However, this compensation is slow, taking weeks to months to fully restore red cell mass.

2.2.2 Cardiac Output

The preceding discussion clearly illustrates that the amount of oxygen delivered to the muscles by a given volume of blood is limited at altitude because of the reduced arterial PO_2. A logical means to compensate for this is to increase the volume of blood delivered to the active muscles. At rest and during submaximal exercise, this is accomplished by increasing cardiac output. Since cardiac output is the product of stroke volume and heart rate, increasing either or both of these variables will increase cardiac output. Upon ascent to altitude, the sympathetic nervous system is stimulated, releasing norepinephrine and epinephrine, the main hormones that alter cardiac function. The increase in norepinephrine in particular persists for several days of acute altitude exposure.

When submaximal exercise is performed during the first few hours at altitude, stroke volume is decreased compared to sea-level values (attributable to the reduced plasma volume). Fortunately, heart rate is increased disproportionately not only to compensate for the decrease in stroke volume but also to slightly increase cardiac output. However, this extra cardiac workload is not an efficient way to ensure sufficient oxygen delivery to the body's active tissues for prolonged periods. Consequently, after a few days at altitude, the muscles begin extracting more oxygen from the blood (increasing the arterial-venous oxygen difference) , which reduces the demand for increased cardiac output, since $\dot{V}O_2 = \dot{Q} \times Ca\text{-}C_{\bar{v}}O_2$ difference. The increase in heart rate and cardiac output peaks after about six to ten days at high altitude, after which cardiac output and heart rate during a given exercise bout start to decrease.

At maximal or exhaustive work levels at higher altitudes, both maximal stroke volume and maximal heart rate are decreased, as is cardiac output. The decrease in stroke volume is directly related to the decrease in plasma volume. Maximal heart rate may be somewhat lower at high altitude as a consequence of a decrease in the response to sympathetic nervous system activity, possibly attributable to a reduction in β-receptors (receptors in the heart that respond to sympathetic nerve activation, thus increasing the heart rate). With a decreased diffusion gradient to move oxygen from the blood into the muscles, coupled with this reduction in maximal cardiac output, it is apparent why both $\dot{V}O_{2\,max}$ and submaximal aerobic performance are hindered at altitude. In summary, hypobaric conditions significantly limit oxygen delivery to the muscles, reducing the capacity to perform high-intensity or prolonged aerobic activities.

2.3 Metabolic Responses to Altitude

Ascent to altitude increases the basal metabolic rate, possibly due to increases in both thyroxin and catecholamine concentrations. This increased metabolism must be balanced by an increased food intake to prevent body weight from decreasing, a common occurrence during the first few days at altitude because appetite declines as well. In individuals who maintain their body weight at altitude, there is an increased reliance on carbohydrate for fuel, both at rest and during submaximal exercise.

Table 11.1 summarizes the acute responses to altitude at rest and during submaximal exercise. Given the hypoxic conditions at altitude, and because any fixed amount of work at altitude represents a higher percentage of $\dot{V}O_{2\,max}$, we would expect anaerobic metabolism to be increased. If this occurs, we would expect lactic acid production to increase at any given work rate above the lactate threshold. This is in fact the case upon arrival at altitude. However, with longer exposure to altitude, the lactate concentration in the muscles and venous blood at a given intensity of exercise (including maximal exertion) is lower, despite the fact that muscle $\dot{V}O_{2\,max}$ does not change with adaptation to altitude. To date, there is no universally accepted explanation for this so-called lactate paradox.

Table 11.1 Effects of Acute Hypoxia (Initial 48 h) on Physiological Responses at Rest and During Submaximal Exercise

System	Acute hypoxic effect at rest	Acute hypoxic effect at a given submaximal exercise intensity
Respiratory and oxygen transport	Immediate increase in ventilation (increased frequency > increased tidal volume) Decreased 2,3-diphosphoglycerate concentration Leftward shift in the oxyhemoglobin dissociation curve Stimulation of peripheral chemoreceptors Respiratory alkalosis	Increased ventilation

continued

System	Acute hypoxic effect at rest	Acute hypoxic effect at a given submaximal exercise intensity
Cardiovascular	Decreased plasma volume Increased heart rate Decreased stroke volume Increased cardiac output Increased blood pressure	Increased heart rate Decreased stroke volume (due to decreased plasma volume) Increased cardiac output Increased $\dot{V}O_2$
Metabolic	Increased basal metabolic rate Decreased $Ca\text{-}C_{\bar{v}}O_2$ difference	Greater utilization of carbohydrates for energy Increased lactate production initially, then lower Decreased blood pH
Renal	Diuresis Excretion of bicarbonate ions Increased release of erythropoietin	

2.4 Nutrition Needs at Altitude

In addition to the alterations in physiological systems and processes already described, several other considerations are important to note with ascent to altitude. At altitude, the body has a natural tendency to lose fluids through the skin (insensible water loss) , the respiratory system, and the kidneys. This water loss is exaggerated with exercise as sweat evaporation increases from the wetted skin to the relatively dry air. These avenues of fluid loss dramatically increase the risk of dehydration, and one should pay careful attention to staying hydrated. A rule of thumb at altitude is to consume at least 3 L of fluid per day; however, this must be tailored to individual needs. It may seem counterproductive to increase fluid intake when the decrease in plasma volume is taking place to help pack red blood cells. However, dehydration can negatively alter the body water balance among fluid compartments, so staying well hydrated and allowing the natural decrease in plasma volume to occur is sound advice.

Appetite decreases at altitude, and decreased food intake often accompanies that decline. This decreased energy consumption coupled with increased metabolic rates can lead to daily energy deficits of up to 500 kcal/day, resulting in weight loss over time. Consuming adequate calories to support exercise and recreational activities is important, and climbers should be instructed to eat more calories than their appetite suggests.

Finally, successful acclimation and acclimatization to high altitude depend on adequate iron stores in the body. Iron deficiency may prevent the increase in red blood cell production that occurs progressively over the first four weeks or so at altitude. Therefore, consumption of iron-rich foods and perhaps even iron supplements is recommended before and during altitude exposure.

3 Exercise and Sport Performance at Altitude

The difficulty of demanding physical exertion at high altitude has been described by many climbers. In 1925, E.G. Norton gave the following account of climbing without supplemental oxygen at 8,600 m: "Our pace was wretched. My ambition was to do 20 consecutive paces uphill without a pause to rest and pant, elbow on bent knee, yet I never remember achieving it—13 was nearer the mark." In this section we briefly consider how exercise and sport performance is affected by altitude.

3.1 Maximal Oxygen Uptake and Endurance Activity

Maximal oxygen uptake decreases as altitude increases (Figure 11.2). $\dot{V}O_{2\,max}$ decreases little until the atmospheric PO_2 drops below 131 mmHg. This decline generally begins at an altitude of about 1,500 m—about the elevation of Denver, Colorado, and Albuquerque, New Mexico. At altitudes between 1,500 m and 5,000 m, the decreased $\dot{V}O_{2\,max}$ is due primarily to the reduced arterial PO_2; at higher elevations, a decreased maximal cardiac output further limits $\dot{V}O_{2\,max}$. $\dot{V}O_{2\,max}$ decreases approximately 8%–11% for every 1,000 m increase in altitude above 1,500 m. The rate of decline may become even steeper at very high altitudes (Figure 11.2).

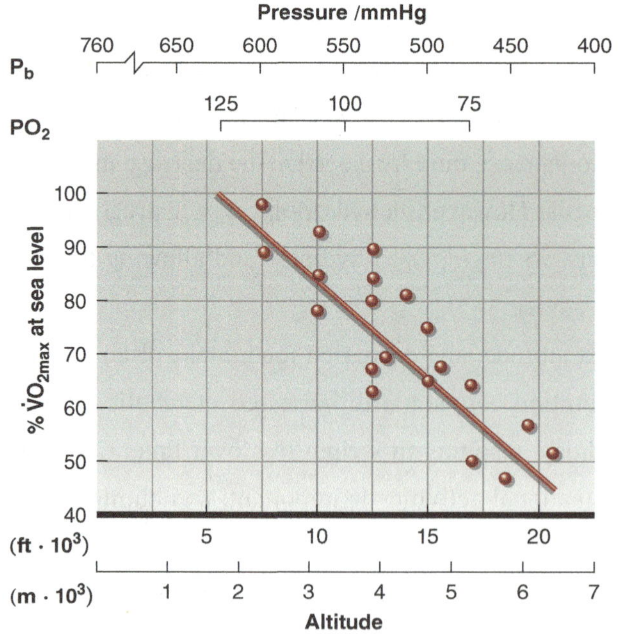

Figure 11.2 Changes in maximal oxygen uptake ($\dot{V}O_{2\,max}$) with decreases in barometric pressure (Pb) and partial pressure of oxygen (PO_2). Values for $\dot{V}O_{2\,max}$ are recorded as percentages of $\dot{V}O_{2\,max}$ attained at sea level (Pb = 760 mmHg). Note that the decline in $\dot{V}O_{2\,max}$ begins at about 1,500 m and is fairly linear. At the altitudes of Mexico City (2,240 m) , Leadville, Colorado (3,180 m) , and Nuñoa, Peru (4,000 m) , one's $\dot{V}O_{2\,max}$ would be significantly below one's capacity at sea level or in Denver, Colorado (1,600 m).

When men and women are matched for their initial aerobic fitness level, there are no sex differences in the rate of decline in $\dot{V}O_{2\,max}$.

As shown in Figure 11.3, men climbing Mount Qomolangma in a 1981 expedition experienced a change in $\dot{V}O_{2\,max}$ from about 62 ml · (kg · min)$^{-1}$ at sea level to only about 15 ml · (kg · min)$^{-1}$ near the mountain's peak. Because resting oxygen requirements are about 3.5 ml · (kg · min)$^{-1}$, without supplemental oxygen these men had little capacity for physical effort at this elevation. A study by Pugh and coworkers, also shown in Figure 11.3, showed that men with $\dot{V}O_{2\,max}$ values of 50 ml · (kg · min)$^{-1}$ at sea level would be unable to exercise, or even to move, near the peak of Mount Qomolangma because their $\dot{V}O_{2\,max}$ values at that altitude would decrease to 5 ml · (kg · min)$^{-1}$. Thus, most normal people with sea level $\dot{V}O_{2\,max}$ values below 50 ml · (kg · min)$^{-1}$ would not be able to survive without supplemental oxygen at the summit of Mount Qomolangma because their $\dot{V}O_{2\,max}$ values at such an altitude would be too low to sustain their body tissues. Enough oxygen would be consumed to barely meet their resting requirements.

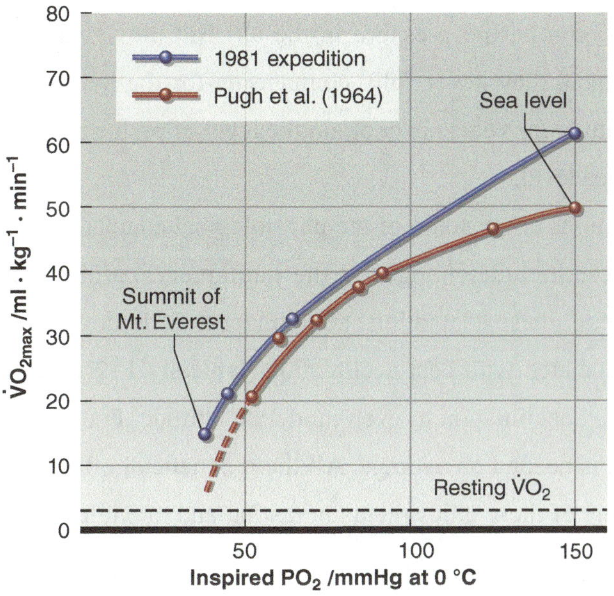

Figure 11.3 $\dot{V}O_{2\,max}$ relative to the partial pressure of oxygen (PO_2) of the inspired air for two expeditions to Mount Qomolangma.

3.2 Anaerobic Sprinting, Jumping, and Throwing Activities

Whereas endurance events are impaired at altitude, anaerobic sprint activities that last less than a minute (such as 100–400 m track sprints) are generally not impaired by moderate altitude and can sometimes be improved. Such activities place minimal demands on the oxygen transport system and aerobic metabolism. Instead, most of the energy is provided through the adenosine triphosphate (ATP) , phosphocreatine, and glycolytic systems.

In addition, the thinner air at altitude provides less aerodynamic resistance to athletes' movements. At the 1968 Olympic Games, for example, the thinner air of Mexico City clearly aided the performances of certain athletes. At Mexico City, world or Olympic records were set or tied in the men's 100 m, 200 m, 400 m, 800 m, long jump, and triple jump events and in the women's 100 m, 200 m, 400 m, 800 m, 4 × 100 m relay, and long jump events. Because similar results occurred in swimming events up to 800 m, some exercise scientists have questioned the role of lower air density in improved sprint performance. Interestingly, while shot put performance was not affected at the altitude of Mexico City, discus performance declined because there is less lift at low barometric pressures.

4 Acclimation: Chronic Exposure to Altitude

When people are exposed to altitude over days, weeks, and months, their bodies gradually adjust to the lower oxygen partial pressure in the air. But, however well they acclimate to the conditions at high altitude, they never fully compensate for the hypoxia. Even endurance-trained athletes who live at altitude for years never attain the level of performance or the $\dot{V}O_{2\,max}$ values that they might achieve at sea level.

The following sections cover some of the physiological adaptations that occur with prolonged altitude exposure. These include changes at the pulmonary, cardiovascular, and muscle tissue (cellular) level. In general, these adaptations take longer to fully develop (several weeks to several months) than those associated with heat acclimation (typically 1–2 weeks). Generally, about three weeks are needed for full acclimation to even moderate altitude. For each additional 600 m altitude increase, another week is needed on average. All these beneficial effects are lost within a month of return to sea level. Many of these adjustments in resting and maximal exercise variables are shown in Figure 11.4.

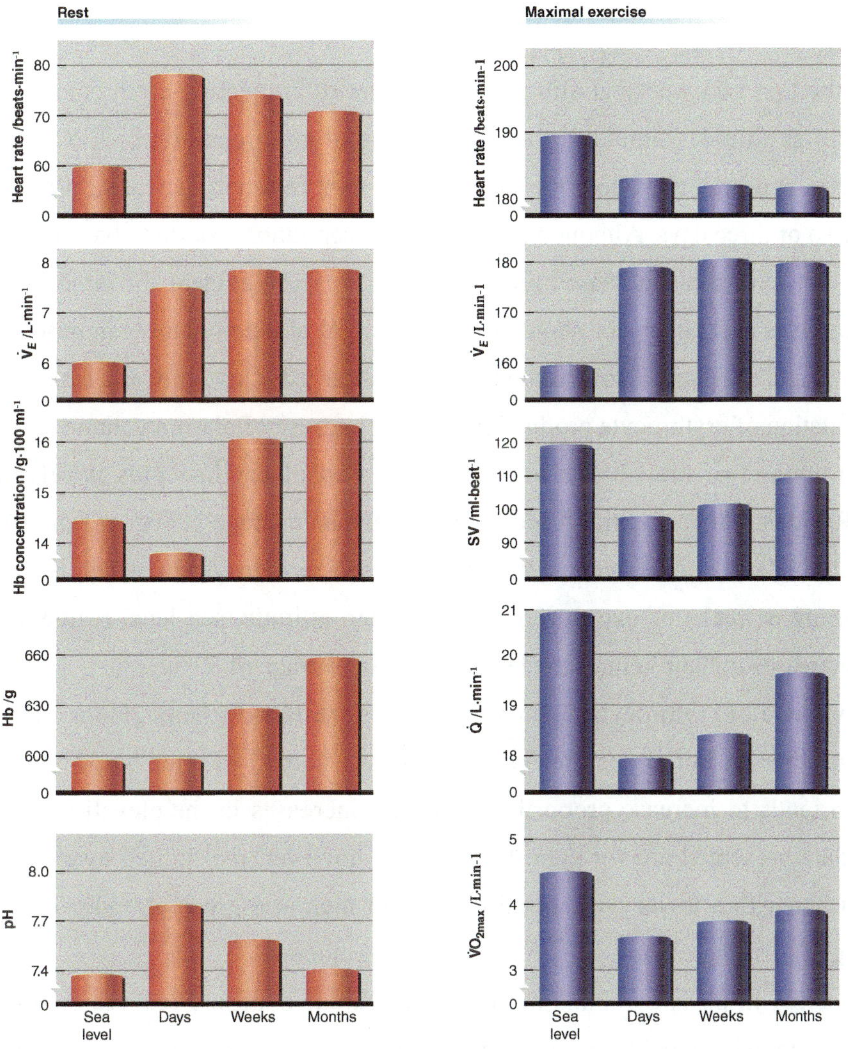

Figure 11.4 Physiological variables measured at sea level, after two or three days at altitude, and after weeks and months at altitude (3,000–3,500 m, or 9,843–11,483 ft). Both resting (left) and maximal exercise (right) variables are shown.

4.1 Pulmonary Adaptations

One of the most important adaptations to altitude is an increase in pulmonary ventilation, both at rest and during exercise. Within three or four days at 4,000 m, the increased resting ventilation rate levels off at a value about 40% higher than at sea level. Submaximal exercise ventilatory rate also plateaus at about 50% higher but over a longer time frame. Increases in ventilation during exercise remain elevated at altitude and are more pronounced at higher exercise intensities.

4.2 Blood Adaptations

During the first two weeks at altitude, the number of circulating erythrocytes increases. The lack of oxygen at altitude stimulates the renal release of erythropoietin or EPO. Within the first 3 h after arrival at a high elevation, the blood's EPO concentration increases; it then continues to increase for two or three days. Although blood EPO concentrations return to baseline levels in about a month, the polycythemia (increased red blood cells) may be evident for three months or more. After a person lives at 4,000 m for about six months, total blood volume (composed mainly of the red cell volume and the plasma volume) increases by about 10%, not only as a result of the altitude-induced stimulation of erythrocyte production but also because of plasma volume expansion.

The percentage of total blood volume composed of erythrocytes is referred to as the hematocrit. Residents in the central Andes of Peru have an average hematocrit of 60%–65%. This is considerably higher than the average hematocrit of sea-level residents, which is only 45%–48%. However, during 6 weeks of exposure to the Peruvian altitude, sea-level residents have shown remarkable increases in their hematocrit levels, up to an average of 59%.

As the volume of erythrocytes increases, so does the blood's hemoglobin (Hb) content (and concentration, after an initial decline; Figure 11.4). As noted in Figure 11.5, blood hemoglobin concentration tends to increase proportionately with increases in the elevation at which people reside. The data presented are for men. For women, however, the limited available data show a similar trend but with a lower concentration than for men at a given altitude. These adaptations improve oxygen-carrying capacity of a fixed volume of blood.

The reduction in plasma volume during acute altitude exposure reduces total blood volume, thus reducing submaximal and maximal cardiac output. But with acclimatization, as plasma volume increases over several weeks at altitude and as red blood cells continue to increase, maximal cardiac output increases. However, it does not return to sea-level values, as shown in Figure 11.4. Thus, overall oxygen delivery capacity is increased with acclimatization but not to the extent needed to achieve sea-level $\dot{V}O_{2\,max}$ values.

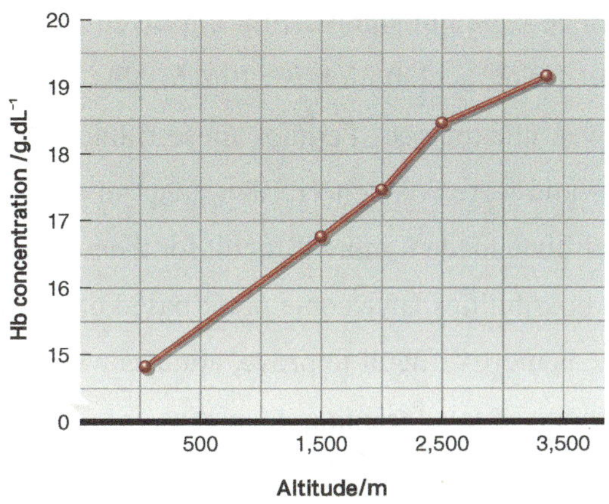

Figure 11.5 Hemoglobin (Hb) concentrations of men living at, and acclimatized to, various altitudes

4.3 Muscle Adaptations

Although few attempts have been made to study muscle changes that occur during exposure to altitude, sufficient muscle biopsy data exist to indicate that muscles undergo significant structural and metabolic changes during ascent to altitude. In a study of climbers experiencing four to six weeks of chronic hypoxia on expeditions, muscle fiber cross-sectional area decreased, thus decreasing total muscle area. Capillary density in the muscles increased, which allowed more blood and oxygen to be delivered to the muscle fibers. Muscles' inability to meet exercise demands at high altitude might be related to a decrease in their mass and their ability to generate ATP.

Several weeks at altitudes above 2,500 m reduce the metabolic potential of muscle, although this may not occur at lower elevations. Both mitochondrial function and glycolytic enzyme activities of the leg muscles (vastus lateralis and gastrocnemius) are significantly reduced after four weeks at altitude. This suggests that, in addition to receiving less oxygen, muscles lose some of their capacity to perform oxidative phosphorylation and generate ATP. Unfortunately, no muscle biopsy data have been obtained from long-term residents at high altitudes to determine whether those individuals experience any muscular adaptations as a consequence of lifelong residence at these elevations.

4.4 Cardiovascular Adaptations

Studies conducted on endurance-trained runners in the late 1960s indicated that the decrement in $\dot{V}O_{2\,max}$ when they first reached high altitude improved little for the duration of their exposure to hypoxia. Aerobic capacity remained unchanged for up to two months at altitude. Although the runners who previously had been exposed to altitude were more tolerant of hypoxia, their $\dot{V}O_{2\,max}$

values and running performance were not significantly improved with acclimation. Because of the many adaptations that occur during acclimation to altitude, this lack of improvement in aerobic capacity and performance was unexpected. Perhaps these trained subjects had already attained maximal training adaptations and were unable to further adapt in response to altitude exposure. Or perhaps the reduced PO_2 of altitude made it more difficult for them to train at the same intensity and volume as at sea level. Both possibilities have some merit based on the available literature. While a ceiling effect on performance is more difficult to prove, athletes who train at altitude routinely have a difficult time maintaining their sea-level training intensities or volumes.

5 Altitude: Optimizing Training and Performance

We have considered the major changes that occur as the human body becomes acclimated to altitude and how these adaptations affect performance at altitude. But is there any advantage to training at altitude to improve performance at sea level? Are there advantages to training at altitude versus training at sea level when one must compete at altitude? And what about the relatively new concept of "live high, train low" to optimize performance?

5.1 Does Altitude Training Improve Sea-Level Performance?

Athletes have hypothesized for decades that training under hypoxic conditions, for example in an altitude chamber or by simply breathing low-oxygen gas mixtures, can improve sea-level endurance performance. Since many of the beneficial changes associated with altitude acclimation are similar to those conferred by aerobic training, can combining the two be even more beneficial? Can altitude training improve sea-level performance?

A strong theoretical argument can be made for altitude training. First, altitude training evokes substantial tissue hypoxia (reduced oxygen supply). This is thought to be essential for initiating the conditioning response. Second, the altitude-induced increase in red blood cell mass and hemoglobin content improves oxygen delivery on return to sea level. Although evidence suggests that these latter changes are transient, lasting only several days, in theory this still should provide an advantage for the athlete.

Studying athletes at altitude poses additional problems because they are often unable to train at the same volume and intensity of effort as when at sea level. This was demonstrated in a group of elite female cyclists who performed self-selected maximum power outputs during high-intensity interval training. They completed trials under the following conditions: breathing atmospheric air (normoxia) and breathing a hypoxic gas mixture simulating 2,100 m. The athletes' sustained (10 min) and short-term (15 s) power outputs at maximal intensity were reduced under hypoxic conditions.

Training at even higher elevations, where acclimatization effects would be even more beneficial, causes even greater disruptions in training.

In addition, living and training at moderate to high altitude often causes athletes to dehydrate and to lose blood volume and muscle mass. These and other side effects tend to diminish the athletes' fitness and their motivation and tolerance for intense training. As a result, studies are difficult to interpret, but the value of altitude training for optimal sea-level performance has not been validated.

5.2 Live High, Train Low

When living and training at altitude, athletes are faced with the problem that the intensity of training is reduced because aerobic capacity and cardiorespiratory function are reduced at altitude. Thus, although athletes gain certain physiological benefits from being at altitude, they lose training adaptations associated with higher intensities of training. One way to get around this problem is to have athletes live at moderate altitude but train at low altitude, where training intensity is not compromised.

Researchers at the Institute for Exercise and Environmental Medicine in Dallas, Texas, conducted a series of studies in the mid-1990s to investigate altitude training for enhancing endurance performance. In one study,15 researchers divided 39 competitive runners into three equal groups: One (the high–low group) lived at moderate altitude (2,500 m) and trained at low altitude (1,250 m) ; one group (high–high) lived and trained at moderate altitude (2,500 m) ; and one group (low–low) lived and trained at low altitude (150 m). Using a 5,000 m time trial as the primary performance outcome measure, the researchers found that the high–low group was the only group to significantly improve their running performance, even though both the high–low and high–high groups increased their $\dot{V}O_{2\,max}$ values by 5% in direct proportion to their increase in red cell mass. Thus, there appear to be performance benefits from living at moderate altitude but going to lower elevations to maximize training intensity.

This was tested more recently by the same scientists working with a group of 14 elite male and eight elite female runners, with all but two ranked in the U.S. top 50 for their event. These athletes lived at 2,500 m and trained at 1,250 m over a period of 27 days. Testing was conducted at sea level both the week before and the week after the 27 days of living at altitude. Sea-level 3,000 m time trial performance increased by 1.1% and $\dot{V}O_{2\,max}$ increased by 3.2% as a result of this intervention.

Multiple studies have now shown a benefit of living and sleeping at high altitudes but training at low altitude for increasing sea-level $\dot{V}O_{2\,max}$ or improving sea-level aerobic performance in elite endurance athletes. These improvements have been linked to an increase in the oxygen-carrying capacity of the blood. Chronic living above 2,500 m induces such ematological acclimatization features in most athletes, although there is some variability. A recent study examined whether there is a minimum threshold "living" altitude for improvements in sea-level performance. That is, do athletes who live at relatively higher altitudes demonstrate greater performance improvements in a live high–train low setting?

In the study, 48 trained distance runners were randomly assigned to live at one of four altitudes: 1,780 m, 2,085 m, 2,454 m, or 2,800 m. The athletes all trained together at altitudes between 1,250 m and 3,000 m. Upon return from the live high–train low altitude camp, red blood cell mass and EPO concentrations increased similarly in all four groups, but EPO returned to baseline sooner in the 1,780 m group. Sea level $\dot{V}O_{2max}$ was improved for all groups as expected (Figure 11.6). However, performance on a 3 km run at sea level was significantly improved only in the groups that had lived at the middle two altitudes.

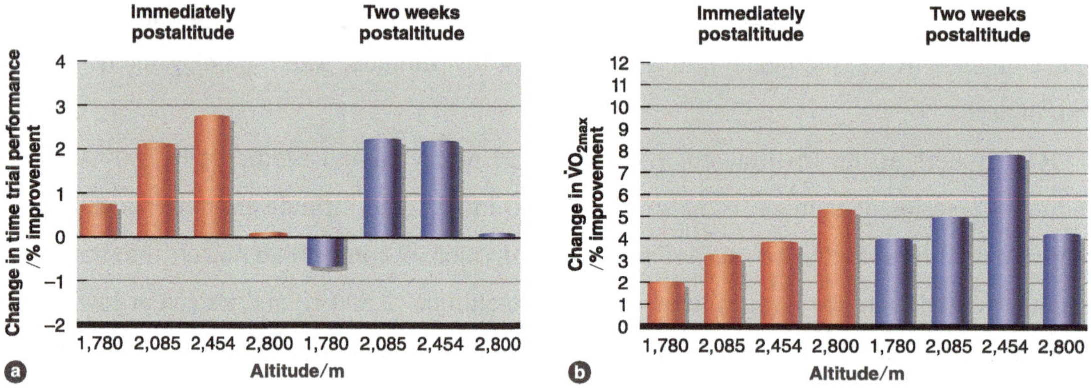

Figure 11.6 (a) Improvement in 3K time trial (%) and (b) $\dot{V}O_{2max}$ immediately upon return to sea level and two weeks later in elite collegiate distance runners after four weeks of living at one of the four altitudes shown but training together as a group. See the text for details.

5.3 Artificial Altitude Training

The favorable results of the studies on living high and training low have stimulated considerable interest in how this concept might be applied without having to send athletes to altitude to live. One approach has been to develop a hypoxic apartment where athletes sleep and live. The gas mixture inside the apartment is adjusted so that nitrogen represents a higher percentage of the inspired air, reducing the percentage of oxygen in the inspired air as well as its partial pressure. Pioneered by Finnish sport scientists, these apartments can simulate altitudes between 2,000 m and 3,000 m as the nitrogen and oxygen percentages in the inspired air are adjusted to reduce the partial pressure of oxygen to those levels associated with 2,000–3,000 m altitude. Hypoxic sleeping devices or tents have also been proposed.

6 Health Risks of Acute Exposure to Altitude

A large proportion of people who ascend to moderate and high altitudes experience symptoms of acute high altitude (mountain) sickness. This disorder is characterized by symptoms such as headache, nausea, vomiting, dyspnea (difficult breathing) , and insomnia. These symptoms can begin anywhere from 6–48 h after arrival at high altitude and are most severe on days 2 and 3. Although not life threatening, acute high altitude sickness can be incapacitating for several days or longer. In some cases, the condition can worsen. The victim can develop the more lethal altitude-related illnesses of high-altitude pulmonary edema or high-altitude cerebral edema.

6.1 Acute High Altitude (Mountain) Sickness

The incidence of acute high altitude high sickness varies with the altitude, the rate of ascent, and the individual's experience and susceptibility. Several studies have been conducted to determine the incidence of acute high altitude sickness in groups of novice hikers (tourists) and more experienced climbers. Results vary widely, ranging from a frequency of less than 1% to almost 60% at altitudes of 3,000–5,500 m (Figure 11.7). Another study showed that at elevations of 2,500–3,500 m, altitudes commonly experienced by recreational skiers and hikers, the incidence of acute high altitude sickness was about 7% for men and 22% for women, but the reason for this sex difference is unclear.

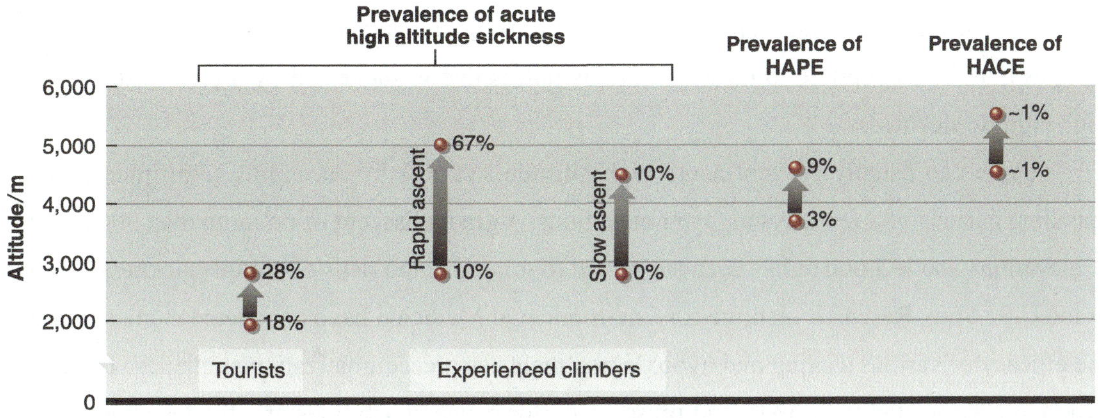

Figure 11.7 Change in the reported prevalence of acute high altitude sickness, high-altitude pulmonary edema (HAPE) , and high-altitude cerebral edema (HACE) as a function of altitude, experience, and, in the case of acute high altitude sickness, rate of ascent.

Although the precise underlying cause of acute altitude sickness is not fully understood, it appears that people who experience the greatest distress also have a low ventilatory response to hypoxia. This inadequate ventilation allows PO_2 to decrease further and carbon dioxide to accumulate in the tissues, and these two factors may induce most of the symptoms associated with altitude sickness.

Headache is the most common symptom associated with ascent to high altitude. Headache is rarely experienced below 2,500 m , but ascent to 3,600 m results in headache in the majority of people. The headache at altitude, which many sufferers describe as continuous and throbbing, is typically worse in the morning and after exercise. Alcohol consumption worsens the symptoms. The precise mechanism is unsubstantiated, but hypoxia causes dilation of the cerebral blood vessels, so stretching of pain receptors in these structures is a likely cause.

Another consequence of acute high altitude sickness is an inability to sleep even if the individual is markedly fatigued. Studies have shown that the inability to achieve satisfying sleep at altitude is associated with an interruption in the sleep stages. Additionally, some people suffer from a pattern of interrupted breathing, called Cheyne-Stokes breathing, which prevents them from falling asleep and remaining asleep. Cheyne-Stokes breathing is characterized by alternating periods of rapid breathing and slow, shallow breathing, usually including intermittent periods in which breathing completely stops. The incidence of this irregular breathing pattern increases with altitude, occurring in 24% of people at 2,440 m, 40% of people at 4,270 m, and almost everyone at altitudes above 6,300 m.

The first few days at high altitude are associated with reduced exercise performance and increased risk of acute mountain sickness (AMS). How can exercisers and athletes prevent acute high altitude sickness? Even athletes who are highly endurance trained before altitude exposure seem to have little protection against the effects of hypoxia, and it is difficult to determine which athletes may be susceptible to these symptoms unless this is suggested by a prior history of acute high altitude sickness.

People can usually prevent acute high altitude sickness by ascending to altitude gradually, spending periods of a few days at lower elevations. A gradual ascent of no more than 300 m per day at elevations above 3,000 m has been suggested to minimize the risks of altitude sickness. Scientists at the U.S. Army Research Institute for Environmental Medicine have conducted studies examining the efficacy of various staging and hypoxia treatments as preacclimatization strategies. To minimize symptoms associated with AMS and preserve performance capabilities at altitudes above 4,000 m, evidence suggests the following:

- Ascending to moderate altitudes of >1,500 m for one to two days induces ventilatory acclimatization
- Six days at 2,200 m substantially reduces AMS and improves exercise performance after rapid

ascent to >4,000 m

- Five or more days at 3,000 m within the last two months significantly reduces AMS
- The longer the residence at moderate altitudes, the better the ventilatory adaptations and prevention of AMS at high altitude
- Exercise training during these preexposures may improve physical performance even more
- Strategies involving hypobaric hypoxia (actual altitude exposures, chambers, and tents) are much more effective that normobaric hypoxia (breathing low-oxygen mixtures at sea level)

Of the drugs that have been used to reduce symptoms in those who develop acute high altitude sickness, acetazolamide started the day before ascent is the only established preventive measure. Acetazolamide is sometimes combined with a steroid such as dexamethasone. Both drugs must be used with medical supervision. Of course, the definitive treatment for severe acute mountain sickness is a retreat to lower altitude, but high-flow oxygen and the use of hyperbaric rescue bags are also effective in severe cases.

6.2 High-Altitude Pulmonary Edema

Unlike AMS, high-altitude pulmonary edema (HAPE) , which is the accumulation of fluids in the lungs, is life threatening. The cause of HAPE is likely related to the pulmonary vasoconstriction resulting from hypoxia, causing blood clots to form in the lungs. Remaining tissue becomes overperfused, and fluid and protein leak out of the capillaries. This seems to occur most frequently in unacclimatized people who rapidly ascend to altitudes above 2,500 m. The disorder occurs in otherwise healthy people and has been reported more often in children and young adults. The fluid accumulation interferes with air movement into and out of the lungs, leading to shortness of breath, a persistent cough, chest tightness, and excessive fatigue. Disruption of normal breathing impairs blood oxygenation and, if it is severe enough, cyanosis (a bluish tint) of the lips and fingernails, mental confusion, and loss of consciousness may occur. High-altitude pulmonary edema is treated via administration of supplemental oxygen and movement of the victim to a lower altitude.

6.3 High-Altitude Cerebral Edema

Rare cases of high-altitude cerebral edema (HACE) , which is fluid accumulation in the cranial cavity, have been reported. The condition is often a subsequent complication of HAPE. This neurological condition is characterized by mental confusion, lethargy, and ataxia (difficulty walking) , progressing to unconsciousness and death. Most cases have been reported at altitudes greater than 4,300 m. Similar to that for HAPE, the cause of HACE involves hypoxia-induced leakage of fluids from cerebral capillaries, causing edema and a resultant pressure buildup in the confined intracranial space. Treatment involves administration of supplemental oxygen, a hyperbaric bag, and prompt descent to a lower altitude. If descent is delayed, permanent impairment may ensue.

IN CLOSING

Activities are seldom conducted under ideal environmental conditions. Heat, cold, humidity, and altitude—alone or in combination—present unique problems that are superimposed on the physiological demands of exercise. This chapter and the preceding chapter summarized the characteristics of these common environmental stresses and how we can cope with them. Much of our discussion thus far has dealt with how physiological variables and environmental stress can hinder our performance.

KEY TERMS

acute altitude (mountain) sickness; barometric pressure (Pb) ; Cheyne-Stokes breathing; high-altitude cerebral edema (HACE) ; high-altitude pulmonary edema (HAPE) ; hypobaric; hypoxemia; hypoxia; partial pressure of oxygen (PO_2) ; polycythemia; respiratory alkalosis

STUDY QUESTIONS

(1) What types of exercise are detrimentally influenced by exposure to high altitude and why?

(2) Differentiate the physiological adjustments that accompany acclimation to altitude over a period of days, weeks, and months.

(3) Would an endurance athlete who trained at altitude be able to perform better during subsequent sea-level performance? Why or why not?

(4) Describe the theoretical advantage of living high and training low.

(5) What are the best strategies for preparing athletes for high-altitude competition?

(6) What are the health risks associated with acute exposure to high altitude and how can they be minimized?

第十一章 高原环境与运动训练

高原因气压降低被称为低压环境或简称低压（低气压）。较低的大气压力意味着空气中较低的氧分压，这限制了氧气从肺部向组织的扩散和输送。

在这一章中，我们将研究低压缺氧环境的独特特征，以及这些特征如何改变休息时以及体力活动、训练和运动表现时的生理反应。我们将讨论机体的急性高原反应，这些反应在人类适应高海拔时的变化特点，以及运动员为提高运动表现的高原训练策略。我们也分析了一些与低氧环境相关的健康危害。

一、高原环境条件

高原效应对于机能表现的影响应注意以下4点：①低海拔高度500～2000米，对于大部分人群的健康没有影响但因机能下降运动表现可能会减弱，尤其是运动员在1500米以上高度的运动表现，但是这些机能下降可以通过适应来克服。②中等海拔高度2000～3000米，不适应环境者其健康会受到影响，最大摄氧量和身体机能都有可能下降。机能最佳状态可能会随着适应恢复，也可能不会。③高海拔高度3000～5500米，对大部分人群的健康有负面影响（包括急性高山病），即使在完全适应之后，机能表现也显著下降。④极端海拔高度5500米以上，严重的缺氧影响。人类可长久居住的最高海拔位于5200～5800米。

在我们的讨论中，高原是指海拔高度在1500米以上，因为在该海拔高度以下，很少看到对锻炼或运动表现的负面生理影响。

1.高原气压

从海平面到高原尽管大气压有所变化，但是我们呼吸的空气中各气体的百分比是不变的，只有不同气体的分压发生了变化。大气中的氧分压会影响到达肺的氧分压以及肺泡和血液之间（氧气被加载的地方）、血液和组织之间（氧气被卸载的地方）的氧分压梯度。

2.高原空气的温度和湿度

水蒸气有自己的分压，称水蒸气压。由于高原的低温，空气中的水蒸气压极低。冷空气容纳的水很少。因此，即使空气完全被水饱和（100%相对湿度），空气中包含的水的实际水蒸气压也很低。高原环境的极低水蒸气压促进了皮肤（或衣物）表面的水分蒸发，导致机体迅速脱水。除此之外，大量的水分通过呼吸系统蒸发。

3.高原的太阳辐射

太阳辐射强度在高原增加有两个原因。第一，在高原地区，太阳辐射（尤其是紫外线）被大气吸收的更少。第二，高原环境的空气中的低水蒸气含量也会增加辐射暴露。雪的反射光可能会进一步增强太阳辐射，这在高海拔地区很常见。

二、急性高原暴露的生理反应

本节讨论人体对于急性高原暴露的生理反应，强调这种生理反应可能会影响人体的锻炼状态和运动表现，主要关注的是呼吸、心血管和代谢反应。

1.呼吸系统的高原反应

充足的氧气供应对于人体的运动表现是至关重要的。氧气从肺部转移到血液，运输到肌肉，并充足地供应于肌肉中。这些步骤中任何一个受限都会降低运动表现。

（1）肺通气。肺通气，即气体分子进入到肺泡的主动运动（呼吸）。人体暴露在高海拔的几秒钟内，通气量都会增加，因为主动脉弓和颈动脉中的化学感受器受到低氧分压的刺激，同时，信号传递到大脑以增加呼吸。通气量增加主要与潮气量增加和明显的呼吸频率增加有关。这种通气量增加与在平原地区发生的过度换气类似，会降低肺泡处的二氧化碳量。二氧化碳的排出引起血液中二氧化碳分压降低，血液pH值增加，这种状况称为“呼吸性碱中毒”。这种碱中毒有两方面影响：一是引起氧离曲线左移；二是有助于抑制由低氧引起的通气量增加。在亚极限运动强度，高原通气量比平原地区更高，但是在极限运动强度通气量相似。为了抵消呼吸性碱中毒，肾脏排出更多的碳酸氢根离子，碳酸氢根离子浓度降低会降低血液的缓冲能力，血液中酸性增强，碱中毒减弱。

（2）肺换气。在安静状态下，肺换气（氧气从肺泡扩散到动脉血）并不限制肺泡和血液之间的气体交换。在高原上气体交换受到限制或削弱，进入血液的氧气就会减少，动脉血低氧分压或低血氧是肺泡低氧分压的直接反映。

（3）肌肉中的气体交换。当人处于海平面高度时，动脉血中氧分压为100毫米汞柱，组织血氧分压在安静状态下一直为40毫米汞柱，动脉血中的氧分压和组织血氧分压之间的压差或压力梯度约为60毫米汞柱。但是在4 300米高度时，动脉血中的氧分压降为42毫米汞柱，组织血氧分压降为27毫米汞柱，压力梯度下降到15毫米汞柱，降低了75%。在5 800米高度时，压力梯度会降低到10毫米汞柱。由于压力梯度负责将血液中血红蛋白中的氧气运输到组织，因此高原上动脉血中氧分压变化对运动表现的影响比肺部血红蛋白饱和度的小幅度降低要大得多。

2.心血管系统的高原反应

由于呼吸系统在高原中受到限制，心血管系统同样经历了实质性变化以弥补低氧引起的动脉血中氧分压的降低。

（1）血容量。在到达高原后的几个小时内，血容量开始减少，并在几周后达到一个平稳状态。血容量的减少是呼吸系统水分丢失和尿量生成增多的共同结果，能够使血容量减少达25%。这种适应使单位血液中的红细胞增多，也使在一定的心输出量下更多的氧气被输送到肌肉。到高原几周后摄入充足的液体，血容量会恢复正常。

持续暴露于高海拔能够刺激肾脏释放促红细胞生成素（EPO），从而增加红细胞总数，并产生更大的血容量。但这种补偿是缓慢的，需要几周到几个月以重塑红细胞数量。

（2）心输出量。由于动脉血氧分压的降低，血液输送到肌肉的氧气量受到限制。机体会增加输送到活动肌肉的血液量。高原上在安静状态下或进行亚极限强度运动时，机体会增加心输出量。心输出量是心脏每搏输出量和心率的乘积，增加这两个变量中的一个或两个都会增加心输出量。到达高原后，交感神经系统兴奋，释放肾上腺素和去甲肾上腺素，改变心脏功能。到达高原后的几个小时内进行亚极限强度运动，心脏每搏输出量会减少（由于血容量减少）。但是心率的急剧增加弥补了心脏每搏输出量不足，还会轻度增加心输出量。在高原几天之后，肌肉已经可以从血液中获得更多的氧气（动静脉血氧含量差增加），这就减少了对增加心输出量的需求，因为$\dot{V}O_2 = \dot{Q} \times Ca^{2+} - C_{\bar{v}}O_2$。心率和心输出量的增加在到高原后的6 ~ 10天到达顶峰；之后，心输出量和心率在一次性运动中开始降低。

在高原的极限强度或者力竭运动中，最大心脏每搏输出量和最高心率均降低，心输出量也一样。心脏每搏输出量的减少与血容量的减少直接相关。在高原地区，交感神经系统活动反应降低，最大心率可能会降低，这可能是由于β受体（心脏中对交感神经激活做出反应的受体）减少所致。

3. 代谢系统的高原反应

到达高原之后基础代谢率提高，可能是因为甲状腺素和儿茶酚胺浓度增加所致。此时需要通过增加食物摄入来平衡体重，但高原反应也会使食欲下降。对于能够在高原维持体重的人群，他们在安静状态和亚极限运动中，都增加了对碳水化合物的依赖。

4. 高原的营养摄入

在高原身体会通过皮肤、呼吸系统和肾脏丢失水分。运动时，水分流失更多。这些液体的流失增加了机体脱水的风险。在高原时，建议运动员每天至少补液3升。在高原，食欲降低会造成体重逐渐降低。是否能成功适应高原环境取决于体内是否有充足的铁。因此，建议高原暴露之前以及到高原后摄入含铁丰富的食物或补充铁剂。

三、高原的锻炼和运动表现

1.最大摄氧量和耐力运动

最大摄氧量会随着海拔增加而降低，最大摄氧量的下降从海拔约1 500米开始。海拔1 500~5 000米，最大摄氧量由于动脉血氧分压降低而降低。5 000米以上，心输出量的降低则进一步限制最大摄氧量的水平。从1 500米开始每增加1 000米高度，最大摄氧量降低大约8%～10%。在更高的海拔处，这个下降率变得更高。

2.无氧短跑、跳跃和投掷运动

虽然耐力运动表现在高原会受损，但持续不到1分钟的无氧短跑运动（如100～400米跑）在中等海拔高度一般不会受到影响，甚至有可能提高。因为这些运动很少需要氧运输系统和有氧代谢，大部分的能量是通过三磷酸腺苷（ATP）、磷酸肌酸和糖酵解系统获得。此外，高原的稀薄空气降低了运动员运动时的空气阻力。例如，1968年奥运会，在墨西哥城刷新的世界纪录集中在男子和女子100米、200米、400米、800米和跳远项目上。有趣的是，虽然铅球成绩没有受到影响，但铁饼的成绩下降，这可能是因为低气压导致对铁饼的上托力量降低所致。

四、长期暴露于高原的适应

当人们一直生活在高原地区时，他们的身体会逐渐适应空气中的低氧分压。但是，无论他们的适应能力如何，都无法完全补偿缺氧。即使是长期生活在高原地区的耐力运动员，运动成绩或最大摄氧量也无法达到海平面高度的水平。通常，高原适应与热习服（通常是1～2周）需要更长的时间（几个星期到几个月）。高度每增加600米，平均需要增加一周的适应时间。机体所发生的变化会在回到海平面高度的一个月内消失。

1.肺适应

高原最重要的适应之一是在休息或运动时肺通气量增加。在4 000米高度的3～4天，静息通气量会增加，比海平面高约40%。而在亚极限强度运动时，通气量也会增加，在很长一段时间的内通气量比海平面高约50%。

2.血液适应

初到高原的2周，循环血中红细胞总量增加。高原缺氧会刺激肾脏释放促红细胞生成素（EPO）。到达高原后的3小时内，血液中EPO浓度增加，一个月内血液中EPO的浓度恢复至原来水平，但红细胞会在3个月内持续增多。在4 000米的高原生活6个月后，总血容量（主要由红细胞和血浆组成）会增加约10%。

血液中的血红蛋白浓度往往随着人们的居住的海拔高度的增加而成比例地增加。随着红细胞比容的增加，血液中的血红蛋白含量和浓度也增加（虽然会经历最初一段时间的下降）。这种适应性变化提高了一定容量血液的携氧能力。

急性高原暴露期间血浆容量的减少，导致总血容量减少，从而降低了次最大和最大心输出量。但随着对高原的适应，以及血浆容量在高原数周内的增加和红细胞的持续增加，最大心输出量会增加。但最大心输出量和总的氧气输送能力仍旧达不到海平面高度时的最大摄氧量水平。

3.肌肉适应

到达高原后，肌肉的结构和代谢都发生了明显的变化。肌肉中的毛细血管密度增加，能够运输更多的血液和氧气到肌纤维。肌纤维的横截面积减少，线粒体功能下降，进行氧化磷酸化和产生ATP的能力下降，这也是肌肉在高原环境下运动能力下降的主要原因。

4.心血管适应

对经过耐力训练的跑步运动员的研究发现，当他们第一次经历长时间高原暴露后其最大摄氧量的下降并没有得到明显改善，在到达高原2个月后，也没有明显变化。在高原低氧习服后，尽管跑步运动员能更加耐受低氧刺激，但他们的最大摄氧量和跑步成绩没有明显提高。虽然多项生理指标开始出现适应现象，但有氧能力和运动表现也没有如预期那样得到提高。也许是这些经过训练的运动员已经达到了最大水平的训练适应；也或许是由于低氧分压，导致运动员无法在高原达到与平原同样的训练强度和训练量。这两种可能都有一定的文献支持。当运动员运动表现达到其“天花板”时，很难再进一步；运动员在高原上的常规训练很难维持在平原时训练强度和量。

五、高原训练方法

几十年来，运动员们一直模拟缺氧刺激进行训练，例如利用低压舱或简单地吸入低氧气体混合物。由于许多与高原适应相关的有益变化与有氧训练相似，那么将两者结合起来，进行高原训练能提高海平面运动成绩吗?

1. 高原训练能增加海平面的运动表现吗?

高原训练是有理论依据的。第一，高原训练引起大量组织缺氧（氧气供应减少），这被认为是启动机体反应的必要条件。第二，高原引起的红细胞数量和血红蛋白含量的增加，改善了返回海平面高度时的氧气输送。但高原训练会带来额外的问题，因为运动员通常无法在高原完成海平面高度的训练量和强度；在海拔更高的地方训练，机体的适应效果会更好，但也会对训练造成更大的干扰。此外，在中高海拔高度生活和训练常会导致运动员脱水以及血容量和肌肉质量减少。这些及其他副作用往往会削弱运动员的体能，以及他们对高强度训练的动力和耐受性。

2.高住低练

在高原生活和训练中，运动员面临着因有氧能力和心肺功能下降而导致训练强度降低的问题。解决此问题的一个方法就是让运动员居住在中等海拔地区，而在更低海拔地区训练，以保证训练强度。

多项研究表明，在高海拔地区生活，在低海拔地区进行训练，可以提高运动员海平面高度最大摄氧量或有氧运动能力。这些改变与血液氧运输能力的提高有关。在一项研究中，48名受过训练的长跑运动员被随机分配居住在4组海拔高度：1 780米、2 085米、2 454米或2 800米。运动员们一起在海拔1 250米～3 000米训练。从“高住低练”训练营返回时，4组运动员的红细胞数量和EPO的浓度均明显增加，但是1 780米组的运动员的EPO在较短的时间内恢复到基线水平。然而，在海平面高度3 000米跑的成绩仅居住在中等海拔高度的两组运动员有明显提高。因此，增加红细胞数量是必要的，但不足以提高运动表现。此外，在这样的环境中，似乎有一个最佳的居住高度以获得最优机能增益。

3.模拟高原训练

“高住低练”研究的良好结果，激发了人们对模拟高原训练的极大兴趣。模拟高原训练的方法之一是开发一个低氧房间，运动员可以在那里睡觉和生活。对房间内的气体进行调整，提高氮气所占的比例，降低了吸入气中氧气的百分比及分压。

六、急性高原暴露的健康伤害

大部分来到中高海拔地区的人都会出现急性高原（高山）病症状。这种疾病的特征是头痛、恶心、呕吐、呼吸困难和失眠。这些症状可在抵达高海拔地区后6～48小时出现，症状最严重的是抵达后的第2天和第3天。虽然没有生命危险，但是急性高原（高山）病可以使人在几天或更长时间内的运动能力下降。在某些情况下还会恶化。部分人群可能患上更致命的高原相关疾病，如高原肺水肿或高原脑水肿。

1.急性高原（高山）病

急性高原（高山）病的发病率随海拔高度、上升速度、个人经历和易感性而不同。有研究在比较一群无经验的远足者（游客）和更有经验的登山者急性高原（高山）病的发病率时发现结果差异很大，在海拔3 000～5 500米的范围发病率从小于1%到近乎60%不等。另一项研究显示，在2 500～3 500米的海拔高度，休闲滑雪者和徒步者中，男性急性高原（高山）病的发病率约为7%，女性约为22%，但这种性别差异的原因尚不清楚。

急性高原（高山）病严重的人，通气量明显降低。不充分的通气使得氧分压进一步降低，二氧化碳在组织中聚集，两因素结合可能诱发与急性高原（高山）病相关的大多数症状。头痛是高原比较常见的症状。在2 500米以下时很少会有人出现头痛，但海拔上升到3 600米会导致大多数人头痛。高原上的头痛，部分人群描述为是持续性和搏动性的，通常在早晨和运动后更严重。

急性高原（高山）病的另一个后果是失眠，即使人体感到明显疲劳，也无法入睡。

人们通常可以通过先在较低海拔地区适应几天，逐渐提高海拔高度的方法来预防急性高原（高山）病。如上升到大于1 500米的中等海拔高度1～2天后会产生通气适应；在2 200米海拔高度待6天基本上能减轻急性高原（高山）病，且改善快速上升到4 000米后的运动表现。中等海拔地区居住时间越长，高海拔地区通气适应和对急性高原（高山）病的预防越好。

在用于减轻急性高原（高山）病患者症状的药物中，乙酰唑胺是唯一确定有效的。乙酰唑胺有时与类固醇如地塞米松联合使用。两种药物都要在医嘱指导下服用。当然，对严重急性高原（高山）病的最终治疗是退到海拔较低的地区，高流量氧气和使用高压救援袋在严重情况下也是有效的。

2.高原肺水肿

不同于急性高原（高山）病，高原肺水肿（HAPE）是肺部水聚集，有生命危险。HAPE的病因可能与缺氧引起的肺血管收缩有关，导致肺内形成血栓。其余的组织过度灌注，液体和蛋白质从毛细血管中溢出。这种情况似乎最常发生在迅速上升到2 500米以上高度未适应的人群。液体积聚会干扰肺部空气进出，导致呼吸急促、持续咳嗽、胸闷和过度疲劳。正常呼吸中断会损害血液供氧，如果病情严重，可能会出现嘴唇和指甲发绀（呈蓝色）、精神错乱和意识丧失。高原肺水肿的治疗方法是给病人补充氧气，并将其转移到较低的海拔地区。

3. 高原脑水肿

高原脑水肿（HACE）发生较少，据报告是液体聚集在颅腔引起的。这种情况通常是HAPE的后续并发症。这种神经系统疾病的特点是精神错乱，昏昏欲睡，共济失调（行走困难），并会最终发展到失去知觉和死亡。大多数病例报告的海拔高度超过4 300米。与HAPE相似，HACE的病因包括缺氧引起的脑毛细血管液体渗漏引起水肿，并在狭窄的颅内空间形成压力。HACE的治疗包括补充氧气，使用高压救援袋，并迅速下降到海拔较低的地区。如果下降延迟，可能对人体造成永久性损伤。

Chapter 12 Exercise in Hot and Cold Environments

The stresses of physical exertion are often complicated by environmental conditions. Performing exercise in extreme heat or cold places an additional burden on the mechanisms that regulate body temperature while supporting continued exercise. Although these mechanisms are amazingly effective in regulating body temperature under normal conditions, mechanisms of thermoregulation can be inadequate when we are subjected to extreme heat or cold. Fortunately, the body is able to adapt to such environmental stresses with continued exposure over time, a process known as acclimation (which refers to a short-term adaptation, e.g., days to weeks) or acclimatization (the proper term when we are referring to natural adaptations gained over long periods of time, e.g., months to years).

In the following discussion, we focus on the physiological responses to acute and chronic exercise in both hot and cold environments. Specific health risks are associated with exercise in both temperature extremes, so we also discuss the prevention of temperature-related illness and injuries during exercise.

1 Body Temperature Regulation

Humans are homeotherms, which means that our internal body temperature is physiologically regulated to keep it nearly constant even when environmental temperature changes.

Whenever this balance is disturbed, body temperature changes.

1.1 Metabolic Heat Production

Only a small part (usually less than 25%) of the energy (adenosine triphosphate, ATP) the body produces is used for physiological functions such as muscle contraction; the rest is converted to heat. All active tissues produce metabolic heat (M) that must be precisely offset by heat loss to the environment to maintain the internal temperature of the body. If the body's heat production exceeds its heat loss, as it often does during moderate- to heavy-intensity aerobic activity, the body stores the excess heat, and internal temperature increases. People's ability to maintain a constant internal temperature depends on their ability to balance the metabolic heat they produce and the heat they gain from the environment with the heat the body loses.

1.2 Transfer of Body Heat to and from the Environment

Let's examine the mechanisms by which heat is transferred between a person and the surroundings. For the body to transfer heat to the environment, the heat produced in the body must first move from deep in the body (the core) to the skin (the shell) , where it has access to the outside environment. Heat is primarily moved from the core to the skin by the blood. Only when heat reaches the skin can it be transferred to the environment by any of four mechanisms: conduction, convection, radiation, and evaporation. These are illustrated in Figure 12.1.

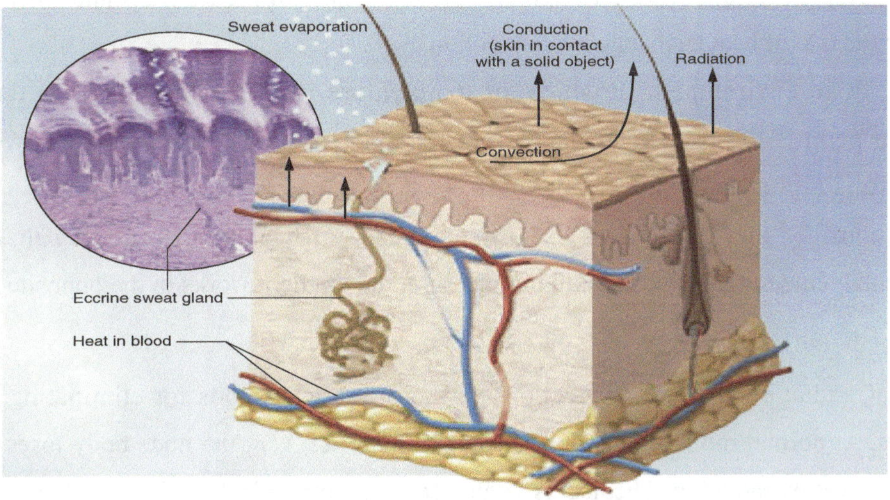

Figure 12.1 The removal of heat from the skin. Heat is delivered to the body surface via the arterial blood and to a lesser extent by conduction through the subcutaneous tissue. When the temperature of the skin is greater than that of the environment, heat is removed by conduction (if the skin is in contact with an object) , convection, radiation, and sweat evaporation; when the environmental temperature exceeds skin temperature, heat can be removed only by evaporation.

1.2.1 Conduction

Heat conduction (K) involves the transfer of heat from one solid material to another through direct molecular contact. As an example, heat can be lost from the body when the skin is in contact with a cold object, as when one sits on cold metal bleachers watching a soccer match on a chilly day. Conversely, if a hot object is pressed against the skin, heat from the object is conducted to the skin and heat is gained by the body. If the contact is prolonged, heat from the skin surface can be transferred to the blood as it flows through the skin and transferred to the core, raising internal (core) temperature. During exercise, conduction is usually negligible as a source of heat exchange because the body surface area in contact with solid objects (for example, soles of the feet on hot playing fields) is small. Therefore, many environmental physiologists treat conductive heat exchange as negligible in their calculations of heat balance and exchange.

1.2.2 Convection

Convection (C) , on the other hand, involves transferring heat by the motion of a gas or a liquid across the heated surface. When the body is still and there is little air movement, a thin unstirred boundary layer of air surrounds the body. However, the air around us is usually in constant motion, especially so during exercise as we move either the whole body or body segments (e.g., the arms pumping as we run) through the air. As air moves around us, passing over the skin, heat is exchanged with the air molecules. The greater the movement of the air (or liquid, such as water) , the greater the rate of heat exchange by convection.

Thus, in an environment in which air temperature is cooler than the skin temperature, convection permits the transfer of heat from the skin to the air (heat loss) ; however, if air temperature is higher than skin temperature, heat is gained by the body through convection. We often consider these processes to be mechanisms of heat loss, forgetting that when the environmental temperature exceeds skin temperature, the gradient works in the opposite direction.

1.2.3 Radiation

At rest, radiation (R) and convection are the primary methods for eliminating the body's excess heat. At normal room temperature (typically 21℃–25 ℃) , the nude body loses about 60% of its excess heat by radiation. The heat is given off in the form of infrared rays, which are a type of electromagnetic wave. Figure12.2 shows two infrared thermograms of an individual.

The skin constantly radiates heat in all directions to objects around it, such as clothing, furniture, and walls, but it also can receive radiant heat from surrounding objects that are warmer. If the temperature of the surrounding objects is greater than that of the skin, the body experiences a net heat gain via radiation. A tremendous amount of radiant heat is received from exposure to the sun.

Taken together, conduction, convection, and radiation are considered avenues of dry heat exchange. Resistance to dry heat exchange is called insulation, a concept known to everyone as it relates to clothing and home heating and cooling. The ideal insulator is a layer of still air (remember that moving air causes convective heat loss) , which we achieve by trapping layers of air in fibers (down, fiberglass, and so on). Adding insulation in this way minimizes unwanted heat loss in cold environments. However, during exercise we want to dissipate heat to the environment, which is best accomplished by wearing thin, light-colored clothing (to limit radiant heat absorption) that allows for a maximally exposed skin surface area. The effect of clothing on sweat evaporation is discussed later.

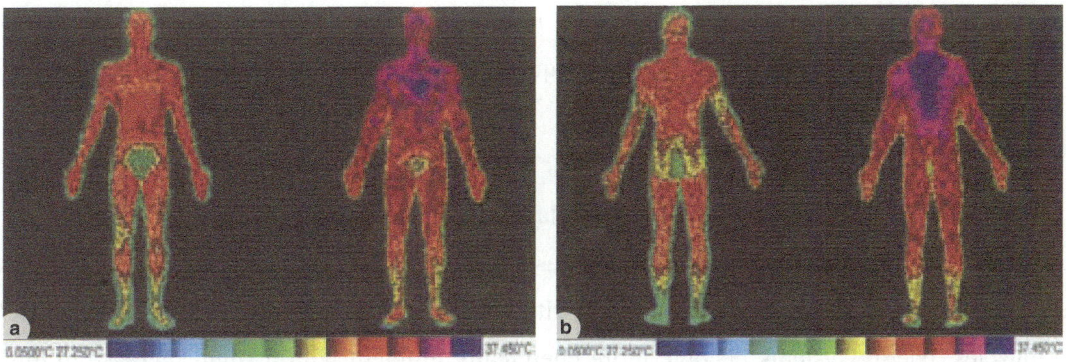

Figure 12.2 Thermograms of the body showing the variations in radiant (infrared) heat leaving the (a) front and (b) rear surfaces of the body both before (left) and after (right) running outside at a temperature of 30 ℃ and 75% humidity. The color scale at the bottom of each photo provides the temperature variation for the changes in color.

1.2.4 Evaporation

By far, evaporation (E) is the primary avenue for heat dissipation during exercise. In fact, when air temperature is close to skin temperature, the only available means of cooling is evaporation. As a fluid evaporates and turns into its gaseous form, heat is lost. An important concept to remember is that sweat must evaporate for any heat loss to occur. Some sweat drips off the body or stays on the skin or in the clothing, especially if the air is humid. This unevaporated sweat contributes nothing to body cooling and simply represents a wasteful loss of body water. Evaporation accounts for about 80% of the total heat loss when one is physically active and is therefore an extremely important avenue for heat loss. Even at rest, evaporation accounts for 10%–20% of body heat loss, since some evaporation occurs without our awareness (termed insensible water loss).

Evaporation of 1 L of sweat in an hour results in the loss of 580 kcal (about 2,428 kJ) of heat. To put the tremendous cooling power of sweat evaporation into perspective, a 70 kg marathon runner who runs a 2:30 marathon will produce about 860 kcal (about 3,600kJ) of metabolic heat.

If every drop of sweat he produced evaporated, he would need to sweat at a rate of about 1.5 L per hour. Because inevitably some sweat drips off, a better estimated sweating rate necessary to maintain core temperature would be 2 L per hour. Without replacing fluids, however, our hypothetical runner would lose about 5 L of water, or over 7% of his body weight!

The water vapor pressure of the air (the pressure exerted by water vapor molecules suspended in the air) plays a major role in evaporative heat loss. Relative humidity is a more commonly used term that relates the water vapor pressure of the air to that of fully saturated air (100% humidity). When humidity is high, the air already contains many water molecules. This decreases its capacity to accept more water because the vapor pressure gradient between the skin and the air is decreased. Thus, high humidity limits sweat evaporation and heat loss, while low humidity offers an ideal opportunity for sweat evaporation and heat loss. But this efficient cooling mechanism can also pose a problem. If sweating is prolonged without adequate fluid replacement, dehydration can occur.

1.3 Thermoregulatory Control

Internal body temperature at rest is regulated at approximately 37 ℃. During exercise, the body is often unable to dissipate heat as rapidly as it is produced. In rare circumstances, a person can reach internal temperatures exceeding 40 ℃, with a temperature above 42 ℃ in active muscles. The muscles' energy systems become more chemically efficient with a small increase in muscle temperature, but internal body temperatures above 40 ℃ can adversely affect the nervous system and reduce further efforts to unload excess heat. How does the body regulate its internal temperature? The hypothalamus plays a central role (Figure 12.3).

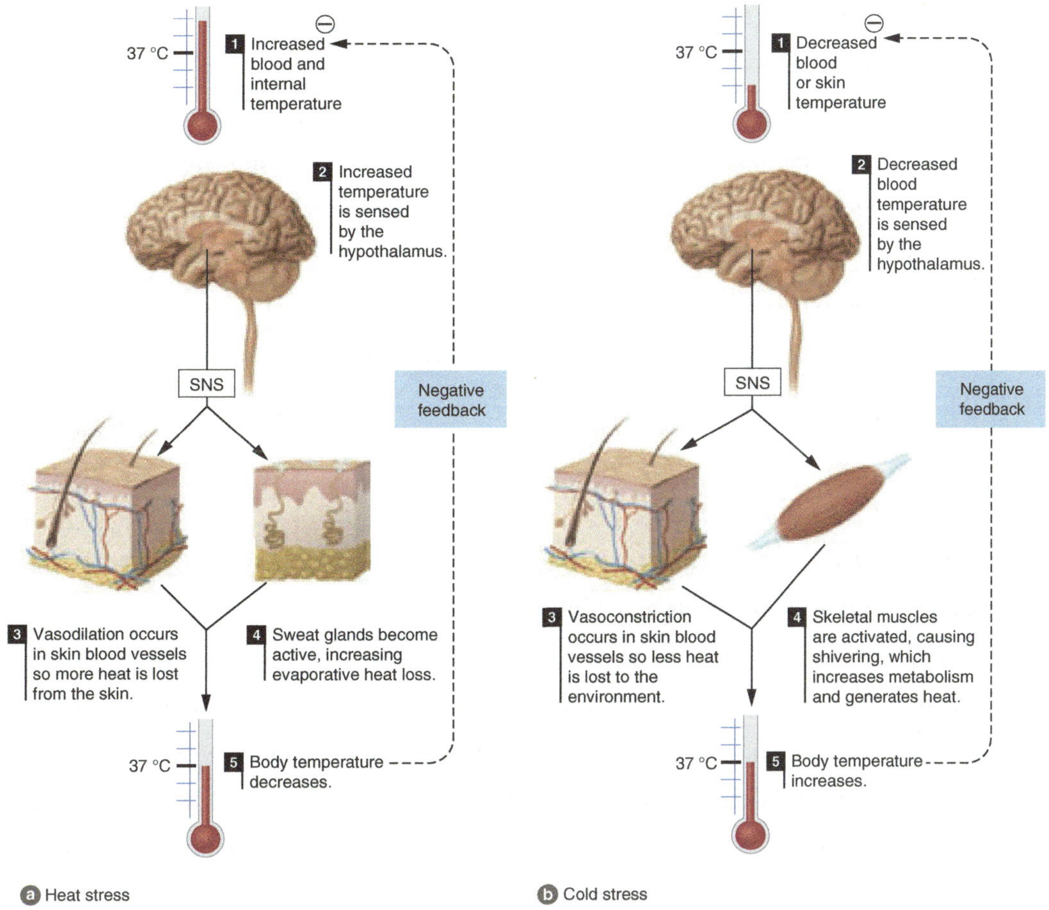

Figure 12.3 A simplified overview of the role of the hypothalamus in controlling body temperature during (a) heat stress and (b) cold stress.

1.3.1 The Preoptic-Anterior Hypothalamus: The Body's Thermostat

A simple way to envision the mechanisms that control internal body temperature is to compare them to the thermostat that controls the air temperature in a home, although the body's mechanisms function in a more complex manner and generally with greater precision than a home heating and cooling system. Sensory receptors called thermoreceptors detect changes in temperature and relay this information to the body's thermostat, located in a region of the brain called the preoptic-anterior hypothalamus (POAH). In response, the hypothalamus activates mechanisms that regulate the heating or cooling of the body. Like a home thermostat, the hypothalamus has a predetermined temperature, or set point, that it tries to maintain. This is the normal body temperature. The smallest deviation from this set point signals this thermoregulatory center to readjust the body temperature.

Thermoreceptors are located throughout the body but especially in the skin and central nervous system. The peripheral receptors located in the skin monitor the skin temperature, which varies with changes in the temperature around a person. They provide information not only to the POAH but also to the cerebral cortex, which allows one to consciously perceive temperature and voluntarily control one's exposure to heat or cold. Because the skin temperature changes long before core temperature, these receptors serve as an early warning system for impending thermal challenges.

Central receptors are located in the hypothalamus, other brain regions, and the spinal cord and monitor the temperature of the blood as it circulates through these sensitive areas. These central receptors are responsive to blood temperature changes as small as 0.01 ℃ and to the rate of change as well. Because of this exquisite sensitivity, very small changes in the temperature of the blood passing through the hypothalamus quickly trigger reflexes that help one conserve or eliminate body heat as needed.

1.3.2 Thermoregulatory Effectors

When the POAH senses temperatures above or below normal, signals are sent through the sympathetic nervous system to four sets of effectors:

(1) Skin arterioles

When skin or core temperature changes, the POAH sends signals via the sympathetic nervous system (SNS) to the smooth muscle in the walls of the arterioles that supply the skin, causing them to dilate or constrict. This either increases or decreases skin blood flow. Skin vasoconstriction results primarily from SNS release of the neurotransmitter norepinephrine, although other neurotransmitters are involved as well, and facilitates heat conservation by minimizing dry heat exchange. Skin vasodilation in response to heat stress is a more complex and less understood process. Increased skin blood flow aids in heat dissipation to the environment through conduction, convection, and radiation (and, indirectly, evaporation as skin temperature goes up). Fine-tuning of skin blood flow is the mechanism by which minute-to-minute adjustments are made in heat balance and exchange. These adjustments are rapid and occur with no real energy cost to the body.

(2) Eccrine sweat glands

When either the skin or core temperature is elevated sufficiently, the POAH also sends impulses through the SNS to the eccrine sweat glands, resulting in active secretion of sweat onto the skin surface. The primary neurotransmitter involved is acetylcholine; thus, we refer to sweat gland activation as sympathetic cholinergic stimulation. Like skin arterioles, sweat glands are about 10 times more responsive to increases in core temperature than to similar increases in skin temperature. The evaporation of this moisture, as discussed earlier, removes heat from the skin surface.

(3) Skeletal muscle

Skeletal muscle is called into action when a person needs to generate more body heat. In a cold environment, thermoreceptors in the skin or core sense cold and send signals to the hypothalamus.

In response to this integrated neural input, the hypothalamus activates the brain centers that control muscle tone. These centers stimulate shivering, which is a rapid, involuntary cycle of contraction and relaxation of skeletal muscles. This increased muscle activity is ideal for generating heat to either maintain or increase the body temperature, because no useful work results from the shivering, only heat production.

(4) Endocrine glands

The effects of several hormones cause the cells to increase their metabolic rates. Increased metabolism affects heat balance because it increases heat production. Cooling the body stimulates the release of thyroxine from the thyroid gland. Thyroxine can elevate the metabolic rate throughout the body by more than 100%. Also, recall that epinephrine and norepinephrine (the catecholamines) mimic and enhance the activity of the SNS. Thus, they directly affect the metabolic rate of virtually all body cells.

2 Physiological Responses to Exercise in the Heat

Heat production is beneficial during exercise in a cold environment because it helps maintain normal body temperature. However, even when exercise is performed in a cool environment, the metabolic heat load places a considerable burden on the mechanisms that control body temperature. In this section, we examine some physiological changes that occur in response to exercise while the body is exposed to heat stress and the impact that these changes can have on performance. For this discussion, heat stress means any environmental condition that increases body temperature and jeopardizes homeostasis.

2.1 Cardiovascular Function

When the need to regulate body temperature is added during exercise in the heat, the burden placed on the cardiovascular system is enhanced. During exercise in hot conditions, the circulatory system has to continue to transport blood not only to working muscle but also to the skin, where the tremendous heat generated by the muscles can be transferred to the environment. To meet this dual demand during exercise in the heat, two changes occur. First, cardiac output increases further (above the level associated with a similar exercise intensity in cool conditions) by increasing both heart rate and contractility. Second, blood flow is shunted away from nonessential areas (like the gut, liver, and kidneys) and to the skin.

Consider what happens during prolonged running on a hot day. The aerobic exercise increases both metabolic heat production and the demand for blood flow and oxygen delivery to the working muscles. This excess heat can be dissipated only if blood flow increases to the skin.

In response to the elevated core temperature (and to a lesser extent, the higher skin temperature) , the SNS signals sent from the POAH to the skin arterioles cause these blood vessels to dilate, delivering more metabolic heat to the body surface. Sympathetic nervous system signals also go to the heart to increase heart rate and cause the left ventricle to pump more forcefully. However, the ability to increase stroke volume is limited as blood pools in the periphery and less returns to the left atrium. To maintain cardiac output under such circumstances, the heart rate gradually creeps upward to help compensate for the decrease in stroke volume.

2.2 What Limits Exercise in the Heat?

At some point, the cardiovascular system can no longer compensate for the increasing demands of continuing endurance exercise and efficiently regulating the body's heat. Consequently, any factor that tends to overload the cardiovascular system or interfere with heat dissipation can drastically impair performance, increase the risk of overheating, or both. Exercise in the heat becomes limited when heart rate approaches maximum, especially in untrained or nonheat-acclimated exercisers. Interestingly, working muscle blood flow is well maintained even at very high core temperatures unless significant dehydration occurs.

Another theory that helps explain limitations to exercise in the heat—especially in well-trained, acclimated athletes—is the critical temperature theory. This theory proposes that, regardless of the rate at which core temperature (and thus brain temperature) increases, the brain will send signals to stop exercise when some critical brain temperature is reached, usually between 40 and 41 ℃.

2.2.1 Precooling and Sport Performance

Two recent meta-analyses (statistically based review of existing studies) addressed that important question, concurring that precooling does effectively enhance sport performance, particularly in hot environments. As expected, precooling had a larger effect during endurance events like cycling time trials, but improvement was also seen for intermittent running or cycling sprints. The effectiveness of precooling on short sprints was minimal. Of the methods compared, ingesting cold drinks was the most promising procedure. Further, the best results occurred in athletes with the highest $\dot{V}O_{2\,max}$.

The second analysis11 concluded that precooling actually impaired sprint performance, which might be expected if active muscle temperature fell. Intermittent activity and endurance performance were both improved with precooling, however. Similarly, cooling maneuvers used during exercise were also successful at improving performance. Whether used before exercise or during exercise, the effectiveness of body cooling procedures depends on both (1) the amount of cooling (intensity and duration) and (2) how much thermal strain is involved in the exercise.

2.2.2 Body Fluid Balance: Sweating

On hot summer days, it is not uncommon for the temperature of the environment to exceed both the skin and deep body temperatures. As mentioned earlier, this makes evaporation far more important for heat loss, because radiation, convection, and conduction now become avenues of heat gain from the environment. Increased dependence on evaporation means an increased demand for sweating.

The eccrine sweat glands are controlled by stimulation of the POAH. Elevated blood temperature causes this region of the hypothalamus to transmit impulses through the sympathetic nerve fibers to the millions of eccrine sweat glands distributed over the body's surface.

The sweat glands are fairly simple tubular structures extending through the dermis and epidermis, opening onto the skin, as illustrated in Figure 12.4.

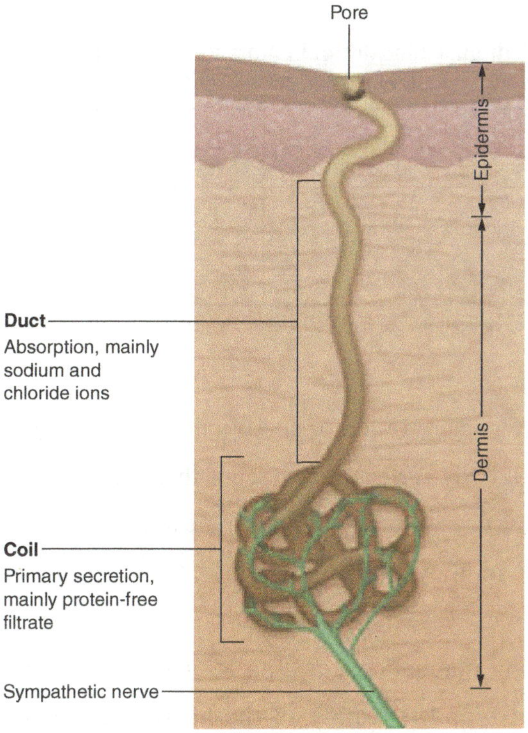

Figure 12.4 Anatomy of an eccrine sweat gland that is innervated by a sympathetic cholinergic nerve.

A second type of sweat gland, the apocrine gland, is clustered in particular regions of the body, including the face, axilla, and genital regions. These are the glands associated with nervous perspiration, and they do not contribute significantly to heat loss by evaporation.

The eccrine sweat glands, on the other hand, play a purely thermoregulatory role. They are located over most of the skin surface, with ~2–5 million covering the whole body. They are most densely distributed on the palms of the hands, the soles of the feet, and the forehead. The lowest densities are found on the forearms, lower legs, and thighs. When sweating begins, there are large regional variations in sweating rate. During exercise, the highest local sweating rates are typically measured on the middle and lower back and on the forehead, while the lowest sweating rates are observed on the hands and feet.

As seen in Table 12.1, the electrolyte concentration of trained and untrained subjects' sweat is significantly different. With training and repeated heat exposure (acclimation) , more sodium is reabsorbed and the sweat is more dilute, in part because the sweat glands become more sensitive to the hormone aldosterone. Unfortunately, the sweat glands apparently do not have a similar mechanism for conserving other electrolytes. Potassium, calcium, and magnesium are not reabsorbed by the sweat glands and are therefore found in similar concentrations in sweat and plasma. In addition to heat acclimation and aerobic training, genetics is a major determinant of both sweating rate and sweat sodium losses.

Table 12.1 Example of Sodium, Chloride, and Potassium Concentrations in the Sweat of Trained and Untrained Subjects During Exercise

Subjects	Sweat Na /mmol · L^{-1}	Sweat Cl^- /mmol · L^{-1}	Sweat K^+ /mmol · L^{-1}
Untrained men	90	60	4
Trained men	35	30	4
Untrained women	105	98	4
Trained women	62	47	4

Individual sweat electrolyte concentrations are highly variable, but training and heat acclimation decrease sodium losses in the sweat.

While performing heavy exercise in hot conditions, the body can lose more than 1 L of sweat per hour per square meter of body surface. This means that during intense effort on a hot and humid day (high level of heat stress) , an average-sized female athlete (50–75 kg) might lose 1.6–2.0 L of sweat, or about 2.5%–3.2% of body weight, each hour. A person can lose a critical amount of body water in only a few hours of exercise in these conditions.

A high rate of sweating maintained for a prolonged time ultimately reduces blood volume. This limits the volume of blood returning to the heart, increasing heart rate and eventually decreasing cardiac output, which in turn reduces performance potential, particularly for endurance activities. In long-distance runners, sweat losses can approach 6%–10% of body weight. Such severe dehydration can limit subsequent sweating and make the individual susceptible to heat-related illnesses.

Loss of both electrolytes and water in the sweat triggers the release of both aldosterone and antidiuretic hormone (ADH) , also known as vasopressin or arginine vasopressin. During acute exercise in the heat and during repeated days of exercise in the heat, this hormone limits sodium excretion from the kidneys.

Similarly, exercise and body water loss stimulate the posterior pituitary gland to release ADH. This hormone stimulates water reabsorption from the kidneys, which further promotes fluid retention in the body.

3 Health Risks During Exercise in the Heat

Despite the body's defenses against overheating, excessive heat production by active muscles, heat gained from the environment, and conditions that prevent the dissipation of excess body heat may elevate the internal body temperature to levels that impair normal cellular functions. Under such conditions, excessive heat gains pose a risk to one's health, as we highlighted in the opening anecdote of this chapter. Air temperature alone is not an accurate index of the total physiological stress imposed on the body in a hot environment. Six variables must be taken into account:

- Metabolic heat production
- Air temperature
- Ambient water vapor pressure (humidity)
- Air velocity
- Radiant heat sources
- Clothing

3.1 Measuring Heat Stress

It has become common to hear about the heat index on local weather channels. The heat index, a complex equation involving air temperature and relative humidity, is a measure of how hot it feels, that is, how we perceive the heat. However, the heat index does not do a good job of reflecting the physiological stress on humans, so its use is limited in exercise physiology. Through the years, efforts have been made to quantify atmospheric variables into a single index that would reflect the physiological heat stress on an individual. In the 1970s, wet-bulb globe temperature (WBGT) was devised to simultaneously account for conduction, convection, evaporation, and radiation (see Figure 12.5). It is based on three different thermometer readings and provides a single temperature reading to estimate the cooling capacity of the surrounding environment.

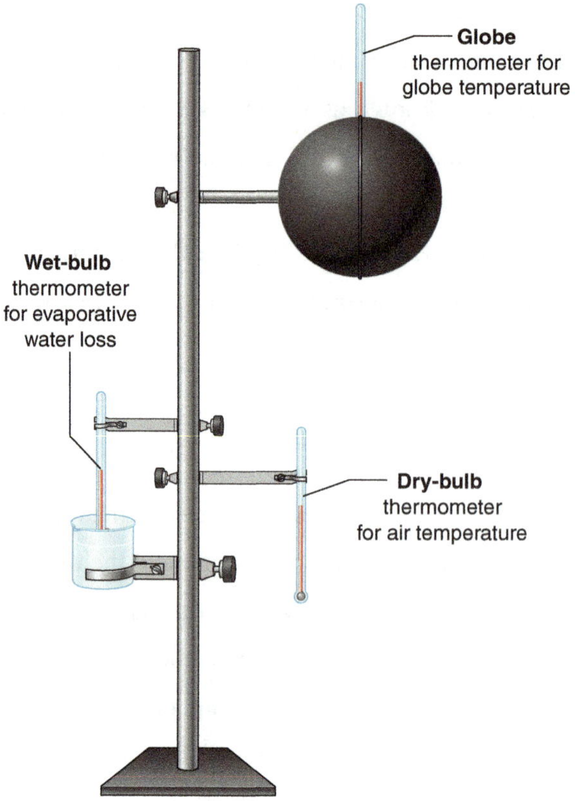

Figure 12.5 A wet-bulb globe temperature stand showing the three separate thermometers for air (dry-bulb) temperature, wet-bulb temperature reflecting the cooling effect of evaporation, and globe temperature, which measures additional effects of radiant heat.

Wet-bulb globe temperature, as an index of thermal stress, is now routinely used by coaches, team physicians, and athletic trainers to anticipate the health risks associated with athletic practices and competitions in thermally stressful environments.

3.2 Heat-Related Disorders

Exposure to the combination of external heat stress and metabolically generated heat can lead to three heat-related disorders: heat cramps, heat exhaustion, and heatstroke.

3.2.1 Heat Cramps

Heat cramps, the least serious of the three heat disorders, are characterized by severe and painful cramping of large skeletal muscles. They involve primarily the muscles that are most heavily used during exercise, and such instances of athletes "locking up" are different from cramps everyone has experienced in small muscles. Heat cramps are brought on by sodium losses and dehydration that accompany high rates of sweating, and thus are most common in heavy sweaters who lose a lot of sodium in their sweat. (A common misconception is that potassium is involved in cramping and that eating potassium-rich foods like bananas will prevent heat cramps.) Heat cramps can be prevented or minimized in susceptible athletes by proper hydration practices involving liberal salt intake with foods and in beverages consumed during exercise. Treatment for these cramps involves moving the stricken individual to a cooler location and administering a saline solution, either orally or intravenously if necessary.

3.2.2 Heat Exhaustion

Heat exhaustion typically is accompanied by such symptoms as extreme fatigue, dizziness, nausea, vomiting, fainting, and a weak, rapid pulse. It is caused by the cardiovascular system's inability to adequately meet the needs of the body as it becomes severely dehydrated. Recall that during exercise in heat, active muscles and skin compete for a share of a limited, and decreasing, blood volume. Heat exhaustion may result when these simultaneous demands cannot be met, and it typically occurs when blood volume decreases as a result of excessive fluid loss from profuse sweating. A second form of heat exhaustion, from sodium depletion, is rare in athletes. Therefore, heat exhaustion can be thought of as a syndrome of dehydration and should be treated as such.

With heat exhaustion, the thermoregulatory mechanisms are functioning but cannot dissipate heat quickly enough because insufficient blood volume is available to allow adequate blood flow to the skin. Although the condition often occurs during moderate to heavy exercise in the heat, it is not necessarily accompanied by extremely high core temperatures. Some people who collapse from heat exhaustion have core temperatures well below 39 ℃. People who are unfit or not acclimated to the heat are more susceptible than others to heat exhaustion.

Treatment for victims of heat exhaustion involves rest in a cooler environment with their feet elevated to facilitate return of blood to the heart. If the person is conscious, administration of salt water is usually recommended. If the person is unconscious, medically supervised intravenous administration of saline solution is recommended.

3.2.3 Heatstroke

Heatstroke is a life-threatening heat disorder that requires immediate medical attention. Heatstroke is caused by failure of the body's thermoregulatory mechanisms. It is characterized by

- an increase in internal body temperature to a value exceeding 40 ℃, and
- confusion, disorientation, or unconsciousness

The latter element—altered mental status—is the key to recognizing impending heatstroke because neural tissues in the brain are particularly sensitive to extreme heat. In heatstroke, cessation of active sweating may also occur, but sweat may remain on the skin. The notion that heatstroke is always accompanied by dry, red skin is outdated, and this sign should never be used to distinguish heatstroke from heat exhaustion.

If heatstroke is left untreated, core temperature will continue to rise, progressing to coma and ultimately death. Appropriate treatment always involves cooling the body as rapidly as possible. In the field, this can best be accomplished by immersing the victim—as much of the body as possible excluding the head—in a bath of cold water or ice water. While cold-water immersion provides the fastest cooling rates, in cases in which cold or ice water is not available, temperate-water immersion is the next best option. Where immersion is not feasible, the combination of wrapping the entire body in cold, wet sheets and fanning vigorously may be used. Cooling methods that place ice bags on small areas, like the armpits, neck, and groin, are not effective in rapidly lowering core temperature because of the small surface area covered.

For the athlete, heatstroke is not just a problem associated with extreme conditions. Studies have reported rectal temperatures above 40.5 ℃ in marathon runners who successfully completed races conducted in temperate and even in cool conditions.

4 Acclimation to Exercise in the Heat

How can athletes prepare for prolonged activity in the heat? Does repeated exercise in the heat make us better able to tolerate thermal stress? Many studies have addressed these questions and have concluded that repeated exercise in the heat causes a series of relatively rapid adaptations that enable us to perform better, and more safely, in hot conditions. When these physiological changes occur over short periods of time, like days to weeks, or if they are artificially induced as in a climatic chamber, those adaptations are termed acclimation (heat acclimation). A similar but much more gradual set of adaptations occurs in people who adapt to hot conditions by living in hot environments for months to years. This is known as acclimatization (note that the word climate is part of this latter term).

4.1 Effects of Heat Acclimation

Repeated bouts of prolonged, low-intensity exercise in the heat cause a relatively rapid improvement in the ability to maintain cardiovascular function and eliminate excess body heat, which reduces physiological strain. This process, termed heat acclimation, involves changes in plasma volume, cardiovascular function, sweating, and skin blood flow that allow for subsequent exercise bouts in the heat to be performed with a lower core temperature and heart rate response (Figure 12.6). Because the body's heat loss capacity at a given rate of work is enhanced by acclimation, core temperature during exercise increases less than before acclimation (Figure

12.6a) , and heart rate increases less in response to standardized submaximal exercise after heat acclimation (Figure 12.6b). In addition, after heat acclimation, more work can be done before adverse symptoms occur or a maximal tolerable core temperature or heart rate is reached.

This series of positive adaptations typically takes a period of 9–14 days of exercise in the heat to fully occur, as shown in Figure 12.6. Well-trained individuals need fewer exposures than untrained individuals to fully acclimate. A critical physiological adjustment that occurs over the first 1–3 days of acclimation is the expansion of plasma volume. The exact mechanism by which plasma volume expands after these initial exercise–heat exposures is not universally agreed upon. The process likely involves (1) proteins being forced out of the circulation as muscles contract, (2) these same proteins then being returned to the blood through the lymph, and (3) fluid moving into the blood because of the oncotic pressure exerted by the increased protein content. However, this change is temporary, and blood volume usually returns to original levels within 10 days. This early expansion of blood volume is important because it supports stroke volume, allowing the body to maintain cardiac output while additional physiological adjustments are made.

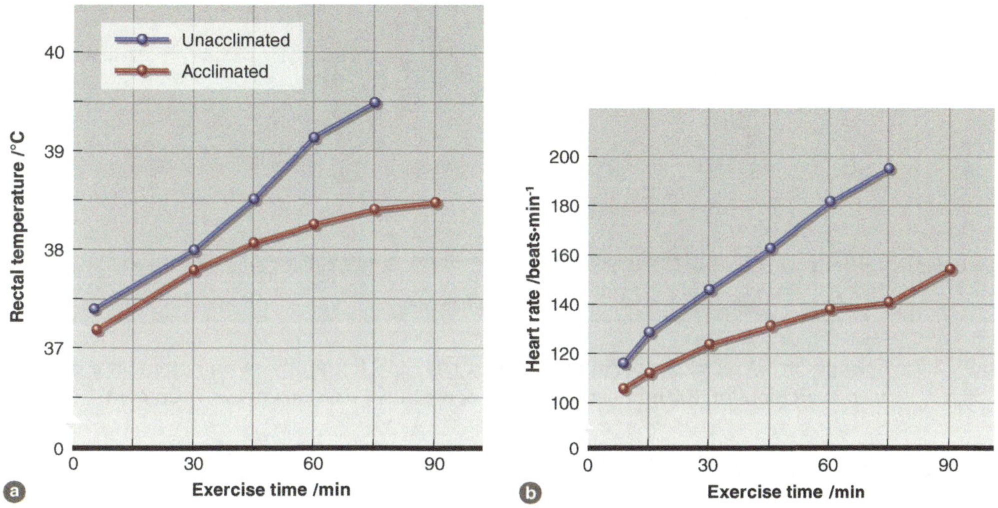

Figure 12.6 Typical (a) rectal temperature and (b) heart rate responses during an acute bout of exercise at the same intensity before and after heat acclimation. Note that, in addition to lower physiological strain, exercise time is usually longer after acclimation.

As shown in Figure 12.7, end-exercise heart rate and core temperature decrease early in the acclimation process, while the increase in sweating rate during exercise in the heat occurs somewhat later. An additional adaptation is a more even distribution of sweat over the body, with increased sweating on the most exposed body areas such as the arms and legs, areas that are most effective at dissipating body heat. At the beginning of exercise, sweating also starts earlier in an acclimated person, which improves heat tolerance, and the sweat that is produced becomes more dilute, conserving sodium. This latter effect occurs in part because the eccrine sweat glands become more sensitive to the effects of circulating aldosterone.

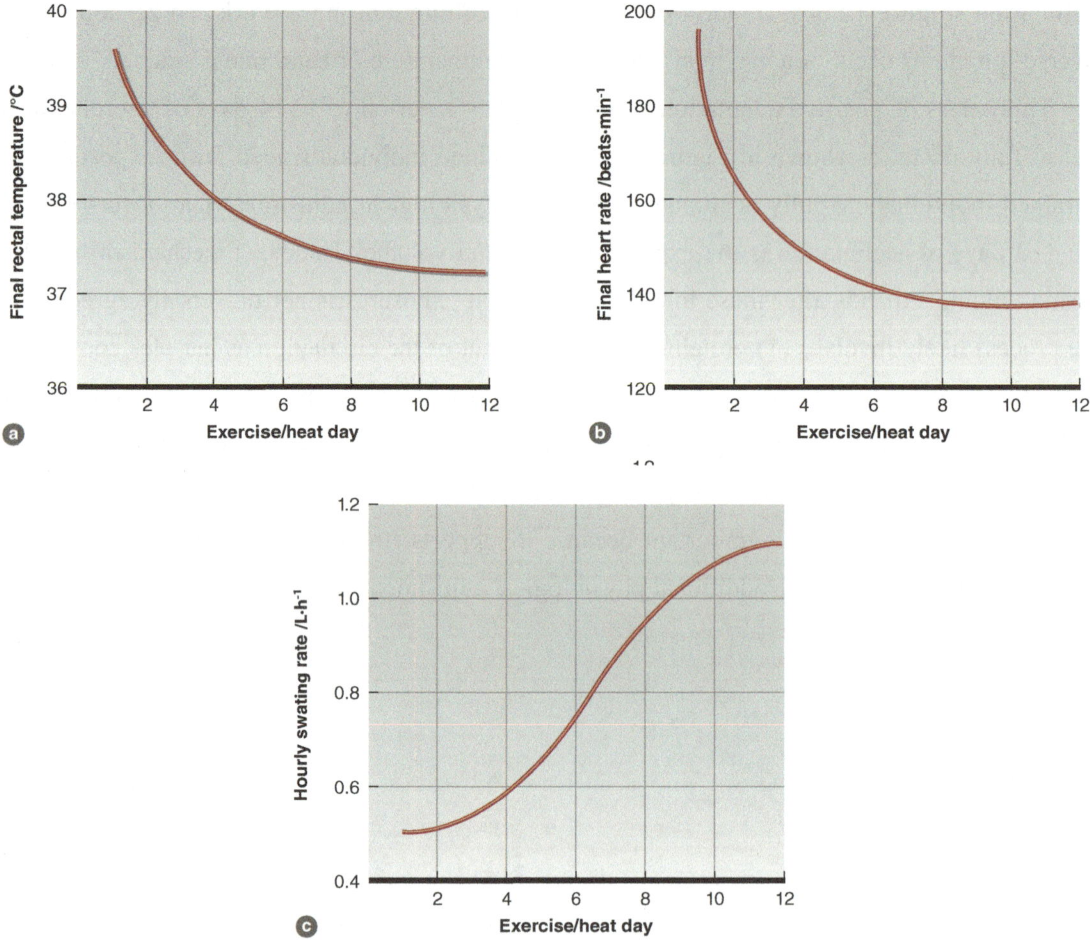

Figure 12.7 Changes in (a) rectal temperature, (b) heart rate, and (c) hourly sweating rate in a group of men exercising for 100 min per day for 12 consecutive days in a hot environment.

4.2 Achieving Heat Acclimation

Heat acclimation requires more than merely resting in a hot environment. The benefits of acclimation, as well as the rate at which we acclimate, depend on

- the environmental conditions during each exercise session
- the duration of exercise-heat exposure, and
- the rate of internal heat production (exercise intensity)

An athlete must exercise in a hot environment to attain full acclimation that sustains exercise in the heat. Simply sitting in a hot environment, such as a sauna or steam room, for long periods each day will not fully or adequately prepare the individual for physical exertion in the heat, at least not to the same extent as will exercising in the heat.

Because body temperature is elevated and sweating occurs, athletes gain partial heat tolerance simply by training, even in a cooler environment. Therefore, athletes are "preacclimated" to heat and need fewer exercise heat exposures to fully acclimate. To gain maximal benefits, athletes who train in environments cooler than those in which they will compete must achieve heat acclimation before the contest or event. Heat acclimation will improve their performance and reduce the associated physiological stress and risk of heat injury.

With a full 14-day heat acclimation schedule (90 min cycling, 40 ℃, 20% relative humidity) , improvements in whole-body heat loss can be demonstrated using direct calorimetry. After 14 days, whole-body heat loss was improved by 11% since sweat rate, and subsequently sweat evaporation, occurred to a greater extent over a shorter period of time. Approximately 70% of the improvements occurred within the first seven days. While heat loss responses improved, there was no effect on core temperature in this study. Once the acclimation protocol was stopped, benefits persisted for up to two weeks.

5 Exercise in the Cold

Humans can be thought of as tropical animals. Most of our adjustments to heat stress are physiological, whereas many adjustments to cold environments involve behavior, like putting on more clothing or seeking shelter. Increased year-round participation in sport has sparked new interest in, and concerns about, exercise in the cold. We define cold stress here as any environmental condition causing a loss of body heat that threatens homeostasis. In the following discussion we focus on the two major cold environments: air and water.

The hypothalamus has a temperature set point of about 37 ℃, but daily fluctuations in the body temperature can be as much as 1 ℃. A decrease in either skin or blood temperature provides feedback to the thermoregulatory center (POAH) to activate mechanisms that conserve body heat and increase heat production. The primary means by which our bodies avoid excessive heat loss (in the order in which they are invoked) are peripheral vasoconstriction, nonshivering thermogenesis, and shivering.

Peripheral vasoconstriction occurs as a result of sympathetic stimulation of the smooth muscle layers of the arterioles in the skin. This stimulation causes the vascular smooth muscle to contract, which constricts the arterioles, reduces the blood flow to the shell of the body, and minimizes heat loss. Even at thermoneutral temperatures, there is tonic (constant baseline) skin vasoconstriction, and continuous adjustment of skin vascular tone occurs at all times to offset small heat imbalances in the body. When changing skin blood flow alone is not adequate to prevent heat loss, nonshivering thermogenesis—stimulation of metabolism by the SNS—is increased. Increasing the metabolic rate increases heat production. The next line of defense of body temperature during cold stress is shivering, a rapid, involuntary cycle of contraction and relaxation of skeletal muscles, which can cause a four- to five-fold increase in the body's rate of heat production.

5.1 Habituation and Acclimation to Cold

People who are regularly exposed to cold environments under which significant body heat loss does not occur typically undergo cold habituation, in which skin vasoconstrictor and shivering responses are blunted, and core temperature is allowed to fall to a greater extent than before the chronic cold exposures. This pattern of adaptation often occurs when small areas of skin—often the hands and face—are exposed repeatedly to cold air.

However, when heat loss is more severe or occurs at a faster rate, total body heat loss may occur. In cases in which increased metabolic heat production alone can sufficiently minimize heat loss, enhanced nonshivering and shivering thermogenesis develop (metabolic acclimation). Yet a third distinct pattern of cold adaptation, called insulative acclimation, tends to occur in situations in which increased metabolism is unable to maintain core temperature. In insulative acclimation, enhanced skin vasoconstriction occurs, which increases peripheral insulation and minimizes heat loss.

5.2 Other Factors Affecting Body Heat Loss

The mechanisms of conduction, convection, radiation, and evaporation, which usually perform effectively in dissipating metabolically produced heat during exercise in warm conditions, can dissipate heat to the environment faster than the body produces it in extremely cold environments.

Pinpointing the exact conditions that permit excessive body heat loss and eventual hypothermia (low body core temperature) is difficult. Thermal balance depends on a wide variety of factors that affect the balance between body heat production and heat loss. Generally speaking, the larger the thermal gradient between the skin and the cold environment, the greater the heat loss. When exercising in the cold, people should not overdress. Overdressing can cause the body to become hot and initiate sweating. As the sweat soaks through the clothing, evaporation removes the heat, and heat is lost at an even faster rate.

A number of additional factors can also influence the rate of heat loss.

5.2.1 Body Size and Composition

Insulating the body against the cold is the most obvious form of protection against hypothermia. Recall that insulation is defined as resistance to dry heat exchange through radiation, convection, and conduction. Both inactive peripheral muscles and subcutaneous fat are excellent insulators. Skinfold measurements of subcutaneous fat thickness are a good indicator of an individual's tolerance for cold exposure. The thermal conductivity of fat (its capacity for transferring heat) is relatively low, so fat impedes heat transfer from the deep tissues to the body surface. People who have more fat mass conserve heat more efficiently in the cold than smaller, leaner individuals.

The rate of heat loss also is affected by the ratio of body surface area to body mass. Larger individuals have a small surface area-to-mass ratio, which makes them less susceptible to hypothermia.

5.2.2 Sex and Age Differences

Women have a slight advantage over men during cold exposure because they have more subcutaneous body fat. But their smaller muscle mass is a disadvantage in extreme cold because shivering is the major adaptation for generating body heat. The greater the active muscle mass, the greater the heat generation. Muscle also provides an additional insulating layer.

True sex differences in cold tolerance are minimal. Some studies have shown that the added subcutaneous fat in women may give them an advantage during cold-water immersion, but when men and women of similar body fat mass and size are compared, no real difference is noted in body temperature regulation during exposure to the cold.

Small children have a large surface area-to-mass ratio compared with adults, leading to proportionately greater heat loss. This makes it more difficult for them to maintain normal body temperature in the cold. On the other end of the age spectrum, elderly individuals often tend to lose overall muscle mass, decreasing tissue insulation and making them more susceptible to hypothermia.

6 Physiological Responses to Exercise in the Cold

We have seen how the body adapts to maintain its internal temperature when exposed to a cold environment. Now consider what happens when the demands of physical performance are added to those of thermoregulation in the cold. How does the body respond to exercise in cold environmental conditions?

6.1 Muscle Function

Cooling a muscle causes it to contract with less force. The nervous system responds to muscle cooling by altering the normal muscle fiber recruitment patterns for force development, which may decrease the efficiency of the muscle's actions. Both muscle shortening velocity and power decrease significantly when muscle temperature is lowered. Luckily, large deep muscles seldom experience such low temperatures because they are protected from heat loss by a continuous supply of warm blood flow.

If clothing insulation and exercise metabolism are sufficient to maintain an athlete's body temperature in the cold, aerobic exercise performance may be unimpaired. However, as fatigue sets in and intensity decreases, so does metabolic heat production. Long-distance running, swimming, and skiing in the cold can expose the participant to such conditions. At the beginning of these activities, the athlete can exercise at an intensity that generates sufficient metabolic heat to maintain core temperature. However, late in the activity, when the energy reserves have diminished, exercise intensity declines, and this reduces metabolic heat production. The resulting decrease in core temperature causes the individual to become even more fatigued and less capable of generating heat. Under these conditions, the athlete may be confronted with a potentially dangerous situation.

Cold conditions affect muscle function in another way. As small muscles in the periphery like the fingers become cold, muscle function can be severely affected.

This results in a loss of manual dexterity and limits the ability to perform fine motor skills like writing and manual labor tasks.

6.2 Metabolic Responses

Prolonged exercise increases the mobilization and oxidation of free fatty acids (FFAs) as a fuel source. The primary stimulus for this increased lipid metabolism is the release of catecholamines (epinephrine and norepinephrine). Exposure to cold markedly increases epinephrine and norepinephrine secretion, but FFA levels increase substantially less than during prolonged exercise in warmer conditions. Cold exposure triggers vasoconstriction in the vessels supplying not only the skin but also fatty subcutaneous tissues as well. The subcutaneous fat is a major storage site for lipids (as adipose tissue) , so this vasoconstriction reduces the blood flow to an important area from which the FFAs would be mobilized. Thus, FFA levels do not increase as much as the elevated levels of epinephrine and norepinephrine would predict.

Blood glucose plays an important role in both cold tolerance and exercise endurance. For example, hypoglycemia (low blood sugar) suppresses shivering. The reasons for these changes are unknown. Fortunately, blood glucose concentrations are maintained reasonably well during cold exposure. Muscle glycogen, on the other hand, is used at a somewhat higher rate in the cold than in warmer conditions.

7 Health Risks During Exercise in the Cold

7.1 Hypothermia

Individuals immersed in near-freezing water will die within a few minutes when their rectal temperature decreases from a normal level of 37 ℃ to 24℃ or 25 ℃ . Cases of accidental hypothermia, as well as data obtained from surgical patients who are intentionally made hypothermic, reveal that the lethal lower limit of body temperature is usually between 23℃ and 25 ℃, although patients have recovered after having rectal temperatures below 18 ℃.

Once core temperature falls below about 34.5 ℃, the hypothalamus begins to lose its ability to regulate body temperature. This ability is completely lost when the internal temperature decreases to about 29.5 ℃. This loss of function is associated with a slowing of metabolic reactions. For each 10 ℃ drop in cellular temperature, the metabolism of the cell decreases by half. As a result, low core temperatures can cause drowsiness, lethargy, and even coma.

Mild hypothermia can be treated by removing the affected person from the cold, providing dry clothing and blankets for insulation, and providing warm beverages. Moderate to severe cases of hypothermia require gentle handling to avoid initiating a cardiac arrhythmia. This requires slowly rewarming the victim. Severe cases of hypothermia require hospital facilities and medical care. Recommendations to prevent cold exposure–related injuries were outlined by the American College of Sports Medicine in its 2006 position stand on cold illness during exercise.

7.2 Cardiorespiratory Effects

The hazards of excessive cold exposure include potential injury to both peripheral tissues and the cardiovascular and respiratory systems. Death from hypothermia has resulted from cardiac arrest while respiration was still functional. Cooling primarily influences the sinoatrial node, the heart's pacemaker, leading to a substantial decrease in heart rate and, ultimately, cardiac arrest.

People have questioned whether rapid, deep breathing of cold air can damage or freeze the respiratory tract. In fact, the cold air that passes into the mouth and trachea is rapidly warmed, even when the temperature of inhaled air is less than −25 ℃. Even at this temperature, when a person is at rest and breathing primarily through the nose, the air is warmed to about 15 ℃ by the time it has traveled about 5 cm into the nasal passage. As shown in Figure 12.8, extremely cold air entering the nose is quite warm by the time it reaches the back of the nasal passage, thereby posing no threat of damage to the throat, trachea, or lungs. Mouth breathing, which often occurs during exercise, may result in cold irritation to the mouth, pharynx, trachea, and even bronchi when the air temperature is below −12 ℃. Excessive cold exposure also affects respiratory function by decreasing respiratory rate and volume.

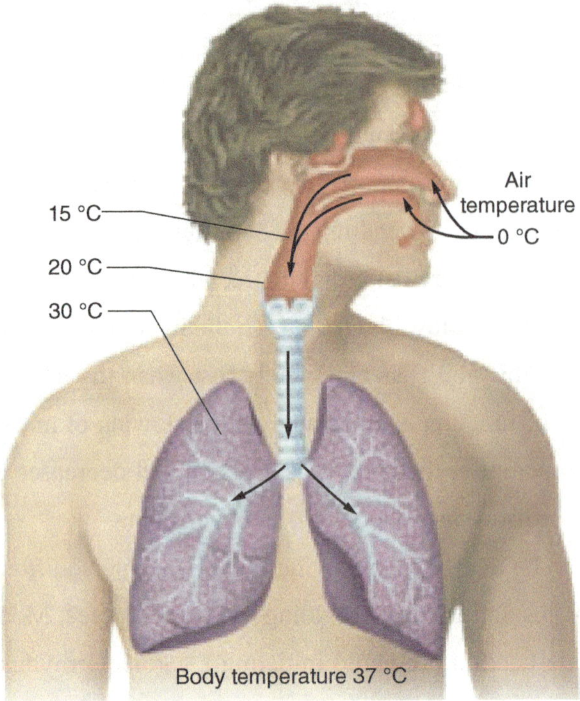

Figure 12.8 The warming of inspired air as it moves through the respiratory tract.

7.3 Frostbite

Exposed skin can freeze when its temperature is lowered just a few degrees below the freezing point (0 ℃). Because of the warming influence of circulation and metabolic heat production, the environmental air temperature required to freeze exposed fingers, nose, and ears is about −29 ℃. Recall from our earlier discussion that peripheral vasoconstriction helps the body retain heat. Unfortunately, during exposure to extreme cold, the circulation in the skin can decrease to the point that the tissue dies from lack of oxygen and nutrients. This is commonly called frostbite. If not treated early, frostbite injuries can be serious, leading to gangrene and loss of tissue. Frostbitten parts should be left untreated until they can be thawed, preferably in a hospital, without risk of refreezing.

7.4 Exercise-Induced Asthma

While not strictly a cold-related illness, exercise-induced asthma is a common problem that affects as many as 50% of winter sport athletes. The main cause of this syndrome is the drying of the airways due to the combination of the high respiration rate associated with exercise and the extremely dry air as temperature drops, although multiple environmental and genetic factors may determine whether a given athlete will experience asthma symptoms as a result.

The resultant airway narrowing often leaves athletes gasping for breath. Luckily, there are preventive medications available such as β-agonists plus inhalers that can quickly deliver corticosteroids and bronchodilating medications to relieve symptoms.

IN CLOSING

In this chapter, we began our examination of how the external environment affects the body's ability to perform physical work. We looked at the effects of extreme heat and cold stress and the body's responses to these conditions. We considered the health risks associated with these temperature extremes and how the body adapts to these conditions through acclimation.

Much of our discussion thus far has dealt with how physiological variables and environmental stress can hinder our performance.

KEY TERMS

acclimation (heat acclimation) ; acclimatization; arginine vasopressin; cold habituation; conduction (K) ; convection (C) ; critical temperature theory; dry heat exchange; eccrine sweat glands; evaporation (E) ; frostbite; heat cramps; heat exhaustion; heatstroke; hypothermia; insulation; insulative acclimation; metabolic; non shivering thermogenesis; peripheral vasoconstriction; preoptic-anterior hypothalamus (POAH) ; radiation (R) ; shivering; thermoreceptors; thermoregulation; vasopressin; wet-bulb globe temperature (WBGT).

STUDY QUESTIONS

(1) What are the four major avenues for loss of body heat?

(2) Which of these four pathways is most important for controlling body temperature at rest? During exercise?

(3) What happens to the body temperature during exercise and why?

(4) Why is water vapor pressure in the air an important factor when one is performing in the heat? Why are wind and cloud cover important?

(5) What factors may limit the ability to continue to exercise in hot environments?

(6) What is the purpose of the wet-bulb globe temperature (WBGT) ? What does it measure?

(7) Differentiate between heat cramps, heat exhaustion, and heatstroke.

(8) What physiological adaptations occur that allow a person to acclimate to exercise in the heat?

(9) How does the body minimize excessive heat loss during cold exposure?

(10) What are the three patterns of cold adaptation and when might each be expected to occur?

(11) What factors should be considered to provide maximal protection when people are exercising in the cold?

第十二章 冷热环境与运动训练

在极热或极冷的环境下进行运动时，机体在维持持续运动的同时，会因调节体温的机制带来额外的负担。虽然这些机制在正常情况下调节体温的效果惊人，但当我们遭受极端的热或冷时，体温调节机制可能就不够充分了。幸运的是，在持续暴露一段时间后，身体能够适应这样的环境压力，这一过程称为习服（指的是一个短期的适应，例如，从天到周）或适应（指在很长一段时间后获得自然适应性，例如，从月到年）。

一、体温调节

人类是恒温动物，即使环境温度发生变化，人的内部体温也会因为生理上的调节几乎保持不变。只有在长时间的剧烈运动、因病发烧或极端炎热或寒冷的条件下，身体温度才会偏离36.1 ~ 37.8 ℃正常的基线范围。体温反映了热量产生和热量流失之间的精确平衡。每当这种平衡被打破时，体温就会发生变化。

1.代谢产热

身体产生的能量（三磷酸腺苷，ATP）中只有一小部分（通常少于25%）用于肌肉收缩等生理功能，剩下的转化为热量。如果身体产生的热量超过了热量的散失，就像在中等强度到高强度的有氧运动中经常发生的那样，身体将多余的热量积聚起来，体内温度就会升高。

2.身体与环境的热量传递

热量主要通过血液从核心转移到皮肤。只有当热量到达皮肤时，它才能通过四种机制中的任何一种传递到环境中：传导、对流、辐射和蒸发。

（1）传导。热传导指热量从一种固体物质通过分子接触直接传递到另一种固体物质。例如，当皮肤与冷物体接触时，身体就会失去热量；相反，如果一个热的物体压在皮肤上，热量从该物体传导到皮肤，身体就获得热量，如果接触时间延长，皮肤表面的热量就会通过皮肤转移到血液中，血流进入到核心部位，进而提高核心部位的温度。在运动中，传导作为热交换的来源通常可以忽略不计，因为其与固体物质接触的身体表面面积（例如，脚底与热的运动场的接触）很小。

（2）对流。对流是指通过气体或液体在受热面上的运动来传递热量。当身体静止且空气很少流动时，身体周围会有一层稀薄的静息空气边界层。然而，我们周围的空气通常是不断流动的，尤其是在我们运动时全身或身体某些部位（例如，我们跑步时手臂摆动）穿过空气的时候。我们周围的空气流动着通过皮肤表面，身体热量与空气分子进行交换。空气（或液体，例如水）的流动速度越快，则通过对流进行的热交换的速率就越快。

（3）辐射。在静止状态下，辐射和对流是消除身体多余热量的主要方法。在正常的室温下（通常是21～25 ℃），裸体通过辐射散失了大约60%的多余热量。热量以红外线的形式散发出来。如果周围物体的温度大于皮肤的温度，身体就会通过辐射获得净热量。大量的辐射热是因太阳照射而吸收的。总的来说，传导、对流和辐射被认为是干热交换的途径。

阻止干热交换被称为隔热，理想的隔热体是一层静止的空气（前面讲过，移动的空气导致对流热散失），我们一般是通过纤维（如羽绒、玻璃纤维等）储存空气层来实现。以这种方式添加隔热材料，可使寒冷环境中的热量损失最小化。然而，在运动过程中，我们想要把热量散发到环境中，最好是通过穿薄的浅色衣服（以限制吸收辐射热）来完成，从而最大限度地暴露皮肤表面。

（4）蒸发。蒸发是运动散热的主要途径。事实上，当空气温度接近皮肤温度时，唯一可用的降温方法就是蒸发。当流体蒸发变成气态时，热量就会散失。一个重要概念是，任何热量散失都会蒸发掉汗水。有些汗从身上滴下来，或者留在皮肤上、衣服上，这些未蒸发的汗水对身体降温没有任何帮助，只说明水分流失了。当一个人进行身体活动时，蒸发约占总热量散失的80%。休息时，蒸发也占身体热量散失的10%～20%。

每小时蒸发1升的汗水会散失580千卡（约2 428千焦）的热量。为了充分了解汗液蒸发带来的巨大冷却作用，一个体重70 千克的马拉松运动员在跑完2小时30分的马拉松时，会产生约860千卡（约3 600千焦）的代谢热。如果他产生的每一滴汗水都蒸发掉了，他就需要以每小时1.5升的速度流汗。因为不可避免地会有一些汗水滴落下来，为了保持核心温度，更接近的估算出汗率应该是每小时2升的水。然而，如果不补充液体，我们假设的跑步者将会损失5升的水，这或许超过他体重的7%！

空气中的水蒸气压力（悬浮在空气中的水蒸气分子产生的压力）在蒸发散热中起着重要作用。相对湿度是指空气中的水蒸气压力与完全饱和水蒸气的空气（100%湿度）压力的相对值。高湿度会限制它接受更多水分的能力，因为皮肤和空气之间的蒸汽压梯度降低了。因此，高湿度限制了汗液的蒸发和散热，而低湿度则为汗液的蒸发和散热提供了理想的机会。

3.体温调节与控制

静息状态下身体的体温约为37 ℃。在运动过程中，身体散发的热量往往不如产生的热量速度快。在极特殊的情况下，人体内部温度可以超过40 ℃，运动中的肌肉温度可以超过42 ℃。肌肉温度的小幅升高会使肌肉中能量系统的化学效率提高，但超过40 ℃会对神经系统产生不利影响，并减少释放多余热量。

（1）视前区-下丘脑前部（POAH）：人体的恒温器。温度感受器感受到温度的变化，并将信息传递给身体的体温调控中枢即大脑的POAH。下丘脑激活调节身体产热或降温的机制。温度感受器遍布全身，尤其是在皮肤和中枢神经系统中。位于皮肤上的外周感受器监测皮肤温度，皮肤温度随着人体周围环境温度的变化而变化。它们不仅向POAH提供信息，也向大脑皮层提供信息，这可以使人有意识地感知温度，并自动控制自己在冷热环境中的暴露。因为皮肤温度的变化比核心温度早得多，所以这些感受器可以为即将到来的热威胁提供早期预警。

中枢感受器位于下丘脑、其他大脑区域和脊髓，当血液在这些敏感区域循环时，它可以监控血液的温度。这些中枢感受器对血液温度变化和变化速率都有反应，即使是0.01 ℃的变化。由于这种细腻的敏感性，流经下丘脑的血液温度的微小变化会迅速触发反射，帮助人们在需要时保存或散失体温。

（2）体温调节的效应器。当POAH感觉温度高于或低于正常值时，信号通过交感神经系统（SNS）发送到以下四组效应器。

①皮肤小动脉。当皮肤或核心温度发生变化时，POAH通过SNS向供应皮肤的小动脉壁的平滑肌发送信号，使其扩张或收缩。这会增加或减少皮肤的血流量。增加的皮肤血流量有助于热量通过传导、对流和辐射消散到环境中。皮肤血液流动的微调是通过这种机制在每时每刻进行的热量平衡和交换中实现的。这些调整是快速的，而且在身体内没有实际的能量消耗。

②小汗腺。当皮肤或核心温度充分升高时，POAH也会通过SNS刺激汗腺，皮肤会出汗。与皮肤微动脉一样，汗腺对核心温度升高的反应比对类似的皮肤温度升高的反应快10倍。水分的蒸发会从皮肤表面带走热量。

③骨骼肌。当骨骼肌收缩工作时，人体就会产生更多的身体热量。在寒冷的环境中，皮肤或核心的温度感受器能感觉到寒冷，并向下丘脑发送信号。下丘脑整合神经输入的反应，激活控制肌肉张力的大脑中枢。中枢刺激产生寒颤，即骨骼肌非自主的快速收缩和舒张循环。增加的肌肉活动是理想的产热方式，用以维持或提高体温。颤抖没有产生任何有用的工作，只产生热量。

④内分泌腺体。有些激素可以使细胞增加代谢率。新陈代谢的增加会影响热量平衡，因为

它会增加热量的产生。比如，甲状腺素可使全身代谢率提高100%以上。同时肾上腺素和去甲肾上腺素（儿茶酚胺）增强了SNS的活性。因此，它们直接影响几乎所有身体细胞的代谢率。

二、在高温下运动的生理反应

在本节中，我们将研究当身体暴露在热环境时，由于运动而产生的一些生理变化，以及这些变化对运动表现的影响。在本节中，热应激指的是任何能增加体温和破坏体内热平衡的环境条件。

1. 心血管功能

在高温环境下锻炼时，调节体温的需求增加，心血管系统的负担也随之加重。在炎热条件下锻炼时，循环系统必须持续运输血液，使其不仅进入工作的肌肉，也进入皮肤。肌肉产生的大量热能可以通过皮肤转移到环境中。在高温运动中，为了满足这种双重需求，会发生两个变化。首先，通过增加心率和心收缩力，心输出量进一步增加（高于在低温条件下相同强度运动时的水平）；其次，血液从非必需部位（如肠道、肝脏和肾脏）分流到皮肤。

作为对核心温度升高的反应，SNS信号从POAH发送到皮肤微动脉，导致这些血管扩张，将更多的代谢热传递到体表。SNS信号也会进入心脏，增加心率，使左心室泵血更为有力。然而，心脏增加每搏输出量的能力是有限的，因为血液储留在外周并且返回左心房的血量较少。在这种情况下，为了保持心输出量，心率逐渐上升，以帮助弥补每搏输出量的减少。

2. 在热环境下运动的限制因素

在某种程度上，心血管系统不能再补偿持续的耐力运动和有效调节身体热量所增加的需求。因此，任何导致心血管系统过负荷或妨碍散热的因素都可能严重损害机体的运动表现，增加身体过热的风险，或两者兼而有之。当心率接近最大值时，高温下的运动就会受到限制，特别是在未经训练或无热适应的锻炼者中。有趣的是，即使在核心温度非常高的情况下，肌肉的血液流动也能保持良好的状态，除非出现严重的脱水。

另一个有助于解释在高温下运动的局限性的理论是临界温度理论，特别是对于训练有素、适应能力强的运动员。这个理论认为，不管核心温度（如大脑温度）以何种速度升高，当大脑温度达到某个临界温度，通常在40～41 ℃时，大脑就会发出停止运动的信号。

（1）预冷和运动表现。预冷确实能有效地提高运动成绩，尤其是在炎热的环境中。预冷在自行车计时赛等耐力项目中效果明显，在间歇跑或短距离自行车赛中也能看到效果。在短距离的冲刺跑中，预冷的效果是最小的。在众多预冷方法中，喝冷饮是最有效的方法。此外，最好的结果往往发生在具有最高最大摄氧量的运动员身上。

（2）体液平衡：出汗。在炎热的夏天，当环境温度超过皮肤和身体深处的温度时，蒸发对于热量散失非常重要，因为辐射、对流和传导这时已经成为从环境中获得热量的途径。增加对蒸发的依赖意味着增加出汗量。

机体通过刺激POAH来控制小汗腺。血液温度的升高使下丘脑的这一区域通过交感神经纤维将冲动传递到分布在身体表面的数以百万计的汗腺。汗腺是相当简单的管状结构，贯穿真皮和表皮，向皮肤开放。当出汗开始时，不同部位的出汗率有很大差异。在运动过程中，出汗率最高的部位通常是中背部、下背部和前额，而出汗率最低的部位是手和脚。

经过训练的受试者与未经过训练的受试者的汗液电解质浓度存在显著差异。通过训练和反复的热暴露（适应），更多的钠被重新吸收，汗水被稀释，部分原因是汗腺对醛固酮激素变得更加敏感。由于钾、钙和镁不会被汗腺重新吸收，因此它们在汗液和血浆中的浓度相似。遗传也会影响出汗率和汗液钠的流失。

在高温条件下进行剧烈运动时，身体每平方米体表面积每小时会流失超过1升的汗液。这意味着，在炎热潮湿的天气（高水平的热应激）进行高强度运动时，一名中等体型的女运动员（50～75千克）每小时可能会流失1.6～2.0升的汗水，或约2.5%～3.2%的体重。在这种情况下，仅仅几个小时的运动就能使人失去大量的水分。长时间的高出汗率最终会降低血容量。这限制了返回心脏的血液量，增加了心率，最终减少了心输出量，这反过来又降低了运动能力表现，尤其是耐力活动。对于长跑运动员来说，排汗量可以达到体重的6%～10%。这种严重的脱水会限制随后的出汗，使人容易患上热相关的疾病。

三、在高温下运动的健康风险

尽管身体可以防止过热，但是肌肉活动产生的过多热量、从环境中获得的热量，以及防止身体多余热量散失的情况，都可能会使体内温度上升到损害正常细胞功能的水平。

1.测量热应激

多年来，人们一直在努力将大气变量量化为一个单一指数，以反映个体的生理热应激。20世纪70年代，人们设计了湿球黑球温度（WBGT）来同时考虑传导、对流、蒸发和辐射的影响。它基于三个不同的温度计读数，并提供一个单一的温度读数，以估计周围环境的降温能力。湿球黑球温度，作为热应力的一个指数，现在经常被教练、团队医生和培训师用来预测在热应激环境下与运动训练和比赛相关的健康风险。

2.热相关疾病

暴露在外部热应激和代谢产热的复合作用下会导致三种热相关的疾病：热痉挛、热衰竭和中暑。

（1）热痉挛。热痉挛是三种热相关的疾病中症状最轻的一种，其特征是大肌群严重而痛苦的抽筋。它主要涉及运动中最频繁使用的肌肉，这种运动员的“闭锁”情况与每个人都经历过的小肌肉抽筋不同。热痉挛是由钠流失和脱水引起的，伴随高出汗率，因此在汗液中流失大量钠的出汗者中最为常见（一个普遍的误解是，钾与痉挛有关，吃富含钾的食物，如香蕉，可以防止热痉挛）。对易受影响的运动员来说，通过适当的水合作用，包括运动期间从食物和饮料中大量摄入盐，可以预防或减少热痉挛。对这类抽筋的治疗包括将受伤的人转移到一个较冷的地方，如有必要可以口服或静脉注射生理盐水。

（2）热衰竭。热衰竭通常伴有极端疲劳、头晕、恶心、呕吐、晕厥和脉搏无力且加快等症状。它是由心血管系统不能充分满足身体的需要引起的，因为机体已经严重脱水。通常发生在由于大量出汗导致过多的液体流失进而导致血容量减少的时候。热衰竭可以被认为是一种脱水综合征，并应予以对症治疗。热衰竭时，体温调节机制虽然能发挥作用，但散热速度不够快，因为没有足够的血容量保证血液流向皮肤。

虽然这种情况经常发生在中高强度的高温运动中，但并不一定伴随着极高的核心温度。一些因热衰竭而昏倒的人的核心温度远低于39℃。未习服或不适应高温的人比其他人更容易发生热衰竭。热衰竭患者的治疗包括在较冷的环境中休息，抬高双脚，以促进血液回流到心脏。如果患者是清醒的，通常建议使用生理盐水；如果患者处于昏迷状态，建议在医生监督下静脉注射生理盐水。

（3）中暑。中暑是一种危及生命的热相关的疾病，需要立即就医。中暑是由于人体体温调节机制失灵而引起的。它的特点是：体内温度上升到超过40 ℃，并伴随混乱、迷惑或无意识等症状。

精神状态的改变是识别中暑发生的关键，因为大脑中的神经组织对极端高温特别敏感。中暑时，出汗活动也会停止，但汗液可能会留在皮肤上。认为中暑总是伴随着皮肤干燥、红肿的观念已经过时了，这个症状不能用来区分中暑和热衰竭。如果中暑得不到及时治疗，核心温度将继续上升，发展为昏迷，最终死亡。

中暑适当的治疗应该包括尽快使中暑者身体降温。在现场，可以通过冷水浸泡中暑者的身体来达到最好的降温效果。虽然冷水浸泡能提供最快的降温速度，但在没有冷水或冰水的情况下，常温水浸泡也是一个较好的选择。当浸泡不可行时，可以用冷、湿的床单包裹整个中暑者的身体并用力扇风。把冰袋放在像腋窝、颈部和腹股沟这样的部位上进行冷却的方法，由于覆盖的表面积小，并不能有效地迅速降低核心温度。

四、高温环境运动的习服

在高温下反复锻炼会导致一系列相对快速的适应，使我们能够在高温条件下表现得更好、更安全。当这些生理变化在短时间内发生，比如几天到几周，或者由人工诱导发生，比如在气候室中，这些适应被称为习服（热习服）。通过在炎热环境中生活数月至数年来适应炎热环境的人，也会经历一种类似的但更为渐进的适应过程，这就是所谓的适应气候。

1.习服的影响

反复在高温下进行长时间、低强度的运动，能较快地提高维持心血管功能和消除体内多余热量的能力，从而减轻生理压力。这个过程被称为热习服，其中包括血浆容量、心血管功能、出汗和皮肤血流量的变化，这些变化使随后在热环境中进行的运动能够以较低的核心温度和心率反应进行。因为在一定的工作速率下，身体的散热能力会通过习服而增强，所以运动期间核心温度的增加比习服前要少，而在习服后，心率对标准化次最高运动强度的反应也要小。

这一系列积极的适应过程通常需要9～14天的高温运动才能完全完成。在最初1～3天的习服中发生的一个重要的生理调整是血浆容量的扩大。这种变化是暂时的，血容量通常在10天内恢复正常。这种早期的血容量扩张是很重要的，因为它可以维持每搏输出量，允许身体在进行额外的生理调整时保持心输出量。

在运动开始的时候，已经习服的人也会更早开始出汗，这提高了他们的耐热性，同时产生的汗液也会变得更稀，身体保留了钠。后一种效应的出现，其部分原因是汗腺对循环中的醛固酮的作用变得更加敏感。

2.习服的实现

运动员必须在炎热的环境中运动，以达到完全的习服，从而在高温下保持运动。仅仅每天花费较长时间坐在一个炎热的环境中，如桑拿房或蒸气房里，也不会完全或充分地为身体在高温环境下的剧烈体力活动做好准备，至少不会像在高温下运动那样达到相同的效果。

对于完整的14天的习服训练计划（90分钟自行车，40 ℃，20%相对湿度），可以使用直接量热法证明全身散热能力的改善。14天后，由于出汗率提高，全身散热能力提高了11%，随后在较短的时间内汗液蒸发的程度更大。大约70%全身散热能力的提高发生在前7天内。一旦停止习服方案，则效果可持续2周。

五、在寒冷中锻炼

人类可以被看作热带动物。我们对热应激的大部分调整是生理学上的，而对寒冷环境的许多调整则涉及行为学，比如穿更多的衣服或寻求庇护等。我们在这里将冷应激定义为任何环境条件造成的威胁体内平衡的身体热量散失。我们将重点讨论两种主要的寒冷环境：空气和水。

下丘脑的温度设定值约为37℃，但体温的每日波动可高达1℃。皮肤或血液温度的下降会向POAH提供反馈，从而激活保存体温和增加热量产生的机制。我们的身体避免过多热量损失的主要方法（按其调用的顺序）是外周血管收缩、非寒颤产热和寒颤产热。

外周血管收缩是由于交感神经刺激皮肤小动脉平滑肌层而发生的。这种刺激导致血管平滑肌收缩，使小动脉收缩，减少了流向身体外周的血液，使热量散失最小化。即使在热中性温度下，皮肤血管也会有紧张性收缩，皮肤血管张力也会不断调整，以抵消体内微小的热失衡。当仅改变皮肤血流不足以防止热量流失时，非寒颤产热——由SNS刺激新陈代谢——就会增加。增加代谢率会增加热量的产生。在寒冷应激下，体温的下一道防线是寒颤，这是一种骨骼肌快速、不自主的收缩和松弛循环，会导致身体产生热量的速度增加4～5倍。

1.对寒冷的熟习和习服

经常暴露在寒冷环境下的人通常会经历冷熟习，在这种环境下，身体热量不会大量流失，皮肤血管收缩和颤抖反应会减弱，核心温度可以下降到比长期暴露在寒冷环境前更大的程度。这种适应模式通常发生在皮肤的小块区域——通常是手和脸——反复暴露在冷空气中时。

然而，当热流失更严重或发生的速度更快时，也可能会发生全身热流失。在仅靠增加代谢热产生就能充分减少热损失的情况下，非寒颤产热和寒颤产热作用会增强（代谢习服）。

2.影响身体热损失的其他因素

热传导、对流、辐射和蒸发的机制，通常在运动中可以有效地散发代谢产生的热量。在温暖的环境中，机体向环境散发热量的速度比身体在极冷环境中产生热量的速度要快。

准确描述身体热量流失过多并最终导致体温过低（核心温度低）的具体情况是困难的。热平衡取决于影响身体产热量和热流失量平衡的多种因素。一般来说，皮肤和寒冷环境之间的热梯度越大，热流失就越明显。在寒冷的天气里锻炼时，人们不应该穿得过多，因为，穿得过多会导致身体发热并开始出汗。当汗水浸透衣服时，蒸发带走了热量，热量以更快的速度流失。

（1）体型和身体成分。使身体与寒冷隔绝是防止体温过低的最明显的保护形式。不活跃的外周肌肉和皮下脂肪都是极好的绝缘体。皮下脂肪厚度的测量是一个人对冷暴露耐受性的良好指标。脂肪的导热系数（传递热量的能力）相对较低，所以脂肪会阻碍热量从深层组织传递到体表。在寒冷环境中，脂肪含量高的人比脂肪含量低的人可以更有效地保存热量。热量散失率也受到身体表面积与身体质量比率的影响。体型较大的个体表面积与质量的比例较小，这使得它们不太容易受到体温过低的影响。

（2）性别和年龄差异。在寒冷的环境中，女性比男性稍微有优势，因为她们有更多的皮下脂肪。但在极冷的环境下，女性较小的肌肉质量是一个劣势，因为颤抖是产生体温的主要适应方式。活跃的肌肉越多，产生的热量就越多。肌肉也会提供额外的绝缘层。

与成人相比，儿童具有较大的体表面积与身体质量比，导致热量流失得更快。这使得他们在寒冷中保持正常体温变得更加困难。在年龄谱的另一端，老年人往往会失去整体肌肉质量，这降低了组织的绝缘性，使他们更容易患低体温症。

六、在寒冷环境中运动的生理反应

在寒冷环境中，除了温度调节，还需要考虑身体运动表现。在寒冷的环境中，身体如何对运动做出反应？

1.肌肉功能

冷却肌肉会使肌肉收缩的力量下降。神经系统应对肌肉温度下降时会通过改变募集肌纤维的方式来产生力量，这可能会降低肌肉活动的效率。当肌肉温度降低时，肌肉的收缩速度和力量均显著下降。在寒冷环境下，如果衣服隔热和运动代谢产热足以维持运动员的体温，则有氧运动的表现可能不会受到影响。然而，随着疲劳的出现和强度的降低，新陈代谢产生的热量也会减少。

2.代谢反应

长时间的运动可以增加游离脂肪酸作为能量来源的动员和氧化。这种脂质代谢的增加主要是受儿茶酚胺（肾上腺素和去甲肾上腺素）释放的影响。冷暴露不仅会引起皮肤血管收缩，也会引起皮下脂肪组织血管收缩，因而影响脂肪组织的动员。因此，游离脂肪酸水平的增加并不像肾上腺素和去甲肾上腺素水平升高所预测的那样多。

七、在寒冷环境中运动的健康风险

1.体温过低

当浸泡在接近冰点的水中，人直肠温度从37℃降至24℃或25℃时，会在几分钟内死亡。一旦核心温度降至34.5℃以下，下丘脑就开始失去调节体温的能力。当核心温度下降到大约29.5℃时，下丘脑调节体温的能力完全丧失。这种功能的丧失与代谢反应的减慢有关。细胞温度每下降10℃，细胞的新陈代谢就减少50%。因此，核心温度过低会导致机体嗜睡、昏睡甚至昏迷。

轻度低温症可以通过将患者从寒冷环境中移走、提供干燥的衣服和保暖毯等方法来治疗；中度到严重的低体温患者需要温和处理，以避免引发心律失常，慢慢地让患者恢复体温；严重的低体温患者需要医院设施和医疗护理。

2.心肺机能的影响

过度冷暴露的危险包括对外周组织以及心血管和呼吸系统的潜在伤害。体温过低导致的死亡是由心脏骤停引起的，而此时呼吸仍然有效。寒冷主要影响窦房结（心脏的起搏点），导致心率大幅下降，最终导致心脏骤停。在运动中经常会用口呼吸，当空气温度低于-12 ℃时，会对口腔、咽部、气管甚至支气管产生冷刺激。过度的冷暴露也会通过降低呼吸速率和呼吸量而影响呼吸功能。

3.冻伤

当温度仅低于冰点（0℃）几度时，暴露在外的皮肤就会结冰。由于循环和代谢产热而变暖的影响，当环境空气温度约为-29 ℃时，暴露在外的手指、鼻子和耳朵才会被冷冻。在极度寒冷的环境中，皮肤中的循环会下降到组织因缺氧和营养而死亡的程度，这通常被称为冻伤。如果不及早治疗，冻伤会很严重，导致坏疽和失去组织。冻伤的部位，最好是在医院或在没有再次冻结的风险时再进行解冻治疗。

4.运动性哮喘

运动性哮喘是一种常见的问题，影响到多达50%的冬季运动项目的运动员。这种综合征的发生主要是因为运动时呼吸频率加快，以及气温下降导致空气的极度干燥，两种因素造成呼吸道干燥引起运动性哮喘。环境和遗传因素可能也是决定一个特定的运动员是否会出现哮喘症状的原因。这些因素导致的气道狭窄常常使运动员无法喘气。幸运的是，有一些预防药物可用，如β–激动剂加上吸入器，可以快速提供皮质类固醇和支气管扩张药物来缓解症状。

Chapter 13 Prescription of Exercise for Health and Fitness

Patterns of today's living have channeled the average person into an increasingly sedentary existence. Humans, however, were designed and built for movement. Physiologically, we have not adapted well to this inactive lifestyle. Research had clearly determined that, for almost everyone, an active lifestyle is important for optimal health.

1 Medical Clearance

1.1 Medical Evaluation

Although a comprehensive medical evaluation is useful and desirable before exercise is prescribed, not all people need one. Many cannot afford the cost of such an evaluation, and the medical system is not prepared to provide this service for the total population, even if money were available. Also, medical evaluation before prescribing exercise for a population presumed healthy has not been proven to reduce the medical risks associated with exercise. For these reasons, guidelines or recommendations have been established that attempt to target moderate- to high-risk individuals. People at moderate risk are those who have no signs or symptoms of, or who have not been diagnosed with, cardiovascular, pulmonary, or metabolic disease but who have two or more risk factors for coronary artery disease (Table 13.1). Those who are at high risk are people with one or more signs or symptoms of cardiovascular, pulmonary, or metabolic disease.

Table 13.1 Coronary Artery Disease Risk Factors for Targeting At-Risk People

Positive risk factors	Defining criteria
Age	Men ≥45 years; women ≥55 years
Family history	Myocardial infarction, coronary revascularization, or sudden death before 55 years of age in father or other male first-degree relative or before 65 years of age in mother or other female first-degree relative
Cigarette smoking	Current cigarette smoker or those who quit within the previous six months, or exposure to environmental tobacco smoke
Hypertension	Systolic blood pressure ≥140 mmHg or diastolic blood pressure ≥90 mmHg, confirmed by measurements on at least two separate occasions, or on antihypertensive medication
Dyslipidemia	Low-density lipoprotein (LDL) cholesterol ≥130 mg/dL (3.4 mmol/L) or high-density lipo-protein (HDL) cholesterol <40 mg/dL (1.04 mmol/L) , or on lipid-lowering medication. If total serum cholesterol is all that is available, use ≥200 mg/dL (5.2 mmol/L).
Impaired fasting glucose (prediabetes)	Fasting blood glucose ≥100 mg/dL (5.5 mmol/L) but <126 mg/dL (6.9 mmol/L) , or impaired glucose tolerance as determined by an oral glucose tolerance test, confirmed by measurements on at least two separate occasions
Obesity	Body mass index ≥30 kg/m^2; or waist girth >102 cm for men and >88 cm for women; or waist/hip ratio ≥0.95 for men and ≥0.86 for women
Sedentary lifestyle	Persons not participating in at least 30 min of moderate-intensity (40%~60% of $\dot{V}O_2R$) physical activity on at least three days of the week for at least three months.
Negative risk factors	Defining criteria
High serum HDL-C	>60 mg/dL (1.5 mmol/L)

Note. It is common to sum risk factors in making clinical judgments. If high-density lipoprotein cholesterol (HDL-C) is high, subtract one risk factor from the sum of positive risk factors, because high HDL-C decreases coronary artery disease risk. $\dot{V}O_2R$ refers to $\dot{V}O_2$ reserve.

1.2 Graded Exercise Testing

A comprehensive medical examination will include an exercise test, usually conducted on a motor-driven treadmill. A cycle ergometer can also be used but is not that common for clinical testing in the United States. The exercise electrocardiogram (ECG) and blood pressure are monitored as the person progresses from low-intensity exercise, such as slow walking, up to maximal-intensity exercise. Maximal intensity might be brisk walking for an older, deconditioned subject or running up a grade for a younger, fit individual. The rate of work is generally increased every 1–3 min until the maximal rate of work is achieved. This progression is referred to as a graded exercise test (GXT). The ECG is monitored to detect heart rhythm and electrical conductivity abnormalities. Blood pressure is monitored to determine if there is a normal increase in systolic blood pressure and little or no change in diastolic blood pressure as the rate of work progresses from low intensity to maximal or near-maximal levels. It is also important to interact with the subject, observing signs and symptoms during and immediately following the exercise test, such as chest pain or pressure (angina) , unusual shortness of breath, light-headedness or dizziness, and inappropriate heart rate response.

The exercise ECG is an important part of the medical evaluation because a small but significant percentage of the adult population have abnormalities in ECGs taken during or following exercise even though they have normal resting ECGs. These abnormalities include arrhythmias (irregular heart rhythms) and ST-segment changes. Figure 13.1 illustrates a normal ECG and an abnormal ECG in which there is depression of the ST segment. Results from an exercise test are considered either positive, when there have been abnormal changes in the ECG, on the contrary, it is negative. Typically, a person with abnormal changes in his or her exercise ECG will be referred for additional tests.

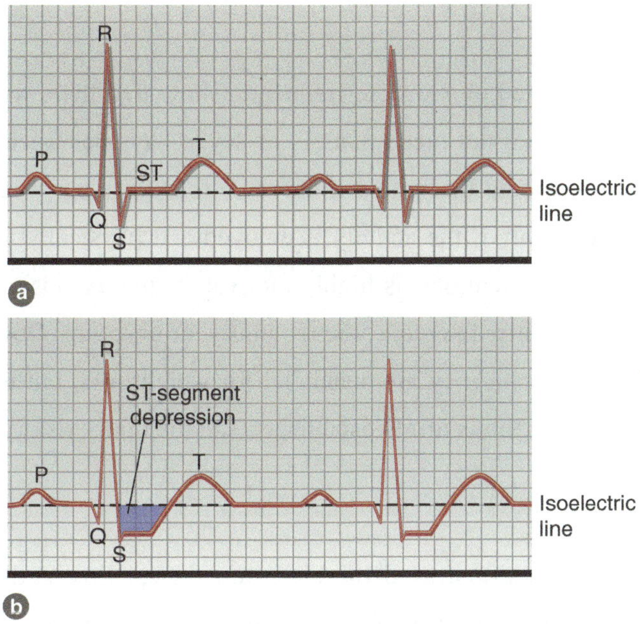

Figure 13.1 Illustration of (a) a normal ECG and (b) an ECG with ST-segment depression, suggestive of the presence of coronary artery disease.

2 Exercise Prescription

The exercise prescription involves four basic factors:

- Mode or type of exercise
- Frequency of participation
- Duration of each exercise bout
- Intensity of the exercise bout

2.1 Exercise Mode

The prescribed exercise program should focus on one or more modes, or types, of cardiovascular endurance activities. Traditionally, the activities prescribed most frequently are walking, jogging, running, hiking, cycling, rowing, and swimming.

For most competitive sport activities, preconditioning with one of the standard endurance activities, such as jogging/running or cycling, is advisable before one undertakes serious competition. Some researchers and clinicians, believe that a basic preconditioning program is essential to bring them up to the level of conditioning needed for the sport or activity and to reduce risk of injury.

2.2 Exercise Frequency

Research studies conducted on exercise frequency show that three to five days per week is an optimal frequency. This does not mean that six or seven days per week won't give additional benefits. Exercise initially should be limited to three or four days per week and increased up to five or more days per week only if the activity is enjoyed and physically tolerated. All too often, a person starts out with great intentions, is highly motivated, and exercises every day for the first few weeks, only to stop from utter fatigue, soreness, injury, or boredom. Obviously, additional days above the three- or four-day frequency are beneficial for weight loss, but this level should not be encouraged until the exercise habit is firmly established and the injury risk is reduced.

2.3 Exercise Duration

Several studies have demonstrated improvement in cardiovascular conditioning with endurance exercise periods as brief as 5–10 min per day. More recent research has indicated that 20–30 min per day is an optimal amount. Again, "optimal" is used here to reflect the greatest return for time invested, and the specified time refers to the time during which one is at one's appropriate exercise intensity. Exercise duration cannot be discussed appropriately without discussion of exercise intensity also. Similar improvements in aerobic capacity are gained with either a short-duration, high-intensity program or a long-duration, low-intensity program if the minimal threshold is exceeded for both duration and intensity. Similar benefits are also gained whether the daily endurance training session is conducted in multiple shorter bouts (e.g., three 10 min bouts) or a single long one (e.g., a single 30 min bout).

2.4 Exercise Intensity

The intensity of the exercise bout appears to be the most important factor. Evidence now suggests that a modest training effect can be accomplished in some people through training at intensities of 40% or less of their aerobic capacities and possibly could lead to health benefits. For most, however, the appropriate minimum intensity appears to be at least 50%–60% $\dot{V}O_{2\,max}$. An upper level for intensity will depend on the purpose for training. Obviously, training for competition requires high intensity. However, training for purposes of attaining and maintaining optimal health would seldom exceed 80% $\dot{V}O_{2\,max}$.

3 Monitoring Exercise Intensity

Exercise intensity can be quantified on the basis of the training heart rate (THR) , the metabolic equivalent (MET) , or the rating of perceived exertion (RPE). Let's examine each of these and their strengths and weaknesses in quantifying exercise intensity.

3.1 Training Heart Rate

The concept of training heart rate (THR) is based on the linear relationship between heart rate and $\dot{V}O_2$ with increasing rates of work. When people are exercise tested, their heart rate and $\dot{V}O_2$ values are obtained each minute and plotted against each other. The THR is established through use of the heart rate that is equivalent to a set percentage of the $\dot{V}O_{2\,max}$. For example, if a training level of 75% $\dot{V}O_{2\,max}$ is desired, 75% of $\dot{V}O_{2\,max}$ is calculated ($\dot{V}O_{2\,max} \times 0.75$) , and the heart rate corresponding to this $\dot{V}O_2$ then is selected as the THR. An important point is that the exercise intensity necessary to achieve a given percentage of $\dot{V}O_{2\,max}$ results in a much higher heart rate than that same percentage of HRmax. As an example, a THR that is set at 75% of the $\dot{V}O_{2\,max}$ represents an intensity of 87% of the HRmax (Figure 13.2).

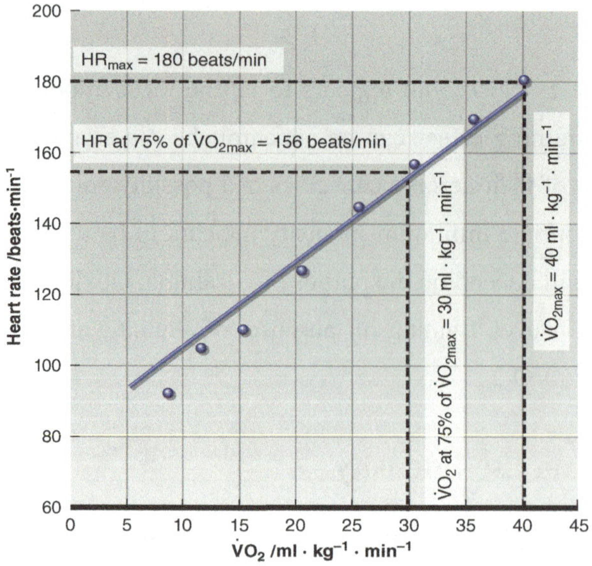

Figure 13.2 The linear relationship between heart rate and oxygen consumption ($\dot{V}O_2$) with increasing rates of work and the heart rate equivalent to a set percentage (75%) of $\dot{V}O_{2\,max}$.

3.1.1 The Karvonen Method

One can also establish the THR by using what is known as the Karvonen concept of maximal heart rate reserve, or the Karvonen method. Maximal heart rate reserve is defined as the difference between HRmax and the resting heart rate (HR_{rest}) :

maximal heart rate reserve = HRmax – HR_{rest}

With this method, the THR is calculated by taking a given percentage of the maximal heart rate reserve and adding it to the resting heart rate. Let's consider an example. For 75% of maximal heart rate reserve, the equation would be as follows:

$THR_{75\%} = HR_{rest} + 0.75\ (HRmax - HR_{rest})$.

The Karvonen method adjusts the THR so that the THR as a specific percentage of the maximal heart rate reserve is nearly identical to the heart rate equivalent of that same percentage of $\dot{V}O_{2\,max}$ at moderate to high intensities, Thus, a THR computed as 75% of maximal heart rate reserve is approximately the same as the heart rate corresponding to 75% of the $\dot{V}O_{2\,max}$. However, there is a substantial difference between the two at low intensities.

3.1.2 Training Heart Rate Range

More recently, appropriate exercise intensity has been established by setting a THR range, rather than a single THR value. This is a more sensible approach because exercising at a set percentage of $\dot{V}O_{2\,max}$ can place people above their lactate threshold, making it difficult for them to train for an extended period of time. With the THR range concept, low and high values are established that will ensure a training response. One starts at the low end of the THR range and progresses through the range as one feels comfortable. Consider the following example. A 40-year-old man has a resting heart rate of 75 beats/min and a maximum heart rate of 180 beats/min, and he is advised to exercise within a THR range of 50%–75% of his maximal heart rate reserve. His training heart rate range would be as follows:

$THR_{50\%} = 75 + 0.50\ (180-75) = 75 + 53 = 128$ beats/min.

$THR_{75\%} = 75 + 0.75\ (180-75) = 75 + 79 = 154$ beats/min.

3.2 Metabolic Equivalent

Exercise intensity also has been prescribed on the basis of the metabolic equivalent (MET) system. The amount of oxygen the body consumes is directly proportional to the energy expended during physical activity. In this system, it is assumed that the body uses approximately 3.5 ml of oxygen per kilogram of body weight per minute [3.5 ml · $(kg \cdot min)^{-1}$] at rest. The MET system, however, is based on this value, and the resting metabolic rate value of 3.5 ml · $(kg \cdot min)^{-1}$ is referred to as 1.0 MET. All activities can be classified by intensity according to their oxygen requirements. An activity that is rated as a 2.0 MET activity would require two times the resting metabolic rate, or 7 ml · $(kg \cdot min)^{-1}$; and an activity that is rated at 4.0 METs would require approximately 14 ml · $(kg \cdot min)^{-1}$. Some activities and their MET values are presented in Table 13.2.

Table 13.2 Selected Activities and Their Respective MET Values

Activity	MET Value	Activity	MET Value
REST AND SELF-CARE ACTIVITIES			
Rest (supine)	1.0	Showering	2.0
Sitting	1.5	General grooming, standing	2.0
Eating	1.5	Dressing or undressing, standing	2.5
Bathing	1.5		
HOME ACTIVITY			
Knitting or hand sewing, light effort	1.3	Vacuuming (general, moderate effort)	3.3
Washing dishes	1.8	Making beds, changing linens	3.3
Ironing	1.8	Cleaning (scrubbing floor, washing car, washing windows)	3.5
Laundry, folding or hanging clothes	2.0–2.3	Sweeping, moderate effort	3.8
Cooking or food preparation	2.0–3.5	Moving furniture, carrying boxes	5.8
Machine sewing	2.8	Scrubbing floors on hands and knees, vigorous effort	6.5

continued

Activity	MET Value	Activity	MET Value
OCCUPATIONAL			
Sitting tasks, office work, working at a computer	1.5	Construction (outside)	4.0
Driving a delivery truck, taxi, school bus, etc.	2.0	Hotel housekeeper	4.0
Cook, chef	2.5	Yard work	4.0
Standing tasks, light to moderate effort	3.0–4.5	Manual or unskilled labor	2.8–6.5
Custodial work	2.5–4.0	Farming, light to vigorous effort	2.0–7.8
Carpentry (general, light to moderate effort)	2.5–4.3	Fire fighter on the job	6.8–9.0
PHYSICAL CONDITIONING			
Walking			
2.5 mph, level	3.0	4.5 mph, level	7.0
3.5 mph, level	4.3	5.0 mph, level	8.3
4.0 mph, level	5.0	5.0 mph, 3% grade	9.8
Jogging or running on level surface 4.0 mph			
4.0 mph	6.0	10.0 mph	14.5
6.0 mph	9.8	12.0 mph	19.0
8.0 mph	11.8	14.0 mph	23.0
Swimming			
Freestyle, vigorous effort	9.8	Breaststroke, recreational/training and competition	5.3/10.3
Freestyle, slow to moderate	5.8	Sidestroke, general	7.0
Backstroke, recreational/training and competition	4.8/9.5		
Cycling			
Leisure, 5.5 mph	3.5	Leisure, 14.0–15.9 mph (vigorous effort)	10.0
Leisure, 10.0–11.9 mph (slow, light effort)	6.8	Racing, 16.0–19.0 mph (vigorous effort)	12.0
Leisure, 12.0–13.9 mph (moderate effort)	8.0	Racing, > 20 mph (vigorous effort)	15.8
RECREATIONAL ACTIVITIES			
Aerobic dance	5.0–7.3	General resistance training	3.5–6.0
Video game activities	2.3–6.0	Rowing machines	4.8–12.0
Stationary cycle ergometer	3.5–14.0	Water aerobics	5.3
Circuit training	4.3–8.0	Video exercise workouts, light to vigorous	2.3–6.0
SPORT ACTIVITIES			
Archery	4.3	Rock or mountain climbing	5.0–8.0
Badminton	5.5–7.0	Roller skating	7.0
Basketball	6.0–9.3	Rugby	6.3–8.3

continued

Activity	MET Value	Activity	MET Value
Bowling/Lawn bowling	3.0–3.8	Skateboarding	5.0–6.0
Football, flag or touch	4.0–8.0	Soccer	7.0–10.0
Golf	4.8	Softball	5.0–6.0
Handball	12.0	Squash	7.3–12.0
Hockey, field	7.8	Table tennis (ping pong)	4.0
Hockey, ice	8.0–10.0	Tennis, singles	7.3–8.0
Horseback riding	5.8–7.3	Tennis, doubles	4.5–6.0
Lacrosse	8.0	Volleyball	3.0–4.0
Orienteering	9.0	Volleyball, competitive	8.0
Racquetball	7.0–10.0	Volleyball, competitive beach	6.0

3.3 Ratings of Perceived Exertion

Ratings of perceived exertion (RPE) also have been proposed for use in prescribing exercise intensity. With this method, individuals subjectively rate how hard they feel they are working. When the RPE scale is used correctly, this system for monitoring exercise intensity has proven very accurate. Using the Borg RPE scale, which is a rating scale ranging from 6–20, the exercise intensity should be between an RPE of 12–13 (somewhat hard) and an RPE of 15–16 (hard). This is a more natural way to prescribe exercise and very efficient if the person is able to relate perceptions of intensity accurately.

Table 13.3 compares the various methods for rating exercise intensity. Let's use them to determine a moderate exercise intensity. As the second column shows, one would want to work within a range of 60%–79% HRmax. If, instead, one is monitoring intensity by $\dot{V}O_{2\,max}$ or using the Karvonen method, this heart rate range is equivalent to 50%–74% of either $\dot{V}O_{2\,max}$ or HRmax reserve, as shown in the third column. With use of the rating of perceived exertion, shown in the fourth column, this is equivalent to an RPE value of 12–13.

Table 13.3 Classification of Exercise intensity Based on 20–60 min of Endurance Activity: Comparing Three Methods

	RELATIVE INTENSITY		
Classification of intensity	HRmax	$\dot{V}O_{2\,max}$ or HRmax reserve	Rating of perceive exertion
Very light	<35%	<30%	<9
Light	35%–59%	30%–49%	10–11
Moderate	60%–79%	50%–74%	12–13
Heavy	80%–89%	75%–84%	14–16
Very heavy	≥90%	≥85%	>16

4 Exercise Program

Once the exercise prescription has been determined, it is integrated into a total exercise program, which is generally only part of an overall health improvement plan. Individual exercise capacity varies widely even among people of similar ages and physical builds. For this reason, each program must be individualized, based on results of physiological and medical tests and, if possible, individual needs and interests.

The total exercise program consists of the following activities:

- Warm-up and stretching activities
- Endurance training
- Cool-down and stretching activities
- Flexibility training
- Resistance training
- Recreational activities

Generally, the first three activities are performed three or four times each week. Flexibility training can be included as part of the warm-up, cool-down, and stretching exercises, or it can be done at a separate time during the week. Resistance training is usually done on alternate days when endurance training is not done; however, the two can be combined into the same workout.

4.1 Warm-Up and Stretching Activities

The exercise session should begin with low-intensity, calisthenic-type and stretching exercises. Such a warm-up period gradually increases both heart rate and breathing, preparing the exerciser for the efficient and safe functioning of the heart, blood vessels, lungs, and muscles during the more vigorous exercise that follows. A good warm-up can reduce the amount of muscle and joint soreness experienced during the early stages of the exercise program. An acceptable warm-up would begin with 5–10 min of stretching, followed by 5–10 min of low-intensity activity using the mode of exercise selected for endurance training. For example, someone who trains by running might start with stretching and then do 5–10 min of light jogging before starting to run.

4.2 Endurance Training

Physical activities that develop cardiovascular endurance are the heart of the exercise program. They are designed to improve both the capacity and efficiency of the cardiovascular, respiratory, and metabolic systems. These activities also help one control or reduce body weight. Activities such as walking, jogging, running, cycling, swimming, rowing, aerobic dancing, box stepping, and hiking are good endurance activities. Sports such as handball, racquetball, tennis, badminton, and basketball also have aerobic potential if they are pursued vigorously.

4.3 Cool-Down and Stretching Activities

The best way to accomplish cooldown is to slowly reduce the intensity of the endurance activity during the last several minutes of a workout. After running, for example, a slow, restful walk for several minutes helps prevent blood from pooling in the extremities. Stopping abruptly after an endurance exercise bout causes blood to pool in the legs and can result in dizziness or fainting. Also, catecholamine levels might be elevated during the immediate recovery period, and this can lead to a fatal heart arrhythmia. After the cool-down period, stretching exercises can be performed to facilitate increased flexibility.

4.4 Flexibility Training

Flexibility exercises usually supplement exercises performed during the warm-up or cool-down period and are useful for those who have poor flexibility or muscle and joint problems, such as low back pain. These exercises should be performed slowly. Quick stretching movements are potentially dangerous and can lead to muscle pulls or spasms. At one time it was recommended that these exercises be performed before the endurance conditioning period. However, recently it has been hypothesized that the muscles, tendons, ligaments, and joints are more adaptable and responsive to flexibility exercises when they are done after the endurance conditioning phase.

4.5 Resistance Training

The importance of resistance training as part of a general health and fitness exercise program has been clearly established. Many health-related benefits can be obtained from resistance training. The ACSM has included resistance training in its recommendations for a general health and fitness program.

The maximum amount of weight one can lift successfully only one time is the 1-repetition maximum, or 1RM. When people begin a resistance training program, they should start with a weight that is exactly one-half of their maximal strength, or 1RM, for each lift. They should attempt to lift that weight 10 consecutive times. If they can lift the weight just 10 times before reaching fatigue, this is the proper starting point. If they can do more repetitions, they should go to the next higher weight for the second set. If, instead, they were able to lift the weight fewer than eight times in the first set, the original weight was too heavy and should be reduced to the next lower weight for the second set.

The number of repetitions they can complete in these last sets will probably decrease as their muscles become fatigued. As strength increases, the number of repetitions they can complete per set will increase. When one reaches 15 repetitions on the first set, one is ready to progress to the next higher weight. This training technique is referred to as progressive resistance exercise.

One can perform two or three sets of each lift per day, two or three days per week, for weight control purposes. Strength gains, however, appear to be fully achieved with just one set per day in previously untrained people. People should select a variety of exercises that tax most or all of the major muscle groups of the upper body, trunk, and lower body. If time is a factor, it is better to reduce the number of sets to one or two and maintain a full-body workout.

4.6 Recreational Activities

Recreational activities are important to any comprehensive exercise program. Although people engage in these activities primarily for enjoyment and relaxation, many recreational activities can also improve health and fitness. Activities such as hiking, tennis, handball, squash, and certain team sports fall into this category.

IN CLOSING

In this chapter, we have seen that the medical community now regards physical activity as vital to maintaining good health and reducing the risk of disease. We looked at the importance and practicality of both a medical examination and an exercise ECG in screening previously sedentary adults before prescribing exercise. We discussed the components of an exercise prescription and methods of monitoring exercise intensity. Finally, we reviewed the components of an exercise program and the role of exercise in rehabilitating patients with disease.

Now that we have seen the importance of exercise in disease prevention, we will look more closely at physical activity as it relates to specific disease states. In the next chapter, we turn our attention to cardiovascular diseases.

KEY TERMS

Borg RPE scale; coronary artery disease (CAD) ; exercise electrocardiogram (ECG) ; rating of perceived exertion (RPE) ; exercise prescription; graded exercise test (GXT) ; sensitivity; Karvonen method; maximal heart rate reserve; training heart rate (THR) ; metabolic equivalent (MET)

STUDY QUESTIONS

(1) What role does the graded exercise test to exhaustion play in medical clearance? Is this test essential for all adults?

(2) What four factors must be considered in the exercise prescription? Which of these is the most important?

(3) Discuss the concept of a minimal threshold for initiating physiological changes with exercise training as it relates to the exercise prescription.

(4) Discuss the various ways of monitoring exercise intensity, and give the advantages and disadvantages of each.

(5) Describe the components of a good exercise program and their importance in the total program.

第十三章 健身运动处方

当今的生活模式使得人们习惯于静坐少动。可是，人体是与运动相适应的，在生理方面，人体很不适应这种不活动的生活方式。研究证实，运动的生活方式对于每个人的最佳健康状态至关重要。

一、医学检查

1.医学评估

尽管在有计划的锻炼之前进行全面的医学评估是有益的，但也不是所有人都需要。这不仅是由于许多人无法承担这项花销，即使经费充足，医疗系统也无法为全部人群提供此项服务。同时，健康人群在有计划的锻炼之前进行医学评估可减少与运动有关的医疗风险，这一说法目前还无法证实。出于上述原因，人们尝试建立了适合中风险人群到高危人群的准则及建议。中风险人群是指没有心血管、肺或代谢疾病体征或症状，或未被诊断患有心血管、肺或代谢疾病，但有两个或两个以上冠状动脉疾病危险因素的人。高危人群则是具有一种或多种心血管、肺或代谢疾病体征或症状的人。

2.递增负荷运动试验

全面的医学检查应该包括运动测试，通常用跑台进行，也可以使用功率自行车。心电图和血压应从低强度运动开始监测，直到最高强度运动。运动速度每1～3分钟逐级递增，直至最大运动速度，这个过程被称为递增负荷运动试验。心电图可以监测心率和心传导异常。运动心电图是医学评估中非常重要的一部分。当运动速度从低到高临近最高强度时，血压监测可以确定收缩压是否正常上升，舒张压是否不变或微变。在运动测试期间或运动后即刻观察各指标或症状，例如有无胸部疼痛或心绞痛、少见的气短、轻微的头晕或晕厥、异常心率反应等，且观察各指标间的相互联系也非常重要。

二、运动处方

运动处方包含四个基本要素：①运动种类；②运动频率；③运动时间；④运动强度。

1.运动种类

运动处方应该包括一种或多种心血管耐力活动的运动种类。一般来说，最常见的运动有步行、跑步、徒步旅行、骑车、划船、游泳等。对于大多数综合性体育项目，最好在比赛之前进行热身活动。

2.运动频率

研究证实，每周运动3～5天是最佳频率，每周运动6天或7天可以获得额外的健康益处。锻炼初始阶段应限制在每周3天或4天，在身体状况允许的情况下可逐步增加到每周5天甚至更多。

3.运动时间

最近的研究显示，每天运动20～30分钟是最佳选择。日常生活中耐力训练可以是多次短时间练习（3次10分钟练习），也可以是一次长时间练习（1次30分钟练习），均可获得相似的效果。

4.运动强度

运动强度是最重要的因素，适宜的最低强度至少为50%～60%最大摄氧量水平。强度上限则依据训练目的制定，为比赛而进行的训练需要较高的强度，而为了达到或维持最佳健康水平而进行的运动则很少需要超过80%最大摄氧量水平。

三、运动强度监控

运动强度可通过靶心率（THR）、代谢当量（MET）、主观体力感觉量表（RPE）等方式进行量化。

1.靶心率

靶心率的概念是基于随着工作效率的增加，心率和耗氧量之间的线性关系产生的。当进行运动测试时，可以得到运动员每分钟的心率和耗氧量指标，同时制图。靶心率是通过心率建立起的，与最大摄氧量的百分比等效，可以通过卡沃宁法和靶心率范围两种方式测得。

2.代谢当量

运动强度也可以用代谢当量表示。身体消耗的氧气量与体力活动消耗的能量成正比。假定人体在安静状态下，每千克体重每分钟消耗3.5毫升氧气（3.5毫升·千克体重$^{-1}$·分$^{-1}$），将安静的代谢率3.5毫升·千克体重$^{-1}$·分$^{-1}$定义为1.0 MET。所有的活动均可根据氧气的需求量进行强度分类。2.0 MET的活动，将需要2倍的安静代谢率即7毫升·千克体重$^{-1}$·分$^{-1}$；4.0 MET的活动，将需要14毫升·千克体重$^{-1}$·分$^{-1}$。

3.主观体力感觉量表

主观体力感觉量表也可以用来确定运动处方的强度。在运动时用这种方法，可以将个人主观评价疲劳感觉给出的数字与运动强度相对应。使用博格（Borg）主观体力感觉量表，感觉尺度为6～20，运动强度应在主观体力感觉量表的12～13（有点吃力）和主观体力感觉量表15～16（吃力）之间。主观体力感觉量表是十分有效的描述运动的方法，并且能够准确地反映运动强度。

四、运动计划

运动处方形成了一个总的锻炼计划，是全面提高健康计划的一部分。不同个体即使是同样的年龄和体型，其运动能力也大不相同。如果要满足个体的需要和兴趣，每个计划在生理学和医学测试的基础上必须满足个性化需求。

完整的运动计划包括下列活动：

· 热身和牵拉活动；
· 耐力训练；
· 整理和牵拉活动；
· 柔韧性练习；
· 抗阻训练；
· 娱乐活动。

通常，前三项活动每周进行3～4次；柔韧性练习可包括在热身、整理和牵拉活动中；抗阻训练通常在不进行耐力训练时隔天进行。柔韧性练习和抗阻训练也可以结合进行。

1.热身和牵拉活动

运动应从低强度的健美操和牵拉等动作开始。在热身阶段逐渐增加心率和呼吸频率，为练习者在接下来更高强度的运动中为心脏、血管、肺、肌肉的工作效率和安全运行做准备。高质量的热身可以在运动早期减少肌肉和关节的酸痛感。适当的热身由5～10分钟的牵拉开始，然后根据耐力训练所选择的运动种类进行5～10分钟的低强度活动。

2.耐力训练

发展心血管耐力的体力活动是运动计划的核心内容。耐力训练不仅可以提高心血管系统、呼吸系统和代谢系统的能力和效率，而且可以控制或减轻体重。像步行、慢跑、骑车、游泳、划船、有氧操、台阶运动和徒步旅行等均是很好的耐力活动。如果需要高强度运动，像手球、壁球、网球、羽毛球和篮球等运动也可作为有氧练习。

3.整理和牵拉活动

完成整理活动最好的方法是在练习的最后几分钟缓慢降低耐力训练的强度。例如，在跑步后，缓慢地步行一段时间，以帮助四肢血液回心。耐力训练后突然停止可能会导致血液停留在下肢，而产生头晕或晕厥。同时，儿茶酚胺水平可能会在即刻恢复期上升，这会导致致命的心律失常。在整理活动后，可进行牵拉活动以提高机体柔韧性。

4.柔韧性练习

柔韧性练习通常是热身阶段或整理阶段的补充练习，对柔韧性较差或腰部疼痛等肌肉关节有问题的人群来说尤为重要。柔韧性练习应该缓慢进行，快速牵拉具有潜在的危险性，会导致肌肉拉伤或痉挛。以往都推荐在耐力训练之前进行这些练习，然而，研究证实了如果在耐力训练之后进行，肌肉、肌腱、韧带和关节对柔韧性练习会更具适应性和反应能力。

5.抗阻训练

抗阻训练在完整运动计划中的重要性不言而喻，美国运动医学学会已将抗阻训练作为健身练习计划的推荐内容。一个人可以成功举起的1次最大重量称为重复1次的最大重量或1RM。当练习者开始抗阻训练计划时，起始重量应为他的最大力量或1RM的一半，尝试举起这个重量10次。如果举起10次刚好达到疲劳状态，这就是正确的起始重量。如果可以举起更多次，第2组则增加重量。相反，如果举起不足8次，说明起始重量过大，第二组则减轻重量。

为控制体重而进行的抗阻训练可以每周进行2～3天，每天2～3组。对未经训练的人来说，为了增加力量而进行的训练只需要每天1组。练习者可以选择多种练习方式去发展上肢、躯干和下肢大部分或全部主要的肌肉。如果考虑时间因素，最好减少1～2组的量以保证全身活动的时间。

6.娱乐活动

娱乐活动对综合性运动计划来说非常重要。尽管练习者的首要目的是娱乐和放松，许多娱乐活动仍然可以提高健康水平，像徒步旅行、网球、手球、壁球和某些团队运动都属于此范畴。

Chapter 14 Cardiovascular Disease and Physical Activity

Most of us consider ourselves to be healthy until we experience some overt sign of illness. With chronic degenerative diseases, such as heart disease, most people are unaware that the disease process is smoldering and progressing to the point that it could cause major complications, including death. Fortunately, early detection and proper treatment of various chronic diseases can substantially reduce their severity and often avert disability and death. Even more important, decreasing the risk factors for a disease often can either prevent the disease or delay its onset. In this chapter, we look at cardiovascular diseases, focusing primarily on coronary heart disease (CHD) and hypertension.

1 Forms of Cardiovascular Disease

There are several different cardiovascular diseases; these are illustrated in Figure 14.1. CHD accounts for the majority (51%) of cardiovascular disease deaths, with stroke a distant second at 17%.

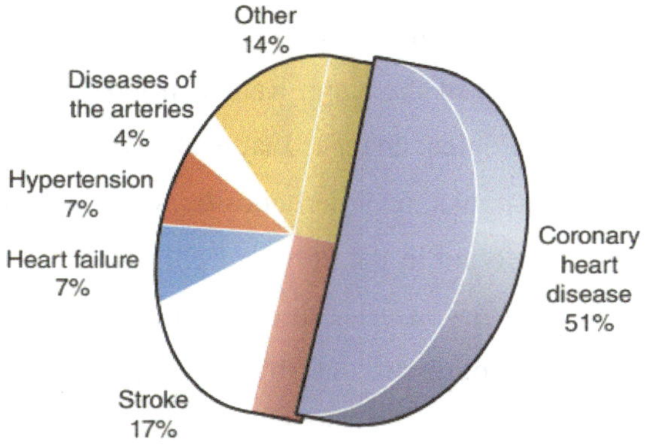

Figure 14.1 The leading causes of death from cardiovascular diseases.

1.1 Coronary Heart Disease

As most humans age, their coronary arteries become progressively narrowed as a result of the formation of fatty plaque along the inner wall of the artery, as seen in Figure 14.2. This progressive narrowing of the arteries in general is referred to as atherosclerosis; and when the coronary arteries are involved, it is termed coronary heart disease (CHD) or coronary artery disease (CAD). As the disease progresses and the coronary arteries become narrower, the capacity to supply blood to the myocardium is progressively reduced.

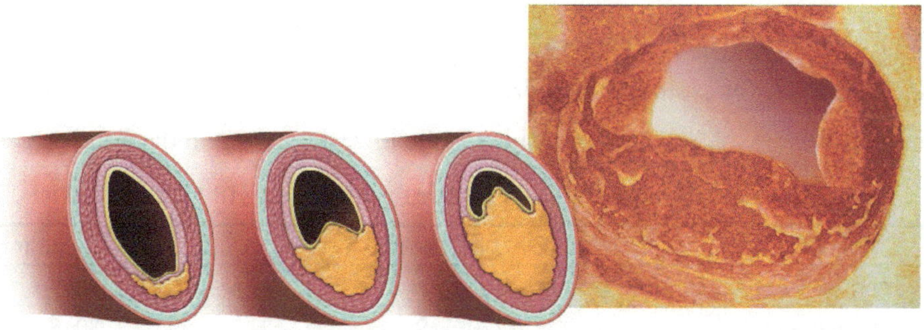

Figure 14.2 The progressive formation of plaque in a coronary artery.

As the narrowing worsens, the myocardium eventually can't receive enough blood to meet all of its needs. When this occurs, the portion of the myocardium that is supplied by the narrowed arteries becomes ischemic, meaning that it suffers a deficiency of blood, or ischemia.

When blood supply to a part of the myocardium is severely or totally restricted, ischemia can lead to a heart attack, or myocardial infarction, because cardiac muscle cells that are deprived of blood for several minutes are thus deprived of oxygen, which leads to irreversible damage and necrosis (cellular death). This can lead to mild, moderate, or severe disability or even death, depending on the location of the infarction and the extent of the damage.

Atherosclerosis is not a disease of the aged. Rather, it is more appropriately classified as a pediatric disease because the pathological changes that lead to atherosclerosis begin in infancy and progress during childhood. Fatty streaks, or lipid deposits, which are thought to be the precursors of atherosclerosis, commonly are found in the aortas of children by age three to five. These fatty streaks start to appear in the coronary arteries during the early teens, can develop into fibrous plaques during one's 20s, and can progress to unstable or complicated lesions during one's 40s and 50s.

Atherosclerosis begins in childhood and progresses at different rates, depending primarily on heredity and lifestyle choices, including smoking history, diet, physical activity, and stress.

1.2 Hypertension

Hypertension is the medical term for high blood pressure, a condition in which blood pressure is chronically elevated above levels considered desirable or healthy for a person's age and size. Blood pressure depends primarily on body size, so children and young adolescents have much lower blood pressures than adults. Hypertension is uncommon during childhood but can appear during mid-adolescence. Clinically, hypertension in these groups is defined as blood pressure values above the 90th or the 95th percentile for the youth's age. For adults, the Joint National Committee on Detection, Evaluation, and Treatment of High Blood Pressure has established guidelines, presented in Table 14.1, for systolic blood pressure, which is the highest pressure in the arteries at any time, and for diastolic blood pressure, which is the lowest pressure in the arteries at any time.

Table 14.1 Classification of Blood Pressure for Adults, Age 18 Years and Older

Category	Systolic /mmHg	Diastolic /mmHg
Normal	<120	<80
Prehypertension	120–139	80–89
Hypertension		
Stage1	140–159	90–99
Stage2	≥160	≥100

Reprinted from: The Seventh Report of the Joint National Committee on Prevention, Detection, Evaluation, and Treatment of High Blood Pressure, 2003, *Journal of the American Medical Association*. 289: 2560–2572.

Hypertension causes the heart to work harder than normal, because it has to expel blood from the left ventricle against a greater resistance. Furthermore, hypertension places great strain on the systemic arteries and arterioles. Over time, this stress can cause the heart to enlarge and the arteries and arterioles to become scarred, hardened, and less elastic. Eventually, this can lead to atherosclerosis, heart attacks, heart failure, stroke, and kidney failure.

1.3 Stroke

Stroke is a form of cardiovascular disease that affects the cerebral arteries, those that supply the brain.

Strokes generally fall into two categories: ischemic stroke and hemorrhagic stroke. Ischemic strokes are the most common (~87% of all cases) and result from an obstruction within a cerebral blood vessel that limits the flow of blood to that region of the brain. Obstructions have one of two causes: cerebral thrombosis and Cerebral embolism.

In cases of ischemic stroke, blood flow beyond the blockage is restricted, and the part of the brain that relies on that supply becomes ischemic, is oxygen deficient, and can die.

Hemorrhagic strokes are of two major types:

- Intracerebral hemorrhage, in which one of the cerebral arteries ruptures in the brain;
- Subarachnoid hemorrhage, in which one of the brain's surface vessels ruptures, dumping blood into the space between the brain and the skull.

In both cases, blood flow beyond the rupture is diminished because the blood leaves the vessel at the site of injury. Also, as the blood accumulates outside of the vessel, it puts pressure on the fragile brain tissue, which can alter brain function. Brain hemorrhages often result from aneurysms, which arise from weak spots in the vessel wall that balloon outward; and aneurysms often arise because of hypertension or atherosclerotic damage to the vessel wall. Arteriovenous malformations are another cause of hemorrhagic strokes.

As with a heart attack, a stroke results in death of the affected tissue. Brain damage from a stroke can affect the senses, speech, body movement, thought patterns, and memory. Paralysis on one side of the body is common, as is the inability to verbalize thoughts.

1.4 Heart Failure

Heart failure is a chronic and progressive clinical condition in which the myocardium becomes too weak to maintain an adequate cardiac output, causing blood to back up in the veins. Hypertension, atherosclerosis, valvular heart disease, viral infection, and heart attack are among the possible causes of this disorder.

When cardiac output is inadequate, blood begins to back up in the veins. This causes excess fluids to accumulate in the body, particularly in the legs and ankles. This fluid accumulation (edema) also can affect the lungs (pulmonary edema) , disrupting breathing and causing shortness of breath. Heart failure can progress to the point of irreversible damage to the heart, and the patient becomes a candidate for a heart transplant.

1.5 Other Cardiovascular Diseases

Other cardiovascular diseases include peripheral vascular diseases, valvular heart diseases, rheumatic heart disease, and congenital heart disease.

Peripheral vascular diseases systemic, rather than coronary, vessels and include arteriosclerosis, varicose veins, and phlebitis. Arteriosclerosis refers to numerous conditions in which the walls of the arteries become thickened, hard, and less elastic. Varicose veins result from incompetency of the valves in the veins, allowing blood to back up in the veins and causing them to become enlarged, tortuous, and painful. Phlebitis is inflammation of a vein and is also very painful.

Valvular heart diseases involve one or more of the four valves that control the direction of blood flow into and out of the four heart chambers. Rheumatic heart disease is one form of valvular heart disease involving a streptococcal infection that has caused acute rheumatic fever, typically in children between ages 5 and 15. Rheumatic fever is an inflammatory disease of the connective tissue and commonly affects the heart, specifically the heart valves. The damage to the valves usually causes difficulty in their opening, hindering blood flow out of that chamber, or difficulty in their closing, allowing blood to flow back into the previous chamber.

Congenital heart disease includes any heart defects that are present at birth, which are also appropriately termed congenital heart defects. These defects occur when the heart or the blood vessels near the heart do not develop normally before birth.

The remainder of this chapter focuses on the two major diseases of the heart and blood vessels: CHD and hypertension.

2 Determining Individual Risk

2.1 Risk Factors for Coronary Heart Disease

The factors associated with an increased risk for premature development of CHD can be classified into two groups: those over which a person has no control and those that can be altered through basic changes in lifestyle. Those that a person cannot control include heredity (family history of CHD), race, male sex, and advanced age. According to the American Heart Association, the primary risk factors that can be controlled or altered include:

- tobacco smoke
- hypertension

- abnormal blood lipids and lipoproteins
- physical inactivity
- obesity and overweight
- diabetes and insulin resistance

Table 14.2 illustrates the ranges of values for some of these risk factors based on the categories of "desirable", "borderline", and "high". These are approximations and vary somewhat by sex and age.

Table 14.2 Level of Risk Associated with Selected Risk Factors for Coronary Heart Disease

		LEVEL OR RISK		
Risk factor		Desirable	Borderline	High
Blood pressure[a]				
Systolic	mmHg	<120	120–139	≥140
Diastolic	mmHg	<80	80–89	≥90
Blood lipids and lipoproteins[a]				
Cholesterol	mg/dL	<200	200–239	≥240
LDL-C	mg/dL	<130	130–159	≥160
HDL-C	mg/dL	≥60	40–59	<40
Triglycerides	mg/dL	<150	150–199	≥200
Overweight/Obesity (BMI)[a]	kg/m^2	18.5–24.9	25.0–29.9	≥30
Fasting plasma glucose[b]	mg/dL	<100	100–125	≥126
Physical inactivity[a, c]	min/day	30–60	15–29	<15

[a]American Heart Association, 2010

[b]Data from the American Diabetes Association: www.diabetes.org/diabetes–basics

[c]Moderate to vigorous exercise on most days of the week

Two classes of lipoproteins of major concern for CHD are low-density lipoprotein (LDL) and high-density lipoprotein (HDL). High concentrations of high-density lipoprotein cholesterol (HDL-C) and low concentrations of low-density lipoprotein cholesterol (LDL-C) place the individual at the lowest risk for CHD. Yet a third class of lipoproteins is called very low-density lipoproteins (VLDL). Very low-density lipoprotein cholesterol (VLDL-C) is becoming increasingly implicated as a risk factor for CHD.

LDL-C is theorized to be responsible for depositing cholesterol in the arterial wall. HDL-C, however, is regarded as a scavenger that removes cholesterol from the arterial wall and transports it to the liver to be metabolized. Because of these very different roles, it is essential to know the specific concentrations of both of these lipoproteins when one is determining individual risk. The ratio of Total-C to HDL-C may be the best blood lipid index of risk for CHD, with values of 5.0 or greater indicating increased risk and values of 3.0 or lower representing low risk.

2.2 Risk Factors for Hypertension

The risk factors for hypertension, like those for CHD, can be classified as ones we can control and ones we cannot. Those we cannot control are heredity (family history of hypertension) , sex, advanced age, and race (increased risk for people of African or Hispanic ancestry). Risk factors we can control are:

- insulin resistance
- obesity and overweight
- diet (sodium; alcohol)
- use of tobacco products
- use of oral contraceptives
- stress
- physical inactivity

Physical inactivity is a risk factor for hypertension. Its role has been conclusively established in epidemiological studies. Furthermore, substantial evidence indicates that increasing physical activity tends to reduce elevated blood pressure.

3 Reducing Risk Through Physical Activity

The role that physical activity might play in preventing or delaying the onset of CHD and hypertension has been of major interest to the medical community for many years. In the following sections, we try to unravel this mystery by examining the following areas:

- Physiological adaptations with training that might reduce risk
- Risk factor reduction with exercise training

3.1 Reducing the Risk of Coronary Heart Disease

3.1.1 Training Adaptations That Might Reduce Risk

The importance of regular physical activity in reducing the risk of CHD becomes apparent when we consider anatomical and physiological adaptations in response to exercise training. For example, exercise training causes the heart to hypertrophy, primarily through an increase in left ventricular chamber size but also through increases in left ventricular wall thickness. This adaptation may be important for improved contractility and increased cardiac work capacity.

The capacity of the coronary circulation appears to increase with training. Studies have shown that the size of major coronary vessels increases, which implies an increased capacity for blood flow to all regions of the heart. In fact, several studies have demonstrated that the peak flow rate in the major coronary arteries increases following an exercise training program.

Evidence is also starting to accumulate suggesting that exercise training increases endothelial function. Endothelial dysfunction is primarily the result of decreased nitric oxide bioavailability. Exercise training has been shown to increase nitric oxide bioavailability. Further, exercise training has been shown to have an anti-inflammatory effect, and we have just learned that atherosclerosis is an inflammatory disease.

Some evidence also suggests that the heart's collateral circulation improves with exercise training. The collateral circulation is a system of small vessels that branch off the major coronary vessels and are important in providing blood to all regions of the heart, particularly when there are blockages in the major coronary arteries.

3.1.2 Risk Reduction with Exercise Training

Many studies have investigated the role of exercise in altering risk factors associated with heart disease. Let's consider the major risk factors and how exercise might affect them.

Exercise possibly exerts its most beneficial effect on blood lipid levels. Although the decreases in Total-C and LDL-C with endurance training are relatively small (generally less than 10%) , there appear to be relatively major increases in HDL-C and major decreases in triglycerides. Cross-sectional studies of athletes and nonathletes alike show unequivocally that people with greater levels of aerobic activity or higher aerobic capacities have higher HDL-C and lower triglyceride levels. Almost all studies, however, have shown that the ratios of LDL-C to HDL-C and of Total-C to HDL-C are decreased following endurance training. This implies a reduced risk.

Exercise plays an important role in weight reduction and control and in the management of diabetes. Exercise also has been reported to be effective for stress reduction and control and for reducing anxiety. Some research supports the use of exercise training in the treatment of depression.

3.2 Reducing the Risk of Hypertension

3.2.1 Training Adaptations That Might Reduce Risk

A number of physiological adaptations that accompany endurance training could affect blood pressure both at rest and during exercise. One of the most important changes associated with endurance training is the plasma volume increase. However, trained muscle has a notable increase in capillaries. Also, the venous system in a trained person has a greater capacity, allowing it to contain more blood. For these reasons, the increased plasma volume following exercise training does not increase blood pressure.

Resting blood pressure is decreased by training in people with hypertension; this is probably attributable to decreased peripheral resistance, but the actual mechanisms are unknown. Exercise also reduces body fat, blood glucose levels, and insulin resistance, factors related to an increased risk for hypertension.

3.2.2 Risk Reduction with Exercise Training

Not only does exercise reduce blood pressure itself, but it also affects other risk factors. Exercise is important in reducing body fat and can increase muscle mass, which may be important in reducing blood glucose levels and thus assisting in better glycemic (blood sugar) control. This could partially explain the reduction in insulin resistance, another risk factor for hypertension, that has been observed in training studies. Exercise training also has been associated with stress reduction.

4 Exercise Training and Rehabilitating Patients with Heart Disease

Can active participation in a cardiac rehabilitation program that has a strong aerobic and resistance exercise component help a heart attack survivor to either survive a subsequent attack or avoid one altogether? Endurance training leads to many physiological changes that reduce the work or oxygen demand of the heart. As we have seen, many of these are peripheral, not involving the heart directly. To recap, training increases the capillary/muscle fiber ratio and plasma volume. Because of these changes, blood flow increases to the muscles. Training also possibly can increase or maintain oxygen supply to the heart.

However, significant changes also may occur in the heart itself. Studies of heart disease patients at Washington University in St. Louis have provided dramatic evidence that intense aerobic conditioning not only can substantially change peripheral factors but also can alter the heart itself, possibly increasing blood flow to the heart and increasing left ventricular function.

It is clear that endurance exercise training can significantly reduce the risk of cardiovascular disease through its independent effect on the individual risk factors for CHD and hypertension. Favorable changes in blood pressure, lipid levels, body composition, glucose control, and stress have been reported in patients undergoing exercise training for cardiac rehabilitation. We have every reason to believe that these changes are just as important to the health of a patient who has had a heart attack as they are for a presumably healthy person.

Resistance training also has substantial benefits when included as a part of a comprehensive cardiac rehabilitation program. Table 14.3 provides a summary comparison of the benefits of resistance training and aerobic training on various physiological and clinical markers of health and fitness. It is obvious that combining the two types of training into a comprehensive rehabilitation program will maximize the overall training benefits.

Table 14.3 Comparison of the Effects of Aerobic Endurance Training and Strength Training on Health and Fitness Variables

Variable	Aerobic exercise	Resistance exercise
Bone mineral density	↑↑	↓↓
Body composition		
% Fat	↓↓	↓
Lean body mass	↔	↑↑
Strength	↔	↑↑↑
Glucose metabolism		
Insulin response to glucose challenge	↓↓	↓↓
Basal insulin levels	↓	↓↓
Insulin sensitivity	↑↑	↑↑
Serum lipids		
HDL-C	↑↔	↑↔
LDL-C	↓↔	↓↔
Resting heart rate	↓↓	↔
Stroke volume	↑↑	↔
Blood pressure at rest		
Systolic	↓↔	↔
Diastolic	↓↔	↓↔
$\dot{V}O_{2max}$	↑↑↑	↑↑
Endurance performance	↑↑↑	↑↑
Basal metabolism	↑	↑↑

Note. HDL-C = high-density lipoprotein cholesterol; LDL-C = low-density lipoprotein cholesterol; ↑ = increase; ↓ = decrease; ↔ = little or no change. The more arrows, the greater the change.

The evidence that physical activity is important in the rehabilitation of the cardiac patient is sufficiently clear. The American College of Sports Medicine issued a position stand that concluded, "most patients with CHD should engage in individually designed exercise programs to achieve optimal physical and emotional health." The recommendation was that such programs include a comprehensive pre-exercise medical evaluation, including a graded exercise test, and an individualized exercise prescription. Such programs should focus on multifactorial risk factor modification by using diet, drugs, and exercise to control blood lipid disorders, diabetes, and hypertension.

IN CLOSING

In this chapter, we have seen how important physical activity is in reducing the risk for cardiovascular diseases, especially CAD and HTN. We discussed the prevalence of these disorders, the risk factors associated with each, and the ways in which physical activity can help reduce our personal risks. In the next chapter, we continue examining the effects of exercise on health as we turn our attention to obesity and diabetes.

KEY TERMS

arteriosclerosis; atherosclerosis; blood lipids; congenital heart disease; coronary heart disease (CHD) ; fatty streaks; heart failure; hemorrhagic stroke; high-density lipoprotein cholesterol (HDL-C) ; hypertension; ischemia; ischemic stroke; lipoproteins; low-density lipoprotein cholesterol (LDL-C) ; myocardial infarction; peripheral vascular disease; primary risk factors; rheumatic heart disease; risk factor; stroke; valvular heart disease; very low-density lipoprotein cholesterol (VLDL-C)

STUDY QUESTIONS

(1) What is atherosclerosis, how does it develop, and at what age does it begin?

(2) What is hypertension, how does it develop, and at what age does it begin?

(3) What is stroke? How does stroke occur? What are the results of stroke?

(4) What are the basic risk factors for coronary heart disease? For hypertension?

(5) What are two basic physiological alterations resulting from exercise training that would reduce the risk of death from coronary heart disease?

(6) In what ways does endurance exercise training alter risk factors for heart disease?

(7) What are two basic physiological alterations resulting from exercise training that would reduce the risk for developing hypertension?

(8) What changes in blood pressure would be expected to result from endurance exercise training in hypertensive individuals?

(9) Of what value is cardiac rehabilitation in treating a patient who has had a heart attack?

第十四章 心血管疾病与体力活动

在出现明显的疾病征兆前，大部分人都认为自己是健康的。对于心脏病等慢性疾病，大多数人并不知道其疾病的发展过程以及包括死亡在内的并发症的严重程度。幸运的是，各种慢性病的早期发现和适当治疗可以大大降低其严重程度，且可预防残疾和死亡。更重要的是，减少疾病的危险因素通常可以预防疾病或延缓疾病发作。在本章中，我们着眼于心血管疾病，主要关注冠心病和高血压。

一、心血管疾病的类型

心血管疾病有许多种类型，如冠状动脉疾病、高血压、中风、心脏衰竭和其他心血管疾病等。

1.冠状动脉疾病

冠状动脉疾病（CAD）指随着年龄的增加，由于脂肪斑块堆积在血管的内壁，而使血管逐渐变窄。这种动脉逐渐变窄常被称为动脉硬化，当涉及冠状动脉时，则被称为冠心病（CHD）或冠状动脉疾病。随着疾病的进展和冠状动脉变窄，其向心肌供血的能力逐渐降低。

当血管狭窄进一步恶化，心肌最终无法获得足够的血液供给以满足其所有需要，由此狭窄动脉所供应的心肌就会缺血，这意味着心肌血供不足或缺血。当部分心肌供血严重或完全受限时，缺血可导致心脏病发作或心肌梗塞，从而导致不可逆转的损伤和坏死（细胞死亡）。这可能导致轻度、中度或严重残疾，甚至死亡，具体取决于梗塞的位置和损伤的程度。

动脉粥样硬化开始于儿童时期，发展速度不同，主要取决于遗传和生活方式，包括年龄、饮食、身体活动和压力。

2.高血压

高血压是血压长期超过个体年龄和体重所需的或健康的状况。血压主要受到体重的影响，所以儿童和青少年的血压比成人低。高血压在儿童身上并不常见，但可能出现在青春期中期。临床上，青少年阶段的高血压是指血压超过同年龄段血压的第90或95百分位数。对于成年人，美国高血压预防、检测、评估与治疗联合委员会建立了相应的指南。

高血压会造成心脏工作负担加重，因为心脏在泵血时，往往需要克服较大的阻力。而且，高血压对动脉和小动脉的管壁有较大的张力。时间一长，将造成心脏扩大，动脉和小动脉损伤、硬化、弹性降低，最终会导致动脉粥样硬化、心脏病、心力衰竭、中风和肾脏衰竭。

3.中风

中风是一种影响到大脑供血动脉的心血管疾病。中风一般分为两类：缺血性中风和出血性中风。其中，缺血性中风较为常见（大约为87%），它起因于大脑血管阻塞，从而限制了大脑的血流。其阻塞的原因主要有两个：大脑血栓和大脑栓塞。发生缺血性中风会造成血流中断，大脑会部分缺血，造成缺氧甚至死亡。出血性中风主要有两种类型：大脑出血和蛛网膜下腔出血。

同心脏病发作一样，中风也会导致受影响组织的死亡。中风导致的脑损伤可能会影响感觉、语言表达、身体活动、思考方式和记忆等。单侧躯体麻痹比较常见，同样常见的还有语言表达障碍。

4.心脏衰竭

心脏衰竭是因心肌无法维持足够的心输出量供给以满足身体对氧的需求的一种临床情况。高血压、动脉粥样硬化、心脏瓣膜疾病、病毒感染和心脏病发作都可能是造成心脏衰竭的原因。

当心输出量不能得到满足时，血液开始滞留在静脉中。这会造成过多的液体潴留在身体内，特别是大腿和脚踝处。液体的潴留也会影响肺部（肺水肿），造成呼吸中断和呼吸短促。

5.其他心血管疾病

其他心血管疾病包括外周血管疾病、心脏瓣膜疾病、风湿性心脏病和先天性心脏病等。

外周血管疾病是全身性的，而不是冠状动脉疾病，它包括动脉硬化、静脉曲张和静脉炎。动脉硬化是指许多动脉的血管壁变厚、变硬且弹性降低的情况。静脉曲张是由于静脉瓣膜功能不全导致的，使血液停留在静脉而造成静脉扩大、弯曲和疼痛。静脉炎则是指静脉发炎。

心脏瓣膜疾病常涉及一个或多个瓣膜，瓣膜控制心脏血流方向，进出心脏的四个腔室。风湿性心脏病是一种心脏瓣膜疾病，是由链球菌感染造成的急性风湿热，易发于5～15

岁的儿童。

先天性心脏病包括出生前心脏任何的缺损，也被称为先天性心脏缺损。这些缺损是由于在出生前心脏或是靠近心脏的血管没有正常发育造成的。

二、个体风险的确定

1.冠状动脉疾病的危险因素

使冠心病早期发展的因素可分为两类：一类是个人可以控制的，它可通过生活方式的根本改变而发生变化；另一类是个人无法控制的，包括遗传（冠状动脉疾病的家族史）、种族、性别和衰老。美国心脏协会认为可以控制或改变的主要危险因素包含：

- 抽烟；
- 高血压；
- 血脂和脂蛋白异常；
- 缺乏身体活动；
- 肥胖和超重；
- 糖尿病和胰岛素抵抗。

与冠心病有关的脂蛋白主要有两种：低密度脂蛋白（low density lipoprotein cholesterol，LDL-C）和高密度脂蛋白（high density lipoprotein cholesterol，HDL-C）。其中，LDL-C参与斑块的形成，而HDL-C可能参与斑块的消退。因此，高浓度的HDL-C和低浓度的LDL-C使个体处于冠心病的最低风险。此外，极低密度脂蛋白胆固醇（VLDL-C）也与动脉粥样硬化的发展有关。总胆固醇（TC）与HDL-C的比值可能是最好的冠心病风险血脂指数，若比值为5.0或更高，则风险增加；若比值为3.0或更低，则风险较低。

2.高血压的危险因素

高血压的危险因素可分为可控制的和不可控制的。不可控制的有遗传（高血压家族史）、性别、衰老和种族（非洲或西班牙血统的人有较高风险）。可控制的危险因素如下：

- 胰岛素抵抗；
- 肥胖和超重；
- 饮食（钠、酒精）；
- 吸烟；
- 口服避孕药；
- 应激；
- 缺乏身体活动。

三、通过体力活动降低风险

1.降低冠状动脉疾病的风险

（1）训练使身体产生的适应可以降低冠状动脉疾病风险。运动训练使人体的解剖结构和生理功能发生适应变化，规律的身体活动对降低冠状动脉疾病风险具有重要作用。运动训练可使心脏肥大，进而提高心肌收缩力，增加心肌的工作能力。运动训练明显增加了冠状动脉循环的能力，改善心脏的侧支循环，进而降低冠状动脉疾病风险。

（2）运动训练降低其他风险因素。运动训练可通过增加HDL-C、降低TC，降低LDL-C/HDL-C和TC/HDL-C的比值，改善血脂，降低冠状动脉疾病风险。此外，运动训练在降低体重、控制体重以及控制糖尿病方面也有着重要的作用，其对心理压力的降低和控制及降低焦虑也有一定影响。

2.降低高血压的风险

（1）训练适应可以降低高血压风险。耐力训练可使身体产生许多生理学适应，影响安静时和运动中的血压。耐力训练可增加血浆容量，促进毛细血管生成，增加静脉系统血液容量，改善血压。高血压患者通过训练可以降低静息血压，可能是由于外周阻力的下降，但实际机制尚不清楚。此外，运动还能降低体内脂肪、血糖水平和胰岛素抵抗，这些因素均与高血压风险增加有关。

（2）运动训练降低高血压的其他风险因素。除降低血压，运动训练还可影响高血压的其他危险因素。运动可降低体脂，增加肌肉质量，这对于降低和协助控制血糖是非常重要的。运动训练还可降低高血压的另一危险因素——胰岛素抵抗。此外，运动训练也可缓解压力。

四、运动训练和心脏病患者的康复

证据显示，身体活动对于心脏病患者的康复而言是相当重要的。美国运动医学学会（ACSM）发表一项立场声明："有冠状动脉疾病的患者应该遵循特殊的个体化运动处方，以达到最佳的身体和心理上的健康。"重点放在改善多项危险因素，通过饮食、药物和运动来控制血脂异常、糖尿病和高血压。

美国圣路易斯华盛顿大学对心脏病患者的研究表明，有氧活动不仅可以改善外周的危险因素，而且会改变心脏本身，从而增加心脏血流和左心室功能。耐力训练可以显著降低心血管疾病的风险，它可以独立影响冠状动脉疾病和高血压的危险因素。对于参与心脏康复的患者来说，耐力训练有利于血压、血脂、身体成分、血糖控制和压力的改善。

此外，抗阻训练作为综合性心脏康复计划的一部分也有很大的益处。将抗阻训练和有氧训练结合到一个综合康复计划中，可以最大限度地提高训练的整体效益。

Chapter 15
Obesity, Diabetes, and Physical Activity

A sedentary lifestyle has been associated with an increased risk for both obesity and diabetes, and both are strongly associated with other diseases that have high mortality rates, such as coronary artery disease and cancer. Furthermore, approximately one-third of all Americans are obese, diabetic, or both. The consequences of these diseases are debilitating, and the costs associated with their treatment are exceedingly high.

1 Understanding Obesity

The terms *overweight* and *obesity* often are used interchangeably, but technically they have different meanings, as discussed next.

1.1 Terminology and Classification

Overweight is defined as a body weight that exceeds the normal or standard weight for a particular person based on height and frame size.

Obesity refers to the condition of having an excessive amount of body fat. Exact standards for allowable fat percentages have not been established. However, men with more than 25% body fat and women with more than 35% should be considered obese. Men with relative fat values of 20%–25% and women with values of 30%–35% should be considered borderline obese.

Body mass index (BMI) is now the most widely used clinical standard to estimate obesity. To determine a person's BMI, body weight in kilograms is divided by the square of body height in meters. Generally, the BMI is highly correlated with body fat and usually provides a reasonable estimate of obesity.

In 1997, the World Health Organization proposed a classification system for underweight, overweight, and obesity based solely on BMI values. This classification system was adopted by the National Institutes of Health in 1998 with several modifications and has been used widely since 2000 (Table 15.1).

Table 15.1 Classification of Overweight and Obesity by BMI, Waist Circumference, and Associated Disease Risk [a]

Classification	BMI / (kg/m^2)	Obesity class	DISEASE RISK [b]	
			Men ≤102 cm Women ≤88 cm	Men >102 cm Women >88 cm
Underweight	<18.5	–	–	–
Normal [c]	18.5~24.9	–	–	–
Overweight	25.0~29.9	–	Increased	High
Obesity	30.0~34.9	I	High	Very high
	35.0~39.9	II	Very high	Very high
Extreme obesity	≥40	III	Extremely high	Extremely high

[a] Disease risk for type 2 diabetes, hypertension, and cardiovascular disease

[b] Relative to normal weight and waist circumference

[c] Increased waist circumference also can be a marker for increased risk even in persons of normal weight.

1.2 Etiology of Obesity

At various times throughout human history, obesity has been thought to be caused by basic hormonal imbalances resulting from failure of one or more of the endocrine glands to properly regulate body weight. At other times, it has been believed that gluttony, rather than glandular malfunction, was the primary cause of obesity. In the first case, a person is perceived as having no control over the situation, and yet in the second, he or she is held directly responsible! Results of recent medical and physiological research show that obesity can be the result of any one or a combination of many factors. Its etiology, or cause, is not as simple as was once believed.

Recent research confirms that there is a significant genetic component in the etiology of obesity. However, it is possible to be obese, attributable basically to lifestyle choices, in the absence of a family history (genetics) of obesity. It is also possible to be relatively lean, even with a genetic predisposition to obesity, through proper diet and activity levels.

1.3 Health Problems Linked with Excessive Weight and Obesity

Before we look at the health problems associated with overweight and obesity, it is necessary to define two terms: morbidity and mortality. Morbidity refers to the presence, or rates of the presence, of a particular disease; mortality refers to deaths or rates of death related to the presence of a disease. Overweight and obesity are associated with an increased overall rate of death (general excess mortality). This relationship is curvilinear, as shown in Figure 15.1. A major increase in risk of death occurs when the BMI exceeds 30 kg/m^2, although BMI values between 25.0 and 29.9 are associated with an increased morbidity risk for many diseases. A number of more recent studies, published between 2005 and 2010, have reported that excess mortality is primarily associated with BMI values of 35.0 and above. Excess morbidity and mortality associated with obesity and overweight are linked with the following major diseases:

- Coronary heart disease
- Hypertension
- Stroke
- Type 2 diabetes
- Certain types of cancer—endometrial, breast, and colon
- Liver and gallbladder disease
- Osteoarthritis
- Sleep apnea and respiratory problems

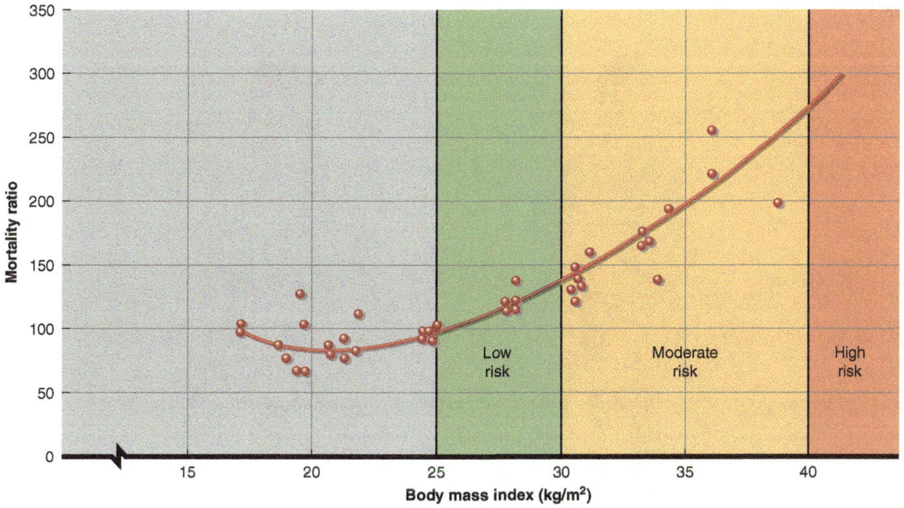

Figure 15.1 The relationship of body mass index to excess mortality. A mortality ratio of 100 represents average mortality. The lowest portion of the curve (body mass indexes under 25) indicates very low risk.

1.3.1 Changes in Normal Body Function

The prevalence and extent of changes in physiological function associated with excess adiposity vary with the individual and with the degree of fatness. Conditions and diseases commonly associated with obesity (especially morbid obesity) include respiratory problems (sleep apnea, chronic pulmonary disease) , abnormal blood clotting (thrombosis) , enlargement of the heart, and congestive heart failure. Obese individuals (and often those who are overweight) typically have decreased exercise tolerance and a lower level of physical fitness due to decreased levels of physical activity. Additional weight gain (and excess adiposity) further reduces activity levels and exercise tolerance decreases.

1.3.2 Increased Risk for Certain Diseases

An increased risk of developing certain chronic degenerative diseases also is associated with obesity. Both hypertension and atherosclerosis have been directly linked to obesity. So have various metabolic and endocrine disorders, such as impaired carbohydrate metabolism and diabetes. Obesity is a problem associated particularly with the onset of type 2 diabetes. Since the 1940s, major sex differences in the way in which fat is stored or patterned on the body have been recognized. As shown in Figure 15.2, males tend to store fat in the upper body, particularly the abdominal area, whereas females tend to store fat in the lower body, particularly the hips, buttocks, and thighs. Obesity that follows the male pattern is referred to as upper body (android) obesity, or apple-shaped obesity, and the female pattern is referred to as lower body (gynoid) obesity, or pear-shaped obesity.

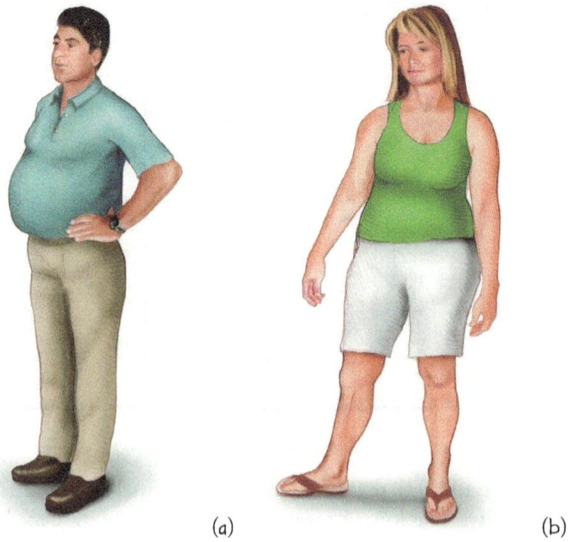

(a) Upper body (android) obesity (b) Lower body (gynoid) obesity

Figure 15.2 Obesity patterns tend to differ by sex.

Research beginning in the late 1970s and early 1980s established upper body obesity as a risk factor for the following conditions:

- Coronary artery disease
- Hypertension
- Stroke
- Elevated blood lipids
- Diabetes

Furthermore, upper body obesity appears to be more important than total-body fatness as a risk factor for these diseases. Waist and hip circumference, or girth, measurements can be used to identify people with increased risk. A waist/hip girth ratio greater than 0.90 for men and greater than 0.85 for women indicates increased risk. With upper body obesity, the increased risk may result from the close proximity of visceral fat depots to the portal circulatory system (circulation to the liver).

1.3.3 Detrimental Effects on Established Diseases

The effects of obesity on existing diseases are not clear. Obesity can contribute to further development of certain diseases and medical conditions, and weight reduction usually is prescribed as an integral part of treatment. Conditions that generally benefit from weight reduction include

- angina pectoris
- hypertension
- congestive heart disease
- myocardial infarction (reduced risk of recurrence)
- varicose veins
- diabetes, and
- orthopedic problems.

1.3.4 Adverse Psychological Reactions

Emotional or psychological problems might be the cause of obesity in some people. Furthermore, emotional or psychological problems can arise from the condition itself. In many societies, obesity carries a social stigma that contributes substantially to the problems of those who have it. Media, especially Western media, typically glamorize only people with extremely lean bodies. Consequently, some obese people might need professional counseling assistance in their efforts to lose weight.

2 Role of Physical Activity in Weight Control

Inactivity is a major cause of obesity in the United States. In fact, a sedentary lifestyle may be just as important in the development of obesity as overeating! Thus, increasing physical activity levels must be recognized as an essential component in any program of weight reduction or control.

2.1 Changes in Body Composition with Exercise Training

Physical training can alter body composition. A person who jogs three days a week for 30 min each day at an 11 km/h pace (slightly over 5.4 min/km) will expend about 14.5 kcal/min, or 435 kcal, for the 30 min run each day. This results in a total expenditure per week of about 1,305 kcal, the equivalent loss of about 0.15 kg of adipose tissue (fat plus connective tissue and water) each week just from the exercise period alone. However, in 52 weeks, providing energy intake remained constant, this person would lose 7.8 kg !

In estimations of an activity's energy cost, typically the average or steady-state rate of energy expenditure for that activity is multiplied by the number of minutes the activity is performed. For example, if the steady-state rate for shoveling snow is 7.5 kcal/min, 1 h of shoveling would require a total of 450 kcal. This would result in an approximate loss of 0.06 kg of adipose tissue.

But examining the energy expended only during exercise does not give us the full picture. Metabolism remains temporarily elevated after exercise ends. This phenomenon is now referred to as the excess post-exercise oxygen consumption (EPOC). Returning the metabolic rate back to its pre-exercise level can require several minutes following light exercise, such as walking; several hours following very heavy exercise, such as playing a football game; and up to 12–24 h or even longer for prolonged, exhaustive exercise, such as running a marathon in a hot and humid environment.

Studies have shown relatively small, but significant changes in both weight and body composition with both aerobic and resistance training, which include

- total weight decrease
- fat mass and relative body fat decrease, and
- either maintained or increased fat-free mass

Although most weight loss studies have used aerobic training, a number of studies have used resistance training and have shown impressive decreases in body fat and increases in fat-free mass. The evidence shows that exercise is an important part of any weight loss program. But to maximize losses in body weight and body fat, it is necessary to combine exercise with decreased caloric intake.

Since the 1990s, abdominal visceral fat has been identified as a major independent risk factor for cardiovascular diseases and obesity. There is now substantial evidence that physical activity reduces the rate of accumulation of visceral fat and that exercise training actually reduces visceral fat stores. This could be one of the most important health benefits of an active lifestyle!

2.2 Spot Reduction

Many people, including athletes, believe that exercising a specific area of the body will use the fat in that area, reducing the locally stored fat. Results of several early research studies tended to support this concept of spot reduction. But later research suggests that spot reduction is a myth and that exercise, even when localized, draws from almost all of the fat stores of the body, not just from local depots.

One such study used outstanding tennis players, theorizing that they would be ideal subjects for studying spot reduction because they could act as their own controls: Their dominant arms exercise vigorously for several hours every day, whereas their nondominant arms are relatively inactive. Researchers postulated that if spot reduction is a reality, the nondominant (inactive) arm should have substantially more fat than the dominant (active) arm. The players' dominant arms had substantially greater girths attributable to exercise-induced muscle hypertrophy. But the subcutaneous skinfold fat thicknesses in the active and inactive arms showed absolutely no differences.

The higher the exercise intensity, the greater the body's reliance on carbohydrate as an energy source. With high-intensity aerobic exercise, carbohydrate can supply up to 90% or more of the body's energy needs. During the late 1980s, various professional exercise groups promoted low-intensity aerobic exercise to increase the loss of body fat. These groups theorized that low-intensity aerobic training would allow the body to use more fat as the energy source, hastening the loss of body fat. Indeed, the body uses a higher percentage of fat for energy at lower exercise intensities. However, the total calories expended does not necessarily change as a result of the body's use of fat.

This is illustrated in Table 15.2. In this hypothetical example, a 23-year-old woman with a $\dot{V}O_{2\,max}$ of 3.0 L/ min exercises for 30 min at 50% of her $\dot{V}O_{2\,max}$ on one day and for 30 min at 75% of her $\dot{V}O_{2\,max}$ on another. The total calories from fat do not differ between the low-and high-intensity aerobic workouts: In both cases she burns about 110 kcal of fat during 30 min. Most important, however, for the higher-intensity workout she expends about 50% more total calories for the same time period.

Table 15.2 Estimation of Kilocalories Used from Fat and Carbohydrate for a Low- and High-Intensity Aerobic Training Bout of 30 min Duration

Exercise intensity	Average $\dot{V}O_2$ /L · min^{-1}	Average RER	% kcal CHO	% kcal fat	kcal for 30 min CHO	kcal for 30 min fat	kcal for 30 min total
Low, 50%	1.50	0.85	50	50	110	110	220
High, 75%	2.25	0.90	67	33	222	110	332

Note. RER = respiratory exchange ratio; CHO = carbohydrate. Subject was a fit but not highly trained 23-year-old woman ($\dot{V}O_{2\,max}$ = 3.0 L/min).

Scientists have determined that there is an optimal zone where rates of fat oxidation are at their highest. The Fat zone, defined as that zone where fat oxidation rates are within 10% of the peak rate, was found to vary from between 55% and 72% of $\dot{V}O_{2\,max}$. This is illustrated in Figure 15.3.

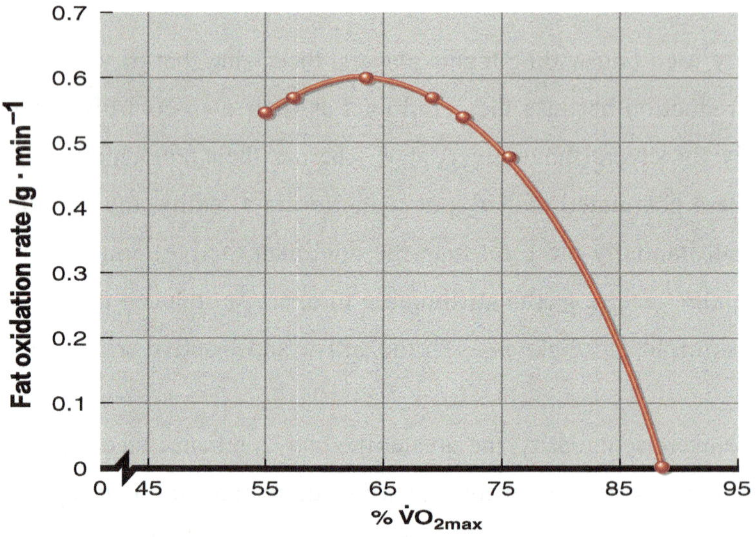

Figure 15.3 Rate of fat oxidation at various exercise intensities, expressed as a percentage of $\dot{V}O_{2\,max}$.

For those who are overweight or obese, their overall risk of death from disease is greatly reduced if they are physically active and fit. An active lifestyle and moderate to high fitness levels can greatly reduce their risk of dying from chronic degenerative diseases, such as coronary artery disease and diabetes.

3 Diabetes

Diabetes mellitus, also called simply diabetes, is a disease characterized by high blood glucose levels (hyperglycemia) resulting from either an inadequate production of insulin by the pancreas, an inability of insulin to facilitate the transport of glucose into the cells, or both.

3.1 Terminology and Classification

Historically, diabetes mellitus was classified into two major categories: juvenile-onset diabetes, or insulin-dependent diabetes mellitus (type 1 diabetes) , and adult-onset diabetes (type 2 diabetes). This classification was based on the age of onset of diabetes.

Type 1 diabetes is caused by the inability of the pancreas to produce sufficient insulin as a result of failure of the β-cells in the pancreas, which is the result of the body's immune system destroying pancreatic β-cells. Thus, this type has also been referred to as insulin-dependent diabetes mellitus (IDDM). Type 1 diabetes accounts for only 5%–10% of all cases of diabetes.

Type 2 diabetes is the result of the ineffectiveness of insulin to facilitate the transport of glucose into the cells and is a result of insulin resistance. It had previously been referred to as non-insulin-dependent diabetes mellitus (NIDDM). Type 2 diabetes accounts for 90%–95% of all cases of diabetes. Insulin resistance refers to the condition in which a "normal" insulin concentration in the blood produces a less than normal biological response. Insulin's primary function is to facilitate the transport of glucose from the blood into the cell, across the cell membrane. With insulin resistance, the body needs more insulin to transport a given amount of glucose across the cell membrane into the cell.

A third type of diabetes, gestational diabetes, is a form of diabetes that develops in pregnant women and their fetuses in about 4% of all pregnancies. Fortunately, it usually disappears in both mother and baby after delivery. Unfortunately, when gestational diabetes is present, there can be complications during pregnancy.

Another category, prediabetes, refers to the condition in those whohave impaired fasting glucose, impaired glucose tolerance, or both. Both type 1 and type 2 diabetes are diagnosed on the basis of a plasma glucose level of greater than 125mg/dL following an 8h fast. Impaired fasting glucose is defined as a plasma glucose level of between 100 and 125mg/dL, again following an 8h fast. Impaired glucose tolerance is determined by a glucose tolerance test. This involves drinking a solution in which 75g of anhydrous glucose is dissolved in water. Plasma glucose levels are measured 2h later. A glucose value of 200mg/dL orhigher is diagnostic of diabetes. Values of 140–199mg/dL represent impaired glucose tolerance, and values below 140mg/dL are considered normal.

There are also symptoms of diabetes that can be used to identify those at risk for diabetes. These include the following:

3.1.1 Type 1 Diabetes

- Frequent urination
- Excessive or unusual thirst
- Unusual, unexplained weight loss
- Extreme hunger
- Extreme fatigue and irritability

3.1.2 Type 2 Diabetes

- Any of the type 1 symptoms
- Frequent infections
- Blurred vision or sudden vision changes
- Tingling or numbness in hands or feet
- Cuts, bruises, or sores that are slow to heal
- Recurring skin, gum, or bladder infections

3.2 Etiology of Diabetes

Heredity appears to play a major role in both type 1 and type 2 diabetes. With type 1 diabetes, the β-cells (insulin-secreting cells) of the pancreas are destroyed. This destruction may be caused by the body's immune system, increased β-cell susceptibility to viruses, or β-cell degeneration.

Type 1 diabetes generally has a sudden onset during childhood or young adulthood. This leads to almost total insulin deficiency, and daily injections of insulin usually are required to control the disease.

In type 2 diabetes, the onset of the disease is more gradual, and the causes are more difficult to establish. Type 2 diabetes often is characterized by any of the following three major metabolic abnormalities: delayed or impaired insulin secretion; impaired insulin action (insulin resistance) in the insulin-responsive tissues of the body, including muscle; or excessive glucose output from the liver.

3.3 Health Problems Linked with Diabetes

Considerable health risks are associated with diabetes. People with this disease have a relatively high mortality rate. Diabetes places a person at increased risk for

- coronary artery or heart disease
- cerebrovascular disease and stroke
- hypertension

- peripheral vascular disease
- kidney disease
- nervous system disease
- eye disorders, including blindness
- dental disease
- amputations
- complications during pregnancy

During the late 1980s, scientists made the important associations among coronary artery disease, hypertension, obesity, and type 2 diabetes. Hyperinsulinemia (high blood levels of insulin) and insulin resistance appear to be the important threads linking these disorders, possibly through insulin-mediated sympathetic nervous system stimulation (increased insulin levels cause increased sympathetic nervous system activity). Again, obesity seems to be the trigger setting off this reaction.

4 Role of Physical Activity in Diabetes

Indirect scientific evidence has clearly established that a physically active lifestyle reduces the risk of developing type 2 diabetes, but there is little evidence to support this for type 1 diabetes. Because there is such a disparity between the characteristics and responses of those with type 1 and type 2 diabetes, we discuss each separately.

4.1 Type 1 Diabetes

The role of regular exercise and physical training in improving glycemic control (regulation of blood sugar levels) in patients with type 1 diabetes has not been clearly defined and is controversial. The most distinguishing feature differentiating type 1 and type 2 diabetes is that those with type 1 have low blood insulin levels attributable to the inability or reduced ability of the pancreas to produce insulin. Those with type 1 diabetes are prone to hypoglycemia (low blood sugar levels) during and immediately after exercise because the liver fails to release glucose at a rate that can keep up with glucose utilization.

Although glycemic control is generally not improved by exercise in most people with type 1 diabetes, there are other potential benefits of exercise for these patients. Because these patients have a two to three times greater risk for coronary artery disease, exercise may help reduce this risk. Exercise may also help reduce the risk for cerebrovascular and peripheral arterial diseases.

People with uncomplicated type 1 diabetes do not have to restrict physical activity, providing that blood sugar levels are controlled appropriately. Monitoring blood sugar levels in an exercising person with type 1 diabetes is important so that diet and insulin dosages can be altered accordingly.

Special attention also should be given to the feet of people with diabetes, as it is common for them to experience peripheral neuropathy (diseased nerves) with some loss of sensation in the feet. Ulcerations and other lesions on the feet account for more than half of all hospitalizations of diabetic patients. Because weight-bearing exercise places additional stress on the feet, the proper selection of footwear and appropriate preventive foot care are important.

4.2 Type 2 Diabetes

Exercise plays a major role in glycemic control for people with type 2 diabetes. Particularly during the early stages of the disease, so the major problem with this form of diabetes is the lack of target cell response to insulin (insulin resistance). Because the cells become resistant to insulin, the hormone cannot perform its function of facilitating glucose transport across the cell membrane, resulting in decreased insulin sensitivity. Muscle contraction has an insulin-like effect. Membrane permeability to glucose increases with muscular contraction. Thus, acute bouts of exercise decrease insulin resistance and increase insulin sensitivity. This reduces the cells' requirements for insulin, which means that people taking insulin must reduce their dosages. Resistance and aerobic training appear to produce similar effects, although some evidence suggests that combining resistance and aerobic exercise is the optimal exercise strategy for reducing insulin resistance. This decrease in insulin resistance and increase in insulin sensitivity may primarily be a response to each individual bout of exercise rather than the result of a long-term change associated with training. Some studies have shown that the effect dissipates within 72 h .

IN CLOSING

In this chapter, we have concluded the role of physical activity in preventing and treating obesity and diabetes. We have seen that exercise can decrease individual risk and also can be an integral part of treatment, improving overall health as well as alleviating some symptoms.

KEY TERMS

obesity; overweight; body mass index (BMI) ; spot reduction; diabetes mellitus; β-cells; type 1 diabetes; type 2 diabetes; insulin-dependent diabetes mellitus (IDDM) ; non-insulin-dependent diabetes mellitus (NIDDM) ; prediabetes; impaired glucose tolerance; insulin resistance

STUDY QUESTIONS

(1) What is the difference between overweight and obesity?

(2) What is ideal body weight, and how is it determined?

(3) What is body mass index? What is its significance?

(4) What are several health-related problems associated with obesity?

(5) What role does exercise play in the prevention and treatment of obesity?

(6) How effective is spot reduction? Low-intensity aerobic exercise?

(7) Describe the two major types of diabetes. How are they caused?

(8) What health risks are associated with diabetes?

(9) Describe the role of exercise in preventing diabetes and in treating patients with type 1 and type 2 diabetes.

第十五章
肥胖、糖尿病与体力活动

静坐少动的生活方式增加了肥胖和糖尿病的患病风险，而此风险又密切关联了如冠状动脉疾病和癌症等许多高死亡率疾病。

一、肥胖

1.术语及分类

超重指超过正常或标准的体重。肥胖指身体脂肪含量过多的一种状态。

体重指数（BMI）与体脂含量密切相关，是目前临床使用最广泛的肥胖评估指标。

2.肥胖的病因

肥胖不只与饮食过量或内分泌失调等单一因素有关。它的病因复杂而综合，并且包含显著的遗传成分，但人们可以通过合理饮食和身体活动管理体重。

3.与超重和肥胖有关的健康问题

以下一些疾病的高发病率和高死亡率与超重及肥胖有关。冠心病，高血压，中风，2型糖尿病，某些类型的癌症——子宫内膜、乳腺和结肠癌，肝脏和胆囊疾病，骨关节炎，睡眠呼吸暂停和呼吸问题等。

（1）正常身体机能的改变。与肥胖相关的生理功能变化因个体和肥胖程度而异。肥胖者通常会有呼吸系统问题、凝血异常、心脏增大和充血性心衰等。肥胖者会由于体力活动减少使运动耐受力和身体健康水平降低，而增加的体重会进一步降低运动耐受力。

（2）增加患病风险。肥胖会增加某种慢性退行性疾病的风险，其中高血压和动脉粥样硬化与肥胖直接相关，从而导致各种代谢或内分泌异常，如糖代谢受损或糖尿病。肥胖与2型糖尿病有关。脂肪在体内的储存存在性别差异，男性的体脂更易储存在腹部而形成上半身肥胖或苹果形肥胖；女性的体脂则更易储存在臀部和大腿而形成下半身肥胖或梨形肥胖。上半身肥胖比全身肥胖的危害更大。

（3）肥胖对疾病的不利影响。肥胖对已患疾病的影响还不清楚。肥胖能加重某些疾病的发展，而减体重是治疗该疾病必要的一部分。减体重通常能改善一些身体条件，如心绞痛、高血压、充血性心脏疾病、心肌梗塞、静脉曲张、糖尿病和骨科疾病等。

（4）负面心理效应。肥胖往往产生负面心理效应并带来相应的社会问题，因而需要专业咨询帮助。

4.体力活动在控制体重方面所起到的作用

缺乏运动是导致肥胖的一个主要原因，提高体力活动水平是减重和控制体重的重要因素。

（1）运动与体成分。运动能改变体成分，将有氧运动和抗阻训练相结合并减少热量摄入将更利于控制体重和优化体成分。

（2）运动形式和局部减脂。运动强度越大，糖供能的比例越高；运动强度越小，脂肪供能比例越高。低强度有氧运动会分解更多的脂肪作为能量来源，但身体脂肪所消耗的总热量不一定改变，而且在同一时间段内，高强度运动比低强度运动消耗的总热量要多。科学家们已证明在一定的区域内脂肪氧化率会达到最高值。脂肪最高氧化域指在脂肪氧化率最高点的10%以内的区域，即运动强度在55%～72%$\dot{V}O_{2\,max}$范围内。

局部运动不能实现局部减脂，因为并不是局部脂肪供能，而是动员全身脂肪分解供能，局部减脂是不可能的。比如，网球运动员的优势手和非优势手的皮下脂肪并不存在差异。

积极的生活方式能大大提升超重和肥胖者的健康水平，降低其患病风险。

二、糖尿病

糖尿病是由于胰腺产生的胰岛素不足，或者胰岛素无法促进葡萄糖进入细胞，或者这两种原因共同导致的血糖浓度过高的疾病。

1.分型

1型糖尿病是由胰腺中β细胞失活而不能产生足够的胰岛素引起的，也被称作胰岛素依赖型糖尿病（IDDM），1型糖尿病仅占所有糖尿病病例的5%～10%。

2型糖尿病是由于胰岛素不能有效地将葡萄糖转运到细胞中而造成的，也是胰岛素抵抗的结果，也被称作非胰岛素依赖型糖尿病（NIDDM）。2型糖尿病占所有糖尿病病例的90%～95%。

3型糖尿病也被称为妊娠糖尿病，大约有4%的孕妇及其胎儿会罹患这种糖尿病，分娩后通常会消失。还有一种类型是糖尿病前期，指的是空腹葡萄糖异常或对葡萄糖耐受异常，或这两种情况兼存。

2.糖尿病的病因

遗传在1型糖尿病和2型糖尿病中都起着重要作用。对于1型糖尿病，胰腺的β细胞被破坏，这可能是由β细胞变性或者免疫问题增加了β细胞的病毒易感性造成的，一般在童年或成年早期突然患病，需要每天注射胰岛素来控制病情。

2型糖尿病发病缓慢，发病原因更难确定，通常伴有代谢异常，如胰岛素分泌延迟或受损、胰岛素抵抗或肝脏葡萄糖输出过多。

3.与糖尿病相关的健康问题

糖尿病会增加患以下疾病的风险：冠状动脉疾病和心脏病，脑血管疾病和中风，高血压，周围血管疾病，肾病，神经系统疾病，视力受损及失明，牙病，截肢，妊娠期并发症。

4.体力活动对于糖尿病的影响

（1）1型糖尿病。1型糖尿病病人因为胰腺功能受损而使血液中胰岛素含量减少，且在运动中或运动后肝脏无法异生葡萄糖，使血糖浓度不能与葡萄糖利用率相持平而出现血糖过低现象，因此运动通常不能改善大多数1型糖尿病病人血糖控制的状况。但运动能降低其患脑血管疾病和周围动脉疾病的风险。

（2）2型糖尿病。运动对2型糖尿病病人的血糖控制起到重要作用，运动减少胰岛素抵抗增加其敏感性。抗阻训练和有氧训练会产生类似效果，通常二者结合进行。但运动的效果主要反映在每次运动中，而不是与训练相关的长期变化上，一些研究显示这种效果会在72小时内消散。